UDENOSAUNEE) ✪ 1780–1794 CHICKAMAUGA ✪ 1790–17[...] P9-AOF-605

[...] ✪ 1806 MEXICO ✪ 1806–1810 SPANISH, FRENCH PRIVATEERS ✪ 1810 SPANISH WEST

[...]AR OF 1812 WITH GREAT BRITAIN) ✪ 1812–1815 DAKOTA SIOUX ✪ 1812–1815 IROQUOIS

[...]LANDS ✪ 1813–1814 MUSKOGEE (CREEK) CONFEDERACY ✪ 1814 SPANISH FLORIDA ✪

[...]H FLORIDA ✪ 1817–1819 SEMINOLE ✪ 1818 OREGON (RUSSIA, SPAIN) ✪ 1820–1861

[...]827 GREECE ✪ 1831–1832 FALKLAND ISLANDS ✪ 1832 SAUK ✪ 1832 SUMATRA ✪

[...]MUSKOGEE (CREEK) ✪ 1838–1839 SUMATRA ✪ 1840 FIJI ISLANDS ✪ 1841 SAMOA ✪

[...]AYUSE ✪ 1849 TURKEY ✪ 1850–1886 APACHE ✪ 1851 JOHANNA ISLAND ✪ 1851 TURKEY

[...]YU, BONIN ISLANDS ✪ 1854–1856 CHINA ✪ 1855 FIJI ISLANDS ✪ 1855 URUGUAY ✪

[...]E ✪ 1855–1858 SEMINOLE ✪ 1856 PANAMA (COLOMBIA) ✪ 1856–1857 CHEYENNE ✪

[...]58–1859 TURKEY ✪ 1859 CHINA ✪ 1859 MEXICO ✪ 1859 PARAGUAY ✪ 1860 ANGOLA

[...]OLOMBIA) ✪ 1866 CHINA ✪ 1866 MEXICO ✪ 1866–1868 LAKOTA SIOUX, NORTHERN

[...]COMANCHE ✪ 1868 COLOMBIA ✪ 1868 JAPAN ✪ 1868 URUGUAY ✪ 1870 HAWAII ✪

[...]XICO ✪ 1874 HAWAI'I ✪ 1874–1875 COMANCHE, APACHE, ARAPAHO, CHEYENNE, KIOWA

[...]NE ✪ 1879–1880 UTES ✪ 1882 EGYPT ✪ 1885 PANAMA (COLOMBIA) ✪ 1888 HAITI ✪

[...] 1891 BERING STRAIT ✪ 1891 CHILE ✪ 1891 HAITI ✪ 1893 HAWAI'I ✪ 1894 BRAZIL ✪

[...]NICARAGUA ✪ 1898 CUBA (SPAIN) ✪ 1898 NICARAGUA ✪ 1898 PHILIPPINES (SPAIN) ✪

[...]PHILIPPINES ✪ 1900 CHINA ✪ 1901–1902 COLOMBIA ✪ 1903 HONDURAS ✪ 1903 SYRIA

[...]04 DOMINICAN REPUBLIC ✪ 1904 TANGIER ✪ 1904–1905 KOREA ✪ 1906–1909 CUBA

[...] 1912 CUBA ✪ 1912–1925 TURKEY ✪ 1912–1933 NICARAGUA ✪ 1914 DOMINICAN

[...]BLIC ✪ 1917–1918 WORLD WAR I (EUROPE) ✪ 1917–1922 CUBA ✪ 1918–1920 RUSSIA

[...]ATEMALA ✪ 1921 COSTA RICA, PANAMA ✪ 1922 TURKEY ✪ 1924–1925 HONDURAS ✪

[...]A/PACIFIC) ✪ 1946 TRIESTE ✪ 1947–1949 GREECE ✪ 1948–1949 BERLIN, GERMANY

[...]975 VIETNAM ✪ 1956 EGYPT ✪ 1958 LEBANON ✪ 1962 CUBA ✪ 1962 THAILAND ✪

[...]DIA ✪ 1967 CONGO (ZAIRE) ✪ 1976 KOREA ✪ 1978 CONGO (ZAIRE) ✪ 1980 IRAN ✪

[...]ANON ✪ 1983 CHAD ✪ 1983 GRENADA ✪ 1986 BOLIVIA ✪ 1986 LIBYA ✪ 1987–1988 IRAN

[...]HILIPPINES ✪ 1989–1990 PANAMA ✪ 1990 SAUDI ARABIA ✪ 1991 CONGO (ZAIRE)

[...]3–1996 HAITI ✪ 1993–2005 BOSNIA ✪ 1995 SERBIA ✪ 1996 LIBERIA ✪ 1996 RWANDA

[...]0 MONTENEGRO ✪ 1999–2000 SERBIA ✪ 2000 YEMEN ✪ 2000–2002 EAST TIMOR

[...]015 PHILIPPINES ✪ 2002– YEMEN ✪ 2003–2011 IRAQ ✪ 2004 HAITI ✪ C. 2004– KENYA

[...]– CENTRAL AFRICAN REPUBLIC ✪ C. 2012– MALI ✪ C. 2013–2016 SOUTH SUDAN ✪

[...]NIGERIA ✪ 2014 DEMOCRATIC REPUBLIC OF THE CONGO ✪ 2014– IRAQ ✪ 2014– SYRIA

[...]BLIC OF THE CONGO ✪ 2017– SAUDI ARABIA ✪ C. 2017 TUNISIA ✪ 2019– PHILIPPINES

"A brisk, sweeping, and utterly persuasive account of the relationship between foreign bases and the U.S. propensity for war. The case that David Vine makes is irrefutable: The former spawn the latter."

Andrew Bacevich, author of *The Age of Illusions: How America Squandered Its Cold War Victory*

"David Vine's *The United States of War* puts a much needed pin to the balloon of American exceptionalism. An invaluable guide to a country that, long before Orwell came along, said war was peace and interventionism was the highest form of anticolonialism. *The United States of War* is especially important now, as we try to make sense of a presidential administration that, in the name of so-called isolationism, has left a trail of global destruction in its wake."

Greg Grandin, author of *The End of the Myth: From the Frontier to the Border Wall in the Mind of America*

"David Vine's newest book connects Fort Lauderdale to Okinawa. It makes me realize I can't make adequate sense of U.S. militarism today if I don't take seriously the history of Native Americans. The book will make us all globally smarter and a lot more curious."

Cynthia Enloe, author of *Bananas, Beaches, and Bases: Making Feminist Sense of International Politics*

"Like David Vine's previous book, *Base Nation*, his new book provides a clear look at rampant U.S. imperialism as exhibited by U.S. overseas basing at 800 locations across the globe. *The United States of War* is an agonizing read even if the myth of U.S. exceptionalism is already badly tattered. In short, 'exceptionalism' only applies if one means unique brutality, violence, ruthlessness, unparalleled pursuit of self-interest, and imperialism of the most blatant and degrading sort—an exceptionalism that has meant the deaths of millions, the maiming of millions more, and the wandering from state to state of even more millions displaced by war. It is not a book to read curled up by a warm winter fire; rather, it's a book that will stir your soul, if you have one left, to action."

Colonel Lawrence Wilkerson, USA (Ret), former chief of staff, U.S. Department of State, and Professor of Government and Public Policy at the College of William and Mary

Named in remembrance of

the onetime *Antioch Review* editor

and longtime Bay Area resident,

the Lawrence Grauman, Jr. Fund

supports books that address

a wide range of human rights,

free speech, and social justice issues.

The publisher and the University of California Press Foundation gratefully acknowledge the generous support of the Lawrence Grauman, Jr. Fund.

THE UNITED STATES OF WAR

THE UNITED STATES

OF WAR

**A GLOBAL HISTORY OF AMERICA'S
ENDLESS CONFLICTS, FROM
COLUMBUS TO THE ISLAMIC STATE**

DAVID VINE

UNIVERSITY OF CALIFORNIA PRESS

The author will donate all proceeds from this book's royalties to nonprofit organizations serving victims of war and other forms of violence.

University of California Press
Oakland, California

© 2020 by David Vine

Maps, except where noted, are by Kelly Martin Design. Earlier versions of some maps first appeared in David Vine, *Base Nation: How U.S. Military Bases Abroad Harm America and the World* (New York: Metropolitan Books, 2015).

Library of Congress Cataloging-in-Publication Data

Names: Vine, David, 1974– author.
Title: The United States of war : a global history of America's endless
    conflicts, from Columbus to the Islamic State / David Vine.
Other titles: California series in public anthropology.
Description: Oakland, California : University of California Press, [2020] |
    Series: California series in public anthropology | Includes
    bibliographical references and index.
Identifiers: LCCN 2020006465 (print) | LCCN 2020006466 (ebook) |
    ISBN 9780520300873 (cloth) | ISBN 9780520972070 (ebook)
Subjects: LCSH: United States—History, Military. | United States—
    History, Military—Social aspects. | United States—Military policy—
    History. | United States—Foreign relations. | United States—History.
Classification: LCC E181 .V65 2020 (print) | LCC E181 (ebook) |
    DDC 355.00973—dc23
LC record available at https://lccn.loc.gov/2020006465
LC ebook record available at https://lccn.loc.gov/2020006466

Manufactured in the United States of America

28 27 26 25 24 23 22 21 20
10 9 8 7 6 5 4 3 2

To my parents and siblings. I love you dearly
and forever.

If we divide reality into two camps—the violent and the nonviolent—and stand in one camp while attacking the other, the world will never have peace. We will always blame and condemn those we feel are responsible for wars and social injustice, without recognizing the degree of violence in ourselves. We must work on ourselves and also with those we condemn if we want to have a real impact.

Thich Nhat Hanh, *Love in Action: Writings on Nonviolent Social Change*

CONTENTS

ILLUSTRATIONS

MAPS

For ease of comparison maps generally use contemporary borders and, unfortunately, Mercator projections. The dates of conflicts and base creation referenced in the maps are often disputed. Additional details and citations for these maps are available in the most recent version of my "Lists of U.S. Military Bases Abroad," available at www.basenation.us/maps.

PREFACE

On that Wednesday night in June, Russell Madden's mother, Peggy Madden Davitt, heard the knock at the door she had dreaded for months. She opened the door and saw a man in full military dress uniform. For a nanosecond Peggy thought there might be good news about her son, who was fighting in Afghanistan. Realizing why the officer was there, she started saying, then crying, "No, no, no, no, no, no, no, no, no, no . . ." Peggy told the man, a U.S. Army chaplain, that he had the wrong house and slammed the door shut.

He knocked again.

"*No*, you have the wrong house!" Peggy screamed.

The chaplain knocked again. When Peggy finally opened the door, the chaplain quickly slid his foot between the door and its frame and forced his way inside.

Private First Class Russell Madden was just twenty-nine years old. According to the Army, on June 23, 2010, Russell was killed in Afghanistan when a rocket-propelled grenade, or RPG, tore through his vehicle's armored hull.

Russell grew up in Bellevue, Kentucky, a town of fewer than six thousand, across the Ohio River from Cincinnati. He ran track, played baseball, and was a high school football star who played six positions for a team that lost one game his senior year. After graduation Russell coached peewee football and was a mentor to his players on and off the field. He volunteered to help elderly neighbors with odd jobs. Russell married his girlfriend, Michelle Lee Reynolds, and in 2006 she gave birth to their child, Parker Lee.

Parker was born with cystic fibrosis, the incurable disease requiring lifetime medical treatment. According to Peggy, Russell struggled to find steady work after high school. Mostly he did some roofing and electrical work, and he didn't have health insurance to cover the treatment. "Where he had been working, he had no benefits or anything like that," his sister, Lindsey, said.[1] Family and friends raised money to send Parker to the world-famous Mayo Clinic in Minnesota. When Russell, Michelle, and Parker arrived, the clinic asked about Parker's insurance. Peggy said the clinic quickly turned them away.

"No one will ever send my son away again," Peggy remembers Russell saying. After returning home, Russell enlisted in the Army. "He joined because he knew that Parker would be taken care of" by the military "no matter what," Russell's sister said.

Russell went to boot camp. The Army sent Russell to advanced training and then to its elite 173rd Airborne Brigade, stationed at military bases in Germany and Italy. Russell deployed to Afghanistan in 2009. Eight months later, Russell's family received his body in a casket at the local airport.

So many people wanted to attend the viewing of Russell's casket that the city moved the viewing to a local ten thousand–seat arena. It lasted for more than five hours. The line to greet the family stretched the entire length of the arena and out the doors. The day of the funeral, a hearse drove Russell's casket to the football stadium at Russell's high school. His former teammates were waiting for him at the fifty-yard line, standing in two lines in football jerseys and suits. A horse-drawn carriage carried Russell's casket through Bellevue, where people lined the streets holding Stars and Stripes flags and signs saying good-bye. A bishop and six priests presided over the funeral. The next day, Russell was on the local newspaper's front page. More than eight hundred people joined a Facebook group created in his honor. The Kentucky state legislature named a highway after Russell.[2]

Before Peggy and I met in 2014, she sent me a photo of Russell in uniform, holding Parker in his arms before he deployed to Afghanistan. Russell was just as Peggy had described: almost six feet tall and two hundred pounds, he could look intimidating with his completely shaved head, but he had a boyish smile and soft, gentle eyes. "That smile," his mother said longingly over the phone. "I miss that smile."

According to the Army, Russell died of severe injuries after the RPG blast fractured his skull in multiple places and caused bruising and bleeding inside and around his brain. The explosion hit Russell's face and fractured his jaw and nasal bones in multiple places. The impact fractured Russell's left clavicle, broke both forearm bones on his right arm, and caused bruising and bleeding around both lungs. Scrapes, cuts, and bruises covered much of his body.[3]

Russell Madden is one of more than 2.7 million people that the U.S. government has sent to fight wars that have raged continuously since the U.S. military invaded Afghanistan on October 7, 2001. Within days of the militant group al-Qaeda's September 11, 2001, attacks on the United States, President George W. Bush declared a "global war on terrorism." Within months U.S. forces were occupying Afghanistan and fighting other militants, with differing connections to al-Qaeda, in the Philippines, Somalia,

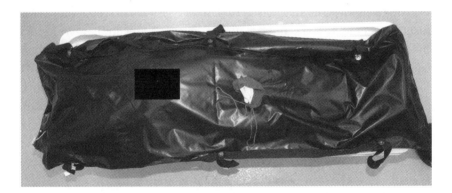

Figure 1. Body bag containing the remains of one of an estimated four million or more dead combatants and civilians, from all nations, in the post-2001 U.S.-led wars in Afghanistan, Iraq, Syria, Pakistan, and Yemen. Tens or, likely, hundreds of thousands more have died in seventeen additional countries where U.S. military forces have fought since 2001.

and Yemen. On March 20, 2003, the U.S. military invaded Iraq. Its leader, Saddam Hussein; its government; and its people had no connection to the September 11 attacks or al-Qaeda. U.S. troops deposed Hussein and occupied the country. President Bush, Vice President Dick Cheney, and members of their administration justified the invasion by claiming an imminent threat from Iraqi chemical, biological, and possibly nuclear weapons; U.S. troops found that no such weapons existed. As in Afghanistan, U.S. forces soon faced an increasingly fierce armed resistance that became a brutal civil war.

In the nearly two decades since U.S. forces invaded Afghanistan and Iraq, the U.S. military has fought in at least twenty-two countries.[4] The actual number is probably higher because of the secretive nature of post-2001 military operations. The words of U.S. leaders suggest that this period of unceasing war will continue for decades. Gen. David Petraeus, who commanded U.S. forces across the Middle East, called the wars "the kind of fight we're in for the rest of our lives, and probably our kids' lives." Other military and civilian officials call the current conflicts the "long war" or the "forever war."[5]

"Do you think it's a forever war?" an NBC News reporter asked one four-star general.

"I don't know if it's—if it's," hesitated Gen. Joseph Votel, "you know, forever war. Define *forever*."[6]

Some tend to think that this period of forever war is exceptional. Some assume, as I did, that it's unusual that most new U.S. military recruits and most new U.S. college students have no memory of a time when their country wasn't at war. To the contrary, this state of war is the norm in U.S. history. According to the government's own Congressional Research Service and other sources, the U.S. military has waged war, engaged in combat, or otherwise employed its forces aggressively in foreign lands in all but eleven years of its existence.[7] Depending on one's definitions, the years at peace may be even fewer. "The people of the United States have arguably never been at peace," says scholar Nikhil Pal Singh.[8]

U.S. forces initiated most of these wars and invasions. Most were aggressive, offensive wars of choice. The Japanese attack on the United States—specifically, on what were then five Pacific Ocean colonies: Hawai'i, the Philippines, Guam, Wake Island, and Alaska—was an exception in U.S. history. The total list of U.S. wars and other combat actions extends into the hundreds. A small fraction appears in most U.S. history textbooks: the Revolutionary War, the War of 1812, the Mexican-American War, the Spanish-American War, World Wars I and II, the Korean War, Vietnam, the 1991 and 2003–11 wars in Iraq, the war in Afghanistan, and the wars against the so-called Islamic State in Iraq and Syria. If histories mention the wars between European settlers and indigenous North American peoples, those wars are generally lumped together as the "Indian Wars." Between U.S. independence and the end of the nineteenth century, Euro-American settlers waged essentially unceasing warfare against the Miami, Shawnee, Delaware, Muskogee (Creek), Seminole, Cherokee, Kiowa, Comanche, Cheyenne, Modoc, Apache, Sioux, Bannock, Piute, and Ute, among many others.*

Even before the conclusion of the Revolutionary War with Britain, soldiers of the soon-to-be independent nation launched another war, to destroy Iroquois Confederacy resistance to settlers and troops in western New York and today's Ohio. The brutal scorched-earth war opened new territories to westward colonization. It also opened the way for more wars. After independence U.S. forces were soon fighting a naval war with France. The U.S. government launched another war against Britain and invaded Canada at least eleven times (the military maintained plans to invade Canada into the 1930s).[9] In the first decades after U.S. independence, the military deployed to fight in places as far flung as Algiers, the Marquesas Islands, Peru, Samoa, Turkey, Angola, China, Haiti, Siberia, Laos, and Somalia.

Across the nineteenth century and into the twentieth and twenty-first, the invasions and wars of aggression generally grew lengthier, deadlier, and larger in scope. Although relatively few today think of California, the Southwest, and parts of Colorado, Utah, and Wyoming as occupied territory, they're controlled by the United States because the U.S. government instigated a war with Mexico in 1846, invading and taking almost half its land. The military invaded and occupied hemispheric neighbors, including Cuba (six times), Honduras (eight times), and Panama (twenty-four times). More fighting followed in China, Cambodia, Laos, Serbia, and Sudan, among others. Elsewhere the U.S. government has waged

* When discussing American Indian/Native American/indigenous nations and peoples, I try to use the name(s) and spelling(s) most commonly used by the group itself, historically and today.

U.S. War(s)

Other U.S. Combat Actions

Map 1. U.S. Wars and Combat, 1776–2020.
Because of space limitations, this map does not reflect all conflicts between U.S. forces
and Native American peoples. See the appendix for a full list. Oceans not to scale. Key
sources: Torreon and Plagakis, *Instances of Use;* Roxanne Dunbar-Ortiz, *An
Indigenous Peoples' History of the United States* (Boston: Beacon, 2014); John
Grenier, *The First Way of War: American War Making on the Frontier, 1607–1814*
(Cambridge: Cambridge University Press, 2005).

proxy wars and backed coups in places such as Guatemala, Iran, Indonesia, Chile, and Afghanistan.

The number of dead from these wars is hard to comprehend. Imagine how many Russell Maddens there have been. In the Revolutionary War, there were between 25,000 and 70,000 U.S. deaths, alone. More than 400,000 died in the U.S. Civil War. There were more than 1.6 million U.S. deaths combined between World Wars I and II; 36,500 U.S. dead in Korea; and more than 58,000 U.S. deaths in Vietnam, Laos, and Cambodia.[10]

In Afghanistan, Russell Madden is one of around 6,100 U.S. military personnel and contractors who have died since the October 2001 invasion. Adding personnel and contractors who died in Iraq, Syria, Pakistan, Yemen, and other countries where the U.S. military has been waging war for almost two decades, the total rises to around 15,000.[11] Hundreds of thousands have returned from these wars with amputations, post-traumatic stress disorder (PTSD), traumatic brain injuries, and other physical and mental damage; as of 2018, 1.7 million veterans had reported a disability connected to wartime deployments.[12]

When one counts the dead on all sides in the history of U.S. wars, combatants and civilians alike, the total runs into the tens of millions. They include what were likely millions of Native Americans killed by battle, disease, and starvation; 200,000 to 1 million Filipinos dead in a fifteen-year U.S. war to assert colonial control beginning in 1898; between 3 and 4 million killed in Korea; and an estimated 3.8 million deaths in the wars in Vietnam, Laos, and Cambodia.[13]

To call attention to all the dead in these and the many other U.S. wars is not to suggest that the U.S. government or the U.S. military—let alone every U.S. citizen—is responsible for all the death and damage caused by these wars. It is, however, to insist that any examination of U.S. wars needs to foreground the damage these wars have inflicted on human beings, regardless of their place of birth or nationality. This is especially important given the tendency of many U.S. news accounts and histories to ignore the suffering of non–U.S. citizens or to whitewash the deadly reality of war altogether.

As terrible as the impact of the post-2001 wars has been in the United States, death, injury, and trauma in the countries where the U.S. military has fought is orders of magnitude worse. An estimated 755,000 to 786,000 civilians and combatants, on all sides, have died in just Afghanistan, Iraq,

Syria, Pakistan, and Yemen since U.S. forces began fighting in those countries. That figure is around fifty times larger than the number of U.S. dead.[14]

But that's only the number of combatants and civilians who have died in combat. Many more have died as a result of disease, hunger, and malnutrition caused by the wars and the destruction of health care systems, employment, sanitation, and other local infrastructures. While these deaths are still being calculated and debated by researchers, the total could reach a minimum of 3 million—around two hundred times the number of U.S. dead. An estimate of 4 million deaths may be a more accurate, although still conservative, figure.[15]

Meanwhile, entire neighborhoods, cities, and societies have been shattered by the U.S.-led wars. The total number of injured and traumatized extends into the tens of millions. In Afghanistan, surveys have indicated that two-thirds of the population may have mental health problems, with half suffering from anxiety and one in five from PTSD. By 2007 in Iraq, 28 percent of young people were malnourished, half living in Baghdad had witnessed a major traumatic event, and nearly one-third had PTSD diagnoses. As of 2019, more than 10 million have likely been displaced from their homes in Afghanistan, Iraq, Yemen, and Libya alone, becoming refugees abroad or internally displaced people within their countries.[16]

Alongside the human damage, the financial costs of the post-2001 U.S.-led wars are so large, they're nearly incomprehensible. As of late 2020 U.S. taxpayers already have spent or should expect to eventually spend a minimum of $6.4 trillion on the post-2001 wars, including future veterans' benefits and interest payments on the money borrowed to pay for the wars. The actual costs are likely to run hundreds of billions or trillions more, depending on when these seemingly endless wars actually end.[17]

Despite the challenge of trying to fathom one trillion anything, let alone $6.4 trillion, it's important to try to grasp what these sums mean (especially for those of us who are paying for the fighting with our taxes). What, for example, could such sums have done to rebuild public schools and public health infrastructure or to provide health care to those, like Russell and Parker, lacking insurance? The roughly $5 trillion that U.S. taxpayers have already spent on the wars could have paid, for example, for eighteen years of health care for the thirteen million U.S. children now living below the poverty line, while simultaneously paying for two years of Head Start for all

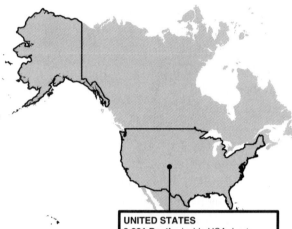

UNITED STATES
3,081 Deaths inside USA due to Islamist Militants since Sept. 11, 2001

14,986 Deaths of U.S. Military Personnel at War (incl. Contractors)

**TOTAL U.S. SPENDING
ON POST-2001 WARS: $6.4 TRILLION**

 War

(20XX–) Years of U.S. Involvement

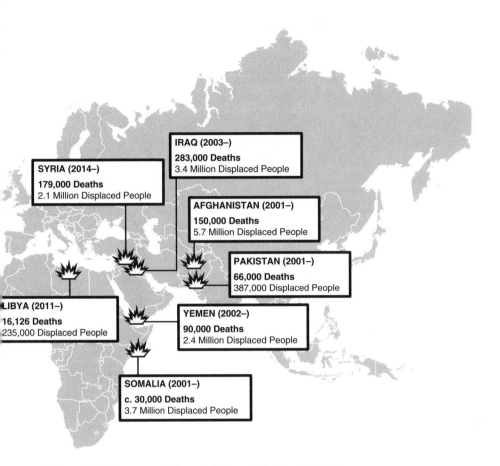

Map 2. The Human and Financial Costs of the Post-2001 Wars.
Deaths include only direct combat fatalities among combatants and civilians of all
nationalities. Total war deaths could be three-to-four, or more, times higher, including
"indirect deaths" caused by the destruction of health and other infrastructure.
Displaced people include refugees and internally displaced peoples, although the
causes of displacement are complex and extend beyond war alone (especially in
Somalia and Pakistan). Financial costs reflect taxpayer funds spent or obligated,
including estimated future veterans' benefits and interest payments. Data is as of
2019–2020. Oceans not to scale. Key sources: see page 349, notes 15 and 16.

those children, while simultaneously funding four-year public college schol-
arships for twenty-eight million students, while also providing twenty years
of health care for one million military veterans, while still having enough to
pay the salaries of four million people working clean energy jobs for ten
years.[18]

The total effects of the post-2001 wars have been so disastrous that
words can't capture the calamity. Numbers certainly can tell us only so
much. Quickly they become numbing. Ultimately, there's no adequate way
to measure the immensity of the damage these wars have inflicted on all
the people in all the countries affected. Imagine how many Yemeni Russell
Maddens there are. Imagine how many mothers who've lost sons, like
Peggy Madden Davitt, there are in Iraq; how many sons without fathers,
like Parker Lee, there are in Somalia; how many widows, like Michelle,
there are in Afghanistan.

Facing the longer history of U.S. wars and their terrible effects, from the
eighteenth century to today, the inescapable question is *why?* Whatever the
motivations behind any individual war, what explains this record of near-
constant warfare? What explains this record of war for a country long portrayed as a beacon of peace and democracy? And does it have to be this way?

POSTSCRIPT, MAY 6, 2020

I made the last substantial edits to this book early this year, before the first
reports of deaths in the United States from the 2019 coronavirus disease
pandemic. How many have died or suffered unnecessarily because the U.S.
government didn't invest in adequate pandemic preparedness? The cost of
assembling an adequate supply of masks and other personal protective
equipment, an adequate ventilator stockpile, robust testing and vaccine-
production capacity, among other public health tools, would have been a
tiny fraction of the $6.4 trillion spent or obligated on the post-September
11, 2001, wars. Responsibility for the COVID-19 disaster doesn't just lie in
one or two or three of the last presidential administrations. Responsibility
lies in large measure in the long history of U.S. wars and what's become a
system of endless war. COVID has further demonstrated the urgency of
changing that system.

A NOTE ON LANGUAGE AND TERMINOLOGY

I've written this book in ways that are different than those of some other books. One difference is that I generally don't adopt conventional names for wars. The names of wars are political and usually reflect one's national perspective or the perspective of the "winner." Commonly used names also tend to trigger commonly held understandings about wars, which tend to shut off curiosity, critical thinking, and the ability to build new understandings about wars' causes, dynamics, and effects.

For example, commonly used names for wars greatly oversimplify the nature of conflicts. The "Spanish-American War" of 1898 is more accurately named the "Spanish–Cuban–Puerto Rican–Philippine–American War," as historian Daniel Immerwahr has noted.[1] Beyond oversimplifying, the conventional name erases the lives of the colonized from history. This happens all too often already. To avoid some of these pitfalls, I generally identify wars by naming major combatants and years of combat (while noting commonly used names to prevent ambiguity when necessary).

Naming all the combatant countries and territories involved in what's generally known as the "Cold War" would make for an impossibly long name. But how can we call a war *cold* that killed an estimated ten million people in Korea, Southeast Asia, Indonesia, and Afghanistan alone?

Calling the war *cold* contributes to ignoring the victims of the war and to ensuring that, as historian Paul Thomas Chamberlin writes, "its constituent conflicts are little more than footnotes in the story of post-1945 international relations."[2] I generally avoid the name and, when necessary, render it as "Cold War" with quotation marks to encourage rethinking its widespread acceptance.

Rethinking naming practices and the myths and assumptions built into them is one of many ways to change how we write, talk, and think about history and the present. With rare exceptions I refer to the government agency responsible for the U.S. armed forces as the "Pentagon" rather than the "Department of Defense." The name of the agency's headquarters is a frequently used and less ideologically loaded shorthand. The degree to which the department actually provides *defense* services is a major subject of this book and should not be assumed. The name of one of the Pentagon's predecessor agencies, the "Department of War," provides a more accurate description of that agency's activities.

For similar reasons, except in quotations, I don't use the language of *national defense* or *national security* or the terms *national security state* or *national security bureaucracy*. The language of *national defense* and *national security* has often obscured and implicitly justified U.S. military, CIA, and other government actions that have frequently been offensive in nature and had little to do with defending or securing the nation. I likewise avoid describing countries as having *national interests*. Doing so suggests that an entire nation could share and agree on common interests. Such language often obscures the specific interests of specific actors and specific groups, making it more difficult to understand how and why things happen in the world. In a similar way, I try to avoid making claims about what the United States writ large has done. Instead, I attempt to be as precise as possible by writing about what specific individuals or groups have done—*U.S. government officials* or *U.S. corporate elites* or specific multinational corporations, for example.

Finally, with the exception of the book's subtitle, I do not refer to Christopher Columbus—an Anglicized name the sailor never used—and instead employ the only documented name he appears to have used, Cristóbal Colón. I do this to question some of the colonialist assumptions built into language and our daily lives. In the United States these assump-

tions include, as historian Roxanne Dunbar-Ortiz points out, an "unconscious belief in manifest destiny," which is equally visible in my city's
name: Washington, District of *Columbia*, celebrates and claims Cristóbal
Colón despite his never having set foot in continental North America.[3] For
similar reasons, outside of the subtitle and quotations, I avoid using
"America" when I mean "United States of America." As Latin American
friends rightly remind us U.S. Americans, "America" means the continents
of South and North America, not the United States alone.

INTRODUCTION

"IF WE BUILD THEM, WARS WILL COME"

There's obviously no easy answer to why the United States—or, more accurately, its government and its military—has been fighting almost without pause since independence. Some might invoke biological metaphors to suggest that the answer to this question lies in the country's DNA, in the soil, in the people's blood. Of course, these are just metaphors. Countries have no DNA; a propensity to wage war doesn't get transmitted through the soil, nor through blood or genes, although the history of a land and the people who live there is critically important.

Some suggest the answer lies in the country's birth in a revolutionary war for independence. Others point to the culture of the United States or the psychology of its people. Some say the record of war has its roots in economic forces or the capitalist system itself. Others link the pattern to the power and influence of the Military Industrial Complex, about which President Dwight D. Eisenhower warned in his famous 1961 farewell address. Some identify domestic politics as providing the answer. Others point to race and racism, gender and hypermasculinity, nationalism and ideas of U.S. "American exceptionalism," or a missionary Christianity exemplified by the idea that the country has a "manifest destiny" to expand.

1

This book offers a new way to think about why the U.S. military seems to fight wars without end. The approach I take is simple but somewhat unusual. Rather than looking primarily at the wars themselves, this book looks at the infrastructure that made the wars possible. Rather than being a book about battles, this book uses military bases as windows to understand the pattern of endless U.S. wars. To fight wars, especially wars far from home, armies and navies generally need bases to organize, support, and sustain combat. Bases are logistical centers for organizing military personnel, weaponry, and supplies and for deploying troops to wage war. Domestic bases serve that role. But if a military wants to fight a war far from home, as the United States has generally done, it needs to move and maintain its forces over long distances. Extraterritorial bases, bases far from home, bases in foreign lands, make this much easier, facilitating the logistics of war hundreds or thousands of miles away.

Since independence the U.S. government has built the largest collection of military bases occupying foreign lands in world history. Today the military controls around eight hundred military bases in some eighty-five countries outside the fifty states and Washington, DC.[1] At other times the total has been higher. While many in the United States take it for granted that the U.S. military maintains hundreds of bases in places as far flung as Germany and Japan, Djibouti and Honduras, Greenland and Australia, the thought of finding a foreign base in the United States is basically unimaginable. For most it's a challenge to imagine what it would feel like to have a single foreign base anywhere near a U.S. border, for example in Mexico, Canada, or the Caribbean, let alone in the United States.

Rafael Correa, then the president of Ecuador, revealed this rarely considered truth when in 2009 he refused to renew the lease for a U.S. base in his country. Correa told reporters that he would renew the lease on one condition: "They let us put a base in Miami—an Ecuadorian base. If there's no problem having foreign soldiers on a country's soil," Correa quipped, "surely they'll let us have an Ecuadorian base in the United States."[2]

From the United States' earliest days, bases abroad have played key roles in launching and maintaining U.S. wars and other military actions. In the eighteenth and nineteenth centuries, hundreds of Army forts beyond U.S. borders launched dozens of wars against Native American peoples, resulting in the conquest of lands across North America and the deaths of millions. In the late nineteenth and early twentieth centuries, the military built bases farther from the North American mainland, in Alaska, Hawai'i, Puerto Rico, the Philippines, Guam, Panama, and Guantánamo Bay, Cuba. During World War II U.S. forces built and occupied two thousand base sites and a total of thirty thousand installations touching every continent.[3] Holding on to hundreds of those bases and building new ones after World War II made it easier to wage war in Korea, Vietnam, and elsewhere in Southeast Asia, as well as to support proxy armies from Central America to the Middle East. The wars the U.S. government launched after October 7, 2001, would have been significantly more difficult to wage without a collection of bases of unprecedented breadth around the globe. Bases in the Middle East, central and southern Asia, the Indian Ocean, and as far as Thailand, Djibouti, Italy, and Germany have played critical roles in allowing U.S. troops to fight in Afghanistan, Pakistan, Iraq, Somalia, Libya, and far beyond.

This book looks at the bases that have enabled U.S. leaders to launch and sustain wars as well as the bases that the U.S. military occupied and retained after the wars ended. Research funded by none other than the U.S. Army indicates that since the 1950s a U.S. military presence abroad is correlated with U.S. forces initiating military conflicts.[4] In other words, there appears to be a relationship between establishing bases outside the United States and the incidence of wars. Notably, the historical record also shows that U.S. wars have often led U.S. leaders to establish more bases abroad. The establishment of more bases abroad, in turn, has often led to more wars, which has often led to more bases, in a repeating pattern over time. Put another way, bases frequently beget wars, which can beget more bases, which can beget more wars, and so on.

By this I don't just mean that the construction of bases abroad has enabled more war. I mean that the construction of bases abroad has actually made aggressive, offensive war *more likely*. Since the revolution that won independence from Britain, the construction and maintenance of extraterritorial bases has increased the likelihood that these bases would be used. They have increased the likelihood that the United States would wage wars of aggression.

Greenland
(Denmark)

Iceland—⊙

Canada (3)

UNITED STATES
OF AMERICA

Puerto Rico (34)
U.S. Virgin
Islands (6)

Bahamas (6)
Cuba

⊙
Johnston
Atoll

Honduras (3)
El Salvador
Costa Rica

Curaçao
(Netherlands)

Aruba (Netherlands)
Colombia

⊙
American Samoa

Peru (2)

Chile—⊙

⊛ U.S. Base(s)

⊛ U.S. Bases (≥25)

⊙ U.S. Small Base(s) Only

U.S. Naval Fleet

U.S. Colonies, Military Occupations in italics

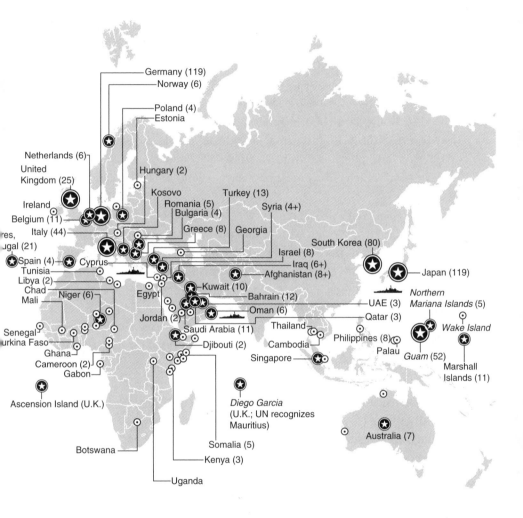

Germany (119)
Norway (6)
Poland (4)
Estonia
Netherlands (6)
United Kingdom (25)
Hungary (2)
Kosovo
Turkey (13)
Ireland
Romania (5)
Syria (4+)
Belgium (11)
Bulgaria (4)
Italy (44)
Greece (8)
Georgia
res,
ugal (21)
South Korea (80)
Spain (4)
Cyprus
Israel (8)
Tunisia
Iraq (6+)
Japan (119)
Libya (2)
Afghanistan (8+)
Chad
Kuwait (10)
Northern
Mali
Niger (6)
Egypt
Bahrain (12)
Mariana Islands (5)
Oman (6)
UAE (3)
Wake Island
Jordan (2)
Qatar (3)
Senegal
Saudi Arabia (11)
Thailand
Philippines (8)
urkina Faso
Djibouti (2)
Cambodia
Palau
Guam (52)
Ghana
Singapore
Cameroon (2)
Marshall
Gabon
Islands (11)
Ascension Island (U.K.)
Diego Garcia
(U.K.; UN recognizes
Mauritius)
Australia (7)
Botswana
Somalia (5)
Kenya (3)
Uganda

Map 3. *U.S. Military Bases Abroad, 2020.*
As of 2020, the United States controlled around eight hundred bases outside the fifty
U.S. states and Washington, DC. The number of bases and the secrecy and lack of
transparency of the base network make any graphic depiction challenging. This map
reflects the relative number and positioning of bases given the best available data.
Oceans not to scale. For details and additional sources, see Vine, "Lists of U.S.
Military Bases." Key source: *Base Structure Report: Fiscal Year 2018.*

Historian and former U.S. Army officer Andrew Bacevich has shown how maintaining "a far-flung network of bases and other arrangements to facilitate intervention abroad" has been an "essential predicate" of U.S. political life and a deeply ingrained, unconscious "matter of faith" about the role of U.S. power in the world "for decades." Bacevich says that "a central purpose of" what elites have called "forward presence"—a euphemism for bases and troops on other people's soil—"has been to project [military] power anywhere on earth." Bacevich traces this tendency to President Theodore Roosevelt's 1904 "corollary" to the Monroe Doctrine. The corollary asserted the U.S. government's right to invade any country in the Western Hemisphere committing what U.S. leaders deemed "chronic wrongdoing," which mostly meant not paying debts to U.S. banks and other businesses.[5]

While Roosevelt's proclamation was bold, the belief in the U.S. military's right to invade other nations and peoples was not new. Invasions of other people's lands have been part of U.S. history since the Revolutionary War (although many refer to them euphemistically and antiseptically as military "interventions," "operations," or "contingencies"). From the creation of the Continental Army and the establishment of the first bases on Native American peoples' lands, most U.S. leaders have shared a deeply held belief in their right to deploy military power into and seize the lands of others. Given the patterns of who invaded whom, this belief was clearly shaped by ideas of white, male, Christian, U.S. American supremacy and socially constructed ideas of masculinity tied to the infliction of violence.

Maintaining bases abroad has not always made war more likely, and it has not always resulted in war. At particular times and in particular places, U.S. leaders avoided, averted, or didn't consider war. War has never been and is not inevitable. Frequently, however, bases beyond U.S. borders have made war and the deployment of military force too easy, too tempting for politicians, high-ranking military and civilian officials, and other elites with the power to shape government decisions. These bases have provided what is by design an easily deployable form of offensive military power. With this offensive power readily available, elites often have been tempted to advocate for its use to advance their own economic and political interests and the interests of fellow business leaders and politicians, land speculators, miners, traders, farmers, and settlers, among others.[6]

For these reasons and reasons related to the immediate profits to be made from building and running military installations, exterritorial bases have been a foundation of U.S. foreign policy since 1776. Bases abroad have become, as some say, foreign policy written in concrete (and, in centuries past, written in wood, brick, iron, and adobe). As anthropologist Catherine Lutz writes, bases abroad, and the military forces that occupy them, have been the main tool in the U.S. foreign policy toolbox. They have been the hammers that have left little room for diplomacy and other foreign policy tools. And when hammers dominate one's toolbox, Lutz says, everything starts looking like a nail.[7] The hammers become all too tempting, especially when mostly male policy makers perceive them, consciously or unconsciously, as visible demonstrations of their masculinity and strength.

Let me be clear. I'm not saying that bases abroad are the sole cause of all U.S. wars or of any one war. I'm saying that bases beyond U.S. borders are a particularly important cause. To focus this book's attention on bases abroad is not to dismiss economic, political, social, ideological, or psychological explanations for the U.S. record of persistent war making. I am not dismissing explanations rooted in capitalism, racism, patriarchy, nationalism, or religious chauvinism. All these dynamics are important parts of the history that follows. Bases abroad, however, provide a lens through which to see the intersection and interaction of these forces, which have together created the United States' history of war. Bases beyond U.S. borders provide a key to help unlock the complex question of why the United States has such a long and consistent record of war.

Specifically, bases abroad show how U.S. political, economic, and military leaders (themselves shaped by the forces of history, political economy, racism, patriarchy, nationalism, and religion) have used taxpayer money to build a self-perpetuating system of permanent war revolving around an often expanding global collection of extraterritorial military bases. These bases have expanded the boundaries of the United States, while keeping the country locked in a state of nearly continuous war that has largely served the economic and political interests of elites and left tens of millions dead, wounded, and displaced.

Military bases need not facilitate war. Bases can be defensive in nature. Bases can protect. For example, the walls and fortifications of castles—a type of base—provided a place of safety from foreign invaders and protected entire cities from attack; during World War II British bases helped protect the British Isles from Nazi invasion. But when bases are occupying foreign lands, history suggests they aren't likely to be defensive in nature. Military and other government leaders often claim otherwise, portraying extraterritorial bases as deterrents and forces of stability and peace. But that is rarely the case.[8] Bases abroad are generally offensive in nature. They are not designed for peace. They are designed to threaten, to deploy military force, and to wage offensive wars. There should be no surprise that, as U.S. history shows, an unprecedented collection of foreign bases has led not to peace but to war.

✪

For millennia empires and other major powers have used extraterritorial bases to wage offensive wars. Powerful leaders have used far-flung bases to conquer territory and protect conquered lands, to extract resources and secure access to markets and labor, and to threaten and exert influence. Bases abroad have been a foundation for empires' control over foreign lands and foreign peoples, from the ancient Egyptian, Chinese, and Roman Empires to empires and regional powers of the second millennium such as the Mongols, Malians, Normans, Incans, Ottomans, and Genoese to the European empires of Spain, France, and Britain. In the Americas in particular, fort construction by European empires after 1492 enabled more than three centuries of deadly colonizing warfare.

That U.S. leaders began building a large collection of extraterritorial forts and embarked on a similar record of warfare helps show the continuity between the U.S. Empire and empires past. Many Revolutionary War–era elites in the thirteen states saw the British, French, and other European empires as models for what the United States should and would become: an expanding nation and expansionist "American Empire." George Washington referred to the United States as a "rising Empire." Thomas Jefferson was one of many who hoped and assumed the country would expand its territory in virtually every direction, including into Canada and

Cuba.[9] U.S. military and civilian leaders began working toward that goal during the revolution, with the Continental Army's attacks on the Iroquois Confederacy. The construction of a growing chain of extraterritorial military bases—army forts—on indigenous peoples' lands became a key tool to waging a century of wars to expand the boundaries of the United States, seize the land and its natural resources, and displace, dispossess, and kill American Indians in frequently genocidal ways. "From the time the first settlers arrived in Virginia from England and started moving westward, this was an imperial nation, a conquering nation," historian Paul Kennedy explains.[10]

Many of us in the United States have long had great difficulty seeing our nation as an empire like others. I certainly have. The country's birth in a revolution against the British Empire and powerful foundational ideologies of democracy, liberty, and freedom, coupled with changing attitudes about empire, have made it hard to accept the reality of U.S. Empire. Some have called the United States an "empire in denial."[11] Since the nineteenth century the language of "manifest destiny" has helped hide U.S. imperialism by suggesting that the country's westward conquest and expansion were inevitable phenomena, the natural or divinely planned progression of history. At other times "the history of territorial expansion that required more than a century of wars with hundreds of indigenous polities," writes Nikhil Pal Singh, "is forgotten or else quietly inscribed as a lasting achievement of US nationhood."[12] If the country was ever an empire, many have learned, it was only briefly and perhaps absentmindedly so around the "Spanish-American War" of 1898 and the conquest of Spain's colonies of Cuba, the Philippines, and Puerto Rico.

But what, if not an empire, is a country that violently conquered lands and displaced, dispossessed, and killed millions clear across North America, before seizing colonies in the Caribbean and on a chain of islands across the Pacific Ocean? What, if not an empire, is a country that since World War II has had the world's most lethal military; that has a near-monopoly on nuclear weapons capable of destroying the planet; and that has launched dozens of coups and overthrown a long series of foreign governments? What, if not an empire, is a country that largely designed the post–World War II international political-economic system; that has had the world's most powerful economy; that can print dollars to pay its debts because the U.S. dollar is the world's reserve currency; that has unparalleled control over the United Nations and other international organizations; and that has had unparalleled media and cultural influence over other nations and peoples, thanks to Hollywood, pop music, the Internet, and social media? What, if not an empire, is a country that has such an unbroken record of warfare since its founding, including, in recent years, the invasion and long-term occupation of two countries, Afghanistan and Iraq, the size of Texas and California, respectively? What, if not an empire, is a country that maintains eight hundred military bases on other people's soil?

Since the U.S. military invaded Afghanistan and Iraq in 2001 and 2003, there's actually been little debate about whether the United States is an empire. While the existence of U.S. imperialism was the subject of ideological arguments during, for example, the U.S. war in Southeast Asia, there's now widespread agreement across the political spectrum about the fact of the U.S. Empire. Today the main debates are about the kind of empire the United States has become and the morality of imperialism.[13]

Imperialism and *empire* are helpful concepts to characterize a type of expansionist power and rule that has recurred across millennia of human history.* At times the language of empire has been used too casually and with too little precision. At times the terminology has been more political rhetoric than a useful lens to help understand the United States or the world. Some use the Roman Empire as a metaphor to describe the United States. But the United States is not Rome. No two empires are alike. If the concept is to be meaningful, if it is to illuminate, the challenge is not just to say that the United States is an empire. The challenge is to explain why the United States is an empire, what kind of empire it has become, and what effects it has had.

Comparing the U.S. Empire to prior empires, one sees continuities and shifts.[14] The United States in the post–World War II era represents a break

---

* Debates about such definitions are contentious. I define *imperialism* generally as the practice by one country, state, or people of forcibly imposing and maintaining hierarchical relationships of formal or informal rule, domination, or control over a significant part of the life of other groups of people such that the stronger shapes, or has the ability to shape, significant aspects of the political, economic, social, or cultural life of the weaker. *Empire* is then the designation reserved for states and other entities practicing imperialism. *Colonialism* is a specific form of imperialism in which citizens of an empire settle in conquered territory.

with previous empires in the extent to which imperial control has been exercised through the base network and not through a large collection of formal colonies.[15] Still, this is not entirely new. Bases abroad have been a frequently overlooked but critical dimension of the U.S. Empire since the earliest days of U.S. history. For the United States, bases have been a crucial imperial tool for launching wars and other military actions to advance profit making and domestic political fortunes; for maintaining systems of alliances; for keeping other nations in subordinate relationships; and, in the post–World War II period, for upholding a global political, economic, military order to the perceived benefit of the United States and its elites. In other words, bases and other military tools have worked in tandem with and undergirded economic and political tools of empire.

That most U.S. leaders have pursued a path of empire since shortly after independence makes the U.S. record of war unsurprising. Just as building bases abroad has made wars more likely, building an empire has done the same. Riffing off the famous line from the baseball movie *Field of Dreams*, one might say, "If we build them, wars will come." Except the reference is to bases and empire rather than baseball: If we build bases abroad, wars will likely come. If we build an empire, wars will likely come. If we use aggressive military force to build an expansionist nation focused on dominating and controlling the lands and lives of others in the pursuit of profit for some, wars will come.

Still, the "if" in "If we build them, wars will come" is an important reminder of the choices involved in both the history and the future of the United States' relationship to war. There was nothing inevitable about the United States becoming an empire. There was nothing inevitable about any single war or the long history of wars. U.S. leaders could have made different choices in the past. At times leaders avoided wars, often as a result of pressure from large groups of people. Today there are choices to be made about the country's future.

Despite many signs that the U.S. Empire is in decline, many government officials and other elites appear content to perpetuate the status quo. Many are undeterred by the pattern of moving from one catastrophic war to the next: from Vietnam to Afghanistan to Iraq to Libya to Syria to Yemen to . . . . During President Donald J. Trump's administration, some senior officials, such as Secretary of State Mike Pompeo and now former

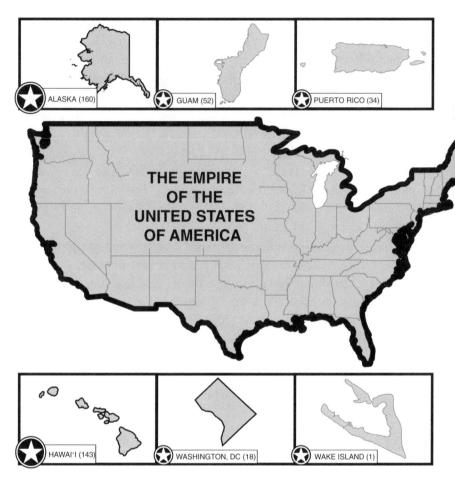

Map 4. The United States of America and Its Empire.

Most maps of the United States are inaccurate. Most depict the fifty U.S. states or, often, just the continental forty-eight and Washington, DC. These maps hide the U.S. Empire. They hide the U.S. colonies (territories), where, by law, people lack full democratic rights. Traditional maps also hide the occupation of lands worldwide by some eight hundred U.S. military bases in around eighty-five countries. This map tries to depict the United States more honestly. Land areas not to scale. Inspired by Daniel Immerwahr, *How to Hide an Empire: A History of the Greater United States* (New York: Farrar, Straus and Giroux, 2019).

 VIRGIN ISLANDS (6)

 N. MARIANA ISLANDS (5)

 AMERICAN SAMOA (1)

COUNTRY	U.S. BASES				
Germany	119	Somalia	5	Chad	1
Japan	119	Bulgaria	4	Chile	1
South Korea	80	Poland	4	Colombia	1
Italy	44	Spain	4	Costa Rica	1
United Kingdom	25	Syria	4+	Curaçao (Netherlands)	1
Portugal	21	Canada	3	Cyprus	1
Turkey	13	Honduras	3	Diego Garcia (U.K.)	1
Bahrain	12	Kenya	3	Egypt	1
Belgium	11	Qatar	3	El Salvador	1
Marshall Islands	11	United Arab Emirates	3	Estonia	1
Saudi Arabia	11	Cameroon	2	Gabon	1
Kuwait	10	Djibouti	2	Georgia	1
Afghanistan	8+	Hungary	2	Ghana	1
Greece	8	Jordan	2	Greenland (Denmark)	1
Israel	8	Libya	2	Iceland	1
Philippines	8	Palau	2	Ireland	1
Australia	7	Peru	2	Kosovo	1
Bahamas	6	Singapore	2	Mali	1
Iraq	6+	Thailand	2	Senegal	1
Netherlands	6	Aruba (Netherlands)	1	Tunisia	1
Norway	6	Ascension Island (U.K.)	1	Uganda	1
Oman	6	Botswana	1		
Niger	6	Burkina Faso	1		
Romania	5	Cambodia	1		

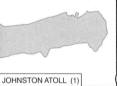 JOHNSTON ATOLL (1)

 NAVAL STATION GUANTÁNAMO BAY, CUBA (1)

U.S. State

U.S. Colony/Base sites in ( ). Base sites in continental 48 states = 3,829.

military adviser John Bolton, have appeared committed to instigating a new conflict. Despite Trump's declared opposition to interventionist wars, he and his administration's actions have brought the country close to war with North Korea, Venezuela, and Iran.

With U.S. troops currently or recently engaged in some form of combat in fifteen or more countries, interventionist military and civilian officials are already planning for what they assume will be another major war.[16] At the Pentagon military leaders no longer talk about the so-called war on terrorism as the "long war." Now they call it "infinite war."[17] Air Force General Mike Holmes predicted in 2018 that, after fighting three wars in Iraq since 1991, "odds are there's another one ten years from now, to go back into the Sunni areas up north. We've been fighting for almost 20 years in Afghanistan. These are infinite wars."[18] More frighteningly, a growing number of government officials, politicians, pundits, and think tank analysts are talking, directly and indirectly, about the inevitability of a future war with China or Russia. (Often one senses a certain sports-like enthusiasm in such talk, despite the potential for millions of deaths, if not planetary nuclear annihilation.)

Alternatively, brave U.S. citizens and leaders can demand the country give up this catastrophic pattern of war. They can demand the country give up on offensive foreign bases and give up on empire. They can demand the country embrace a foreign policy built around diplomacy, cooperation, and respect, and principles that are at the heart of the best traditions in U.S. history: democracy, equity, and justice.

✪

The United States of War is divided into five parts that reflect five distinct periods of U.S. imperialism.* Part I uncovers the roots of the U.S. Empire. It shows the connections and similarities between the U.S. Empire and its imperial predecessors, dating to the arrival of Cristóbal Colón in Guantánamo Bay in 1494. Like its predecessors, the U.S. Empire has been

---

* Others identify three, four, or more periods. Periodization is always somewhat arbitrary, and the dividing lines between periods are almost always blurrier than they are presented.

defined significantly by the now long-debunked pseudoscientific idea of race and the racist belief in white supremacy as justification for the conquest of those deemed "not white." That the U.S. government's conquest of territory has almost always involved the territory of non-European people of color is no coincidence. Race and racism have been defining features of contemporary imperialism since the emergence of race as a concept around the sixteenth and seventeenth centuries.

Part II tells the story of the growth of the U.S. Empire from independence to the wars the U.S. military waged against forces of the dwindling Spanish Empire and locals in Cuba, the Philippines, and Puerto Rico beginning in 1898. At the beginning of this period, the first U.S. bases abroad—forts located on the territories of Native American peoples—helped enable the violent conquest of territory and peoples across North America. Near-constant offensive warfare allowed the U.S. Army to push the country's borders westward. U.S. soldiers effectively served as an advance guard and protection service as Euro-American settlers colonized lands across the continent. The result was the dispossession and death of millions. Other nineteenth-century bases helped enable invasions and wars in Canada, Spanish Florida, Mexico, Central America, the Caribbean, and as far as the Middle East and beyond. Unlike some histories, *The United States of War* treats the U.S. wars beginning in 1898 not as an aberration or historical disjuncture or the birth of U.S. imperialism but rather as a continuation of linked processes of war and empire, profit seeking and expansion.[19]

The third part of *The United States of War* corresponds with the third period of the U.S. Empire, from the end of the wars of 1898 to the start of World War II. This period featured a new, less territorially focused imperialism, during which there was less formal expansion of U.S. territory and the addition of a relatively small number of bases abroad. This period is marked by greater use of economic tools of imperial control, symbolized by "Open Door" trade policies initiated in China around the time of the "Boxer" Rebellion and backed by frequent military invasions and occupations of countries in Latin America and the Caribbean.

Part IV, covering the fourth period of the U.S. Empire, stretches from before the United States formally entered World War II to the early twenty-first century. Beginning with President Franklin Roosevelt's 1940

"Destroyers-for-Bases" deal acquiring ninety-nine-year leases on military bases in eight British colonies, U.S. leaders built the world's largest-ever collection of foreign bases by the end of World War II. After the war, in the era of decolonization, U.S. officials invented a new, more discreet form of empire. This new form of empire relied heavily on foreign bases working in tandem with economic and political tools and other forms of military power, such as periodic military invasions and wars, the threat of nuclear war, CIA-backed coups and political meddling, and support for proxy armies. The foreign base network became a major mechanism of U.S. imperial control, helping to keep wayward nations within the rules of an economic and political system favorable to U.S. corporations and elites and allowing the control of territory vastly disproportionate to the land actually occupied.[20]

Part V focuses on the current period of the U.S. Empire, which began with the U.S. invasion of Afghanistan on October 7, 2001, and the launch of the so-called global war on terrorism. In many ways this period has seen a continuation of the same imperial tools and trends in evidence since World War II. But this period is distinct because it features the emergence of a *hyperimperialism* marked by (1) unprecedented levels of military spending despite the absence of an imperial competitor akin to the Soviet Union or any comparable threat; (2) unprecedented levels of power and influence for the Military Industrial Complex as a result of and reinforcing skyrocketing military expenditures; (3) unprecedented breadth in the deployment of U.S. military bases and troops abroad, with installations now in around eighty-five countries and territories and a growing number of secretive special operations forces in nearly every country on Earth; and (4) unprecedented U.S. military intervention, base construction, and warfare in the Greater Middle East, resulting in levels of death, injury, displacement, and destruction not seen since the U.S. wars in Southeast Asia. U.S. leaders' increasing reliance on the U.S. military has also been a reaction to escalating geopolitical-economic competition with Europe, Russia, India, other rising powers, and especially China, at a time when the U.S. Empire has been weakened by deindustrialization, economic instability, mounting inequality, escalating national debt, and astronomically costly wars.

The story that follows is the culmination of eighteen years of research about foreign military bases and their relationship to U.S. wars. During this research I visited more than sixty current and former bases in fourteen countries and territories, including Cuba, Ecuador, El Salvador, Germany, Great Britain, Guam, Honduras, Italy, Japan, Mauritius, the Northern Mariana Islands, the Seychelles, South Korea, and the United States. In these places I conducted more than one hundred formal interviews, had hundreds of informal conversations, and engaged in ethnographic participant observation with current and former U.S. government officials, U.S. military personnel and their family members, and locals living near U.S. bases abroad. I coupled this work with extensive archival research in the U.S. National Archives, the Lyndon B. Johnson and John F. Kennedy Presidential Libraries, the U.S. Navy's archives, and the National Archives in Britain. Given the breadth of the story that follows, this book and I owe a great debt to the excellent work of countless historians, social scientists, journalists, advocates, lawyers, and filmmakers, among others.

In the chapters that follow, I have tried to weave these disparate sources into a portrait of everything from British forts occupying colonial Boston to one of the earliest U.S. bases abroad, on the Kansas prairie. Elsewhere I describe visits ranging from Germany to Guam to Guantánamo Bay. In London and around Washington, DC, I introduce military base contractors and senior government officials who show how the Military Industrial *Congressional* Complex has helped sustain the global collection of bases and a system of imperial war. I offer these descriptions of contemporary life in tandem with descriptions of the past to emphasize the connections between the past and the present. I do so also to stress the role of individual agency in the past, as well as the contingency of history and the future. While people and countries are shaped by historical patterns and political-economic and ideological forces, futures are in no way predestined, inevitable, or leading to some ultimate goal. Any suggestion to the contrary erases the ability of human beings, however constrained and shaped by larger structures, to shape and change the world around them. Ultimately, I am writing this book with the hope of contributing to such change.

I start my tour of bases and the infrastructure of U.S. wars in Guantánamo Bay, Cuba. The naval station there has long been the best-known U.S. base overseas. It has also been the most infamous since it began hosting a prison in 2002, shortly after the start of the George W. Bush administration's self-declared global war on terrorism. While some describe Guantanamo Bay Naval Station as the oldest U.S. base abroad, my two trips to Guantanamo helped me see that the history of U.S. foreign bases and the relationship between the United States and war goes far deeper, dating to a time before the existence of the United States of America.

PART I **IMPERIAL SUCCESSION**

1 CONQUEST

"Gitmo passengers!" the Air Sunshine representative called out, breaking the 5:00 a.m. silence of a largely deserted Fort Lauderdale airport. Miami and Fort Lauderdale are the only two airports that offer commercial flights to the Guantanamo Bay Naval Station for anyone with a military entry clearance. My flight left from the city named after forts the U.S. military built around 1835, during wars to displace the Seminole people and other remaining indigenous communities from Florida. Most of the passengers on the flights to "Gitmo" are civilian contractors and family members living on base with Navy personnel.* Lawyers and journalists representing or writing about people held at the prison can also gain permission to visit. Thanks to this $500 flight, I was joining a group of U.S. and European journalists for a multiday tour.

Responding to the call to board the plane, ten tired passengers quickly got in a line. We had been waiting in front of the Air Sunshine ticket desk since our check-in at 3:30 a.m. *sharp,* in the bowels of the airport, where

---

* To distinguish Guantánamo Bay and the nearby Cuban city of Guantánamo from Guantanamo Bay the military base (which discarded the accent mark), I typically refer to the base as "Gitmo." This is its commonly used military nickname and the pronunciation of the base acronym, GTMO.

small commuter airlines offer flights to places like the Bahamas, Puerto Rico, and Jamaica. Most of the other passengers in line that morning were civilian base employees returning from vacation. Some were family members, including a young girl carrying a pink and brown camo bag.

A redheaded pilot appeared and told the line to follow him. We passed through a single door and stepped directly onto the tarmac. In front of us was our white thirty-seat, two-propeller plane, decorated only with its tail markings. Suddenly I realized that, while check-in had involved being weighed on a scale to ensure a proper weight balance for the plane, we were flying to the world's most infamous base without passing through a Transportation Security Administration (TSA) security screening.* Minutes later we were in the air above the bright lights of Fort Lauderdale, heading out over the ocean and into the pitch-black sky toward Cuba.

✪

"Ladies and gentlemen, welcome to Guantánamo," the Air Sunshine pilot announced a little after 8:00 a.m., toward the end of our three-and-a-half-hour trip. The flight felt strangely like riding a school bus, given that everyone shared a single final destination in common. When we stepped off the plane onto the airport's tarmac, the air was hot and thick with humidity. There was a spotty drizzle in a place that almost never sees rain. From the tarmac about all we could see was a fence about six feet high, topped with another three feet of razor wire, lining the airport's perimeter. I followed the rest of the plane's passengers, who seemed like they knew what they were doing, and walked into a large hangar to get in line.

One by one we approached a rickety wooden desk. We showed our passports and security clearance paperwork to a Filipino man wearing a polo shirt emblazoned with the name BREMCOR. The latest in a line of military contractors at Gitmo, BREMCOR was hired to run much of the operations, maintenance work, and daily life in a ten-year Pentagon contract, potentially worth $128,052,773.[1]

Before we entered the tiny airport terminal next to the hangar, Navy guards finally made us go through a security screening. Inside the terminal

---

* When I returned two years later, a TSA screening was required before boarding.

Sgt. Fred Ortiz, a Public Affairs officer, greeted me.* Sergeant Ortiz was wearing the Navy's digital-patterned blue camouflage (or BDU, for "battle dress uniform"). He was around six feet tall and two hundred pounds, with a broad head and face. He said to call him Fred. He told me that he or someone else from Public Affairs would be with me every waking hour until "wheels up" on my return flight to Florida. The only exception would be in my room at the Navy lodging hotel. They did this, Fred said, "as a courtesy." The surveillance didn't surprise me, given the pages-long list of rules I had to agree to follow to get permission to visit the prison.

While Fred and I waited for a ferry to the other side of the bay, where most of the base is centered, he told me was born on one of Cuba's neighboring islands, Puerto Rico. Fred noted that Puerto Rico's seizure by the United States was entirely a "strategic, military decision." U.S. troops launched their invasion of Puerto Rico from Guantánamo Bay not long after they arrived in 1898. In April of that year, the United States declared war on Spain after the mysterious sinking of the USS *Maine* provided a pretext for intervening in the Cuban Revolution. (The explosion that catastrophically damaged the *Maine* is now widely assumed to have been an accident, not Spanish sabotage. The Cuban government has long suggested that the U.S. government likely caused the explosion to justify intervention.)[2] Planning its invasion, the Navy decided that Guantánamo Bay would make a good coaling station and base for future operations. Others also saw the long-term advantages of Guantánamo. "The fine harbor there will make a good American base," wrote the *New York Times*.[3]

After the U.S. military quickly defeated Spanish troops, U.S. officials offered Cuban leaders thinly disguised U.S. rule in exchange for Cuba's official independence and the withdrawal of U.S. troops. It was an offer Cuban representatives couldn't refuse. As part of the deal, the two sides signed a lease giving the U.S. military "complete jurisdiction and control" over forty-five square miles of Guantánamo Bay—more than twice the size of Manhattan. Tellingly, the "lease" had no termination date. Effectively, Cuba was ceding territory. "We regard the [Cuban] coaling stations as ours," stated President Theodore Roosevelt.[4] The United States agreed to build a fence, prevent commercial or industrial activities within the base, and pay

---

* Fred Ortiz is a pseudonym.

a meager yearly fee of $2,000 in gold coins. Under Fidel Castro's rule, Cuba's government stopped cashing checks, worth around $4,085 each; for years the uncashed checks apparently went directly into Castro's desk.[5]

When the two governments updated the Guantánamo Bay agreement in the 1930s, it stipulated that Cuba could never force the United States to leave: the lease can be terminated only if both governments chose to do so or if the U.S. military chooses to leave. Renters everywhere wish they had such eviction-proof leases.[6] In other words, the "lease" for Guantánamo Bay is a fig leaf, an attempt to obscure colonial occupation and de facto U.S. sovereignty. In a 1953 history of the base, Gitmo's then commander, Rear Adm. Marion Emerson Murphy, wrote plainly, "Guantánamo Bay is in effect a bit of American territory, and so it will probably remain as long as we have a Navy, for we have a lease in perpetuity to this Naval Reservation and it is inconceivable that we would abandon it."[7]

✪

Once the Gitmo ferry arrived, Sergeant Ortiz and I got on board for the two-mile trip across the bay. On our right the water stretched over the horizon toward Jamaica, as the main part of the base slowly came into view. At the ferry landing the sounds of Filipino Tagalog and the lilt of Jamaican English and Patois carried across the parking lot from some of the hundreds of imported civilian contract workers on base. Sergeant Ortiz's Public Affairs colleague, Sgt. Jim Green, met us with a large white passenger van. We climbed into the van, its air conditioning on full blast in the Cuban heat, for a tour of the base.

The most well-known and notorious of U.S. bases overseas, the Guantanamo Bay Naval Station makes most people think of its high-security prison created by the George W. Bush/Dick Cheney administration in 2002.* After the administration launched its so-called global war on terrorism, the prison became an international symbol of the administration's policies of brutal torture and indefinite detention without trial.

---

* Numerous sources make the case that Cheney was the most powerful vice president in U.S. history, frequently overshadowing the power of Bush, especially on matters of war. As such, I generally refer to the 2001–9 administration as the Bush/Cheney administration.

Since the emergence of images of orange jumpsuit–clad prisoners being held in what were initially outdoor prisons, the facility has imprisoned around 780 individuals, aged thirteen to ninety-eight. Most were guilty of nothing more than being in the wrong place at the wrong time: more than 85 percent of about 700 detainees transferred out of the prison were not suspected of committing terrorist acts.[8]

To the surprise of many, the prison occupies a tiny corner of the base. While some may know the base's undulating fence line walling off the rest of Cuba, as seen in the Jack Nicholson movie *A Few Good Men,* few have seen the vast majority of the base. Ironically enough, it offers a good picture of bases worldwide. Like most bases, Gitmo resembles a U.S. town, in this case plopped down on the Cuban coast. Since at least the 1950s, military leaders have designed most bases abroad to look something like idealized versions of suburbia.[9] Gitmo, like many other bases, features suburban-style housing developments with names like Deer Point and Villamar. They have wide, looping roads and cul-de-sacs lined with single-family homes featuring driveways, garages, and spacious backyards dotted with grills and play toys. Almost everywhere teams of workers—often low-paid Filipinos— keep expansive lawns meticulously groomed. Using racialized language reflecting the racial hierarchy on base and the racial organization of labor, some military personnel call these men "lawn ninjas."

Most bases, like Gitmo, have schools, hospitals, movie theaters, gyms, golf courses, yoga studios, bowling alleys, entertainment centers, fast-food and other restaurants, barber and beauty shops, post offices, chapels, and other places of worship. Along the main two-lane road through the center of base known as "downtown," a sun-bleached set of McDonald's golden arches stands above most of Gitmo's landscape. (The McDonald's, along with the other shops and stores, violates the ban on commercial activities in the original base agreement.) Like many bases, Guantanamo Bay is on prime waterfront property, meaning the base enjoys gorgeous, uncrowded Caribbean beaches.

Military leaders' hope has been to make it as easy as possible for troops and family members to cycle between bases around the globe and to quickly feel at home. The generous amenities are also a kind of costly taxpayer-funded employment benefit, in addition to salaries, free univer-sal health care, GI Bill educational benefits, pensions, and an array of other benefits designed to keep people in the military. The on-base perks have become especially important since the end of the draft in 1973, after which Pentagon leaders have had to work harder to ensure a labor supply. (People in the U.S. armed services are laborers, even if their work is usually obscured with the language of "service.")

The amenity-rich lifestyle is particularly pronounced at Guantanamo Bay because military personnel and their family members can't leave— that is, they can leave only by flying back to the U.S. mainland. Since the Cuban Revolution of 1959, military personnel have been unable to cross the fence line. On base people ironically describe being "locked down." Many refer to the base itself as "the island." Until recently the only people allowed to cross the fence line were a handful of Cuban workers who had been working on base for decades, commuting to and from the city of Guantánamo on a daily basis. The last two such employees retired a few years ago, choosing to remain on the Cuban-controlled side of the fence. A small number of Cuban employees long ago chose to live on the base permanently. This generally meant permanently separating from Cuban family members and friends. As non–U.S. citizens, they can't move to the United States. As traitors to Cuba (in the view of the Cuban government), they can't return home. As a result, Guantanamo Bay is probably the only military base in the world with an assisted-living facility. The Cuban employees live in a kind of stateless netherworld reflective of the base's ambiguous legal status.

In many ways Guantanamo Bay feels surreal—as if it is both in the United States and not in the United States, both in Cuba and not in Cuba.[10] This is true of many bases. Most are insulated worlds unto themselves that one never has to leave. Air Force personnel can be deployed to city-sized Ramstein Air Base in Germany and never step foot off base; lederhosen and other German souvenirs are even on sale at the Ramstein mall. In other ways Gitmo feels more like a gated community, or perhaps a country club or one of the colonial plantations that once ruled the island: the base features stark segregation and inequities between U.S. military personnel and the low-paid Filipino and Jamaican guest workers who do most of the cleaning, cooking, and everyday maintenance to keep the base running.

This is not unique to Gitmo. On most bases overseas there's a class of people called "third-country nationals"—the citizens of countries other than the United States and the host nation—who keep bases running. Often they are citizens of the Philippines, a former U.S. colony. At the other end of the colonial base hierarchy, officers are disproportionately white Euro-Americans. While much of the U.S. and global economy remains hierarchically organized by race and ethnicity, the sharply colonial nature of the labor system on base contributes to the feeling that the Guantanamo Bay Naval Station is a place that's not just out of place but also out of time. Admittedly, that feeling may have been particularly pronounced because my tour of the base stopped at the tiny, little-visited museum to Gitmo's history, tucked within a sixty-foot-tall, copper-domed lighthouse along the Caribbean coast.[11]

Sergeant Green pushed open the small wooden door to the lighthouse keeper's cottage, which is now home to the museum. As fluorescent lights flickered on, we walked into a room filled with dusty bric-a-brac, its walls lined with photos dating to the days of Teddy Roosevelt's Rough Riders capturing Cuba. Along the windows sat an old glass-bottle collection. A natural history museum–style display of local flora and fauna featured taxidermy snakes, birds, and banana rats. A copy of the menu for December 22, 1903, listed "slum" (beef stew) and coffee for breakfast; beef, potatoes, and gravy for lunch; "apple (dried) sauce" and "salt horse" (salted beef) for dinner.[12]

As I walked into the museum's last cramped room, I saw a glass case with a collection of base yearbooks, much like one would see in a high school. The cover of one read "1494/1964." I asked Fred about the 1494 reference. He said it was the year Christopher Columbus landed in Guantánamo Bay on his second voyage to the Americas. This was news to me. Somehow, though, it made sense that Cristóbal Colón landed in a bay that reveals so much about the United States as an empire. Somehow it wasn't surprising that the base celebrated the beginning of the colonization and conquest of the Western Hemisphere.[13]

✪

Cristóbal Colón landed his ship, the *Santa Clara,* formerly named the *Niña,* in the bay he called Puerto Grande. Once ashore he and his men found a feast in the midst of preparation. Fish, iguanas, rabbit-like *utias,* and other food were still cooking over the flames. No one was in sight. The local indigenous people who had been preparing the meal had disappeared into the surrounding forest. The sailor and his crew were ecstatic at their discovery. Foreshadowing events to come across the Americas, they decided to help themselves to the feast.[14]

Two years earlier, on the night of Christmas Eve, 1492, on Colón's first voyage to what he and other Europeans would call the "new world," Colón ran his ship, the *Santa María*, aground. He and the other men on board found themselves on the island now called Hispaniola, in today's Haiti. The ship was lost, but Colón ordered the construction of a fort using the vessel's splintered timbers. It became the first European fort in the hemisphere. Colón had heard the island was rich with gold. He named the fort La Navidad—Christmas.

The local Taino people welcomed Colón and his men. They gave the visitors masks and ornaments of gold and wood. They even helped in the fort's construction, "little dreaming," as Washington Irving's largely mythic biography of Colón notes, "that they were assisting to place on their necks the galling yoke of perpetual and toilsome slavery."[15] Before departing for Spain Colón selected thirty-nine men—many apparently intrigued by the Tainos' peaceful way of life—to remain at the fort. He charged them with finding the island's gold, mines, and spices and promised to return in a year on his second voyage.

Colón returned with seventeen ships and 1,200 men intent on conquest. The fort was in ashes. He found the bodies of some of the men on the beach.[16] Some say the sailors mistreated the Tainos, and the locals killed the men in revenge. Others say there was an insurrection among the men. Before sailing off in search of China, only to find Guantánamo Bay and other parts of nearby islands, Colón created a new fort, Santo Tomás. The fort was in the interior of Hispaniola and would serve as a base for further colonization. Colón and the military garrison enslaved and killed hundreds of locals and took their gold. The ruins of Fortaleza Santo Tomás can still be seen in grainy photographs from as late as 1893. Archaeologists continue to explore the site today. A 2017 excavation discovered as many as nine indigenous sites nearby. The authors remarked on the lack of prior "discussions and understanding of the functioning of Fort Santo Tomás and its impact on the indigenous" peoples of the area.[17]

Before Colón's arrival and his fort, there were likely one million or more Tainos. By 1510, there were fifty thousand. Ten years later there were fifteen thousand. By 1530, five thousand remained. By the midpoint of the sixteenth century, less than sixty years after Colón's arrival, weapons and disease had wiped out all but a few hundred Tainos.[18] The horrific rate at which people died is hard to fathom.

❁

For millennia military bases have been a foundation for imperial conquest and control over foreign lands and foreign peoples.[19] "Empires have required outposts beyond their homeland, places from which they could project their awesome and frequently gruesome power," writes former Air Force officer and academic base expert Mark Gillem. "These outposts have existed to support the implementation of power."[20] Bases have been known by many names throughout history: fort, fortress, garrison, stronghold, castle, camp, citadel, cantonment, installation, facility, and outpost, to name a few. The Egyptian Middle Kingdom positioned military strongholds on the borders of its empire. Throughout antiquity fortified cities were the norm across the fertile Middle East, from Babylon to Troy to Jerusalem. The Greek word *acropolis,* associated today with the hilltop home of the Parthenon in Athens, originally referred to mountaintop citadels of the kind that appear from Masada in Israel/Palestine to Machu Picchu in today's Peru.[21]

Rome was itself an acropolis. During the expansion of its empire, the Roman military built temporary "Caesar's camps" for marching soldiers and *castra stativa,* or permanent stone and wood bases of operation, to the outer reaches of its empire. Some Roman fortresses later provided foundations for the castles built by the Norman invaders who conquered England in 1066.[22] William's army quickly erected a castle in Hastings soon after crossing the channel separating England and France. After marching from the castle to their victory at the Battle of Hastings, William's Norman nobles built another base, Pevensey Castle, within the walls of a fourth-century Roman fort.[23] The Tower of London, today one of Britain's iconic symbols, was originally William the Conqueror's military and administrative headquarters following his army's conquest.[24]

Within twenty years Norman elites, with the help of forced labor, con-structed some five hundred castles, and perhaps as many as one thousand, to control English territory and stamp out rebellions. The Normans "built castles far and wide throughout the land," reported the *Anglo-Saxon Chronicle* in 1067, "oppressing the unhappy people, and things went ever from bad to worse."[25] English castles subsequently played key roles in state administration and in the conquest and subjugation of more terri-tory in Ireland, Scotland, and parts of France.[26]

Elsewhere around the globe one finds similar histories. The Arab and Berber armies of the Umayyad Caliphate built fortifications during the eighth-century conquest of Iberia, or what became known as al-Andalus. In the thirteenth century the Mongol Empire established bases in Korea and Vietnam to invade Japan and Southeast Asia. The Chinese Ming Dynasty's "eunuch admiral" Zheng He used bases as far as East Africa and the Persian/Arabian Gulf to dominate trade routes in the Indian Ocean in the fifteenth century. Around the same period, in the Mediterranean Sea, major regional powers Venice and Genoa jockeyed with the Ottoman and Spanish Empires for control of strategically located bases and, with them, control over regional trade.[27]

The pursuit and protection of profit making through trade were central to the function of bases. Especially in the cases of Venice, Genoa, Portugal, and the Netherlands, bases were often colocated with entrepôts and other kinds of trading posts. The British East India Company, one of the main mechanisms of British colonization, "made extensive use of bases in order to pursue trade in far-flung overseas areas."[28] In the years prior to and fol-lowing Colón's first voyages, the major European powers started compet-ing for bases across much of the globe as keys to building colonial empires. Throughout history "fortifications have been a key tool by which contend-ing empires and rival nations have sought to gain an advantage over foes."[29] The Portuguese were the first to deploy their military and eco-nomic power on a global basis. In the fifteenth and sixteenth centuries, Portuguese bases could be found in, for example, the Azores, Cape Verde, São Tomé, Recife, Zanzibar, Mombasa, Goa, Timor, Macao, and Nagasaki. "Both the Portuguese fleets and its bases were deeply involved in economic activity," explains foreign bases expert Robert Harkavy. "Many bases were also *feitorias*, 'factories,' trading posts, and hubs for a variety of economic

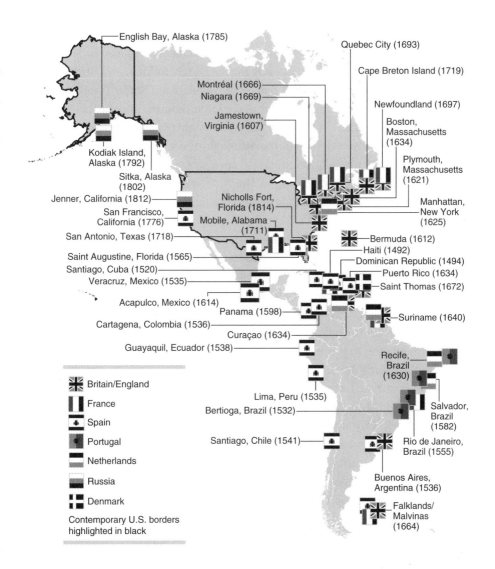

Map 5. Major European Bases in the Americas since 1492.

European empires built hundreds of forts, castles, armories, garrisons, and other military bases in the Americas. Particularly significant installations are depicted here. Place names are generally from European conquerors. Key source: Harkavy, *Strategic Basing.*

functions. Portuguese warships convoyed ships involved in commodity trade. Bases/entrepôts in West Africa in particular served also as slaving stations, as they would subsequently for the Dutch, French, and British."[30]

In the Americas Colón's first two forts, Navidad and Santo Tomás, were followed by more Spanish, Portuguese, Dutch, French, and British forts. From Canada to the Carolinas to Chile, the remains of these fortresses have often become tourist destinations. Although rarely intended this way, the bases are unintentional monuments to once powerful empires and the role forts played in the colonization of the Americas. In the case of Spanish colonial Cuba, Guantánamo Bay became a strategic colonial hub. "It served as a portal for the trade of enslaved Africans," Amy Kaplan explains, "and in the nineteenth century, Caimanera, one of its port cities, became the end point for the railroad that transported sugar and molasses from the plantations of the region to be exported abroad."[31] The Spanish monarchy created other fortified settlements in Florida and San Juan, Puerto Rico. Bases in Cartagena, Havana, and the Canary Islands were important nodes in shipping silver from the colonies to Spain—"perfectly illustrat[ing] the role of bases in relation to trade."[32]

On the North American mainland, France established the first bases: Charles Fort near Paris Island, South Carolina, in 1562, and Fort Caroline on the Saint Johns River in Florida, in 1564. English settlers built bases first in North Carolina in 1584 (Fort Raleigh) and later from Virginia to Massachusetts and well beyond. Within a month of arriving at Jamestown in 1607, immigrants at the first continuous English settlement on the continent felled trees and stripped the trunks of bark to build a basic triangular fort.[33] In 1664 English military forces took over Fort Amsterdam, near the southern tip of Manhattan, as Dutch officials surrendered their New Amsterdam colony. British bases would appear across much of northern North America, including in Boston, Plymouth, Oswego Bay, and Baltimore, during Britain's battles with Spain, France, and American Indian nations for control of the continent.

✪

There are few better illustrations of the role bases have played in the rise and fall of empires and other major powers than the former key to the

British Empire, Malta. For more than two thousand years, powerful peoples, kingdoms, and empires have sought to control the island at the center of the Mediterranean, south of Italy, as a naval base in an effort to control the entire sea and its surrounding lands. In that time Malta has been ruled or controlled by, among others, Phoenicians, Persians, Carthaginians, Romans, Byzantines, Vandals, Goths, Aghlabid and Fatimid North Africans, Normans, Genoese, Swabian Germans, Angevin and Aragonian and Castilian Spaniards, the Holy Roman Empire, the Kingdom of Sicily, the Knights of Saint John, and the Ottoman, Spanish, French, and British Empires (with a period of U.S. and Allied military control during World War II, prior to Maltese independence in 1964).

For millennia, in Malta and around the globe, rising powers frequently have usurped power from predecessors by displacing them from foreign bases. "The idea of empire or impulse of expansion seems to outlast specific polities or dynasties," writes archaeologist of ancient empires Carla Sinopoli. "Later empires often build on the cultural traditions and strategies and infrastructure of rule of earlier polities."[34] Around the Indian Ocean, for example, from Indonesian islands in the east to Sri Lanka and India in the north to Hormuz and Aden in the west, bases first occupied by Zheng He's Chinese fleet were later occupied by a succession of Portuguese, Dutch, and British military forces.[35]

In 1769, at the isolated center of the Indian Ocean, a French lieutenant named La Fontaine led the first naval survey of Diego Garcia. "A great number of vessels might anchor there in safety," La Fontaine reported to his superiors in France about Diego Garcia's lagoon.[36] Two hundred years later, almost to the day, U.S. Navy Admiral John F. McCain (grandfather of the late Republican senator) described the same island with similar enthusiasm: "As Malta is to the Mediterranean, Diego Garcia is to the Indian Ocean."[37] The U.S. Navy was soon building a major military base on the island. At the time, the U.S. and Soviet Empires were competing for supremacy around the Indian Ocean, including for bases in some of the same locations first occupied by Zheng He. Ever since, the U.S. base on Diego Garcia has played key roles in nearly all the U.S. wars in the Middle East.

There was nothing inevitable about these examples of imperial succession, of one empire replacing another at a base. Histories tend to make the past seem that way sometimes, as if history has a genealogy, with a biblical succession of one empire begetting another, begetting another.[38] To the contrary, the process of replacement has almost always been a violent, deadly one. The death in war has often been obscured by the focus on the victorious emperors, kings, and "big men" of the past.

Centuries before the creation of the U.S. base in Guantánamo Bay, Cristóbal Colón's arrival in today's Cuba came at the start of a process whereby a succession of European powers would violently conquer indigenous peoples and lands, kill millions, and extract resources and wealth across the Americas. At times empires such as Colón's patron Spain have secured foreign bases critical to conquest through diplomatic negotiations, usually involving some degree of coercion, threat, or bribery.[39] Most often empires have obtained foreign bases through conquest and occupation—so it is with the U.S. presence in Guantánamo Bay. The U.S. military seized the bay from Spain in 1898 through military conquest and has occupied it against the will of the Cuban people, revealing the domination at empire's core.

As I left Cuba, I realized I needed to see how, a century prior to replacing the Spanish Empire in Cuba, a rising U.S. Empire replaced the British Empire in Boston and elsewhere in North America. In the first days of the American Revolution, British soldiers tried to prevent this imperial succession by holding on to their control of Boston from Fort William, a base on Castle Island in Boston Harbor.[40] After Gen. George Washington surrounded Boston with his newly formed army in the spring of 1776, the Redcoats retreated and the revolutionaries occupied the fort. Today the base, known as Fort Independence, is a Boston tourist attraction.[41] Built in 1634, the base remained in continuous military operation until World War II.

2 OCCUPIED

Like Boston's Fort William, the public park known as the Boston Common dates to 1634. Several years ago I found myself in the Common to support my best friend I've known since birth, who was running the Boston Marathon. The park was buzzing with activity in preparation for the race, held annually on Patriots' Day. I had a hard time imagining Boston Common occupied not by runners and race spectators but by foreign soldiers, as it was in the fall of 1768.

On the first day of October 1768, it was supposed to be peacetime. Seven hundred British Redcoats came ashore with bayonet-tipped muskets charged and ready and a train of artillery in tow. Behind them fourteen British warships were anchored in Boston Harbor near Fort William. The warships' cannons were pointed at the city.

Shocked Bostonians, unaccustomed to the presence of an occupying army in their midst, watched as the soldiers encamped on Boston Common. Hours after their arrival a British officer stood in front of the municipal building at the corner of Tremont and Winter Streets and requested quarters for two of his regiments. The building's tenants responded by barring and bolting the doors. The troops withdrew, but when the British colonel waved a demand for quarters at city selectmen,

Boston's leaders complied. By nine that night Redcoats were marching into Faneuil Hall, the city's famous market.

"We now behold the Representatives' Chamber, Court-House, and Faneuil-Hall, those seats of freedom and justice, occupied with troops, and guards placed at the doors; the Common covered with tents, and alive with soldiers, marching and countermarching," observers reported two days later. "In short, the town is now a perfect garrison."[1]

☉

The garrisoning of troops in Boston was set in motion by King George's Quartering Act of 1765. The royal act required the colonies "to billet and quarter" British troops in "barracks provided by the colonies." If there wasn't enough room in the barracks, the colonies were required to provide quarters "in inns, livery stables, ale-houses, victualling-houses," and other shops. If there still wasn't enough room, the colonies were forced to lodge the troops in "uninhabited houses, outhouses, barns, or other buildings."[2]

Incensed by the military occupation, a group of anonymous authors smuggled regular reports out of Boston about the British presence and "the riots, outrages, robberies, etc. that are daily perpetrated among us." Although no one ever established the authors' identities, some think they may have included prominent revolutionaries like Samuel Adams and his cousin and future president, John Adams.[3]

A week after Boston received the quartering demands, the mysterious authors reported that British troops had seized private lands to build a new military post at the entrance to the city. Their reports soon read like a crime blotter:

> October 29: The inhabitants of this town have been of late greatly insulted and abused by some of the officers and soldiers, [and] several have been assaulted.

> December 29: A number of robberies have been lately committed by the soldiers.

> January 22: The common soldiers continue their robberies and violences.

March 18: A woman of this town was struck down the other evening . . . and
much abused and wounded by a soldier; another woman . . . was served in
the same brutal manner, and then robb'd of a bundle of linen . . . as was also
a peddler coming into town, from whom they took about forty dollars.[4]

Throughout 1769, reports of assaults, robbery, harassment, and rape by
soldiers were commonplace.

On a Tuesday morning in June, Sarah Johnson collapsed while walking
to Boston's South Market to go shopping. Sarah was from Bridgewater, a
small town twenty-five miles south of Boston, founded thirty years after
the *Mayflower* landed in Plymouth. She started feeling faint when she was
just steps from the elm that would soon become known as the "Liberty
Tree" for its role as a center of revolutionary organizing. People at Chase
and Speakman's Distillery, near the corner of Essex and Washington
Streets, saw Sarah in distress and quickly rushed to her aid. They brought
her water and had her sit down. When they helped Sarah to her feet, she
collapsed a second time. She would not get up again. She died before their
eyes. A coroner and a team of physicians conducted an autopsy and an
inquest into Sarah's death. From the collected evidence and marks on her
body, they concluded that Sarah had been violently raped by three unknown
British soldiers and that it "probably was the cause of her death."[5]

The anger provoked by such crimes and by troops in Boston and other
coastal cities built for months. On March 5, 1770, British soldiers fired on a
crowd, taunting them in front of Boston's Customs House. Five locals were
killed in what became known as the Boston Massacre. The killings were
another spark leading toward revolution. The movement toward armed
revolt in the colonies gained more momentum in 1774, when King George III
enacted a new Quartering Act, allowing his colonial governors to seize privately owned homes and buildings for use by British troops. In 1775
Redcoats based in Boston clashed with American militias at Lexington and
Concord. Almost 125 were dead. The revolution that would give birth to the
United States had begun. The British retreated to Castle Island and Fort
William to try to maintain hold of their thirteen rebellious colonies.

On July 4, 1776, the signers of the Declaration of Independence proclaimed, "He has kept among us, in times of peace, Standing Armies without

the Consent of our legislatures" and "quarter[ed] large bodies of armed troops among us." These were among the "long train of abuses and usurpations" committed by King George III, which the Declaration listed as cause for declaring the independence of the thirteen colonies. When thinking about the Declaration today, many forget that several of the "long train of abuses and usurpations" focused on the king's imposition of an undemocratic, violent foreign military presence. When the signers declared the colonies' intention to separate from Britain, they had in mind soldiers' crimes against Sarah Johnson and others in and beyond Boston. King George, the signers declared, had "protected [soldiers], by a mock Trial, from punishment for any Murders which they should commit on the Inhabitants of these States." The Declaration of Independence's list of the king's abuses continued:

> He has affected to render the Military independent of and superior to the Civil Power.
>
> He has abdicated Government here, by declaring us out of his Protection and waging War against us.
>
> He has plundered our seas, ravaged our coasts, burnt our towns, and destroyed the lives of our people.
>
> He is at this time transporting large Armies of foreign Mercenaries to comple[te] the works of death, desolation, and tyranny, already begun with circumstances of Cruelty and Perfidy scarcely paralleled in the most barbarous ages, and totally unworthy the Head of a civilized nation.

Patrick Henry, famous for helping inspire the U.S. revolution with his "Give me liberty or give me death!" speech to the Virginia legislature, called the basing of foreign troops in the thirteen colonies "one of the principal reasons for dissolving the connection with Great Britain."[6] So powerful were sentiments against the imposition of military forces on civilian populations that they were enshrined in the oft-forgotten Third Amendment to the Constitution: "No Soldier shall, in time of peace be quartered in any house, without the consent of the Owner, nor in time of war, but in a manner to be prescribed by law."

✪

Following the outbreak of the Revolutionary War in 1775, British troops retreated from their quarters around Boston to the safety of Castle Island's Fort William. Gen. George Washington marched his newly organized army to lay siege on the fort and evict the British from the city. After eleven months the Redcoats retreated, destroying the fort as they left Boston Harbor.[7] The reconstruction and occupation of the fort by U.S. troops under Lt. Col. Paul Revere marked a turning point in the war and in the history of North America. English troops built the first fort on Castle Island to protect shipping lanes into Boston in 1634. A century and a half later, their occupation of the city was no more. Over the next seven hard, deadly years of war, the revolutionaries—with crucial military aid from the government of France and some of Britain's other European enemies— would slowly push the British military from the thirteen newly independent states. (British soldiers continued to occupy thirteen forts on the U.S. side of the Canadian border, creating a source of tension for several years after the Treaty of Paris formally ended the war.) Estimates of the revolution's death toll from combat, disease, and other causes for combatants and civilians vary widely, with low estimates around 50,000 and high estimates up to around 160,000.[8]

British troops would return to U.S.-claimed soil after the new nation instigated a war with its former colonial ruler in 1812. Since that war it's been two centuries since an enemy power quartered soldiers or controlled a military base on U.S. soil. The one exception was Japan's World War II occupation of the U.S. colonies of Guam, the Philippines, parts of Alaska, and Wake Island.

The independence of the United States marked the beginning of an imperial transition from the British Empire to what would soon be a rapidly expanding U.S. Empire. Just as Redcoats occupied Boston with the help of Fort William, U.S. troops would use a growing number of forts and other bases on the edges of and beyond U.S. borders to occupy lands and peoples across the continent and, eventually, beyond. These bases would play a critical role in expanding U.S. borders and launching the long succession of wars that continues to this day.

The invasion of foreign lands and the occupation of bases on foreign soil began almost immediately after the colonies declared their independence. The invasions would target not just Native American peoples' lands. The invasions would target Canada as well. Mexico would follow. In the wake of the Revolutionary War, concerns about foreign military occupation disappeared for many of the leaders of the newly independent United States. The U.S. government and U.S. troops were soon committing "abuses and usurpations" similar to those listed by the signers of the Declaration of Independence as having been inflicted by King George and his troops.

Few thought to extend to others the democratic principles of the Declaration of Independence and the U.S. Constitution, including its Third Amendment barring the quartering of a soldier "without the consent of the Owner" except "in a manner to be prescribed by law." Ideas about white supremacy and about the superiority of Christianity and the United States as a chosen nation helped male leaders sustain these contradictions and overlook the hypocrisy involved when occupying lands that, with a brief exception in Canada, were inhabited by peoples who, in the minds of most U.S. leaders, were considered "racially inferior."

Such contradictions are still embedded in the Declaration of Independence and the U.S. Constitution. The Declaration's signers called their neighbors "merciless Indian Savages." The Constitution embraced slavery, the idea that enslaved African Americans counted for three-fifths of a person, and the restriction of full citizenship rights to white, Euro-American, property-owning men. These contradictions, embedded in the political-economic, legal, and social foundations of the United States, would play important roles in shaping wars to come.

PART II **EXPANDING EMPIRE**

3 WHY ARE SO MANY PLACES NAMED *FORT*?

I suspect I'm not alone among people who grew up in the United States and never thought about how frequently the word "Fort" appears in the names of cities, towns, and other locales across the country. According to the U.S. Geological Survey, there are more than four hundred populated places in the United States containing the word *fort* (long one of the U.S. Army's preferred terms for a base).[1] We've seen and heard the names so often that most of us in the United States don't register the military meaning of cities called Fort Lauderdale, Fort Worth, and Fort Knox or less prominent places such as Fort Carson and Fort Collins (Colorado), Fort Lee (New Jersey), Fort Myers (Florida), Fort Wayne (Indiana), and at least thirteen places in ten states called "Old Fort."

Many of the actual forts in these cities and towns disappeared well over a century ago. Even where the forts remain as National Park Service sites or, in rare cases, as functioning forts, the military roots of the names are easily forgotten. Several years into my research, I realized I've lived in Fort Greene (Brooklyn), picnicked and gone to concerts at Fort Reno (Washington, DC), enjoyed the beach at Fort Funston (San Francisco), and passed through the Fort McHenry Tunnel (Baltimore) hundreds of times driving up and down the East Coast. But rarely did I think about the military significance of these names—or of similar names such as Washington, DC's Military Road and Battery Kemble Park, where I went sledding as a child. In total, there are more than eight hundred past or present military sites in the United States that have *fort* in their name.[2] The evidence that forts played a critical role in this country's history is there for all to see, but it is, as anthropologist Catherine Lutz says, "hidden in plain sight."[3]

Most people studying U.S. bases outside the United States, myself included, have tended to devote little if any attention to forts within today's contiguous forty-eight states.[4] Scholars and others often say that the first U.S. base abroad was in Guantánamo Bay or perhaps the Philippines, Puerto Rico, or Guam. But U.S. Army forts and posts (the Army's other preferred term) of the eighteenth and nineteenth centuries were built on Native American territory that was very much *abroad* at the time.

By overlooking U.S. forts in North America, many scholars have inadvertently contributed to naturalizing U.S. expansion, warfare, and colonization across the continent. Ignoring the construction of U.S. forts on Native American peoples' lands has likewise made it more difficult to see the United States as an empire. Some scholars of empire have tended to make a similar mistake by marking the U.S. war with Spain in 1898 and the acquisition of colonies outside North America as the beginning of the era of U.S. imperialism. In these histories the genocidal conquest of American Indians and the ongoing occupation of indigenous lands get little attention. So too there's been little attention directed toward the role that early bases abroad played in enabling a near-constant series of wars that expanded U.S. domination across North America and eventually beyond.

Rather than distinguishing between periods of continental and extra-continental expansion, it's important to understand the relative continuity in the pattern of base construction, warfare, and territorial expansion from independence until the start of World War II. The U.S. Army was what one historian calls the "advance agent" and "pry bar" of Euro-American conquest.[5] And it was a rapidly expanding chain of western forts that provided the iron for that pry bar, while marking the line of westward expansion.

✪

From the perspective of the indigenous peoples of North America, all the military bases of the United States and other European colonizers—whether within the original thirteen states or otherwise—are *foreign* bases. These bases have, after all, occupied the territory of the original inhabitants of the land. The first bases outside the thirteen states of the colonists who declared independence in 1776 appeared even before the signing of the Declaration of Independence. The bases were in British-controlled Canada. After the clashes in Massachusetts at Lexington, Concord, and Bunker Hill started the war in 1775, the newly appointed Commander in Chief of the Continental Army, Gen. George Washington, and other revolutionary leaders hoped an invasion of Canada would encourage what they considered the fourteenth colony to join their rebellion. Some of the pro-independence leaders considered the expansion of the thirteen colonies into Canada inevitable. In the summer of 1775, the Continental Congress instructed Maj. Gen. Philip Schuyler to seize Montréal, Saint Jean, and "any other parts of the country" if "practicable, and not disagreeable to the Canadians."[6] Shortly after, patriot military forces invaded Canada south of Montréal.

The invasion was a disaster. In late 1775 the invading troops captured Fort Saint Jean, across the Saint Lawrence River, south of Montréal. They entered Montréal unopposed and established a garrison there during a little-remembered occupation that would last until the summer of 1776. Pro-independence troops would get little farther. An attempt to take Quebec City failed in the face of more numerous British troops and Canadian militiamen, inadequate supplies, starvation, disease, desertions, and drownings in the Saint Lawrence. With the contracts of about half the enlistees set to expire on New Year's Day, a final attempted siege on December 30, in the middle of a blizzard, collapsed. The general leading the attack on Quebec City, Richard Montgomery, was killed. Another of the leaders, Col. Benedict Arnold, was wounded. Arnold would infamously change sides later in the war. Only two regiments of Canadians, totaling around two thousand men, changed sides to join the rebellion. By mid-July 1776, just days after the Declaration of Independence, disorganized and defeated troops left Canada and returned to Fort Ticonderoga, in today's upstate New York.[7] Despite the disaster, the invasion of Canada would prove just the first of many attempts to expand U.S. territory by

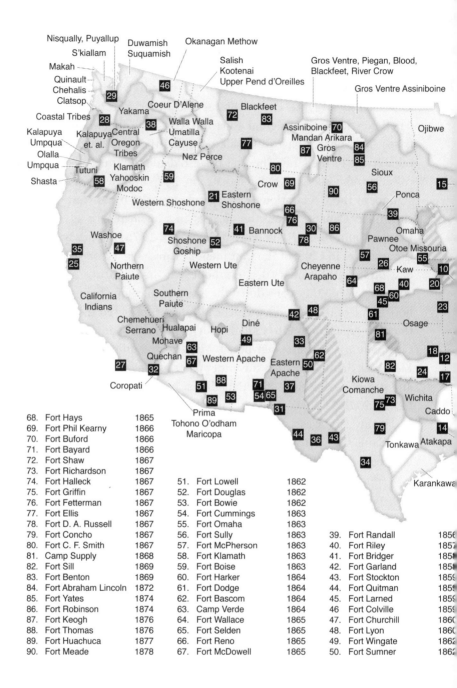

Nisqually, Puyallup
S'kiallam
Duwamish
Suquamish
Okanagan Methow
Makah
Quinault
Chehalis
Clatsop
Coastal Tribes
Kalapuya
Umpqua
Olalla
Umpqua
Shasta
Salish
Kootenai
Upper Pend d'Oreilles
Gros Ventre, Piegan, Blood,
Blackfeet, River Crow
Gros Ventre Assiniboine
Yakama
Coeur D'Alene
Blackfeet
Kalapuya Central
et. al. Oregon
Tribes
Walla Walla
Umatilla
Cayuse
Nez Perce
Assiniboine
Mandan Arikara
Gros
Ventre
Ojibwe
Tutuni
Klamath
Yahooskin
Modoc
Western Shoshone
Eastern
Shoshone
Crow
Sioux
Ponca
Washoe
Shoshone
Goship
Bannock
Omaha
Pawnee
Otoe Missouria
Northern
Paiute
Western Ute
Cheyenne
Arapaho
Kaw
California
Indians
Southern
Paiute
Eastern Ute
Chemehueri
Serrano Hualapai
Mohave
Quechan
Coropati
Hopi
Diné
Western Apache
Eastern
Apache
Osage
Kiowa
Comanche
Wichita
Caddo
Prima
Tohono O'odham
Maricopa
Tonkawa Atakapa
Karankawa

No.	Fort	Year
68.	Fort Hays	1865
69.	Fort Phil Kearny	1866
70.	Fort Buford	1866
71.	Fort Bayard	1866
72.	Fort Shaw	1867
73.	Fort Richardson	1867
74.	Fort Halleck	1867
75.	Fort Griffin	1867
76.	Fort Fetterman	1867
77.	Fort Ellis	1867
78.	Fort D. A. Russell	1867
79.	Fort Concho	1867
80.	Fort C. F. Smith	1867
81.	Camp Supply	1868
82.	Fort Sill	1869
83.	Fort Benton	1869
84.	Fort Abraham Lincoln	1872
85.	Fort Yates	1874
86.	Fort Robinson	1874
87.	Fort Keogh	1876
88.	Fort Thomas	1876
89.	Fort Huachuca	1877
90.	Fort Meade	1878

No.	Fort	Year
51.	Fort Lowell	1862
52.	Fort Douglas	1862
53.	Fort Bowie	1862
54.	Fort Cummings	1863
55.	Fort Omaha	1863
56.	Fort Sully	1863
57.	Fort McPherson	1863
58.	Fort Klamath	1863
59.	Fort Boise	1863
60.	Fort Harker	1864
61.	Fort Dodge	1864
62.	Fort Bascom	1864
63.	Camp Verde	1864
64.	Fort Wallace	1865
65.	Fort Selden	1865
66.	Fort Reno	1865
67.	Fort McDowell	1865

No.	Fort	Year
39.	Fort Randall	1856
40.	Fort Riley	1857
41.	Fort Bridger	1858
42.	Fort Garland	1858
43.	Fort Stockton	1859
44.	Fort Quitman	1859
45.	Fort Larned	1859
46.	Fort Colville	1859
47.	Fort Churchill	1860
48.	Fort Lyon	1860
49.	Fort Wingate	1862
50.	Fort Sumner	1862

Delaware, Eel River, Miami, Potawatomi, Wea

Delaware, Eel River, Miami, Potawatomi

Odawa

Ojibwe, Lenape, Eel River, Kaskaskia, Kickapoo, Miami, Odawa, Piankashaw, Potawatomi, Wea, Wyandot

Odawa, Ojibwe, Wyandot, Potawatomi

Chippewa, Lenape, Munsee, Odawa, Potawatomi, Shawnee, Wyandot

Abenaki

Mohican

Menominee

Ojibwe

Six Nations of the Iroquois

22

Ho-Chunk

va, Ojibwe, Potawatomi 5

Susquehanna

Narraganset, Wampanoag, Wappinger, Massachuset, Pequot, Mohegan

13 8

9

Potawatomi Wyandot

Lenape (Delaware)

ac and Fox

11 Miami

1

19 Kickapoo

2 Uninh

13 original states

niwek Lenape Piankashaw Shawnee

Miami

Wea

Tutelo

onfederation (Delaware)

hawnee

Powhattan

sage

4 Cherokee

Catawba

6 Chickasaw

Quawpaw

3 Choctaw

Muskogee (Creek)

7 Chitimacha

Seminole

Natchez

16 Calusa

1.	Fort Harmar	1785
2.	Fort Washington	1789
3.	Fort McHenry	1789
4.	Post at Knoxville	1793
5.	Detroit Barracks	1796
6.	Fort Pickering	1797
7.	Post at N. Orleans	1803
8.	Fort Dearborn	1803
9.	Fort Madison	1805
10.	Fort Osage (Clark)	1808
11.	Fort Edwards	1814
12.	Fort Smith	1817
13.	Fort Armstrong	1819
14.	Fort Jessup	1822
15.	Fort Snelling	1822
16.	Fort Brooke	1824
17.	Fort Towson	1824
18.	Fort Gibson	1824
19.	Jefferson Barracks	1826
20.	Fort Leavenworth	1827
21.	Fort Hall	1834
22.	Fort Atkinson	1840
23.	Fort Scott	1842
24.	Fort Washita	1842
25.	Presidio San Francisco	1847

26.	Fort Kearney	1848
27.	San Diego Barracks	1849
28.	Fort Vancouver	1849
29.	Fort Steilacoom	1849
30.	Fort Laramie	1849
31.	Fort Bliss	1849
32.	Fort Yuma	1850
33.	Fort Union	1851
34.	Fort Clark	1852
35.	Mare Isl. Shipyard	1853
36.	Fort Davis	1854
37	Fort Stanton	1855
38.	Fort Walla Walla	1856

6. *Native Lands and Early U.S. Military Bases Abroad.*
Army forts enabled the expansion of the U.S. Empire across North America. This map depicts r forts and the lands controlled by indigenous nations and peoples at the time of U.S inde- lence in 1776. Map by John Emerson and Siobhán McGuirk. Sources: Sam B. Hilliard, ian Land Cessions," *Annals of the Association of American Geographers* 62, no. 2 (1972): 374; ard W. Stewart, ed., *American Military History*, vol. 1, *The United States Army and the ing of a Nation, 1775–1917*, 2nd ed. (Washington, DC: Center of Military History, 2005), . 14. An earlier version was published in David Vine, *Base Nation: How U.S. Military Bases ad Harm America and the World* (New York: Metropolitan, 2015).

invading neighboring nations north, south, west, and east. The defeat in Canada led General Washington and other revolutionary leaders to focus mostly—but not entirely—on evicting British troops from the thirteen colonies. The war stretched on for seven more years. With the signing of the Treaty of Paris in 1783, British troops left their last fortifications in Savannah, Charleston, and New York City.

Throughout the war for independence, the Continental Army and local militias and settlers pursued an interrelated series of relatively "small but brutal wars" with indigenous nations and peoples.[8] The wars were waged primarily in the Ohio Valley and western New York. There, historian Roxanne Dunbar-Ortiz explains, colonists fought "Indigenous resisters who realized it was not in their interest to have a close enemy of settlers with an independent government, as opposed to a remote one in Great Britain." These conflicts were part of an already two-centuries-old war between Euro-American settlers attempting to take land and the inhabitants of the land. From the seventeenth century "generations of settlers, mostly [male] farmers, gained experiences as 'Indian fighters' outside of any organized military institution," Dunbar-Ortiz writes. Bounties paid by colonial governments for Native people's scalps provided an immediate financial incentive for expansionism and extreme violence.[9]

When the thirteen North American colonies began moving toward independence from Britain in the middle of the eighteenth century, the colonies' leaders looked to the European empires as models for what the colonies might become. An "expansionist consensus" helped unify the revolutionaries around the "notion of a pre-emptive right to the continent" and the vision of a united continental empire stretching across North America.[10] Perceptions of difference rooted in the developing pseudoscientific idea of *race* meant that few Euro-Americans considered the idea that the land might rightfully belong to Native groups.

Anglo settlers' aggression had been on the rise particularly since the British Empire's victory in 1763 over the French Empire in the "French and Indian War." Amid growing land speculation settlers began pushing westward into the Ohio Valley by the early 1770s. The Shawnee Nation responded to the encroachment by raiding some of the settlements. The British governor of Virginia (himself a speculator) used militia and ranger forces to retaliate by destroying Shawnee towns and arms supplies and "distress[ing] them in every other way that is possible."[11] Three decades of warfare between Anglo settlers and the Shawnee and their indigenous allies followed. A longer century of warfare and colonization was likewise set in motion from the Ohio Valley to the Pacific. A clear pattern formed: vanguard farmers and Euro-American "Indian fighters" entered into and settled on indigenous lands and then called on the government and military forces to protect them.[12]

In 1777 the Shawnee resistance allied with Britain to try to hold off the colonizers. The Shawnees pushed some of the settlers from their territory. When pro-independence forces started gaining the upper hand in the revolution, the Continental Congress launched a campaign to wipe out the Shawnee and any nearby Indian communities, whether allied with the Shawnee or not. The Congress gave orders to "destroy such towns of hostile tribes of Indians as . . . will most effectively chastise and terrify the savages, and check their ravages on the frontiers." Militiamen and Army regulars waged what has been called a "genocidal campaign" against combatants and noncombatants alike. In eastern Ohio, in a neutral Delaware village that had been Christianized by Moravian missionaries, Pennsylvania militia forced more than ninety women, men, and children into two houses before slaughtering them with a large hammer and other weapons.[13]

The commander of nearby Fort Pitt, Col. Daniel Brodhead, attacked another nearby Moravian town, killing fifteen men and taking twenty old men, women, and children prisoner. Brodhead and his men took the captives back to Fort Pitt. Described as "humane and chivalric" in a report later submitted to Congress, Brodhead had the men taken to the outskirts of town, where their captors killed and scalped them.[14]

Air Force officer and professor of history at the U.S. Air Force Academy John Grenier writes that while atrocities were "frequent" before the massacre, they "became commonplace thereafter." From the Carolinas southward to the western reaches of Virginia, Pennsylvania, and New York, gruesome, "extravagant violence" and reciprocal raiding, scalping, and killing between settlers and Native Americans became the norm. Conflicts became "unrestrained struggles for the complete destruction of the enemy."[15] A scorched-earth campaign of terror by the Continental Army, local militias, and frontiersmen, coupled with the westward flight of indigenous communities, left no doubt about who experienced the preponderance of suffering.[16] Throughout the Revolutionary War, writes Dunbar-Ortiz, "armed settlers waged total war against Indigenous people, largely realizing their objectives." Grenier argues that the frontier wars developed "America's first way of war" and that this mode of warfare has remained part of U.S. military practice until today. This is a mode of warfare that "condoned the use of violence against noncombatants," Grenier explains. Indeed, it focused on "attacking and destroying Indian noncombatant populations," and regularly employed tactics included "razing and destroying enemy villages and fields; killing enemy women and children; raiding settlements for captives; intimidating and brutalizing enemy noncombatants; and assassinating enemy leaders."[17]

The roots of this way of war can be traced further back in history. Some of the leaders of the first settlements in North America, such as John Smith in Jamestown, were mercenaries who arrived on the continent with experience fighting in brutally violent European religious wars of the sixteenth and seventeenth centuries. They brought with them the kinds of tactics in which burning entire towns and targeting noncombatants were common. "Tragically for the Indian peoples of the eastern seaboard" and for indigenous peoples who would be the victims of subsequent colonialists who inherited this way of war, "the mercenaries unleashed a similar way of war in early Virginia and New England."[18]

Gen. George Washington was not exempt from these historical patterns. When the Mohawk and Seneca Nations decided to side with Britain during the war for independence, Washington sent orders to Maj. Gen. John Sullivan: "Lay waste all the settlements around, that the country may not be merely *overrun* but *destroyed*. . . . You will not by any means, listen to any overture of peace before the total ruin of their settlements is effected."[19] Sullivan replied, "The Indians shall see that there is malice enough in our hearts to destroy everything that contributes to their support."[20]

Beyond a way of warfare, this mode of total genocidal war became important to the development of a distinct U.S. American identity. This identity in turn has played some role in shaping later wars and the conduct of those wars, especially against peoples deemed to be supposedly racially inferior. "Successive generations of Americans, both soldiers and civilians, made the killing of Indian men, women, and children a defining element of their first military tradition, and thereby part of a shared American identity," writes Grenier. Racism and violence were deeply intertwined. Grenier shows, however, that violence largely led to racism rather than vice versa. The idea of *race* and defined "white" and "Indian" *races* solidified only in the mid-eighteenth century, long after the cycles of brutality and settlers' "shockingly violent campaigns to achieve their goals of conquest" were well underway. "Only after seventeenth- and early-eighteenth-century Americans made the first way of war a key to being a white American," explains Grenier, "could later generations of 'Indian haters,' men like Andrew Jackson, turn the Indian wars into race wars."[21]

✪

In 1785, little more than a year after the end of the war for independence, the U.S. Army was starting what would become a century-long continent-wide fort-construction program. The first base was Fort Harmar. It was located near present-day Marietta, Ohio, roughly equidistant from Columbus and Pittsburgh. At the time it was in the "Northwest Territory." This was the area of today's Midwest United States, beyond the thirteen states that Britain included in generous territory it had previously claimed and ceded to the newly independent nation at the end of the revolution. Of course, the land was still occupied by Native peoples.

In 1784 the Continental Congress deployed Col. Josiah Harmar to the frontier in the Northwest Territory. Harmar's charge was to discourage U.S. settlers from moving into the Ohio Territory before the government could survey the land and put it up for sale. In October 1785 Harmar ordered his men to build a fort near the junction of the Ohio and Muskingum Rivers. Rather than discourage settlement, the fort did the opposite: it encouraged more settlers to push westward in the belief that the fort would protect them from attacks by Native Americans.[22]

At the time the new nation was in a relatively strong position militarily. After the end of the war with Britain, there was "little actual military

threat to the United States," explains an Army military history.[23] Having
agreed to an end to its American war, the British monarchy had no desire
to renew hostilities in an attempt to reconquer its lost colonies. British
leaders, along with their Spanish colonial counterparts in North America,
sought mostly to prevent the United States from expanding beyond the
new nation's borders. The breadth of the Atlantic Ocean presented a
major impediment to any European power who would have contemplated
invading the United States. Commander in Chief of the Continental Army
George Washington called for the creation of a permanent army of just
over 2,600 men, aided only by small, relatively informal state militias.

"Fortunately for us our relative situation requires but few" soldiers, he
explained in a 1783 letter to the Continental Congress. "The same circumstances which so effectually retarded, and in the end conspired to
defeat the attempts of Britain to subdue us, will now powerfully tend to
render us secure. Our *distance* from the European States in a great degree
frees us of apprehension, from their numerous regular forces and the
Insults and dangers which are to be dreaded from their Ambition."
Washington outlined a plan to maintain military posts along the borders
with Canada, Spanish Florida, and the western frontier "to awe the
Indians, protect our [pelt and fur] Trade, prevent the encroachment of
our Neighbours of Canada and the Florida's, and guard us at least from
surprizes [*sic*]." He noted that a "strong post" in the Northwest Territory,
near today's Columbus, Ohio, would be "indispensably necessary for the
security of the present Settlers" who were likely to "*immediately* settle
within those Limits."[24]

U.S. settlers would, indeed, immediately settle within and beyond the
nation's limits. Most of the Indian peoples affected by the often violent
movement of immigrants resisted fiercely. Some launched raids on settlements near the advancing line of colonization, but none were in a position
to retake significant territory or otherwise threaten the United States.[25] To
try to prevent U.S. expansion, Britain provided some support to allied
Native peoples; until 1796 British troops remained in a series of forts on
the territory near the Canadian border that Britain had technically ceded
to the United States in the Treaty of Paris. As settlers pushed westward,
they demanded protection from the new federal government.[26] The Army
built a growing number of forts to counter British, Native American,

French, and Spanish influence. Most of the new installations were in the Northwest Territory, where they were intended to oppose British fur traders, protect U.S. trading posts, and assert U.S. dominance in the face of British and Indian settlements.[27]

In January 1790 President George Washington gave his first annual address to Congress. Washington called for a buildup of the size of the Army and the military presence along the frontier. A movement of Native peoples in the Northwest Territory had been growing powerful, united by the desire to retake their homelands. With British forts in the Great Lakes region providing arms and supplies, Washington feared that U.S. expansion would be blocked by the Miami Confederacy. Congress authorized an increase in the size of the regular Army. Secretary of War Henry Knox ordered now General Josiah Harmar to lead a force of regulars backed by militiamen to attack a powerful coalition of mostly Miami and Shawnee in a rapid show of force aimed at destroying their forces and food supplies. This would prove the start of five years of warfare in Ohio country.[28]

Fort Washington, built in 1789 in what is now Cincinnati, provided the base from which Harmar and his troops launched their invasion. They reached Kekionga, a major Miami town and trading post (in today's Fort Wayne, Indiana), and several nearby Miami, Delaware, and Shawnee villages. They found Kekionga and the other villages abandoned. Some of Harmar's troops began looting.[29] After his commanders brought the men under control, Harmar divided his forces to look for their enemy. Over a period of four days, they were twice ambushed. Almost two hundred U.S. fighters lay dead. Harmar was forced to retreat while the Miami and Shawnee celebrated pushing back the invaders.[30] The battle became known as "Harmar's Humiliation."

After Harmar and his surviving men retreated to Fort Washington, Congress authorized a second, larger invasion force in 1791. The expedition would be led by the governor of the Northwest Territory, the newly named Major General Arthur St. Clair. According to one history of U.S. military strategy, St. Clair's campaign made Harmar's Humiliation "look like [a] masterpiece."[31] The general's expedition earned a name of its own: "St. Clair's Shame." The often sickly troops marched about one hundred miles from Fort Washington. In the early morning hours of November 4, around

1,000 Indians attacked, killing 637 and wounding 263 more. Less than half of St. Clair's force returned to Fort Washington physically unharmed.[32]

Some in the new nation now called for an end to the wars against Native peoples and the acceptance of an Indian buffer state proposed by British officials. President Washington would have none of it. He ordered a third invasion into Indian territory, and Congress authorized a doubling of the size of the Army. Washington appointed a general who had gained military fame during the revolution to lead the expedition, despite concerns that Maj. Gen. "Mad" Anthony Wayne was "addicted to the bottle." Wayne had also recently been removed from Congress for election irregularities after he sought office to escape prosecution from large debts incurred after the war.[33]

In the spring of 1793, Wayne took a large force to Fort Washington. The base would again serve as the launchpad for his army's invasion. After trying to get his Indian opponents to surrender, Wayne marched his troops to confront the allied Native nations from across the Northwest. Along his route he and his men methodically built new forts and smaller, reinforced blockhouses, which provided protected firing positions for riflemen. He systematically burned Indian villages and destroyed their crops.

When combined Indian forces attempted to stop the destruction by confronting Wayne's army in open battle, they suffered a devastating defeat at the "Battle of Fallen Timbers." Wayne considered attacking the nearby British base Fort Miamis. It had previously provided protection to Britain's Native American allies. But Wayne thought better of the idea, given the fort's strength and his fear of setting off another war with the British.[34] Wayne's forces spent the next three days turning villages along the Maumee River valley into a state of "general devastation and conflagration," as Wayne later described it. A week later U.S. troops did the same to villages in the nearby Auglaize River valley. Wayne then marched his troops back to a collection of blockhouses he called Fort Defiance, "laying waste the villages and cornfields for about fifty miles on each side of the Miami [River]."[35] On the site of Kekionga, Wayne's men built another new fort, soon to be called Fort Wayne.

A similar pattern continued throughout the borderlands of the country. "US genocidal wars against Indigenous nations continued unabated in the

1790s," writes Dunbar-Ortiz. In the Northwest Territory and beyond, "brutal counterinsurgency warfare would be the key to the army's destruction of the Indigenous peoples' civilization."[36] In the Ohio Valley in the summer of 1795, the shattered tribes of Wyandots, Delawares, Shawnees, Odawas, Chippewas, Potawatomis, Miamis, Eel Rivers, Weas, Kickapoos, Piankashaws, and Kaskaskias signed the Treaty of Greenville. In exchange for peace, they gave up large swaths of Ohio River valley lands to the United States.[37]

The situation for Native Americans in the region only got worse. Shortly before the signing of the Treaty of Greenville, the conditions of the 1794 U.S. treaty with Britain were announced. "Jay's Treaty" (U.S. Supreme Court Justice John Jay signed for the United States) effectively meant that Britain had ceded sovereignty over the Northwest to the United States. British officials finally agreed to abandon the thirteen forts within the boundaries of the United States that British troops had been occupying since the end of the Revolutionary War. With the departure Britain abandoned its support for its Native American allies. Holding off U.S. settlers became increasingly difficult. The settlers quickly moved farther into Indian-claimed lands in Ohio Territory. Many settlers soon wanted more.

In Spanish-controlled Florida, a similar story was underway. Spanish colonial officials withdrew support for Native peoples in the South, clearing the way for further U.S. expansion and settlement. To aid in the process, the War Department shifted U.S. forces from Ohio to what would become a growing number of forts on and beyond the southern frontier.[38]

Fueled by expansionist desires, surging feelings of nationalism, a growing population, land speculation, and government leaders wanting to pay off the country's war debts by selling western lands (still inconveniently occupied by Native Americans), waves of settlers and speculators moved westward after independence. The colonizers pushed Indians progressively away from the East Coast. "Land and more land" is what settlers and many state governments wanted, writes Reginald Horsman. To the settlers Native peoples were mere obstacles "to drive out or annihilate"; their land claims were simply "invalid."[39]

Map 7. *U.S. Bases, Wars, and Expansion Abroad, 1776–1803.*
Significant bases, combat, and expansion outside U.S. states are shown. U.S. borders are for 1803.
Key sources: Dunbar-Ortiz, *Indigenous Peoples' History;* "Fort Wiki," accessed June 13, 2019,
www.fortwiki.com; Grenier, *First Way of War;* "North American Forts, 1526–1956," accessed June
13, 2019, www.northamericanforts.com; Barbara Salazar Torreon and Sofia Plagakis, *Instances of
Use of United States Armed Forces Abroad, 1798–2018* (Washington, DC: Congressional Research
Service, 2018).

As settlers moved westward and expanded the boundaries of U.S.-controlled lands, the Army helped enable the process with a growing number of forts. Within about a decade of the establishment of Fort Harmar in the Northwest Territory in 1785, U.S. troops occupied the major Fort Detroit and around a dozen smaller bases in the region, including Forts Defiance and Washington.[40] Hundreds more frontier forts would follow.

✪

Forts were never ends in themselves. Army posts played critical roles in opening access to natural resources, land, new markets, and trading relationships. They were particularly important in challenging British, Spanish, French, and Native American influence and power. Forts were especially vital in helping U.S. settlers and businesses challenge and supplant the dominance of British traders, while also protecting and advancing the profit-making interests of U.S. settlers and businesses more broadly. As the example of Fort Harmar illustrates, even when some military officials may have conceived of forts as purely defensive or as tools to hold settlers back and keep the peace, rarely (if ever) was that the case. Settlers saw the forts as protection. Forts helped embolden them to push farther westward in search of land, resources, and profit.

Forts played an especially critical role in the economic growth and geographic expansion of the U.S. fur trade. This expansion in turn helped encourage and almost literally pave the way for other settlers moving westward. "Viewed in the broadest sense," writes David Wishart, "the fur trade was the vanguard of a massive wave of Euro-American colonisation."[41] Fur trappers played a role in westward colonization similar to that which artists have played much more recently in the gentrification of urban neighborhoods: artists have developed businesses and business opportunities, brought police protection, and made the "gentry" feel safe enough to follow them into poorer neighborhoods that wealthier classes formerly saw as scary. (The comparison between colonization and gentrification may seem inappropriate; gentrifiers' frequent use of frontier, pioneer, and cowboy-and-Indian metaphors suggests otherwise.)[42]

U.S. bases in the late eighteenth and nineteenth centuries were even more deeply intertwined with economic interests because many forts were really as much armed trading posts as they were strictly military installations. In this way U.S. military bases of the day often resembled the colonial entrepôts, *feitorias,* and other colocated bases–cum–trading posts of earlier empires and powers, such as Portugal and Genoa.

On January 18, 1803, "for the purpose of extending the external commerce of the United States," President Thomas Jefferson asked Congress for a small and seemingly insignificant appropriation of $2,500. The money was to fund an expedition led by "an intelligent officer, with ten or twelve chosen men, fit for the enterprise, and willing to undertake it, taken from our [military] posts, where they may be spared without inconvenience."[43] Congress soon approved the funds for what became the Lewis and Clark Expedition. Historians, textbooks, and politicians have often uncritically celebrated the expedition purely as an expedition and key moment in early U.S. history—the work of brave adventurers venturing into the unknown of the West (unknown to Euro-Americans at least). One celebratory history writes, "The Lewis and Clark Expedition has become an enduring symbol of the American spirit, selfless service, and human achievement."[44]

What most have forgotten is that the expedition was a military expedition planned prior to the Louisiana Purchase, with which it is generally linked. The expedition's leaders were a U.S. Army captain, Meriwether Lewis, and a former infantry company commander, William Clark. "The Lewis and Clark Expedition (1803–1806) was a military mission from start to finish," writes an official Army history. "The US Army furnished the organization and much of the manpower, equipment, and supplies. Over the course of two years, four months, and ten days, the soldiers traveled 7,689 miles and brought back invaluable geographic and scientific data, including the first detailed map of the region."[45] Unsurprisingly, the geographic and scientific data from the expedition were more than of purely academic interest. The information was critical to future military operations, including fort construction, natural resource exploitation, and westward colonization by settlers. Two subsequent expeditions to the Mississippi headwaters and the Southwest by Capt. Zebulon Pike were similarly important.

As Jefferson's letter to Congress shows, the president was carefully plotting the future commercial and demographic expansion of the United States. That the expedition "should incidentally advance the geographical knowledge of our own continent" was never the primary aim but *"an addi-*

tional gratification.[46] The expedition's main aim was to investigate and develop trading relations with Native peoples from the Mississippi River clear to the Pacific Ocean in the interest of extending a chain of federal trading houses for the exchange of furs and pelts. U.S. politicians and others elites "believed that US fur traders could work within the existing trade networks to pave the way for US expansion," writes Wishart. President Jefferson in particular saw the fur trade as the first stage in the settlement process. It would be an "overture" to encourage westward colonization.[47]

With the Lewis and Clark Expedition underway, the westward colonization process was greatly eased for Euro-Americans when Jefferson purchased around 530 million acres of western land from the French government. In 1800 Spain had secretly ceded control of the Louisiana Territory to France. News of the transfer worried Jefferson and other U.S. leaders. They now faced a strong colonial power, France, as a neighbor rather than the declining Spanish Empire. Jefferson began to investigate the purchase of Louisiana. His timing was auspicious, as Napoleon Bonaparte needed an infusion of cash in anticipation of a new war with Britain and other European powers. In April 1803 the two governments signed a draft treaty for the sale. By year's end the U.S. Army formally took possession of the territory. The Army established a small garrison in New Orleans and proceeded to occupy former Spanish forts along the lower Mississippi River.[48] Many more forts would soon follow across the West.

Just as Jefferson hoped and planned, fur trappers and fur companies came to play a "catalytic role" in colonizing western lands. The Lewis and Clark Expedition reported that the headwaters of the Missouri River were "richer in beaver and otter than any country on earth." Even before they returned to Saint Louis in September 1806, U.S. fur traders were traveling up the Missouri to build trading relationships with Mandan villages, which had previously been trading territory monopolized by the British-Canadian North West Company.[49] Urged on by George Washington, U.S. officials moved to create a "factory system" in the northern plains along the Mississippi and Missouri Rivers: at Forts Osage, Madison, Shelby, Armstrong, and Snelling, among other base-trading posts, "Indian agents" sold manufactured goods to Native buyers in exchange for furs and pelts. Initially, Native American peoples "vied with one another to attract U.S. forts with which to trade."[50]

Unsurprisingly, the rise in trapping and associated hunting reduced the availability of game for peoples who had long depended on it, including the Iowa, Omaha, Otoe, Missouria, Pawnee, Sac, and Sioux.[51] The trade also led to wide-scale deforestation along the upper Missouri River as a result of demand for wood to fuel, build, and heat the steamboats and trading posts. While populations of beaver, otter, mink, sable, deer, martens, weasels, raccoons, bears, wolves, foxes, and other game experienced short-term declines, most would rebound with the help of conservation efforts. By contrast, across the West, the buffalo moved rapidly toward extinction. The arrival of the railroads in the 1870s later allowed the fastest killing spree. By 1890 fewer than one thousand buffalo remained.[52]

Beyond the killing of the buffalo, "the fur trade," writes Wishart, "set the pace for subsequent Euro-American activity in the West. The attitude of rapacious, short-term exploitation which was imprinted during the fur trade persisted . . . as the focus shifted from furs to minerals, timber, land, and water" over the course of the nineteenth century. The profits in fur were so great that, as early as 1810, New York–based business magnate John Jacob Astor began trying to build an "international trade empire" on the Pacific coast. Astor hoped to take on British and Russian competitors, then dominating the lucrative sale of furs to markets in China. By 1811 his Pacific Fur Trading Company established itself at its own armed trading post, Fort Astoria, at the mouth of the Columbia River, in Oregon. But the company soon folded around the start of the War of 1812, when it was clear that it was too far west to receive protection from the U.S. military.[53] Astor had in effect moved too quickly westward for the protection services of the U.S. military to keep up. Astor's failure shows how the intertwined and interdependent relationship between bases and businesses was never automatic and far from seamless; thousands of settlers and settler businesses failed due to bankruptcies, deaths, and other calamities.

Christian missionaries joined those seeking fortunes in attaching themselves to the fur trade. Missionaries used fur-trading posts and fur-company steamships for transportation to gain access to Native peoples they sought to convert. Through conversion and other missionary work, missionaries further catalyzed the colonization process. This had the general effect of further disrupting indigenous societies, assisting with Euro-American conquest and the settlement of indigenous lands. Wishart concludes, "The fur trader undermined the Indian societies and paved the way for a settlement process that would eventually result in the dispossession of the Indians' lands and in the shattering of Indian culture[s]."[54] Small numbers of American Indians profited in the short term, mostly through trade. The cumulative effect of the processes associated with settler colonialism—base creation, warfare, disease epidemics, the fur trade and other resource extraction, capitalist economic transformation, environmental damage, and religious conversion—was catastrophic for indigenous peoples.

✪

Around 1806 tensions between the United States and Spain were growing over the location of the border between the newly purchased Louisiana Territory and Spanish-controlled North America. President Jefferson deployed militiamen and one thousand soldiers to the Sabine River amid rumors that Spain was massing soldiers in East Texas. A tense standoff and small skirmishes followed, but the commanders on both sides averted war or any greater bloodshed.[55] Averting war in East Texas is a reminder that the wars enabled by bases and the larger colonization process weren't inevitable. U.S. leaders and settlers could have pursued other relations with Native American peoples, for example. British leaders did. Some in the new nations also called for a different, more peaceful path.

Still, in just two decades since declaring independence and fighting an eight-year war with Britain, the U.S. military fought with Canadians, Spaniards, and even Revolutionary War ally France. More than against any other foe, U.S. military forces fought repeatedly and with special ferocity against dozens of Native American nations. U.S. Army forts were catalysts in many of these wars and battles. Today few know the military history of the hundreds of places in the United States named *fort:* how forts beyond the thirteen states helped propel Euro-American conquest of Native peoples' lands, how forts helped expand natural-resource extraction, how forts helped dominate trade, and how forts helped contribute to the deaths of probably millions of indigenous people and tens of thousands of settlers, soldiers, and militiamen. U.S. forts beyond the frontier did none of this alone. They did, however, play a critical catalytic role in these interlinked dimensions of the colonization process.

With the history of forts in North America and the wars and conquest they have enabled often "hidden in plain sight" in the names of cities and towns across the country, I was surprised when I started to see depictions of a fort on a license plate, of all places. The state of Maryland issued the plates to mark the two hundredth anniversary of the war the United States launched against Great Britain in 1812, with another invasion of British-controlled Canada. The invasion followed congressional approval of a declaration of war against Britain. A separate vote to wage a simultaneous war against France failed in the Senate by just two votes.

4 INVADING YOUR NEIGHBORS

In 2010 I began noticing them on the roads around the Washington, DC, area. For the two hundredth anniversary of the War of 1812, the state of Maryland was changing its standard-issue license plates to plates commemorating the war. The license plate features a red, white, and blue image of Baltimore's Fort McHenry with an even larger rendering of the Stars and Stripes flag waving atop the fort. In the air above it all are shimmering bursts of red that look like the fireworks one sees above most city skylines on July Fourth—except that the bursts represent the real "bombs bursting in air" that Francis Scott Key wrote about in his poem celebrating the defense of Fort McHenry against British attack. The poem would become the country's national anthem, "The Star-Spangled Banner."

The anthem and Maryland's license plate offer sanitized, bloodless visions of war. While some of those bombs may have burst in air, others burst through the bodies of human beings defending Fort McHenry, as well as the bodies of British troops ordered to attack the fort. How is it that Maryland's leaders decided to celebrate the War of 1812 on the license plate and in official commemorative events? Some state officials surely thought it would be a boon for Maryland's tourist industry. But most in the United States know little about the war. I was one of them before starting this book. When I saw the license plates, I remember asking myself, What was that war really about?

The war probably got only a brief mention in my history classes. I had a sense that whatever story I was told while growing up was severely limited. Mostly I remember learning that the war was a "tie" and that Andrew Jackson defeated the British in a battle in New Orleans that took place two weeks after the war had ended. Many characterize the war as a tie, employing the language of sports that's so often used to describe wars—as if a country or people could "win" when hundreds, thousands, or millions die and are injured. Of course, some do win in war—most often politicians, high-ranking military officials, business elites, and others who claim fortune or fame thanks to war. The vast majority, on all sides, suffer. The history books tend to depict Jackson's "victory" in New Orleans as a quirky detail of the war that propelled Jackson to the presidency as a war hero and that reflected the slow speed of communications at the time. The many hundreds of deaths and injuries on both sides of what was a tragic and unnecessary battle are generally ignored.

U.S. historians began writing about the war shortly after it ended. Their nationalist portrayals framed the war as a kind of second war for independence, with the United States as plucky underdog finally and forever overcoming the former colonial master. Perhaps these sorts of depictions explain in part why it took me about fifteen years of researching U.S. bases abroad before I thought to investigate a war in which U.S. forces invaded both Canada and Spanish- and indigenous-occupied Florida, occupying bases in both. Actually, that's not entirely accurate. U.S. forces attempted ten invasions of Canada between 1812 and the war's end in 1814. "Nearly all," writes historian J. C. A. Stagg, "ended in miserable and often bloody failures."[1]

The U.S. War of 1812 was a war for expansion, a war for the conquest of neighboring lands, a war for empire. And it was widely resisted. The minority Federalist Party opposed the war vehemently. Some in New England considered secession from the United States. The militias of Maine and Connecticut refused the call to war. Militiamen from New York, Ohio, and beyond refused orders to fight in other states or to cross an international border to invade Canada. Some state courts ruled that the federal government did not have the power to require militias to fight in another country. In 1812 militiamen in the Northwest Territory refused to fight until they were paid.[2] Thousands of enslaved men, women, and children fled captivity for sanctuary with British troops, who promised freedom. (Many of the formerly enslaved would ultimately resettle in Canada.)[3]

As the resistance indicates, the war was avoidable. The result could have been the dissolution of the United States just three decades after independence. "Tragic on a scale of vastness previously inconceivable to Americans," writes Stagg of the death and destruction involved in a war that did almost nothing to change the status quo between the United States and Great Britain.[4] During the war U.S. General Zebulon Pike's army burned York, Canada (now Toronto), and its parliament. British troops torched Washington, DC, as revenge. Before their failed attack on Baltimore, British forces easily overran disorganized U.S. troops defending the nation's capital. President James Madison; his wife, Dolly Madison; and other government leaders fled Washington, DC, for their lives. British troops burned the Capitol, parts of the Library of Congress, the Departments of War, State, Navy, and Treasury, and the President's House. (The presidential mansion got the name White House after white paint had to be used to paint over the burn marks.) British Admiral George Cockburn raised the Union Jack over the city and marched his men down the middle of Pennsylvania Avenue. When an onlooker yelled, "You could not have done this" if George Washington were alive, Cockburn retorted that Washington wouldn't have "left his capitol defenseless, for the purpose of making conquest abroad."[5]

Before he became president, James Madison opposed war. He believed in a president with limited powers. He supported vesting the power to make war in the legislative branch. The executive branch, he wrote to Thomas Jefferson prior to his presidency, "is the branch of power most interested in war and most prone to it." Once president, however, Madison felt the temptation of the political capital to be won with war. With the encouragement of House of Representatives Speaker Henry Clay and other "war hawks," Madison became the first president to ask Congress for a declaration of war. Congress agreed. Over two centuries presidents would find it easier and easier to wage war, with or without congressional approval. Just as Madison had previously feared, war became, over time, the "true nurse of executive aggrandizement."[6]

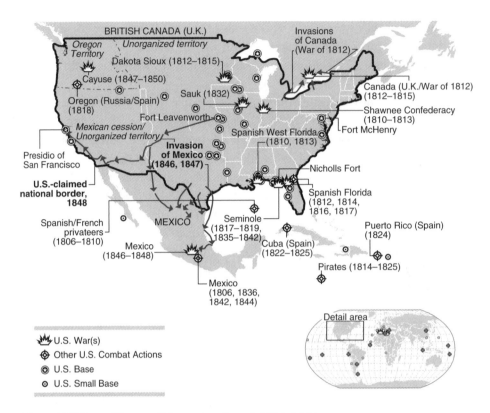

Map 8. *U.S. Bases, Wars, and Expansion Abroad, 1804–1848.*

Significant bases, combat, and expansion outside U.S. states are shown. Because of space limitations, this map does not reflect all conflicts between U.S. forces and Native American peoples. Some bases were occupied for only part of this period. U.S. borders are for 1848. Key sources: Dunbar-Ortiz, *Indigenous Peoples' History;* "Fort Wiki," accessed June 13, 2019, www.fortwiki. com; "North American Forts, 1526–1956," accessed June 13, 2019, www.northamericanforts. com; Barbara Salazar Torreon and Sofia Plagakis, *Instances of Use of United States Armed Forces Abroad, 1798-2018* (Washington, DC: Congressional Research Service, 2018).

The war itself was at least five U.S. wars fought simultaneously. First, there was the country's second war with the British Empire. Second, there was a war for Florida fought against the Spanish Empire and the Creek (or Muskogee) Confederacy, made up of Muskogee, Choctaws, Cherokees, Chickasaws, and other speakers of Muskogean languages from Florida to New Orleans. Third, U.S. forces fought members of the Six Nations Iroquois (Haudenosaunee), who were allied with the British and supported by additional Iroquois allies. Fourth and fifth, there were two wars interrelated with the Six Nations Iroquois war: one with a collection of indigenous peoples from the Algonquian-language group (mostly from the eastern parts of the Northwest Territory and northward into today's Ontario, Canada) and another with the Dakota Sioux and related peoples in the vicinity of the upper Mississippi River.[7]

The lines between and within each of these conflicts were blurry at best. Members of some indigenous groups fought far from home at times. So too, the Native peoples were far from homogenous groups. Each had its own complicated internal dynamics and relations with other indigenous and Euro-American peoples as a result of two centuries of prior displacement and death, warfare and disease, and societal fracturing accompanying these traumas. Intermarriage with other Native Americans and peoples of European and African ancestry further complicated the picture. It is little surprise that some American Indian peoples allied with the United States. Most allied with the British, given perceptions that they were more likely to slow or stop Euro-American westward migration into their lands. Some changed allegiances over time.[8]

Following the withdrawal of British forces to Canada and other parts of the British Empire at war's end, Native peoples' ability to resist U.S. expansion weakened further. The vicious "first way of war" was again the "engine of conquest." Widespread land expropriations and the enforced separation of Indians and whites followed. To most settlers Indians were mere obstacles to drive out or annihilate.[9]

✪

In 1813 Maj. Gen. Andrew Jackson of the Tennessee militia wrote the Secretary of War to say he would "rejoice at the opportunity of placing the American eagle on the ramparts of Mobile, Pensacola, and Fort St. Augustine" in Spanish- and Native American–controlled Florida.[10] Jackson's request reflected growing expansionist desires among many settlers, which contributed to the pressure to wage war against Britain two years before that war. Such feelings were already on display in Florida. In 1810 former Revolutionary War soldier Philemon Thomas led seventy-five Euro-American rebels into Spain's Fort San Carlos in Baton Rouge, in what was then Spanish-controlled western Florida (today's Louisiana). The attackers killed five Spanish soldiers. The other Spaniards surrendered or fled.[11]

Thomas and fellow leaders of the revolt declared independence from Spain and the creation of what would be the short-lived West Florida Republic. The rebellion's leaders formed a West Florida Assembly, created a blue and white Lone Star flag, and elected as governor the more or less aptly named Fulwar Skipwith. The assembly commissioned Thomas as a general of the republic's army and ordered him to conquer as much Spanish territory as possible. Thomas seized lands from the Mississippi River to the Pearl River, which today forms the boundary between Louisiana and Mississippi. After seventy-four days of independence, President James Madison announced the annexation of the former Spanish territory to the United States.[12] The leaders of the rebellion got exactly what they wished. Other rebels would follow in the decades to come, declaring independent states in Texas (1835), in California (1846), and across the South (1861), spurring the U.S. Civil War.

In the rest of Spanish Florida, however, Congress refused Andrew Jackson's request to invade with his Tennessee militia. Instead, U.S. leaders felt confident enough about the war with Britain to divert troops to form an invasion force to enter that part of Florida's Gulf Coast still disputed by the United States and Spain. The U.S. Army conquered Mobile. It occupied the town's fort, whose name changes alone tell Mobile's colonial history: under France, it was Fort Condé; under British rule, Fort Charlotte; under Spain, Fort Carlota; and under U.S. rule, Fort Charlotte, once more.[13]

Jackson was left out of the fight but saw an opportunity when parts of the Muskogee Nation rebelled against an influx of thousands of Euro-American settlers into its territory. In August 1813 a splinter group of

Muskogee, called the "Red Stick" movement, attacked and destroyed Fort Mims, near the border of the Mississippi Territory and West Florida. They killed hundreds of men, women, and children inside, including Euro-Americans, enslaved African Americans, and other Muskogee. Jackson now had cause to reassemble his militia. After nearly being defeated by the Red Sticks, U.S. Army troops returned to the region, allowing Jackson to take on nine hundred Muskogee warriors with three times that number of soldiers and allied Muskogee and Choctaw forces. Jackson's troops overran the Red Sticks' fortified camp on the Tallapoosa River, killing the vast majority of those inside. "I lament that two or three women and children were killed by accident," Jackson later said sarcastically.[14]

Jackson forced Muskogee representatives to sign the Treaty of Fort Jackson. The terms gave the United States more than half the Muskogee land—twenty-two million acres in today's Alabama and Georgia—including land belonging to Jackson's own Muskogee and Cherokee allies. When President Madison ordered Jackson to return the land the following year, Jackson refused the president's order. The Madison administration backed down for fear of Jackson's popularity. The War Department named Jackson a major general in the U.S. Army, in command of the southern frontier. His defeat of British forces invading New Orleans in January 1815 earned him acclaim across the United States. "In the public mind," writes Daniel Howe, "Andrew Jackson had won the war." Even when people learned that U.S. and British officials had signed a peace treaty two weeks earlier, the celebratory feelings remained. "The incompetence, confusion, cowardice, and humiliations of the fall of Washington were forgotten." Nationalism surged. The war quickly became known as a second war for independence. The greatness of the United States was once again clear to many. "Seldom has a nation so successfully practiced self-induced amnesia," notes historian Bradford Perkins.[15]

In the wake of the battle for New Orleans, Jackson imposed martial law on the city and kept it in place for more than two months after the battle. He had six militiamen executed after they tried to leave their militia before the end of their terms of service. He put a judge in jail who dared challenge his dictatorial powers.[16]

✪

Under Jackson's leadership war would beget bases, which would beget more war. In 1816 Jackson ordered the construction of Fort Scott, near the border between Georgia and Florida. Jackson wanted to use the fort to launch an attack on Nicholls Fort (also called the British Post) in Florida. British troops had abandoned the fort at the end of the war and left it in the hands of their allies in Florida—Seminoles and African Americans who had taken refuge in Florida after escaping from slavery in Georgia and elsewhere. Anglos began derisively calling the fort "Negro Fort."

In July 1816 Jackson directed an invasion force to blow up the fort "regardless of the ground it stands on" and "restore the stolen negroes and property to their rightful owners."[17] With the help of Native American allies, U.S. forces destroyed the fort, killing 270 men, women, and children. The survivors were captured, tortured, and either killed or sold into slavery in Georgia and Alabama. This violated a U.S. law prohibiting the importation of enslaved people across an international border.[18] Along with other military commanders, Jackson and the troops under his command had become a kind of de facto slave patrol army and protector of the "property rights" of slaveholders in the region. Like several presidents, Jackson was an "owner" of enslaved people—to the extent that one can own another human. His business in the trade of the enslaved helped Jackson amass the wealth to buy 420 acres of land in Nashville; when he died, as many as 150 people worked in the enslaved labor camp that Jackson called "The Hermitage."[19]

In 1817, the year after destroying the "Negro Fort," Jackson launched another invasion southward. Secretary of War John C. Calhoun issued orders to subdue Seminoles and Muskogee who were resisting settler incursions with raids into U.S.-controlled territory from Spanish Florida. Jackson interpreted his orders "liberally," as historian Daniel Feller puts it. He ordered the construction of a new fort on the ruins of the "Negro Fort." He proceeded to destroy "village after village" of the Seminoles' Miccosukee band, before seizing Spanish forts at Pensacola and Saint Marks. Seminoles, including those of mixed Seminole and African ancestry, fled farther south into Florida.[20]

Jackson was publicly criticized for going beyond his orders. However, claiming Florida from Spain was a long-term foreign policy goal for some politicians and elites dating to before 1812. In 1819 President James

Monroe's Secretary of State John Quincy Adams secured a treaty with Spanish representatives, giving control of Florida to the United States. In exchange the U.S. government agreed to pay up to $5 million in U.S. citizens' claims against the Spanish government and to define the border between Louisiana Purchase lands and what remained of Spanish-controlled North America (today's Texas-Louisiana border).[21]

Jackson's conquests and a series of eleven enforced treaties with Native American peoples ethnically cleansed large parts of the South for Euro-American settlement.[22] This was a precursor to the forced removal of Cherokees and others during Jackson's presidency. According to one estimate, Jackson opened lands to Euro-Americans equivalent to three-quarters of today's states of Florida and Alabama, one-third of Tennessee, one-fifth of Georgia and Mississippi, and smaller parts of North Carolina and Kentucky.[23] In short, Jackson was a driving force behind what historian Howe calls a long-term "struggle by the United States to secure white supremacy over a multiracial and multicultural society [in the South] that included Native Americans, African American maroons, French and Spanish Creoles, and intermixtures of all these peoples with each other and white Americans."[24] For Jackson and others, securing total white supremacy meant the extermination or displacement of all indigenous people in the region.[25]

✪

Just ten days after news arrived in Washington, DC, that U.S. and British representatives had signed a peace treaty ending the 1812 war, President Madison asked Congress to declare war again. And so the congressmen did. The declared adversary this time was the North African state of Algiers. The Barbary Coast states of Algiers, Tripoli, and Tunis had long demanded tribute—taxes—from the vessels of states and peoples trading in the Mediterranean. If money was not paid, Barbary warships attacked trade ships, taking cargoes and ships and holding sailors for ransom or selling them into slavery.

Between 1801 and 1805 Thomas Jefferson had already deployed U.S. naval vessels to the North African coast in what are known in the United States as the Barbary Wars. During a series of naval clashes, U.S. Marines and a U.S. Army lieutenant led a group of mercenaries to capture and occupy Tripoli's port of Derna. The battle would be memorialized in Marine Corps lore as part of its hymn, which begins, "From the halls of Montezuma to the shores of Tripoli." ("Montezuma" refers to the 1846 war the U.S. government instigated with Mexico. Tripoli would prove the first of many occasions when U.S. forces would occupy Muslim lands in the greater Middle East.) In 1815, in the aftermath of war and amid renewed Barbary Coast attacks on U.S. trading vessels, Madison deployed two Navy squadrons to the Mediterranean. U.S. warships quickly captured two Algiers warships. U.S. officers enforced peace terms and an end to the tribute payments. This result was a boon to U.S. shipping and trading companies doing business in the Mediterranean.

The powers controlling North Africa's Barbary Coast are often called the "Barbary pirates." But these were no more pirates than any state that claims taxes, tariffs, or fees in exchange for the right to trade in a given area.[26] Most states, generally speaking, just don't resort to the kind of overt violence—essentially a protection racket—that the North African powers used to enforce such payments. This is important because it shows that when the U.S. military deployed to the Mediterranean, it did so to protect U.S. citizens' individual and corporate economic interests in distant lands. Much as Army forts would support fur trappers, traders, and other business interests as settlers pushed westward, far-off naval stations helped advance the profit making of particular individuals and businesses, as well as the political-economic influence of the U.S. government far beyond North America. On the Barbary Coast the Navy was helping to open new markets to U.S. businesses, while serving as something of a protection service in its own right to ensure U.S. businesses maintained preferential trading access.

The war that the U.S. government started in 1812 was in no small part about competition with Britain and other European empires for commercial opportunities on the high seas. The war was motivated to a significant degree by the expansionist desires of some U.S. politicians, business leaders, and other elites looking for a new excuse to invade Canada and expand U.S. borders while the British military was distracted waging wars in Europe with Napoleon. The war was also a response to years of harassment of U.S. trade ships by both British and French warships, which is why senators came within two votes of declaring war on France as well as Britain.

The U.S. government had fought on-and-off naval battles with France between 1798 and 1800 (known in the United States as the "Quasi-Wars"). During these battles U.S. Navy frigates deployed to and operated from ports on several Caribbean islands. Their aim was to challenge French warships that were seizing U.S. merchant ships and their cargo to claim unpaid U.S debts from the war for independence.[27] While some think of the U.S. Empire as attaining global status only around 1898, the Navy began establishing fleet stations across five continents shortly after the signing of the 1814 peace treaty with Britain.[28] To support what were still relatively small fleets, the Navy generally leased strategically located port warehouses and repair facilities—"leasehold bases"—in places such as Rio de Janeiro; Valparaiso, Chile; Magdalena Bay, Mexico; Panama City; Portugal's Cape Verde; Spain's Balearic Islands; Luanda, Angola; Hong Kong; and Macau.

Two prominent military analysts explain that the patrol bases were positioned "close to the 'nexus of US security and economic interests,' namely, important overseas markets."[29] Notably, the analysts don't explain how bases thousands of miles from the United States advanced U.S. security. Their assertion reflects the frequent conflation of the economic interests of U.S. businesses and elites with U.S. "national security." It also reflects the frequently unsubstantiated claim that advancing corporate and elite profit making automatically advances U.S. security.

Through the middle of the nineteenth century, the Navy would use some of these and other temporary bases to support military interventions and operations in Taiwan, Uruguay, Japan, Holland, Mexico, Ecuador, China, Panama, and Korea.[30] The bases also allowed U.S. sailors to spend winter months in, for example, Spain's Mediterranean island of Menorca, which had a reputation among sailors for warmth and "indulging low and vicious habits."[31] By the time of the U.S. Civil War, the Navy had a relatively small fleet of just forty-two ships. With little to no threat to U.S. shores from European competitors, "most . . . were patrolling thousands of miles away."[32] The creation of U.S. bases and U.S. fleets patrolling in support of U.S. business interests the world over reflected the aspirations of economic elites and U.S. politicians to global political-economic influence and power. These bases and fleets foreshadowed the hundreds of U.S. bases, stations, posts, and forts that would encircle the globe in the century to come, as well as the economic interests served and supported by those installations.

First, U.S. leaders would lay claim to the Western Hemisphere. In 1823 President James Monroe claimed exclusive right to colonize and dominate affairs across the Americas, warning European powers from interfering. "The American continents," the Monroe Doctrine proclaimed, "are henceforth not to be considered as subjects for future colonization by any European powers." The U.S. government would treat any European intervention as "dangerous to our peace and safety." The Monroe administration was declaring the United States the leading power in the Western Hemisphere and that it was not to be messed with.[33]

The Monroe Doctrine contained another proviso, committing the United States to a policy of nonintervention in European wars or "internal concerns." Following the wars of the prior decade, this was notable. The main author of the doctrine, Secretary of State John Quincy Adams, had famously warned of the dangers of looking for enemies abroad. The United States, he said in an Independence Day address in 1821, "goes not abroad in search of monsters to destroy." If it were to do so, Adams cautioned, the country "would involve herself, beyond the power of extrication, in all the wars of interest and intrigue, of individual avarice, envy, and ambition, which assume the colors and usurp the standard of freedom."[34]

For Adams this stance did not mean isolationism. Rather, he said, the country should support the causes of freedom and independence for other nations. But it should do so through "the countenance of her voice, and the benignant sympathy of her example" rather than with military power. If the country involved itself in foreign wars, Adams said, "the fundamental maxims of her policy would insensibly change from liberty to force. The frontlet upon her brows would no longer beam with the ineffable splendor of freedom and independence; but in its stead would soon be substituted an imperial diadem, flashing in false and tarnished lustre the murky radiance of dominion and power. She might become the dictatress of the world," said Adams. But "she would be no longer the ruler of her own spirit."[35]

In 1825 Adams became president. In contrast to the expansionist visions of Monroe and Jackson, who preceded and followed him in office, Adams proposed broad improvements to the nation's infrastructure of roads and canals; investments to support science, invention, and enterprise; and global efforts toward improving humanity. He refused to sign a treaty that would have dispossessed the Muskogee Nation of its lands in Georgia. Unfortunately, Adams's skills as a politician never matched his ideas and his ideals. Much of his agenda was never implemented. He became a one-term president. (Adams returned to serve in the House of Representatives. He was a passionate abolitionist who won the famous case representing the enslaved people who rebelled aboard the slaving ship *Amistad* and attempted to return to Africa. Adams died on the floor of the House in 1848, decrying the invasion of another neighbor, Mexico.)

Adams was defeated in 1828 by the general known for New Orleans fame and ethnic cleansing in the Southeast, Andrew Jackson. In the age of supposed Jacksonian democracy, ideas about the War of 1812 as a defensive war marked by Fort McHenry's salvation in Baltimore and Jackson's triumph in New Orleans became further entrenched. A fairer and more historically accurate depiction of the war on the license plate of Maryland or another state would probably depict the burning of Washington, Jackson's expulsion of the Muskogee, or perhaps his invasion and occupation of forts in Spanish Florida. Such images probably wouldn't be as good for states' tourist industries today.

In the era of Jackson, the dispossession of Native Americans would accelerate. In contrast to Adams's opposition to displacing the Muskogee, the new president continued his pattern of ethnic cleansing. Jackson and Congress used a chain of forts to move indigenous nations westward and establish a "permanent Indian frontier" on the Missouri River. The permanent frontier would soon prove not so permanent.

5 THE PERMANENT INDIAN FRONTIER

I met Kelvin Crow on a crisp April day in rolling Kansas prairie territory at one of the first major U.S. bases abroad. "History is Everything," read the button on Crow's office wall at the U.S. Army's Fort Leavenworth. Crow is a white-bearded, boot-wearing civilian historian posted to the Army's elite Command and General Staff College. With Crow's own time in the military and that of his father and brother, his family has a combined hundred years of military service. His daughter, son, and daughter-in-law have since followed them into the Army, adding to the family's total. He actually urged his children not to join the military, he told me. They did anyway. They pointed out that when they were kids, he sat them on top of tanks when they were playing together. "What do you expect?" they asked, about their choice to follow his path.

On the day we met, Crow was leading a tour of Fort Leavenworth for a class of students from Missouri. He kindly let me tag along. After the tour he showed me where my grandparents had lived when my grandfather was stationed at Fort Leavenworth during World War II. As German Jews who fled Nazi Germany shortly before the war, my grandparents lived in a home on base that was within sight of the prison where German prisoners of war were held.

Built by the Army in 1827, Fort Leavenworth is the oldest continuously operating U.S. base west of the Appalachian Mountains. The base is located on a bluff 150 feet above the western bank of the Missouri River that divides Kansas and Missouri. In the eighteenth century, the same bluff was home to France's Fort de Cavignal, which protected French fur traders in the region. Almost forty years after French troops abandoned the fort, Col. Meriwether Lewis and Capt. William Clark stopped near the site as they followed the course of the Missouri River toward its source. Fort Leavenworth would become one of the most well-known bases in U.S. history. The fort is home to what is certainly the best-known U.S. military prison after only Guantánamo Bay: it has held the likes of My Lai's William Calley and WikiLeaks's Chelsea Manning.[1] (The city of Leavenworth, Kansas, is also home to a federal penitentiary, a state correctional facility, and a nearby prison labor outsourcing facility.)

On the tour Crow invoked a common ethnocentric trope of the day to explain that when the Army built the fort, it was the dividing line between "desert" to the west and "civilization" to the east. The U.S. government declared this the "permanent Indian frontier." "All the white guys," Crow said, were going to put up cattle and grow tobacco to the east. And "all the Indians" would be to the west to ride horses and hunt buffalo. "And never the twain shall meet."

Or at least that was supposedly the idea, he said.

✪

The base that marked the supposed "western edge of civilization" was soon enabling the westward migratory invasion of Euro-American settlers beyond the "permanent Indian frontier" by protecting the start of the Santa Fe and Oregon Trails. Army expeditions and a growing chain of forts led the way for settlers sweeping westward in streams of wagon trains. As the migrants settled farther and farther west, the Army built new forts and abandoned older ones no longer needed. In the three decades after the end of the War of 1812, one historian explains, "the Army pushed westward ahead of the settlers, surveying, fortifying, and building roads. Stockades and forts built and garrisoned in Iowa, Nebraska, and Kansas became the footholds of settlement in the wild frontier; just outside the walls could be found gristmills, sawmills, and blacksmith shops, all of them erected by the troops."[2]

By the middle of the nineteenth century, there were 60 major forts west of the Mississippi River and 138 Army posts in the western territories. Trappers, traders, farmers, miners, and (soon) railroads followed in their wake. The primary mission of these bases was to aid these colonizing settlers, who, at the time, were tellingly called "emigrants." Fort historian Alison Hoagland explains that "travelers stopped at the forts for supplies, relied on them for protection, or at the least saw them as landmarks on their journey." For the most part forts west of the Mississippi were not the high-walled circular forts of Hollywood Westerns and other cowboy-and-Indian clichés. Forts were for the most part open and rarely faced attack. "Fort Union [in Dakota Territory] had a wall," writes Hoagland, "but its gates were closed nightly only to corral the livestock, and were opened by day to gladly welcome in Assiniboine, Cree, and Crow Indians to trade."[3]

Much as today, forts like Fort Leavenworth played important economic roles, both to advance nearby individual, family, and corporate profit making and as economic centers in their own right. Forts were marketplaces and trading hubs for the colonists. They offered contracts to settlers to provide supplies for the installation. And they hired settlers for short-term construction and other work. "Settlers did not view forts as remote, Indian-focused establishments outside their realm, but rather as accessible resources, there to serve them, buy from them, or hire them," says Hoagland.[4]

In addition to having these oasis-like qualities for settlers—Kelvin Crow's depiction of white settlers seeing the West as "desert" was accurate—Fort Leavenworth and the other forts were the source of destruction for those peoples who saw the land not as desert but as their home. Forts enabled the disappearance of Indian-controlled lands during near-constant warfare; they facilitated the concentration of Indians on Army-controlled reservations; they brokered a series of broken treaties that the government sometimes signed with no intention of honoring; they accelerated the extermination of beloved buffalo; and they assisted in the dissolution of Native American societies, involving the dispossession and death of millions.[5]

In the presidential election of 1828, eligible white male voters ousted John Quincy Adams and elected the man who would define the term "Indian hater." Among Euro-Americans Jackson got the nickname "Old

Hickory" because of his perceived toughness. "Sharp Knife" is what the Cherokee Nation and others called him. Many U.S. history books credit new President Andrew Jackson and the new Democratic Party with bringing an era of expanded democracy to the country, thanks to the expansion of voting rights to all white adult men. It's difficult to call the system democratic at all given its clear limitations along racial and gender lines.

The invasion of white settlers and the demands of many for the removal of Native Americans accelerated in 1829 with the discovery of gold on indigenous lands in Georgia. "The lands in question belong to Georgia. She must and she will have them," the Georgia state legislature declared in an 1827 report about Cherokee Territory.[6] In 1830 Congress passed President Jackson's "Indian Removal Policy" to force all Native groups east of the Mississippi River to give up their lands in exchange for land farther west. The Indian Removal Act, as the law was formally and euphemistically known, called for the ethnic cleansing of the Choctaw, Seminole, Muskogee, Chickasaw, and Cherokee Nations from the southern homelands to Oklahoma. New Army forts played a critical role in enforcing the forced deportations.[7]

Support for the removals was far from universal. Many in the U.S. Congress and beyond vehemently resisted the law, which passed the House of Representatives by only five votes and the Senate by a twenty-eight to nineteen vote. Speaking about the Cherokee, Maine Senator Peleg Sprague questioned the right of the United States "to drive them from all their lands—or to destroy the Cherokee nation, to strike it out of existence; and, instead of managing for their 'benefit,' to annihilate 'their affairs,' as a body politic." Sprague reminded the Senate that the United States had signed fifteen treaties with the Cherokees alone since 1785 that guaranteed their land and freedom.

> By several of these treaties, we have unequivocally guaranteed to the Cherokees that they shall forever enjoy

Map 9. The Trans-Mississippi West: Some Posts, Tribes, and Battles of the Indian Wars, 1860–1890. (Map appears on the following pages.)
Reproduced from U.S. Army map. The names, spellings, and locations of Native American peoples and nations are not necessarily accurate. The years indicate the date of post/fort creation and battles. Source: Stewart, *American Military History*, 1:329.

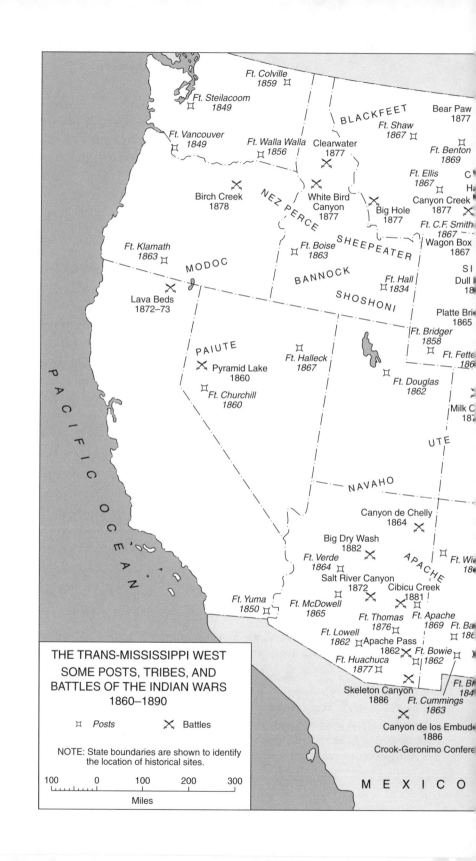

Ft. Colville
1859 ⊨

Ft. Steilacoom
⊨   1849

BLACKFEET

Bear Paw
1877

Ft. Shaw
1867 ⊨

Ft. Vancouver
⊨   1849

Ft. Walla Walla   Clearwater
⊨ 1856   1877
                ✕

⊨
Ft. Benton
1869

Ft. Ellis
1867   C'
      ⊨   Ha

Birch Creek
1878
✕

N E Z

✕
White Bird
Canyon
1877

Canyon Creek
1877   ✕

P E R C E

Big Hole
1877

Ft. C.F. Smith
1867
Wagon Box
1867

Ft. Klamath
1863 ⊨

M O D O C

Ft. Boise   SHEEPEATER
⊨ 1863

B A N N O C K

Ft. Hall
⊨ 1834

S I
Dull I
18

SHOSHONI

Lava Beds
1872–73
✕

Platte Bri
1865

Ft. Bridger
1858
⊨   Ft. Fette
      186

PAIUTE
✕ Pyramid Lake
1860

⊨
Ft. Halleck
1867

⊨
Ft. Douglas
1862

⊨
Ft. Churchill
1860

Milk C
18

U T E

NAVAHO

Canyon de Chelly
1864 ✕

Big Dry Wash
1882
✕

A P A C H E

⊨ Ft. Wi
18

Ft. Verde
1864 ⊨

Salt River Canyon
1872   Cibicu Creek
✕   ✕ 1881
              ⊨

Ft. Yuma
1850 ⊨

Ft. McDowell
1865
⊨

Ft. Thomas   Ft. Apache
1876 ⊨   1869 Ft. Ba
                  ⊨ 186

Ft. Lowell
1862 ⊨ Apache Pass
        1862 ✕ Ft. Bowie
Ft. Huachuca   ⊨ 1862
1877 ⊨

✕

Ft. B
184

Skeleton Canyon
1886   Ft. Cummings
            1863
            ✕

Canyon de los Embud
1886

Crook-Geronimo Confere

M E X I C O

THE TRANS-MISSISSIPPI WEST
SOME POSTS, TRIBES, AND
BATTLES OF THE INDIAN WARS
1860–1890

⊨   Posts   ✕   Battles

NOTE: State boundaries are shown to identify
the location of historical sites.

100   0   100   200   300
Miles

P A C I F I C   O C E A N

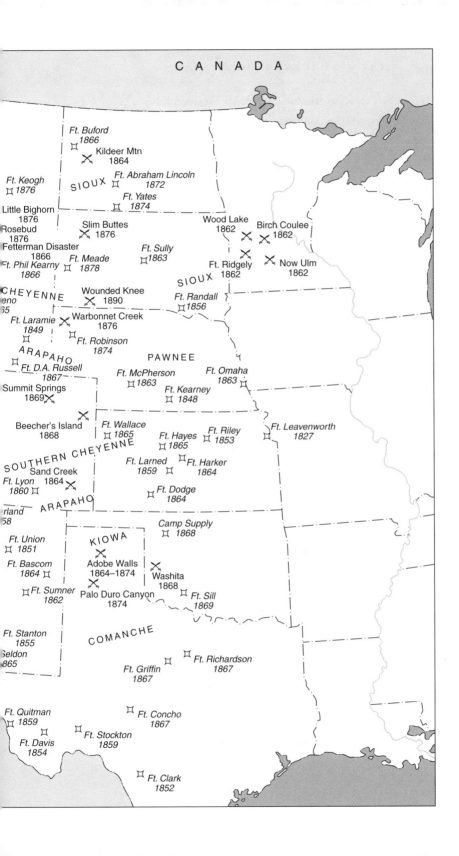

CANADA

Ft. Buford
1866

Kildeer Mtn
1864

Ft. Keogh
1876

SIOUX

Ft. Abraham Lincoln
1872

Ft. Yates
1874

Little Bighorn
1876

Rosebud
1876

Slim Buttes
1876

Wood Lake
1862

Birch Coulee
1862

Fetterman Disaster
1866

Ft. Meade
1878

Ft. Sully
1863

Ft. Phil Kearny
1866

SIOUX

Ft. Ridgely
1862

Now Ulm
1862

CHEYENNE
eno
65

Wounded Knee
1890

Ft. Randall
1856

Ft. Laramie
1849

Warbonnet Creek
1876

Ft. Robinson
1874

ARAPAHO

Ft. D.A. Russell
1867

PAWNEE

Ft. McPherson
1863

Ft. Omaha
1863

Summit Springs
1869

Ft. Kearney
1848

Beecher's Island
1868

Ft. Wallace
1865

Ft. Hayes
1865

Ft. Riley
1853

Ft. Leavenworth
1827

SOUTHERN CHEYENNE

Ft. Larned
1859

Ft. Harker
1864

Sand Creek
1864

Ft. Lyon
1860

Ft. Dodge
1864

rland
58

ARAPAHO

Camp Supply
1868

Ft. Union
1851

KIOWA

Ft. Bascom
1864

Adobe Walls
1864–1874

Washita
1868

Ft. Sumner
1862

Palo Duro Canyon
1874

Ft. Sill
1869

Ft. Stanton
1855

Seldon
865

COMANCHE

Ft. Griffin
1867

Ft. Richardson
1867

Ft. Quitman
1859

Ft. Concho
1867

Ft. Stockton
1859

Ft. Davis
1854

Ft. Clark
1852

1st.   Their separate existence, as a political community;

2nd.   Undisturbed possession and full enjoyment of their lands . . . ;

3rd.   The protection of the United States, against all interference with or encroachments upon their rights by any people, state, or nation.[8]

After the law's passage, Jackson told Congress, "It gives me pleasure to announce . . . that the benevolent policy of the Government, steadily pursued for nearly thirty years, in relation to the removal of the Indians beyond the white settlements is approaching to a happy consummation."[9] Jackson of course intended no irony in his use of the word "happy." The racism of Jackson and many of his contemporaries that underlay the removal policy was on full display when the president told Congress in 1833.

That those tribes cannot exist surrounded by our settlements and in continual contact with our citizens is certain. They have neither the intelligence, the industry, the moral habits, nor the desire of improvement, which are essential to any favorable change in their condition. Established in the midst of another and superior race, and without appreciating the causes of their inferiority or seeking to control them, they must necessarily yield to the force of circumstances and ere long disappear.[10]

When the Cherokee Nation tried to block the removals in court, Jackson ignored Supreme Court rulings and proceeded with the expulsions with the help of the U.S. Army and forts throughout the Southeast.

Unsurprisingly, Native peoples resisted outside the courtroom as well. In Florida in 1835 the Seminoles fought back against their removal to Arkansas, attacking and burning settler sugar plantations. The U.S. Army reinforced Forts Brooke and King in central Florida—two of at least twenty-three forts across Florida at the time—to prepare for war. To uproot the Seminoles the Army employed extermination tactics, including the destruction of villages and food supplies. The war between the Seminoles and the United States continued for twelve years. Despite employing a total of around forty thousand troops and $30 million, the Army failed to drive the last Seminoles out; hundreds held out in the Florida swamps.[11]

Despite fierce resistance, the Cherokees and most of the other remaining Native American groups in the East were forced into camps and reservations in the newly declared "Indian Territory" in Oklahoma. Some of the soldiers from the "Second Seminole War" redeployed to Alabama and Georgia to assist with the expulsion of the Cherokee.[12] Between 1838 and 1839 the Army and local militias forced approximately sixteen thousand Cherokee to move one thousand miles westward, mostly by foot, from Alabama, Georgia, Tennessee, and North Carolina. Without extra food, clothing, or blankets, conditions were horrific. As many as 25 percent— four thousand people—on the march may have died. The Cherokee called it "Nunna dual Isunyi," or the Trail of Tears. "Trail of Death" would be an equally appropriate name.* In total forty-six thousand Native Americans were driven from twenty-five million acres of their lands in the East. At least six thousand died from smallpox, starvation, and exposure. As planned, white settlers took over most indigenous lands.

✪

The deportation and dispossession continued throughout the West, and Fort Leavenworth was at the center of this process. A string of U.S. Army expeditions set out from the fort to make treaties with Native Americans of the Great Plains and to protect westward-moving trading caravans. The government honored many of the treaties only briefly, if at all. An official Army history explains that by the 1840s the Army's "prime consideration was to help the American settlers pouring westward."[13] Tens of thousands had already moved into Texas, which the United States would annex in 1845.

Fort Leavenworth's central parade grounds for soldiers' exercises hosted negotiations between the Army and Indian representatives. It also served as a location for the distribution of goods owed—but often withheld—as treaty obligations.[14] After once-free nations were confined to reservations, the Army created forts, mostly west of Leavenworth, to encircle them, keeping Native peoples in and Euro-Americans out.

---

* For grim context, the sixty-six-mile, more deadly sounding Bataan Death March during World War II probably killed 5–15 percent of the estimated seventy-five thousand Filipinos and U.S. soldiers forced to march by the Japanese military. Some estimates approach 25 percent. See "About Bataan," Bataan Memorial Death March, accessed February 13, 2020, https://bataanmarch.com/about-bataan/.

Frequently, the reservations soon faced new white encroachment.[15] Fort Leavenworth's post commander, Col. Stephen Watts Kearny, was well known for protecting settlers along the Oregon, Mormon, and Santa Fe Trails. Fort Leavenworth had become the departure point not just for wagon trains and caravans of colonizers but also for expeditions, led by Kearny and others, to patrol the trails and resupply more isolated frontier posts, providing protection farther west.[16] As it had been in the East, the U.S. Army was effectively a protection service for settlers.

In 1846 Kearny received new orders from President James Polk. At Fort Leavenworth Kearny mustered three thousand men, mostly from the East, and wagonloads of supplies as the Army of the West. They readied to deploy. President Polk had already ordered Gen. Zachary Taylor to deploy four thousand troops to the Rio Grande. He ordered the Navy's Pacific Squadron to sail for northern Mexico's California coast, with orders to seize Yerba Buena—later known as San Francisco—in the event of war. Tensions had been high between Mexico and the United States since the United States annexed Texas in 1845. Indeed, tensions had been high for several years; in 1842 part of the U.S. Navy's Pacific Squadron invaded and briefly captured the capital of Mexican California, Monterrey, when its commander mistakenly thought the two countries were at war.[17]

After the Texas annexation Mexico cut off diplomatic ties to the United States. The government had threatened to declare war if its northern neighbor annexed its territory. Mexican officials had yet to follow through on the threat and appeared unlikely to do so facing their stronger neighbor. In contrast to the demarcated and walled border today, the Rio Grande was at the southern edge of a large border area disputed by the United States and Mexico. Polk's deployment of U.S. troops into the area was clearly a provocative move. It became even more provocative when Taylor built a strong fort on the river, opposite the Mexican town of Matamoros, and called it Fort Texas.[18]

Polk was hoping to provoke a war with Mexico.[19] The president— another slaveholder—was a fierce expansionist and had dreams of annexing California and other territories in the West. Wherever U.S. migrants settled, he declared in his inaugural address, the federal government should provide them with protection.[20] Polk was far from alone in this view. He was also not alone in holding an even more expansionist national vision of at least continental reach. Shortly before Polk's administration annexed Texas, one of the country's most popular magazines, the *Democratic Review*, argued for annexation in words that would themselves become justification for further expansion. The incorporation of Texas into the United States, the magazine wrote, would represent the "fulfilment of our manifest destiny to overspread the continent allotted by Providence for the free development of our yearly multiplying millions."[21] The religious, messianic language reflected a growing pattern of millenary Protestant Christianity in the United States. Millenary Christianity would be another impetus for expansion, along with the economic interests of slaveholders, land speculators, farmers, and others interested in making money through territorial expansion.[22] "We do but follow out our destiny," wrote South Carolina poet William Gilmore Simms in 1846,

As did the ancient Israelite—and strive
Unconscious that we work at His knee
By whom alone we triumph as we live.[23]

Others opposed such expansionist views and argued vehemently against a war with Mexico. Many feared that expansion would be a way to create more slave states. Former president John Quincy Adams was one who protested in Congress; he suffered a massive stroke on the House floor while arguing against the war. Abraham Lincoln in part made a name for himself challenging President Polk to identify where on U.S. soil U.S. troops had been attacked.[24] Henry David Thoreau's classic essay "Civil Disobedience" was inspired by his opposition to the war and the night he spent in jail for refusing to pay a poll tax to support it.

"We have not one particle of right to be here," U.S. Colonel Ethan Allen Hitchcock wrote from near the Rio Grande on March 26, 1846. "It looks as if the government sent a small force on purpose to bring on a war, so as to have a pretext for taking California and as much of this country as it chooses; for, whatever becomes of this army, there is no doubt of a war between the United States and Mexico."[25] A young soldier at the time, future general and president Ulysses Grant said, "I do not think there was ever a more wicked war than that waged by the United States on Mexico."[26] Today even the U.S. State Department acknowledges that U.S. troops instigated the war that ensued.[27]

After the first shots were fired, Polk used what he knew to be false claims that Mexico had "invaded our territory and shed American blood on American soil" to ask for and win a congressional declaration of war.[28] Kearny led his army on an eight-hundred-mile march from Fort Leavenworth to the Southwest. First they seized Santa Fe. Next they claimed the rest of Nuevo México, renaming it the New Mexico Territory. Locals briefly resisted U.S. occupation but were crushed when elite New Mexicans allied themselves with U.S forces. Newly promoted General Kearny and his army marched to the Pacific, capturing San Diego and Los Angeles.[29]

Once the war started many soldiers questioned the invasion of a neighbor posing no threat to the United States. Angry volunteer troops from Virginia, Mississippi, and North Carolina mutinied. Thousands of soldiers deserted. Some of the resistance was due to casualty rates that were unusually high for U.S. forces. They were higher for Mexicans, including civilians subjected to U.S. bombardment and wartime atrocities. Commanding generals employed the same tactics of inflicting "extravagant violence" against Native American noncombatants that had become the U.S. "way of war."[30] "Murder, robbery, and rape on mothers and daughters, in the presence of the tied-up males of the families, have been common all along the Rio Grande," reported U.S. General Winfield Scott in 1847.[31] The atrocities were motivated "in large measure by bitter racism and anti-Catholicism" among U.S. troops, writes historian Steven Hahn. Some soldiers specifically targeted Catholic churches for plunder, desecration, and arson.[32] Several hundred Irish American soldiers switched sides during the war to fight for Catholic Mexico in the San Patricio Battalion. They faced considerable anti-Catholic and anti-Irish sentiment in the military (as elsewhere in the United States). Most were killed during fighting that quickly turned against Mexican forces; U.S. troops hanged many of the rest.[33]

As fighting continued, U.S. troops captured the major cities of Monterrey, Yerba Buena (San Francisco), Vera Cruz, Puebla, and finally Mexico City. From September 1847 until June 1848, the Army occupied the Mexican capital. During this time commanders established bases to support and resupply the occupation forces in the capital and to contain Mexican guerilla forces who refused to surrender. An Army post of 2,200 soldiers occupied the major Mexican city of Puebla; almost 25,000 occupied central Mexico.[34]

When U.S. and Mexican officials signed a treaty to end the war in 1848, the U.S. government paid $15 million and agreed to pay up to $3.25 million in Mexican government debts in exchange for almost half of Mexico's prewar territory. This included around 525,000 square miles that today are the states of Arizona, Utah, Nevada, and California and parts of New Mexico, Colorado, and Wyoming. President Polk had wanted even more territory: he had plans to invade the Yucatán Peninsula and also hoped to buy Cuba from Spain.[35] Some expansionist Democrats in Polk's party pushed for annexing all of Mexico.

The Polk administration expanded U.S. borders farther into the Northwest shortly after the outbreak of the war with Mexico. In an 1846 treaty with Great Britain, the United States took complete control of the Oregon Territory, which included parts of today's states of Oregon, Washington, and Idaho and portions of Montana and Wyoming. The country would expand further in 1853, when Mexico agreed to what the U.S. government calls the Gadsden Purchase. The purchase involved a swath of Mexican-controlled, but still indigenous-occupied, land in today's Arizona and New Mexico that's larger than West Virginia.

As the government annexed each new territory, scores of Army bases followed, from Fort Bliss, Texas, to Fort Huachuca, Arizona, and from the Presidio in California to the Vancouver Barracks in Oregon Country. Like earlier bases, the new installations would continue to protect Euro-American pioneers, prospectors, California gold miners, and other settlers.

❂

Any vague pretense of the U.S. government's maintaining a "permanent Indian frontier" disappeared after 1846. Following the expulsion of Native peoples from the Southwest to Oklahoma, the War Department designed plans to create a line of forts running from north to south along

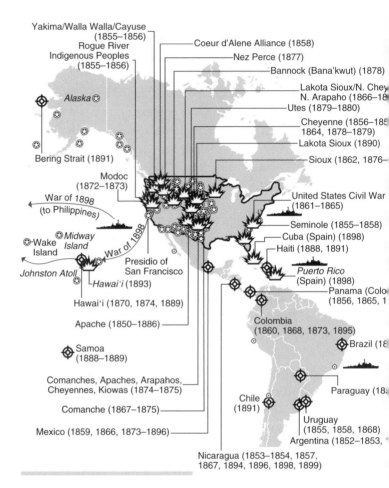

Yakima/Walla Walla/Cayuse (1855–1856)
Rogue River Indigenous Peoples (1855–1856)
Coeur d'Alene Alliance (1858)
Nez Perce (1877)
Bannock (Bana'kwut) (1878)
Lakota Sioux/N. Chey N. Arapaho (1866–18
Utes (1879–1880)
Cheyenne (1856–185 1864, 1878–1879)
Lakota Sioux (1890)
Sioux (1862, 1876–
Alaska ⊛
Bering Strait (1891)
Modoc (1872–1873)
War of 1898 (to Philippines)
United States Civil War (1861–1865)
Seminole (1855–1858)
⊛ Midway Island
⊛ Wake Island
War of 1898
Johnston Atoll
Presidio of San Francisco
Hawai'i (1893)
Hawai'i (1870, 1874, 1889)
Cuba (Spain) (1898)
Haiti (1888, 1891)
Puerto Rico (Spain) (1898)
Panama (Colo (1856, 1865, 1
Apache (1850–1886)
Colombia (1860, 1868, 1873, 1895)
Samoa (1888–1889)
Brazil (18
Comanches, Apaches, Arapahos, Cheyennes, Kiowas (1874–1875)
Chile (1891)
Paraguay (18
Comanche (1867–1875)
Uruguay (1855, 1858, 1868)
Mexico (1859, 1866, 1873–1896)
Argentina (1852–1853,
Nicaragua (1853–1854, 1857, 1867, 1894, 1896, 1898, 1899)

💥 U.S. War(s)

◎ Other U.S. Combat Actions

⊛ U.S. Base

⊙ U.S. Leasehold/Patrol Base

⚓ U.S. Naval Fleet or Squadron

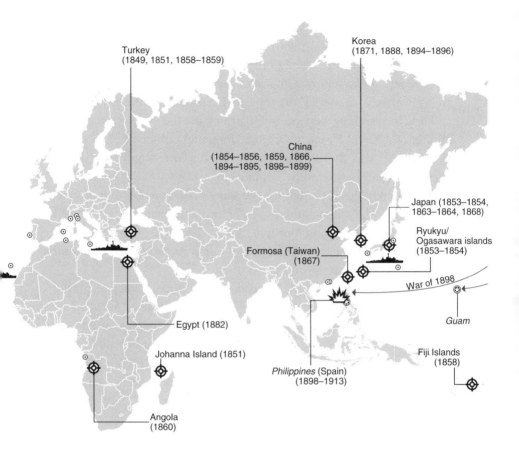

Map 10. *U.S. Bases, Wars, and Expansion Abroad, 1849–1898.*
Significant bases, combat, and expansion outside U.S. states are shown. Because of
space limitations, this map does not reflect all conflicts between U.S. forces and
Native American peoples. Some bases were occupied for only part of this period. U.S.
borders are for 1898. Oceans not to scale. Key sources: Roxanne Dunbar-Ortiz, *An
Indigenous Peoples' History of the United States* (Boston: Beacon, 2014); "Fort Wiki,"
accessed June 13, 2019, www.fortwiki.com; "North American Forts, 1526–1956,"
accessed June 13, 2019, www.northamericanforts.com; Barbara Salazar Torreon and
Sofia Plagakis, *Instances of Use of United States Armed Forces Abroad, 1798–2018*
(Washington, DC: Congressional Research Service, 2018).

the permanent Indian frontier. Fort Leavenworth was one of the major forts in the chain, along with Forts Wilkins, Snelling, Scott, Gibson, Towson, and Washita, among others. Once the United States acquired Oregon and then California and other territories taken from Mexico, settlers effectively "shattered" the supposed permanency of the frontier.[36]

Forts in Wyoming were central to protecting the northern wagon trails through the Great Plains to Oregon, Utah, and California. "Protection of these routes was the original reason for the army's intrusion into the West," Hoagland says starkly. "Establishing a presence over as much of the region as possible accounted for the army's construction of hundreds of posts." The U.S. Army acquired some of the bases from fur-trapping companies, trading posts, and Mormons. Often the settlers demanded protection from the government. Members of Congress responded by authorizing appropriations for new fort construction.[37]

Secretary of War John B. Floyd described a new policy of placing a larger number of smaller forts near colonization trails: "A line of posts running parallel with our frontier, but near to the Indians' usual habitations, placed at convenient distances and suitable positions, and occupied by infantry, would exercise a salutary restraint upon the tribes, who would feel that any foray by their warriors upon the white settlements would meet with prompt retaliation upon their own homes."[38] In the 1850s there were major forts and minor posts in as many as 138 locations in the western territories.[39]

The traditional occupants of the Great Plains saw animal and other food sources and natural resources decimated by the immigrants coming into their lands. The Sioux, Cheyenne, Arapaho, Crow, Assiniboine, Gros Ventre, Mandan, and Arikara signed a treaty with the United States to protect specific areas of land for each group in exchange for compensation in the form of annual payments of goods for a period of a mere ten years. The treaty specified the right of the federal government to build additional roads and forts in the region.[40]

Thousands of colonizers continued to move westward. In 1852 and 1853 alone, an estimated sixty thousand people passed by Fort Laramie, in Wyoming. During the 1850s the fort "served as staging grounds for expeditions against the Indians," writes Hoagland, including full-scale campaigns, smaller patrol actions, and armed escorts for specific travelers.[41] As Native peoples throughout the West found themselves herded onto reservations to control their movement, the Army positioned forts and troops nearby to maintain control. In some places the Army positioned forts to protect settlers from "wild Indians" not yet confined to reservations. In California the Army established new forts in response to Indian attacks and "depredations" against settlers—language long used to justify attacks against indigenous peoples.[42]

"No man except themselves can say what wrongs they do to the Indians by robbery, by violence, or by dispossessing them of districts of country which they have occupied unmolested for centuries," Gen. John Pope would later observe of settlers. "What the white man does to the Indian is never known. It is only what the Indian does to the white man (nine times out of ten in the way of retaliation) that reaches the public."[43]

In 1853 a government agent who delivered treaty money described how the Cheyennes, Arapahos, and many Sioux were "actually in a starving state."[44] The agent described the "system of removals and congregating tribes in small parcels of territory" as "the legalized murder of a whole nation. It is expensive, vicious, and inhuman, and producing these consequences, and these alone. The custom, being judged by its fruits, should not be persisted in."[45] Shawnee leader Tecumseh said of the encroaching "civilization": "We gave them forest-clad mountains and valleys full of game. And in return, what did they give our warriors and our women? Rum and trinkets and a grave."[46]

✪

During the United States' Civil War, the U.S. military's attacks on indigenous peoples continued unabated. After Southern rebels' seizure of Fort Sumter in South Carolina started the war in 1860, the Army's focus changed. President Abraham Lincoln transferred soldiers to the East to fight against the Southern states. During five years of fighting, other than temporary "field camps" used to launch offensive actions, new base construction was often defensive in nature. Washington, DC, became one of the world's most fortified cities: the Army built a series of sixty-eight forts and ninety-three weapons batteries to encircle the nation's capital.[47] Back in the West Lincoln and the War Department recruited volunteers to take the place of the

Army's professional soldiers battling the secessionist states. "Having few Confederates to fight," writes Roxanne Dunbar-Ortiz of the new western recruits, "they attacked people closer to hand, Indigenous people."[48]

"We remember the Civil War as a war of liberation that freed four million slaves," says historian Ari Kelman. "But it also became a war of conquest to destroy and dispossess Native Americans."[49] In Nevada, Utah, Arizona, and New Mexico, volunteer Army units and other militias terrorized Native peoples including the Shoshone, Bannock, Ute, Apache, and Navajo. In March 1864 the U.S. Army forced around eight thousand Navajos to march three hundred miles over eighteen days to what was effectively a military-run concentration camp, Bosque Redondo, at New Mexico's Fort Sumner. The Navajo would refer to the forced march as the "Navajo Long Walk." The people remained interned there for four years. At least one-fourth died of starvation.[50]

In Colorado, in late 1864, around 700 volunteer soldiers attacked a military reservation near Fort Lyon in southeastern Colorado. Around 1,000 displaced Cheyennes and Arapahos had been living in the reservation since 1861 as captives in what they thought was a government-promised "place . . . of safety." During the attack at least 108 women and children and 28 men were "butchered in cold blood by troops in the service of the United States," the federal Commissioner of Indian Affairs later reported. As many as 150 may have died, while the others fled for their lives. The killings became known as the Sand Creek Massacre. The commander of the volunteers, Col. John Chivington, claimed a great victory over a well-armed enemy and "almost an annihilation of the entire tribe." Later a congressional committee found Chivington had "deliberately planned and executed a foul and dastardly massacre" and "surprised and murdered, in cold blood," Cheyennes and Arapahos who "believe[d] that they were under [U.S.] protection."[51]

One of Chivington's captains reported what happened: "Hundreds of women and children were coming towards us, and getting on their knees for mercy." Instead, they were shot and had "their brains beat out by men professing to be civilized." The soldiers mutilated the bodies and decorated their weapons and hats with severed ears, penises, breasts, vulvas, fetuses. In Denver some of the body parts were publicly displayed to celebrate the supposed battle.[52]

In the Minnesota Territory during the Civil War, the federal government carried out the largest mass execution in U.S. history. On Lincoln's orders 38 men were hanged in a public square. They were not Confederate soldiers. Not a single Confederate general or official was executed after the war.[53] The hanged were Dakota Sioux who briefly tried to rise up against settlers in 1862, amid a series of broken treaties and stolen land. Lincoln spared the lives of 265 Dakotas originally sentenced to die by a military tribunal. The president and Congress exiled the Dakota and Winnebago, who were not involved in the uprising, from their lands in Minnesota. General Pope would not have been so merciful. "It is my purpose utterly to exterminate the Sioux if I have the power to do so," he said.[54]

Dunbar-Ortiz points out that "these military campaigns against Indigenous nations constituted foreign wars during the US Civil War." The Civil War's conclusion "did not end" these foreign wars. Indeed, the process of dispossession and the unabashed extermination of indigenous peoples accelerated. After the war large numbers of Euro-Americans were again migrating westward, from the defeated South and Union states alike. The federal government granted 1.5 million homesteads, representing almost 300 million acres of indigenous land. Railroad companies claimed large parcels of land from the government and were free to sell the lands for profit. "As a far more advanced killing machine and with seasoned troops" from the war, writes Dunbar-Ortiz, "the army began the slaughter of people, buffalo, and the land itself," decimating the food supplies of indigenous nations.[55]

Commanding General of the U.S. Army William T. Sherman brought the system of scorched-earth total warfare to the wars in the West. Sherman employed the tactics—long favored by U.S. and colonial troops battling Native Americans in the East—during his Army's march from Atlanta to Savannah, Georgia, aimed at frightening the South into submission. With ethnic cleansing and extermination in mind, the U.S. Army thus went after the Apache, Cheyenne, Comanche, Kickapoo, Kiowa, Sioux, Ute, and other nations. Soldiers and government officials destroyed food supplies, burned villages, carried out more massacres, displaced and incarcerated entire communities in reservations, and separated Indian children from their families to send them to now-notorious boarding schools aimed at forced assimilation and Christian conversion.[56]

Between 1865 and 1898, the U.S. Army fought no fewer than 943 distinct engagements against Native peoples, ranging from "skirmishes" to full-scale battles in twelve separate campaigns.[57] In 1874 and 1875, for example, the Army used bases in Texas, New Mexico, and the Indian Territory (later Oklahoma) to uproot the Arapahos, Cheyennes, Comanches, and Kiowas from a refuge in the Texas panhandle. Soldiers launched raids, destroying horses, property, and supplies, forcing the groups to surrender and relocate to reservations. "The Indian, in truth, has no longer a country," General Pope wrote. "His lands are everywhere pervaded by white men; his means of subsistence destroyed and the homes of his tribe violently taken from him; himself and his family reduced to starvation, or to the necessity of warring to the death upon the white man, whose inevitable and destructive progress threatens the total extermination of his race."

"Whatever may be the right or wrong of the question," Pope continued, "the Indian must be dispossessed. The practical question to be considered is how the inevitable can be accomplished with the least inhumanity to the Indian. We are surely not now pursuing such a course, nor are the means used becoming to a humane and Christian people."[58]

In California, Native Americans suffered what Daniel Howe calls a "shocking process of expropriation, disease, subjugation, and massacre that historians today sometimes call genocide."[59] Even if some resist using the word *genocide* in the broader U.S. context, writes historian Russell Thornton, "California is the one place in the United States where few would dispute that a genocide of Native Americans occurred."[60] Extermination-driven policies led to a decimation of the indigenous population, from an estimated 150,000 to 50,000 between 1845 and 1855. By 1870 it would be 30,000, and by 1890, just 18,000.[61] "The assumption of white supremacy permeated" policies of expansion often justified by the language of "manifest destiny," explains Howe. "It never occurred to US policymakers to take seriously the claims of nonwhite or racially mixed societies to territorial integrity."[62]

Supposed racial differences and ideas of inherent racial superiority and inferiority became a justification for further conquest in an era when the pseudoscientific idea of *race* solidified itself in the minds of Euro-Americans (since the mid-twentieth century, scientists have widely debunked the idea of race as a biological reality or valid scientific concept). Ideas of human hierarchy were also frequently expressed through the related language of "civilization" versus "savagery" or "barbarism," promulgated by anthropologists and other race scientists. "The great battle between civilization and barbarism" is how Gen. William T. Sherman described the Army's mission in the West. The work of civilizing and eradicating supposed barbarism justified what can only be called savage, barbaric violence.

U.S. soldiers, settlers, and citizens were not alone. This was the classic age of late nineteenth-century European imperialism. European empires and their citizens would increasingly invoke ideas of race and the civilizing effects of colonization during their conquests of territories in Africa and Asia. The U.S. government would do much the same in the Philippines and other colonies after 1898. Adolf Hitler's Nazi Germany, among others in the twentieth century, drew on U.S. racial "science" to justify persecution, murder, and, ultimately, the extermination of entire peoples.

❂

The beginning of the end of the wars between the U.S. government and Native American peoples and the last remnants of freedom for the few indigenous nations not yet forced onto reservations came in 1876. One hundred years after independence, President Ulysses Grant's Secretary of the Interior gave the War Department carte blanche: "Said Indians are hereby turned over to the War Department for such action on the part of the Army as you may deem proper."[63]

In 1877 and 1878 what's now Fort Leavenworth's airfield became a prisoner-of-war camp for the Nimíipuu (Nez Perce), who had been trying to flee to the safety of Canada.[64] By 1879 "Indian Territory"—the land supposedly reserved for Native Americans' exclusive use—had been whittled down to today's Oklahoma. It was home to Apaches, Arapahos, Caddos, Cherokees, Cheyennes, Chickasaws, Choctaws, Comanches, Creeks, Delawares, Kaws, Kichais, Kickapoos, Kiowas, Miamis, Modocs, Nimíipuu, Odawas, Osages, Pawnees, Peorias, Poncas, Potawatomis, Quapaws, Sacs and Foxes, Seminoles, Senecas, Shawnees, Tawakonis, Wacos, Wichitas, and Wyandots. Gradually, the indigenous nations were forced into the eastern part of the territory. Euro-American settlers took over the rest. A lottery for land parcels and a race begun with the shot of a federal official's pistol helped divide up the land. Soon settlers were moving into Native Americans' lands in the eastern part of what became the state of Oklahoma (the name appropriates a Choctaw word meaning "red people").[65]

The Army's attempt to quash some of the remaining Indian resistance led to the deaths of Lt. Col. George Custer and his entire Seventh Cavalry at Little Big Horn. The Army responded with a ruthless revenge campaign. The campaign led to the last major battle in what were effectively almost 115 consecutive years of U.S. wars against indigenous nations. In 1890, in the Dakota Territory, at a place called Wounded Knee, U.S. soldiers massacred as many as three hundred disarmed and starving Lakota Sioux.

With conquest across the continent complete and major Native armed resistance dwindling, the government began consolidating many of its western forts. Between 1880 and 1890 the number of forts declined from around 187 to 118.[66] Still, U.S. forts and troops continued to assist Euro-Americans pushing westward.[67] Soldiers focused on exploring and mapping of the type performed since Lewis and Clark's expedition, along with road construction and railroad expansion. The main functions of forts changed from protecting settlers to facilitating the actual settlement process.[68]

Bases continued to protect or advance specific business and economic interests. For example, the Army built Fort Warren (originally D. A. Russell) in Wyoming to protect the construction of the First Transcontinental Railroad. "Even after the completion of the transcontinental railroad," writes Alison Hoagland, "travelers continued to pass by and through the forts." Thousands passed through Fort Laramie, for example, on their way from the railroad station in Cheyenne to a gold rush in the Black Hills of North Dakota between 1875 and 1877.[69] Elsewhere the government instructed the Army to establish new bases to quell anti-Chinese riots along the construction route for the Union Pacific Railroad. Back east major cities witnessed the construction of a growing number of hulking, castle-like armories, as economic and political elites sought to send a message to working-class neighborhoods and to quash class conflict.[70] In Denver the Army built a fort at the urging of those who thought it would help the local economy.[71] Fort Warren remained open and actually saw new investment when many other bases closed. The growth was thanks almost entirely to the power of one Wyoming senator, who conveniently happened to chair both the Senate's Military Affairs and Appropriations Committees. His name was Francis E. Warren.[72]

The change of the fort's name from D. A. Russell to Warren came in 1930, following the senator's death, as an unsurprising tribute to Warren's largesse in funneling taxpayer dollars to the fort.[73] Fort Russell would foreshadow the development of the Military Industrial Congressional Complex after World War II, including the tendency of bases abroad to take on lives of their own, sustaining careers and profits, irrespective of strategic or military needs.[74]

The construction of a growing number of bases outside North America will likewise illustrate how base creation has almost always been closely linked to the advancement of economic interests of one kind or another— be they the interests of individual entrepreneurs or specific businesses and industries. Bases were never ends in themselves. They were always aimed at ensuring access to markets, natural resources, land, and investment opportunities in new lands.[75] They also enabled future military invasions and conquest to advance these same ends.

✪

In the cemetery at Fort Leavenworth, there are more than twenty-three thousand graves from every U.S. war since 1812.[76] The cemetery is officially closed to new burials, Kelvin Crow told me. But, he said, there are a few spaces reserved for "the inevitable casualties for inevitable future wars." The end of my tour with Crow led us to Fort Leavenworth's chapel. There plaques on the walls memorialize the deaths of Custer and the Seventh Cavalry, once based at the fort. Other plaques memorialize more than one hundred soldiers who perished in the Indian Wars.

There are no memorials to Indian dead. The closest thing comes in an ironic memorial outside the fort's gates in the depressed town that bears the same name as the fort. Many of Fort Leavenworth's streets, which are lined with dilapidated homes, pawn shops, liquor stores, and payday lenders, bear the names of some of the defeated nations: Choctaw, Cherokee, Delaware, Shawnee, Seneca, Miami, Osage, Pottawatomie [sic], Ottawa [sic.], Kickapoo, Kiowa, Dakota, Pawnee, Cheyenne, and Iowa.

Inside the gates of the fort feels like a quaint, idealized East Coast town. Kelvin Crow compared it to a "gated community," with its schools, groomed golf course, tranquil ponds, and horse stables. Flags fly outside each perfectly maintained home on shaded streets commemorating the names of some of the generals who brought death and destruction to the West's original inhabitants: Kearny, Grant, Sherman, Sheridan, McClellan, Pope, Scott, and Custer. "They made us many promises, more than I can remember," a Sioux elder said of the white man in 1890. "But they never kept but one: they promised to take our land, and they took it."[77]

Estimates of Native American numbers in the present territory of the United States before Cristóbal Colón's arrival vary widely, from one to twelve million. Their numbers by the end of the nineteenth century are widely accepted: 250,000.[78] "Somehow, even 'genocide' seems an inadequate description for what happened," writes Dunbar-Ortiz, "yet rather than viewing it with horror, most Americans have conceived of it as their country's manifest destiny."[79] The conquest and destruction of territory and peoples across North America was enabled by aggressive fort construction at every step. Forts in the West would soon enable new conquests. For the first time those conquests would be found outside North America.

6 GOING GLOBAL

When you visit the Presidio of San Francisco today, you can imagine why the Spanish Empire decided to build its northernmost military outpost in the Western Hemisphere there when Spanish troops arrived in 1776. The base sits atop a dramatic, breezy hill overlooking the narrow mouth of massive San Francisco Bay, near one side of the iconic Golden Gate Bridge. The bay is the largest on the West Coast and has since given birth to the city that bears its name as well as the neighboring metropolises of Oakland, Berkeley, San Jose, and the heart of the tech economy, Silicon Valley.

U.S. forces first occupied the base in 1846, around the start of the war with Mexico. The Presidio quickly became one of the Army's largest and most important bases in North America. It remained that way until the Pentagon closed the base in 1994 amid antimilitarism protests and the consolidation of bases following the dissolution of the Soviet Union. Since that time the Presidio has been converted into almost 1,500 acres of verdant parkland, forest, hiking trails, and a rare coastal prairie grassland integrated with civilian housing, schools, museums, restaurants, a hotel, and office space. Parts of the base remain as a National Park Service tourist site. On a sunny and typically windy spring day in San Francisco, I visited the old Commandant's Headquarters. Beneath a parking lot lie archaeological remains of the work camp where enslaved and other indigenous Californians built the adobe headquarters beginning in 1776. Nearby I saw the houses of Officers' Row, built in 1862 to replace some of the original adobe buildings inherited from the Spanish and Mexican militaries. Pershing Hall is the large Georgian-style bachelor officers' housing built in 1903, as tens of thousands of troops were deploying from the Presidio to the Philippines. Another intact building is where military officials directed the internment of Japanese Americans during World War II.

As I walked the grounds, I stumbled across several Spanish imperial cannons displayed around the base as war trophies. An iron San Domingo was cast almost four hundred years earlier in 1628, in Spanish-controlled Peru. Another was an Ordóñez gun. Filipino rebels captured it from their Spanish colonial occupiers, only for U.S. forces to seize it while attacking Filipino troops at Subic Bay in 1899. Newspaper owner, editor, and yellow journalism proponent William Randolph Hearst acquired the cannon and had it transported back to San Francisco. Hearst's *New York Journal* helped push the country into war in 1898. The city of San Francisco originally installed the cannon, appropriately enough, in Columbus Square Park, before the Army moved it to the Presidio in 1973.[1]

The cannons from Peru and Subic Bay symbolize the continuity of U.S. Empire both from empires past and from periods of continental to extracontinental conquest. It's no coincidence that U.S. forces seized a gun forged in a major colonial capital of the empire that once dominated the Western Hemisphere. It is no coincidence that Hearst acquired a gun captured by U.S. forces in a war his newspaper helped start and that he transported that gun, like a souvenir, back to one of the launchpads of the war, San Francisco. The U.S. Empire has literally inherited the presidios and other bases, the cannons and weaponry, and the land of empires past—Spanish, French, British, and Russian, among others.

While the conquest of the Philippines and Guam—the other distant Spanish-controlled island in the Pacific—may seem to be a major break in U.S. history and patterns of U.S. imperialism, these conquests were a relatively smooth extension of U.S. imperialism. In North America, forts on and beyond the borders of the thirteen original states helped launch wars that enabled the conquest of more territory, which enabled the creation of new frontier forts, which enabled new wars and territorial conquest.

There should be little surprise that the Presidio, one of the bases seized from Mexico during the midcentury war, would later become one of the major launchpads for the U.S. war in the Philippines. The invasion and seizure of Cuba was likewise launched from the port of Tampa Bay, which the United States had taken from the Spanish Empire early in the nineteenth century. Within weeks of U.S. forces' landing at Guantánamo Bay, it would be the deployment point for invading and seizing Spanish-controlled Puerto Rico.

There was nothing inevitable about the seizure of the Philippines or Cuba or Puerto Rico or about the succession of U.S. wars enabling greater conquests. But the territorial conquest and these wars were no absent-minded or accidental "stumble" into empire either, as some historians and pundits have suggested. The expansion and conquest of the United States across vast Native American lands make it unsurprising that the United States would expand into the waters of the Caribbean and the Pacific, near and far alike. It is less surprising still given that for more than a century prior to 1898, the U.S. military, U.S. businesses, and individual U.S. investors were active far beyond the bounds of North America.

✪

Many histories and popular myths about the U.S. war with Spain in 1898 depict President William McKinley's "splendid little war" and the subsequent acquisition of colonies in the Philippines, Puerto Rico, Guam, and Wake Island as the United States' one flirtation with empire, or the "Great Aberration," as historian Samuel Flagg Bemis called it.[2] This was the age of imperialism, the story often goes. The European powers were carving up Africa and other parts of the globe as colonies. The United States, this version says, got in on the game in a passing "flight of carelessness." Even if perhaps the country was guilty of dabbling in colonialism, at least it freed the Cuban people from the Spanish Empire in the process. Plus, compared to the British Empire in India or the French in West Africa, the collection of colonies could be portrayed as "too small to count as a true empire."[3]

"This compelling moral fable," writes Thomas McCormick, "of a little sin and a great redemption enabled later historians to picture subsequent American wars, both hot and cold, as confrontations fought with clean hands by an exceptional nation, untainted by ulterior motives of aggression and aggrandizement, seeking merely to defend and promote democracy and civilization against Old World Pathologies.[4] A more critical telling of the history thus holds that the War of 1898 was the start of a new form of U.S. overseas empire. This was the fundamental turning point, when the United States began to acquire colonies outside North America for the first time.

Neither of these accounts is accurate. The 1898 U.S. war with Spain and the seizure of colonies outside the continent was no accident, nor was it the emergence of a new form of U.S. Empire. Rather, the war was the culmination of the first period of U.S. imperialism postindependence, which saw the country expand across the continent with the help of U.S. Army forts and near-continuous war. Politicians and other economic and military elites had an interest in seizing territory or otherwise extending U.S. influence beyond the continental United States from the country's earliest days. Coveted lands included Cuba and parts of Asia. Despite the original thirteen states' location confined to the East Coast of North America, "from the first days of the Republic," historian Steven Hahn explains, "power in the Pacific had been central to the continental ambitions of American leaders and policy makers." These elites were "well aware of the already thriving trade in eastern and southern Asia—and of the intense jockeying among the British, French, Spanish, and Dutch" for their cut of the Asian market. U.S. elites "saw the Pacific as a vast source of economic enrichment and the Pacific coast of North America as a gateway to its riches."[5] As early as the 1780s, New England merchants were actively trading in Asian ports. Like the factory system in North America, U.S. businesspeople created the "American Factory" in Guangzhou (Canton) in 1801. Whaling ships from New England, like the fictional *Pequod* in Herman Melville's *Moby Dick*, were regularly cruising the northern Pacific Ocean and visiting the Hawaiian Islands by the 1830s.[6]

With U.S. merchants trading in ports worldwide long before today's age of globalization, the Navy established fleet stations in key strategic locations across five continents shortly after the signing of the 1814 peace treaty with Britain.[7] These were the "leasehold bases" the Navy created in places from Hong Kong to the San Francisco Bay to Rio de Janeiro to Spanish Menorca and beyond.[8] In 1842 the Secretary of the Navy was calling for a major naval buildup and installations from Hawai'i to the west coasts of South and North America.[9] By 1844 U.S. traders and military forces had access to five Chinese ports as a result of one of the many "unequal treaties" that European and U.S. governments would force on China. Sixty-four more ports would follow. These were, in effect, sovereign U.S. enclaves in China.

The most dramatic example of these Euro-American minicolonies was the "American Concession" in Shanghai. It merged with the British Concession to form the Shanghai International Settlement in 1863. It was what one writer has called "Chinatown reversed": much like U.S. bases abroad today, it was "part of a city that was once home to thousands of Europeans and Americans, who could live there in their own slice of home in the middle of the Far East." The Shanghai International Settlement remained foreign territory in China until the end of World War II; China regained sovereignty after Japanese forces occupied the settlement between 1941 and their defeat in 1945.[10]

Elsewhere in Asia, in 1853, Navy Commodore Matthew Perry paid fifty dollars for a plot of land on what's now called Chi Chi Jima, near Iwo Jima in the western Pacific. He wanted the island to become a U.S. coaling station—necessary for new steamship travel and steam-powered military operations. Perry also created the first U.S. military base in the Kingdom of Okinawa, almost one hundred years before the island would be dotted with dozens of U.S. installations. Although it lasted for only a year, Perry used the base to help create U.S. enclaves in Japan and impose unequal treaties on both Okinawa and Japan, opening the latter to the United States and European powers for the first time. U.S. officials ensured similar extraterritorial powers in Borneo, Siam, Korea, and Tonga between 1850 and 1886.[11]

An ocean away U.S. businesses and investors had opened up Cuban markets, and some wanted the United States to take the island from Spain. U.S. leaders had long looked jealously upon the strategic and economic value of the largest island in the Caribbean; many saw it as a "natural appendage of North America."[12] In 1823 Thomas Jefferson called Cuba "the most interesting addition that could ever be made to our system of States."[13] Jefferson did not recommend trying to take Cuba, acknowledging that the United States could acquire the island only through war,

Fort St. Michael

Fort Gibbon
Fort Yukon

Fort Davis

Fort Egbert

Kenai Peninsula

Fort Seward

Fort Wrangell

Kodiak Island
Alaska (U.S.)
Fort Liscum

Castle Hill

Midway Island (U.S.)

Hawai'i (U.S.)
Pearl Harbor

UNITED STATES OF AMERICA

Cuba Guantánamo Bay

Haiti Cap-Haïtien

Puerto Rico (U.S.)
Fort Buchanan

Danish West Indies
St. Thomas

Mexico
Magdalena Bay

Panama
Panama City

Panama
Fort DeLesseps

American Samoa (U.S.)
Pago Pago

Peru
Callao

Brazil
Rio de Janeiro

Chile
Valparaíso

Argentina
Buenos Aires

⊛ U.S. Base

⚓ U.S. Naval Fleet
or Squadron

⊙ U.S. Patrol Base or
Other Small Installation

France
Villefranche-sur-Mer

Spain
ort Mahon

Italy
La Spezia

Italy *Pisa*

raltar
(U.K.)

gal
bon

Malta

Japan
Nagasaki

Japan
Yokohama

China
Macau

Japan
Chi Chi Jima

Guam (U.S.)
Apra Harbor

Hong Kong
(China/U.K.)

Cape Verde
Porto Praya

Philippines
(Spain/U.S.)
Manila

Angola
Luanda

nary
ands
nerife

Map 11. U.S. Military Bases Overseas, 1776–1903.
Fleet stations, patrol and leasehold bases, and other installations beyond North
America are shown. Some bases were occupied for only part of this period. For easy
comparison of base maps over time, borders are contemporary. Oceans not to scale.
Key sources: "Alaskan Command: ALCOM Facts," Joint Base Elmendorf-Richardson,
accessed March 1, 2020, www.jber.jb.mil/Units/Alaskan-Command/; "North
American Forts, 1526–1956," accessed June 13, 2019, www.northamericanforts
.com; Pettyjohn, *U.S. Global Defense Posture.*

which would antagonize Britain. By the 1840s and 1850s, presidential administrations tried to purchase the island from Spain or undermine its rule by backing private mercenaries and rebels seeking independence.[14] When President James Polk seized around half of Mexico's territory in 1848, he wanted more of Mexico, and Cuba too.

Prior to the Civil War, as debates escalated over slavery and whether new states would be admitted to the Union as states allowing or prohibiting slavery, some southerners dreamed of building an empire in the Caribbean, Central America, and Mexico based around enslaved labor and new slaveholding territories. Some led filibustering campaigns in the 1850s into Mexico and Central America, although all failed.[15] (In the 1830s a small-scale invasion of Canada by a private U.S. "filibustering" force inspired some politicians and military officials to want to invade Canada again.)[16]

The most infamous of the filibusterers was William Walker, who led a private army, composed mostly of southerners, in an 1853 campaign into Mexico's Baja Peninsula. He declared himself president of what he called the Republic of Sonora. After Mexicans forced him to retreat to California, Walker led at least six separate campaigns in Nicaragua between 1855 and 1860. For a brief period he declared himself president of Nicaragua, earned recognition from expansionist President Franklin Pierce, declared English the national language, legalized slavery, invaded Costa Rica, and announced his intention to take over all of Central America. Twice the U.S. Navy captured him and returned him to the United States; in 1859 the administration of President James Buchanan ordered him released. Walker soon landed in Honduras during another attempt to take over Nicaragua. This time Hondurans captured Walker, tried him, and executed him with a firing squad.[17]

While U.S. officials generally opposed private interventions like Walker's, the U.S. military intervened in Latin America and the Caribbean throughout the second half of the nineteenth century. U.S. forces invaded or otherwise demonstrated their power in Nicaragua in 1853, 1854, 1857, 1867, 1894, 1896, 1898, and 1899; in Panama (then part of Colombia) in 1856, 1860, 1865, 1873, 1885, and 1895; and in Haiti in 1888 and 1891.[18]

✪

After the Civil War U.S. officials increased the nation's Pacific presence and naval power, thanks to shit—bird and bat shit, to be precise. The method of claiming new territories would provide a precedent for future colonization efforts. In the second half of the nineteenth century, "guano mania" hit U.S. farmers, after the first shipment of the rich fertilizer, consisting of bird and bat feces, arrived in the United States in 1844. Prices hit seventy-six dollars per pound by 1850.[19]

Private citizens and businesses went searching the Atlantic, Pacific, and Indian Oceans for small, generally uninhabited islands full of the "white gold." The U.S. government usually recognized their claims. The U.S. government claimed Palmyra, Jarvis, Baker, Howland's, and Midway Islands to mine guano deposits and serve as naval coaling stations.[20] From 1859 to this day, the United States has claimed control over La Navase (Navassa Island), off the Haitian coast. African American workers from Baltimore mined guano there under "grotesque" slavery-like conditions into the late nineteenth century (some revolted and killed five white managers).[21]

In total, under the Guano Islands Act, the U.S. government recognized ninety-four guano islands as "appertaining" to the United States, with private individuals claiming yet more islands.[22] What "appertaining" meant was another matter. No one really knew, the State Department later acknowledged. The ambiguity allowed the U.S. government to treat such islands as neither part of the United States nor foreign. This allowed the government to avoid the burdens of sovereignty while exercising the benefits of occupation. Beyond guano, small islands became useful for cable-relay stations and other communications, meteorological monitoring, and coaling and other small naval bases, as well as World War II landing strips.[23]

As Christina Duffy Burnett points out, the race to collect islands "appertaining" to the United States is not just a funny historical oddity. U.S. officials learned from the European powers of the late nineteenth century (and later likely from the United States' own colonial experience in the Philippines) the value of a more discreet, indirect form of imperialism avoiding sovereignty over dependent lands. European powers were finding "ways to take control over territory while avoiding many of the responsibilities that sovereignty implies": Britain, France, Italy, Germany, and others created "protectorates" rather than colonies in Africa and Asia; the Austro-Hungarian Empire and Britain annexed

Bosnia-Herzegovina and Cyprus, respectively, disguised as leases. The colonizers thus gained flexibility and freedom "while depriving people of their land (and more) by all manner of deception and subterfuge." Soon the United States would do much the same with the imposed "lease" on Guantánamo Bay and de facto U.S. colonization of Cuba. Numerous other examples of "annexation without sovereignty" would follow in the twenti-eth and twenty-first centuries.[24]

First, however, in 1867, the Stars and Stripes flag rose over a base sit-ting atop a much, much larger territory for the first time. Secretary of State William Seward had negotiated the purchase of Alaska from Russia for $7.2 million. The flag raising and territorial transfer took place at Russia's Baranof Castle, in Sitka. Before the arrival of the Russians, the place that's now called Castle Hill was an indigenous Tlingit fort. The imperial succession and purchase involved the acquisition of territory larger than any in U.S. history except the Louisiana Purchase. The Alaska Territory, as it was soon known, was about twice the size of Texas. U.S. bases soon followed—including Forts Liscum, Davis, Saint Michael, Gibbon, Yukon, Egbert, Seward, and Wrangell and installations on Kodiak Island and the Kenai Peninsula. U.S. military power was suddenly on the northern edge of Asia.

Around the same time Seward and the military tried but mostly failed to create naval bases in the Caribbean.[25] Competition with Britain, France, and Germany was ramping up in anticipation of the construction of a Central American canal connecting the Atlantic and Pacific. Control over the Caribbean Sea would shape construction of any canal and future traf-fic through sea lanes connecting the oceans. With an eye to acquiring bases peacefully, Seward completed a treaty with Denmark to purchase its colony the Danish West Indies (today's U.S. Virgin Islands), only for Congress to reject the pact. (The two countries signed another treaty in 1900. This time the Danish parliament rejected it. The sale of the colony finally went through during World War I.) U.S. officials also considered buying Danish Greenland and Iceland.[26]

In 1869 Seward nearly negotiated the annexation of the Dominican Republic. This time the principal aim was the creation of a naval base in the large and strategically located Samaná Bay. Dominicans supported annexation in a referendum (although turnout was just 30 percent), and the country's leaders signed an annexation treaty in 1870. It never went into effect after ratification efforts in the Senate failed, largely because of Euro-American senators' concerns about incorporating a "mixed race" population into the United States and the effects of "the tropics" on the "Anglo-Saxon race."* Similar sentiments led to Congress's failure to pass an 1871 joint annexation resolution, as it had in annexing Texas. The two governments later signed a lease on the bay, but it was quickly canceled after a new Dominican government took power. In the absence of direct annexation, U.S. officials would rule the Dominican Republic after 1898 through a variety of barely disguised colonial devices, much as in Cuba and Haiti.[27]

In Haiti, on the other side of the island of Hispaniola, where Cristóbal Colón first landed, U.S. leaders had designs on another location for a major Caribbean naval base and coaling station. Môle Saint-Nicholas was a large and protected port, and U.S. officials started to pressure Haiti's government into giving the United States access, through both diplomatic threats and the deployment of gunboats to Port-au-Prince as a threat of invasion in 1889. Haitian officials refused and suffered the imposition of harsh tariffs as a result.[28] In the nineteenth century U.S. naval vessels invaded or otherwise violated Haitian waters at least fifteen times.[29] The pace of intervention only grew in the twentieth century.

By the 1870s U.S. public opinion clearly supported expansion beyond the continent, just as Euro-Americans had generally, if not universally, supported westward expansion. Across a variety of social, political, and economic sectors and classes, people increasingly viewed expansion into foreign markets as the solution to recurring economic crises in the latter half of the nineteenth century.[30]

✪

Foreign markets, naval power, and bases were the trinity of the man they called the "prophet." Historian and president of the Naval War College Capt. Alfred Thayer Mahan was read as "gospel" by everyone from future

---

* I put this racial terminology in quotation marks to emphasize that these are social ideas and categories rather than legitimate or valid scientific categories or biological realities.

president Theodore Roosevelt to imperial Germany's Kaiser Wilhelm II.[31] Mahan derived his belief in foreign markets, naval power, and bases from his historical scholarship. His scholarly aim was to identify the factors in history that have allowed some empires to achieve global preeminence over others. Mahan's interests weren't purely academic. He spread his gospel in popular U.S. magazines such as the *Atlantic* and had access to some of the United States' most powerful men. Mahan wanted to shape U.S. policy in the late nineteenth century and for the century to come.

In Mahan's attempt to understand imperial history as a guide to U.S. policy, he focused on the struggle between imperial Britain and France in the seventeenth, eighteenth, and nineteenth centuries. "If navies, as all agree, exist for the protection of commerce," Mahan writes, "it inevitably follows that in war they must aim at depriving their enemy of that great resource, nor is it easy to conceive what broad military use they can subserve that at all compares with the protection and destruction of trade."[32] Applying these historical lessons to the United States, Mahan and his supporters argued for the maintenance of a navy at least equal to Britain's that was able to operate globally. Mahan argued that great powers require strong navies capable of protecting a country's commercial shipping and opening foreign markets to trade. And, to have a strong navy, a great power needs a far-flung network of support bases. "The maintenance of suitable naval stations," Mahan wrote, "when combined with decided preponderance at sea, makes a scattered and extensive empire, like that of England, secure."[33]

Mahan was concerned when he compared the United States to the British Empire. Unlike the British Navy's three hundred ships and thirty bases circling the globe, Mahan warned that, without "foreign establishments, either colonial or military," U.S. warships "will be like land birds, unable to fly far from their own shores."[34] In the era of coal-powered steamships, having access to coaling stations was critical to maintaining a navy capable of patrolling far from home (petroleum plays the same role today, except on nuclear-powered aircraft carriers). "Fuel is the life of modern naval war," wrote Mahan. "It is the food of the ship; without it the modern monsters of the deep die of inaction."[35]

Mahan argued that the country had to acquire islands and other coastal locations in the Pacific, the Caribbean, and the Gulf of Mexico to create coaling stations and other naval bases. To justify a major naval buildup, he painted a scary picture of a country with huge undefended coastlines and aggressive European powers ready to seize bases and coaling stations in the Western Hemisphere. The military would first have to improve "fortifications and coast-defense ships" along the U.S. Atlantic and Pacific coasts to give the Navy the security needed to patrol far from U.S. shores. Second, the country would have to prevent European powers from "acquir[ing] a coaling position within three thousand miles of San Francisco." Third, and above all, the country would have to build up its "naval force, the arm of offensive power."[36] This meant a major shipbuilding campaign and the acquisition of new coaling stations and ports. Mahan's argument for *offensive* power as the only adequate response to a world he portrayed as teeming with danger presaged aggressive post–World War II strategies of "forward deployment" and "containment," which saw U.S. officials deploy bases and troops globally in a world they depicted as full of Soviet and communist threat.

The ultimate aim for Mahan and other military, political, and economic leaders, such as Roosevelt, Secretary of State Seward, and Massachusetts Senator Henry Cabot Lodge, was claiming islands or territory not for territory's sake but for coaling and provisioning stations with a yet larger aim: they would be the literal way stations, as Mahan said, "along the way to the greater prize of foreign markets." Here Mahan's theories about naval power intersected with the popular view about the need for expansion into foreign markets to forestall stagnation and recurring economic recessions. "We must have new markets unless we would be visited by declines in wages and by great industrial disturbances," said Lodge. Channeling Mahan, Lodge continued, "The old theory of competing in foreign markets merely by the price of the product is no longer practicable [and] a navy, coaling stations, and ports in the East . . . have become essential conditions in our time."[37]

Thanks in no small part to the lobbying of Mahan and his supporters, by the first decade of the twentieth century, the U.S. Navy was the world's second largest—second only to the subject of Mahan's study and admiration, Great Britain.[38] Although Mahan's expansive proposals were never fully realized because of their expense, his influence led Navy officials to push for the creation of more coaling and repair stations, especially in the

Pacific, to support U.S. business in Asia.[39] An official U.S. Army history jealously captures the Navy's growth in the period: "The historical writings of Alfred T. Mahan were particularly influential in establishing the framework of a global, blue-water fleet focused on the dominance of the Navy, the establishment of refueling bases, and the aggressive protection of commerce."[40]

By 1888 the United States had signed agreements to lease naval stations in the Kingdom of Samoa and in the Hawaiian Kingdom's Pearl Harbor. Congress initially failed to provide the funds to build the bases. It meant only a temporary delay. In 1893 the government's representative in Hawai'i and U.S. marines backed the overthrow of the Hawaiian monarchy by Euro-American sugar planters and settlers. The government of President Grover Cleveland acknowledged the illegality of the "act of war" and called for restoring the monarchy. The coup plotters refused. They declared an independent state in 1894 and seized around 1.8 million acres of the kingdom's lands.[41] The son of a missionary family, Sanford B. Dole, assumed the role of president. His first cousin would soon come to the islands and establish the Hawaiian Pineapple Company. It's now known as the Dole Food Company.

In 1898, just days after the explosion of the USS *Maine* and President William McKinley's request for a declaration of war against Spain, McKinley asked Congress to annex Hawai'i. The islands of the previously independent kingdom offered a large coaling station and naval base halfway across the Pacific from which to deploy military power in support of U.S. businesses in Asia. They would also offer a base from which to control the Philippines. "We need Hawaii just as much [as] and a good deal more than we did California," said McKinley. "It is manifest destiny."[42] Congress approved the annexation of Hawai'i in 1898, as well as the islands of the newly named American Samoa and tiny, uninhabited Wake Island in 1899. Naval bases and coaling and cable stations appeared almost immediately.[43] Coup supporter Sanford Dole became Hawai'i's first territorial governor.

McKinley's push to annex the Philippines was driven by its proximity to the economic markets of China. Lodge and others feared being cut out of profit-making opportunities by the European powers then busy dividing up China. They believed it critical "to establish ourselves with a large port and with territory in the East."[44] Mahan acolyte Assistant Secretary of the

Navy Theodore Roosevelt issued the orders to Adm. George Dewey to attack the Spanish fleet in Manila Bay with Dewey's Asiatic Squadron, based in Hong Kong. Manila Bay was the Philippines' key harbor and one of the most important in the region.[45] Roosevelt sent the orders when his boss, Secretary of the Navy John D. Long, was away at a doctor's appointment. Long was shocked by the plans for transoceanic war but let the orders stand, probably for fear that newspapers would portray him as weak. The decision was "influenced in part by [Mahan's] doctrine."[46] On May 1, 1898, in a matter of hours, Dewey's squadron sank the entire Spanish fleet protecting Manila.

✪

By the middle of July, a little more than a month after the first U.S. marines landed in Guantánamo Bay (and one week after the annexation of Hawai'i), the Stars and Stripes was flying over Santiago de Cuba. The Cuba Libre flag was not. This was the flag of the multiracial group of Cuban revolutionaries who had been trying to overthrow Spanish rule for decades. When arranging the terms of the Spanish Empire's surrender, U.S. officials ensured that Spain surrendered to the United States—*not* to the rebels. The aim of intervention for McKinley and his supporters had always been to install a government to the liking of U.S. officials to ensure U.S. political and economic dominance over the island. McKinley couldn't directly annex and rule Cuba as he and the U.S. government had done with Alaska, Hawai'i, and other U.S.-claimed colonies. Anti-interventionist and anti-imperialist sentiments were powerful forces at the time. As part of Congress's declaration of war against Spain, anti-imperialists and anti-annexationists had won a small victory by inserting an amendment renouncing any steps by the U.S. government "to exercise sovereignty, jurisdiction, or control" over Cuba.[47]

Unable to ensure direct rule, President McKinley's administration got the next best thing: U.S. officials offered Cuban leaders thinly disguised U.S. rule in exchange for Cuba's official independence and the withdrawal of U.S. troops. McKinley would get direct colonial rule in Puerto Rico, the Philippines, Guam, Wake Island, and American Samoa. With U.S. troops still on the island, McKinley's offer was one that Cuban representatives

couldn't refuse. In 1901 they begrudgingly allowed the U.S.-penned Platt
Amendment to be inserted into the new Cuban Constitution. The amendment allowed the United States to invade Cuba at will to ensure stability
and so-called Cuban independence. It prevented Cuba from freely making
treaties with other governments and from acquiring debt. And it permitted
the construction of U.S. "coaling or naval stations," including on the forty-
five-square miles of Guantánamo Bay, over which the United States would
soon have "complete jurisdiction and control."[48] A political cartoon of
the day portrayed a man representing Cuba tied to a post marked "Platt
Amendment" and President McKinley using a hot iron to brand his back
"US."[49]

Cubans had freed themselves from Spanish colonial rule only to find
their island a colony again, with the trappings of sovereignty. The U.S.-
appointed military governor Leonard Wood wrote to President Theodore
Roosevelt, "There is, of course, little or no independence left Cuba under
the Platt Amendment."[50] "None of us thought," Cuban rebel Gen. Máximo
Gómez said, "that [peace] would be followed by a military occupation by
our allies, who treat us as a people incapable of acting for ourselves, and
who have reduced us to obedience, to submission, and to a tutelage
imposed by the force of circumstances."[51]

Massachusetts Senator Henry Cabot Lodge predicted the seizure of
Cuba in the years leading up to 1898 and echoed Mahan in calling for a
buildup of naval bases and a navy of such size to protect U.S. business
interests on a global basis. "Commerce follows the flag," he wrote famously.
So it did with the Stars and Stripes flying high in Guantánamo Bay (and
somewhat more subtly in the rest of Cuba). In the 1890s U.S. investors
already had $50 million on the island. The United States was Cuba's main
trade partner.[52] After the occupation of Guantánamo Bay, U.S. firms built
up the economy of eastern Cuba, in particular, where economic output
had been relatively small prior to 1898. U.S. sugar companies quickly
dominated—much as they would dominate in Hawai'i and Central
America. Between 1902 and 1929 sugar production in the east grew from
15 percent to nearly 70 percent of Cuba's total production. United Fruit
Company towns operated, as historian Jana Lipman explains, "largely
outside Cuban law as quasi-independent enclaves within eastern Cuba."
The city of Guantánamo has long been overshadowed by the base. Within

a few decades of U.S. occupation, the town's elite consisted almost exclusively of U.S. expats involved in the sugar industry and locals who made money off the base.[53]

The hoisting of the U.S. rather than the Cuba Libre flag in Santiago de Cuba mirrored the scene thousands of miles away in the Philippines. After the U.S. Navy destroyed the Spanish naval fleet in Manila Bay, anti-Spanish Filipino rebels assumed U.S. forces would be their allies. They were mistaken. U.S. forces took over Manila and struck a deal with its Spanish defenders to orchestrate a surrender and prevent the revolutionary army from entering the city.[54]

At the time there was debate in the United States about whether or not to seize all of the Philippines. There were more than seven thousand islands and a population of seven million, which was the equivalent of nearly 20 percent of the entire U.S. population. Some "imperial pragmatists" thought it best to establish only "a naval base and a coaling station."[55] Others called for full annexation. Many invoked racist ideologies to support annexation of the Philippines and other Spanish colonies. They argued, for example, that the country had a duty to "educate the Filipinos, and uplift and civilize and Christianize them." Others emphasized the "enormous material benefits" that annexation would bring. There should be no hesitancy about seizing colonies, one senator argued: "We have had colonies in this country ever since we ceased to be colonies ourselves."[56]

Others opposed annexation. Calling themselves *anti-imperialists*, prominent figures such as Jane Addams argued that "forcible subjugation" of other peoples was tantamount to "open disloyalty to the distinctive principles of our government." The Democratic Party and its candidate for president in 1900, William Jennings Bryan, would campaign on a platform that "no nation can long endure half republic and half empire."[57] Racism shaped the thinking of anti-imperialists as it did that of imperialists like Roosevelt. Drawing on popular ideas about race and social Darwinism (now debunked), many believed non-European populations to be inherently "inferior" to Euro-Americans, meaning they could not be governed or integrated into the country.[58]

Other anti-imperialists, such as civil rights activist Ida B. Wells-Barnett, argued that black people should oppose expansion abroad until the government could protect their rights at home. The African American newspaper the *Washington Bee* described the country as "busy on a hair-brained attempt to go into the colonizing business against its own Declaration of Independence."[59] Lodge acknowledged that if the anti-imperialists proved correct, "our whole past record of expansion is a crime."[60]

The McKinley administration sided with annexation, in part motivated by fears about German and Japanese interest in the other islands of the Philippines archipelago. In negotiations with the Spanish government, McKinley also claimed Guam and Puerto Rico, which would offer more locations for coaling stations, naval bases, and cable relay sites. "Being good pragmatists," writes Thomas McCormick, U.S. officials declined the Spanish Crown's offer to sell the rest of the Mariana Islands and the Caroline Islands.[61] Spain sold them to Germany. On Guam the Navy designated a small Spanish military garrison and the entire island a U.S. naval station in 1899—technically Guam became one large military base. Admirals served as governors and generally ran Guam like a ship. Signs appeared reading, "English Only Will Be Spoken Here."

In February 1899 the U.S. Congress passed a resolution explicitly prohibiting the people of the Philippines from U.S. citizenship. Another resolution that would have given the Philippines independence after the creation of a stable local government failed by a single vote.[62] In a series of cases, the Supreme Court ruled that the people of Guam, Puerto Rico, and the Philippines were entitled to neither U.S. citizenship nor the full protection of the Constitution. They were to be considered "US nationals" living in, as Daniel Immerwahr puts it, "extra-constitutional zones."[63] (The colonies remain extraconstitutional zones: People born in Puerto Rico got citizenship only when the military needed soldiers to fight in World War I; residents of Guam had to wait until after World War II. All the colonies have been denied statehood, the right to vote for president, and voting representation in Congress. Samoans remain "US nationals" who don't get citizenship by birth.)

The McKinley administration and white Euro-American leaders saw the new colonies (a word not shunned at the time) through a racial lens. They believed Filipinos, Guam's indigenous CHamoru people, Puerto Ricans, and Cubans were not "fit" for self-governance. (These attitudes remain today, as the islands' political status alone reveals.) U.S. troops and diplomatic officials in the Philippines called the Filipinos "n****rs" and "gugus." "Why those people are no more fit for self-government than gun-powder is for hell," one U.S. Army general in Cuba declared. Another said, "They are no more capable of self-government than the savages of Africa."[64]

In the Philippines rebel leader Emilio Aguinaldo declared independence and established a government near Manila. With U.S. leaders unwilling to cede their new conquest, the United States had a new war on its hands. Fighting broke out between U.S. forces and Filipino rebels in early 1899. McKinley initially sent five thousand troops to occupy Manila in the summer of 1898. One year later there were almost forty thousand U.S. troops. Deployments eventually reached seventy thousand and generally averaged around forty-five thousand until 1913. The War Department deployed most of the troops to small garrisons or "stations." In September 1899 there were 53 stations in the Philippines. The following September there were 413. By 1902 the number was 492.[65] U.S. forces also took over the Spanish fort at the port of Subic Bay. The military soon began expanding the naval station there. After World War II and Filipino independence, it would become the largest U.S. base outside the United States.

Aguinaldo's insurgent army turned to guerilla warfare to uproot their new colonial occupiers. U.S. troops turned to the kind of ruthless, scorched-earth warfare honed horrifically against Native Americans. Hahn points to soldiers like Maj. Gen. Adna Chafee, who fought against the Comanche, Kiowa, Apache, and Cheyenne, before deploying to the Philippines. He "brought the Indian Wars with him to the Philippines and wanted to treat the recalcitrant Filipinos the way he had the Apaches in Arizona—by herding them onto reservations." This would prove hard with a population of seven million, but U.S. troops imprisoned large numbers of Filipinos in concentration camps. Soon-to-be president Theodore Roosevelt saw similar parallels: "Every argument that can be made of the Filipinos could be made for the Apaches. . . . Every word that can be said of Aguinaldo could be said of Sitting Bull."[66]

Perhaps no soldier better embodies the continuity in racialized imperial domination from North America to the Philippines than Nelson A. Miles, one of the commanding generals of the U.S. Army during the occupation. After fighting in the Civil War, Miles spent most of the rest of the century fighting in the West against Kiowa, Comanche, Sioux, Nez Perce, and Apache. In 1894 Miles was in charge of putting down the railroad

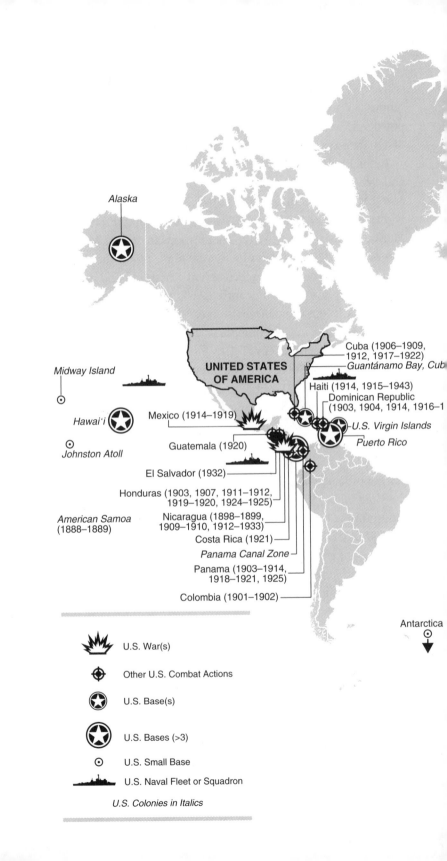

Alaska

Midway Island

Hawai'i

Johnston Atoll

American Samoa
(1888–1889)

UNITED STATES
OF AMERICA

Mexico (1914–1919)

Guatemala (1920)

El Salvador (1932)

Honduras (1903, 1907, 1911–1912,
1919–1920, 1924–1925)

Nicaragua (1898–1899,
1909–1910, 1912–1933)

Costa Rica (1921)

Panama Canal Zone

Panama (1903–1914,
1918–1921, 1925)

Colombia (1901–1902)

Cuba (1906–1909,
1912, 1917–1922)
Guantánamo Bay, Cub

Haiti (1914, 1915–1943)
Dominican Republic
(1903, 1904, 1914, 1916–1

U.S. Virgin Islands

Puerto Rico

Antarctica

U.S. War(s)

Other U.S. Combat Actions

U.S. Base(s)

U.S. Bases (>3)

U.S. Small Base

U.S. Naval Fleet or Squadron

U.S. Colonies in Italics

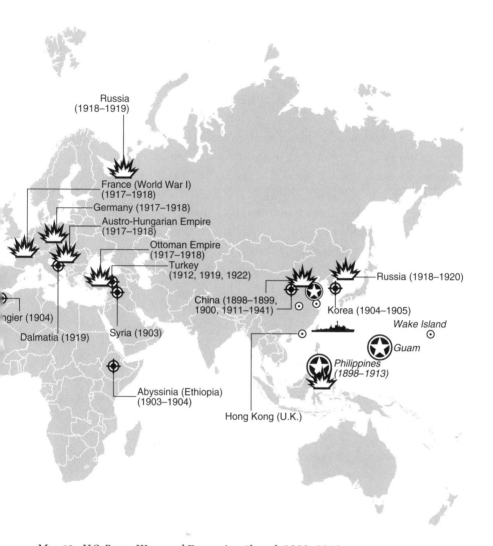

Russia
(1918–1919)

France (World War I)
(1917–1918)
Germany (1917–1918)
Austro-Hungarian Empire
(1917–1918)
Ottoman Empire
(1917–1918)
Turkey
(1912, 1919, 1922)
China (1898–1899,
1900, 1911–1941)
Russia (1918–1920)
Korea (1904–1905)
ngier (1904)
Wake Island
Dalmatia (1919)   Syria (1903)
Guam
Philippines
(1898–1913)
Abyssinia (Ethiopia)
(1903–1904)
Hong Kong (U.K.)

Map 12. U.S. Bases, Wars, and Expansion Abroad, 1899–1940.
Significant bases, combat, and expansion outside U.S. states are shown. Some bases
were occupied for only part of this period. Oceans not to scale. Additional bases
existed during frequent invasions and occupations of Latin American countries in this
period, including Honduras, Guatemala, Costa Rica, and El Salvador. U.S. forces
occupied Nicaragua in 1909–10 and 1912–1933. Key sources: "Fort Wiki," accessed
June 13, 2019, www.fortwiki.com; Robert E. Harkavy, *Strategic Basing and the Great
Powers, 1200–2000* (London: Routledge, 2007); "Alaskan Command: ALCOM
Facts"; "North American Forts"; Pettyjohn, *U.S. Global Defense Posture;* Torreon and
Plagakis, *Instances of Use;* U.S. Army Center of Military History, *The Panama Canal:
An Army's Enterprise* (Washington, DC: Center of Military History, 2009).

workers strike in Pullman, Illinois. He compared the strikers to Confederate and Indian enemies. This was another "war of civilization" against those who would bring "famine, pestilence, and death." Miles asked for permission to open fire on the striking workers. At Wounded Knee Miles did not ask for permission. There at Pine Ridge, on December 29, 1890, he was the officer who gave the orders to Gen. George Custer's former Seventh Cavalry to carry out the massacre of up to three hundred Lakota Sioux.[67]

In the Philippines, under the leadership of men like Miles, U.S. military forces fought a devastating counterinsurgency war. Torture, atrocities, and massacres were common. Under U.S. occupation and a war to crush the Philippines independence movement that formally lasted until 1902, hundreds of thousands of Filipino civilians died from direct violence in war, disease, and starvation. Tens of thousands of Filipino combatants and more than 4,200 U.S. soldiers died.[68] Fighting continued sporadically until 1913, likely taking thousands more lives. Most of the deaths occurred in the Muslim-majority southern islands of Mindanao. (The U.S. military would return to fight Muslim rebels on some of the same islands almost ninety years later.) U.S. forces "easily quelled" the Muslim resistance with "'liberal use of ammunition,' which achieved 'very excellent results against the semi-savages,'" writes Patricio Abinales, noting the racism that shaped the war.[69] In one three-day "battle," U.S. troops led by former Cuban Rough Rider major general Leonard Wood killed at least six hundred Moro Muslims, including hundreds of women and children. Twenty U.S. men reportedly died.[70] Some U.S. news media and critics, including the likes of Mark Twain and his Anti-Imperialist League, expressed horror about the "slaughter," as some had after Wounded Knee.[71] Criticisms "were quickly shunted aside by the politics of the imperial age," writes historian Joshua Gedacht.[72]

Massacres by U.S. forces were a recurring feature of U.S. warfare. From Wounded Knee to the Philippines, Gedacht writes, "the US Army's colonial campaigns produced recurring yet distinct incidents of extreme bloodshed." During the period from 1890 to the 1920s, when the United States was joining the most powerful militaries and empires in the world, "nearly half of all officers who rose to command the US Army had been implicated in colonial massacres." The massacres "had at least one thing in common": the killing of generally non-Christian, nonwhite colonized peoples.[73]

One of the imperialists, Albert Bushnell Hart, explained in *Harper's Magazine* in 1899 that the annexations of 1898 were "not signs of a new policy, but the enlargement of a policy long pursued." The United States, he wrote, "for more than a hundred years has been a great colonial power" in its rule over American Indians. "Whatever is done in the future," he predicted accurately, "will be based on the habits of the past."[74]

❂

Before his retirement Lt. Gen. Nelson Miles returned to the Presidio of San Francisco in 1902 as commanding general of the U.S. Army. The Presidio remained the main deployment and return point for U.S. forces in the Philippines. One of Miles's successors at the Presidio would soon marshal ten thousand soldiers to invade Mexico once more, in search of Pancho Villa, who had been conducting raids along the U.S. border. But first, troops would deploy from the Presidio to help crush a rebellion in China in a bid to open Chinese markets to U.S. businesses.

U.S. bases and troops could now be found from the Caribbean to the Pacific and beyond. The country's bases mirrored the rapid expansion of the country's borders and its leaders' aspirations for further economic, political, and military power. In this classic period of European imperialism, when Europe's empires were competing for colonies in Africa and Asia, the U.S. government claimed the Philippines, Guam, and Puerto Rico from Spain and annexed Hawai'i, American Samoa, and Wake Island. The United States had a collection of new colonies and a de facto colony in Cuba, moving the country into the company of the world's largest and most powerful empires.[75]

PART III **IMPERIAL TRANSITIONS**

7 THE MILITARY OPENS DOORS

When I visited Guam in 2012, I met a man who introduced himself as the "Prime Minister of the Sinåhi Archipelago." At the time I knew that many in Guam refer to the island by its indigenous CHamoru name, Guåhan, but I was unfamiliar with the name Sinåhi Archipelago.* (I later learned that a *sinåhi* is a type of clamshell necklace once worn by the CHamorus' ancestors. Activists in the twentieth century brought back the tradition.) The CHamoru prime minister told me that he had declared his independence from the United States and was Sinåhi's only citizen: "I was never a U.S. citizen. I'm a citizen of the Sinåhi Republic."

The ancestors of today's CHamorus arrived on Guåhan as the island's first human inhabitants between 1500 and 2000 BCE. For the past nearly five hundred years, CHamorus have not enjoyed full political independence. Spanish conquistadors arrived in 1521 and claimed Guåhan/Guam as a Spanish possession three decades later. Like the indigenous peoples of the Americas, CHamorus were decimated by disease and violence.[1]

* With hesitancy I employ the name more widely used for legal and political purposes: Guam.

Spain ruled Guam as a colony until U.S. and Spanish negotiators agreed to include the island in the settlement that ended the 1898 war.

The war with Spain initially seemed to many in the United States to be a "splendid little war." Rapidly defeating Spain and capturing its colonies had catapulted the United States into direct competition with the most powerful empires of Europe. Soon, however, the many challenges of colonial conquest in Guam, Puerto Rico, and the Philippines became apparent to U.S. leaders. In the Philippines the war quickly transformed into a deadly and costly counterinsurgency conflict. Tens of thousands of U.S. troops would deploy for years on end to this new, little-known colony, with its roughly seven thousand islands and seven million people, thousands of miles from North America. The war in the Philippines continued until 1913. Thousands of U.S. troops came home wounded or in coffins, and the war soon grew unpopular in the United States (much as the wars in Afghanistan and Iraq grew increasingly unpopular in the past two decades).

Confronting the challenges of colonial rule, including both violent and peaceful opposition in the new colonies and protest from a powerful anti-imperialist movement at home, U.S. leaders developed new ways to exert power and control. The strategies U.S. government officials developed in the first years of the twentieth century became a template for imperial strategies still practiced today. Following the conquests of 1898, U.S. leaders began to pursue a new kind of imperialism. This was an imperialism that generally avoided formal colonization and the bald-faced seizure of territory. This was an imperialism characterized in part by informal assertions of dominance exemplified by "Open Door" policies in China.[2]

While the Open Door became an important template for the extension of U.S. power abroad, the period between 1899 and World War II also featured frequent, largely underestimated demonstrations of force, military interventions, and the long-term basing of forces abroad.[3] It was U.S. military intervention in China in 1901 that put U.S. leaders in a position to propose the strategies of the Open Door. In the years that followed, Latin American countries were by far the most frequent targets of intervention. In Central America and most of the Caribbean in particular, the United States would not create more colonies but instead impose a kind of de facto colonization without the burdens of sovereignty and the growing international and domestic criticism accompanying colonial rule.

❂

With the conquest of the Philippines, U.S. power was situated firmly in Asia. U.S. businesses and political leaders had long been "mesmerized" by China, given the enormous size of its population—that is, the size of its potential consumer market—and the success of early U.S. exports there, such as tobacco, textiles, and kerosene.[4] The lucrative Chinese opium trade likewise made fortunes for merchants such as Boston elites Warren Delano (Franklin Delano Roosevelt's grandfather) and members of the Forbes family, among others. At the end of the nineteenth century, U.S. officials faced the challenge of competing in China when other powers were far better positioned to dominate business opportunities. Britain, France, Germany, Russia, and Japan had already carved up the Chinese coast, creating de facto colonial enclaves complete with exclusive rights to trade, mining, banking, and railroads. U.S. citizens had enjoyed the privileges of enclaves like the Shanghai International Settlement, but the United States clearly lagged behind its European and Asian competitors in economic, political, and military power and influence in China.

Building up the U.S. military presence in the region was a first step. In the Philippines this meant as many as seventy thousand troops and a growing naval base at Subic Bay. Around 1900 China's rebellion of "Boxers" (a rough translation of the movement of Yihequan, the Righteous and Harmonious Fists) broke out against colonial occupation. This threatened U.S. and other foreign businesses, and the McKinley administration responded by deploying five thousand troops to China from the Philippines and the Presidio in San Francisco. Tens of thousands of additional troops in the Philippines remained at the ready for further deployment given the sporadic fighting in the archipelago.

While U.S. troops helped put down the rebellion with other foreign forces, U.S. leaders knew they lacked the military strength to control China or any significant part of it unilaterally. The distance from the West Coast, the size of China's territory and population, and the advantages enjoyed by the European powers and Japan were too much to overcome.

Plus there was the danger of a larger military buildup arousing more Chinese nationalism or triggering clashes between the colonial powers. U.S. leaders wanted another solution to ensure U.S. businesses had access to Chinese markets and prevent the Europeans and Japanese from dividing China among themselves. The solution was the economic policy known as the Open Door. This was "an updated version of Britain's old Open Door policy for China," explains Thomas McCormick. But rather than carving up China into enclaves and spheres of influence, U.S. officials proposed a kind of collaborative strategy of economic imperialism in which foreign powers would compete on an even playing field while cooperatively funneling investment into the country.[5]

The U.S. version of the Open Door never came to fruition in China. Nonetheless, it became a model for using Open Door–style economic and political tools to exert imperial influence over other nations in the twentieth and twenty-first centuries. In the background, undergirding the political-economic strategies, military power was always lurking. In 1903, after the Boxer movement was no longer a threat, the Navy created a South China Patrol at bases in the British colony of Hong Kong and in Canton (Guangzhou). It also created Yangtze Patrol and a Marine patrol at a garrison in the British-U.S. International Settlement in Shanghai and later at Hankow.[6] The Army sent most of its soldiers back to the Philippines but left a small regiment in Peking (Beijing). In 1912 the Army created a garrison in Tientsin (Tianjin) along the railroad running to Peking. A regiment of around one thousand soldiers remained there for twenty-six years.

U.S. officials abandoned any plans for a larger military presence in the western Pacific after imperial Japan demonstrated the power of its navy in defeating the Russian Empire in their 1905 war. Military leaders concluded that U.S. bases and warships were too vulnerable so far from the United States to justify greater investment. On the other hand, Theodore Roosevelt secured funding in 1907 to build a fortified naval hub in the middle of the Pacific, at Hawai'i's Pearl Harbor. A year later Roosevelt started a major naval buildup to create the "most powerfully armed and longest-range battleships afloat." He would send his "Great White Fleet" of sixteen battleships on a round-the-world voyage to demonstrate U.S. military and economic power.[7]

Presidents William McKinley and Roosevelt showed similar military restraint and imperial guile in Latin America. In Central America there was long-standing interest among U.S. elites to build a canal to speed trade between the Atlantic and Pacific Oceans. U.S. leaders were unhappy when Colombia's government rejected a U.S.-proposed treaty to build the canal across Panama, which was then a province of Colombia. In retaliation U.S. officials and Navy warships helped Panamanian secessionists declare independence in 1903. In the same year that U.S. officials secured permanent access to Guantánamo Bay by another kind of "unequal treaty," the U.S. government also pressured the Panamanian government into signing a canal treaty. If the Panamanian legislature failed to ratify the treaty, U.S. officials threatened to withdraw U.S. Navy warships protecting the new country from the Colombian Navy.

The treaty gave the United States de facto sovereign rights in perpetuity to 553 square miles that became the Panama Canal Zone. The cost was $10 million and yearly rent of $250,000.[8] The treaty authorized extensive powers including those of land expropriation outside the Canal Zone and the authority to build bases. As in Cuba, Panama's Constitution allowed the United States to intervene militarily "in any part of the republic of Panama to reestablish public peace and constitutional order in the event of their being disturbed."[9] The country eventually hosted more than one hundred bases.[10] Between 1856 and the 1989 U.S. war in Panama, the U.S. military invaded the country twenty four times.[11] The Canal Zone bases also served as launchpads for invasions elsewhere in Latin America. Panama, like Cuba, was a U.S. "colony in all but name."[12] The Canal Zone, like Guantánamo Bay, was a colony, full stop.*

A year after signing the canal treaty, President Roosevelt announced his "corollary" to the Monroe Doctrine. The new doctrine was really a threat. The United States, he declared, had the right to intervene in any of the nations of Latin America if their indebtedness threatened European intervention, if they committed "chronic wrongdoing," or if they displayed "impotence which results in a general loosening of the ties of civilized society."

---

* In a 1936 treaty, the U.S. government renounced the right to intervene anywhere in Panama. In 1999, the year U.S. forces left bases in the Canal Zone, Panama gained full control over the canal.

Using the gendered language for which he became famous, Roosevelt had effectively declared the countries of Latin America protectorates of the United States, whose independence and ability to prevent U.S. intervention depended on abiding by rules set by U.S. leaders.[13] "Any country whose people conduct themselves well can count upon our hearty friendship . . . [and] need fear no interference from the United States," the president said with faux, patronizing generosity.[14]

Under Roosevelt and subsequent presidential administrations, other countries in the hemisphere had every reason to fear U.S. interference. Roosevelt euphemistically called such unilateral action "international police power."[15] Cuba would soon see the return of U.S. troops and an occupation by the Army of Cuban Pacification for almost three years, from 1906 to 1909. U.S. troops occupied the country again in 1912 and for five years from 1917 to 1922. The U.S. military occupied the Dominican Republic in 1903, 1904, 1914, and for eight years, from 1916 to 1924. Neighboring Haiti suffered occupation in 1914 and for nearly twenty years from 1915 to 1934.

In Central America, where U.S. businesses had been dominant since the late nineteenth century, Honduras experienced eight invasions and occupations, in 1903, 1907, 1911, 1912, 1919, 1920, 1924, and 1925. The U.S. military occupied Nicaragua for two years in 1909–10 and for around two decades from 1912 to 1933. Elsewhere U.S. troops invaded Guatemala in 1920, Costa Rica in 1921, and El Salvador in 1932.[16] The military occupations depended on the establishment or use of local military bases, camps, and garrisons to station U.S. troops. In Nicaragua, for example, between 1930 and 1932, there were at least eight U.S. garrisons.[17] This was in addition to the U.S. warships that entered Latin American ports some six thousand times between the mid-nineteenth century and 1930, in classic gunboat diplomacy style.[18]

Frequent military invasions coupled with profound economic and political influence meant that U.S. imperial control was more pervasive in Central America and the Caribbean than anywhere else in the world. "Yet apart from the Panama Canal Zone [and Guantánamo Bay]," Victor Bulmer-Thomas points out, control "did not depend on colonies. Control was exercised through protectorates in Nicaragua and Panama and client states elsewhere," including Costa Rica, El Salvador, Guatemala,

Honduras, Cuba, Haiti, and the Dominican Republic. In 1920, Bulmer-Thomas notes, Franklin Roosevelt "boast[ed] that the United States controlled the votes of all six Central American countries in the proposed League of Nations."[19]

Mexico was similarly the "perfect embodiment" of informal, Open Door imperialism, at least until its revolution in 1910. After losing nearly half of its territory in the war with the United States, Mexico had been an Open Door to U.S. economic and political influence. Since 1876 especially, Mexico was as much of an economic dependency of its northern neighbor as it had been to its Spanish colonizer: mines were controlled by U.S. firms; railroads were designed to ship the wealth of the mines from south to north; the oil industry was dominated by John Rockefeller, Andrew Mellon, and other oil giants; the peso was pegged to the dollar; and Mexico was deeply indebted to U.S. banks by the turn of the twentieth century.[20] The instability and weakness generated by the economic and political control emanating from the north helped trigger the Mexican Revolution. In 1914 President Woodrow Wilson became embroiled in the revolution and sent U.S. troops to occupy Vera Cruz. Two years later a "punitive expedition" deployed from the Presidio to invade Mexico again; the troops spent half a year searching unsuccessfully in northern Mexico for the revolutionary leader Pancho Villa.[21]

Even after the revolution's end, Mexico struggled to assert its control over its natural resources and economy in the face of U.S. corporate power. Open Door imperialism has remained a "recurring reality" for Mexico as a result of indebtedness to U.S. banks, the role of Mexicans as a cheap reserve labor supply for U.S. businesses, low-wage maquiladoras, the North American Free Trade Agreement, tensions over immigration and the border, and U.S. drug war policy, among other political, economic, and military dynamics over the past century.[22]

✪

The Marine Corps played a significant role in many of the invasions of Mexico and other parts of Latin America. One of the most decorated officers in Marine Corps history later regretted his role in the wars and the ends they served. "I spent 33 years and four months in active military service and during that period I spent most of my time as a high-class muscle man for Big Business, for Wall Street and the bankers," wrote the oft-quoted two-time Medal of Honor winner Maj. Gen. Smedley Butler. "In short, I was a racketeer, a gangster for capitalism."

> I helped make Mexico and especially Tampico safe for American oil interests in 1914. I helped make Haiti and Cuba a decent place for the National City Bank boys to collect revenues in. I helped in the raping of half a dozen Central American republics for the benefit of Wall Street. I helped purify Nicaragua for the International Banking House of Brown Brothers in 1902–1912. I brought light to the Dominican Republic for the American sugar interests in 1916. I helped make Honduras right for the American fruit companies in 1903. In China in 1927 I helped see to it that Standard Oil went on its way unmolested.

Butler reflected, "Looking back on it, I might have given Al Capone a few hints. The best he could do was to operate his racket in three districts. I operated on three continents."[23]

Each of the invasions and occupations led by men like Butler couldn't have happened without bases to launch, support, and maintain military operations. In classic imperial style these bases, and the wars and military interventions that bases enabled, usually helped stabilize conditions to protect U.S. corporate investments and to open up new markets and profit-making opportunities abroad. "The search for markets, and for access to natural resources, is as central to American history as it has been to the history of every great power in every age," writes Stephen Kinzer.[24] Bases, troops, and war helped ensure smooth operations for U.S. businesses and capitalism more broadly. Forts in the western territories claimed by the United States did much the same a century prior, but they did so generally on a smaller scale: the U.S. Army made land available and (relatively) safe for settlement and Euro-Americans' individual and familial enrichment. So too the Army protected major trading posts, trade routes, railroads, and eventually growing cities to support Euro-American profit making and ensure the smooth operation of capitalism in North America.

Honduras helps illustrate the new imperial pattern: as Butler says, he "helped make Honduras right for the American fruit companies in 1903."[25] Following this and seven more U.S. invasions and occupations between 1907 and 1925, a group of increasingly powerful "banana men" and U.S. banana companies basically took over the country.[26] By 1913 two-thirds of Honduran exports were in the hands of one of the most powerful banana men, Samuel Zemurray, and his closest rivals, the Vacarro brothers from New Orleans (their Standard Fruit Company later merged with Dole, one of the Euro-American settler companies that dominated Hawai'i). The banana companies "bought up lands, built railroads, established their own banking systems, and bribed government officials at a dizzying pace," writes historian Walter LaFeber. "If Honduras was dependent on the fruit companies before 1912, it was virtually indistinguishable after 1912. . . . In 1914, the leading banana firms held nearly a million acres of the most fertile land. Their holdings grew during the 1920s until the Honduran peasants had no hope of access to their nation's good soil. In 1918, dollars became legal tender in Honduras." The wealth of the country and its yellow gold were being "carried off to New Orleans, New York, and later Boston." Hondurans were left with low-wage jobs in the banana groves and export duties, which were mostly pocketed by a small group of Honduran elites, when they weren't evaded entirely (in an economic structure that remains largely intact today).[27]

Honduras became, as LaFeber says, "the original 'banana republic,'" under the near-complete domination of the U.S. banana companies and their political and military muscle, the U.S. government.[28] In popular usage *banana republic* calls to mind (clothing company aside) buffoon-like "third world" despots in the mold of Woody Allen's film *Bananas.* Many forget the term's original meaning. Writer O. Henry coined the term after living in Honduras. He used it to refer to weak, marginally independent countries facing overwhelming foreign economic and political domination. In other words, a banana republic is a de facto colony—which is what Honduras and some other countries in Latin America had become. In an irony that would likely anger him profoundly, Butler's name now adorns a Marine Corps base in Okinawa, Japan: the island has been a de jure and de facto colony of both Japan and the United States for most of the past 150 years.

U.S. imperialism after 1898 became less dependent on the creation of new formal colonies and more dependent on informal, less overtly violent— but violent nonetheless—political and economic tools backed by military might, including bases abroad. "In this mode" of imperialism, writes McCormick, "the major means of control are largely economic and the chief actors are not the state but private American traders and investors, albeit backed by government influences and military power if need be."[29] As revisionist historians and others have emphasized, this was the new kind of Open Door imperialism. But it was an Open Door framed and undergirded by frequent military invasions, lengthy military occupations, gunboat diplomacy, and permanent bases from Cuba, Panama, and Puerto Rico to Alaska, Hawai'i, and the Philippines to Guam, Samoa, and China.

Missionaries again played an important role in this new U.S. imperialism: in the thirty years between 1890 and 1920, the number of U.S. missionaries abroad jumped from nine hundred to more than fourteen thousand. As with other imperial powers, many in the United States had a growing sense of the nation pursuing a global humanitarian mission.[30] So too, many U.S. Americans embraced a belief in spreading democratic ideals. Both missions had powerful racial (and racist) content. Ideas of white supremacy and the "white man's burden" to civilize "lesser," nonwhite, non–Anglo-Saxon Protestant peoples infused much of the missionary idealism of U.S. leaders and millions of other citizens. "The day is not far distant when," President William Taft declared, "the whole hemisphere will be ours in fact as, by virtue of our superiority as a race, it already is ours morally."[31]

This intertwined sense of racial, religio-spiritual, and national superiority has its roots at least as deep as the first Puritan settlers in New England. As Richard Mather and John Cotton articulated, Puritans believed they were fulfilling God's prophecy as God's chosen people, special and superior to all others.[32] In the nineteenth and early twentieth centuries, an even more expansive vision of racial, religious, and national superiority became embodied by the language of "manifest destiny" and the idea that the United States was divinely predestined to conquer and rule others.

Ideas about a distinct "American" mission shaped political discourse and decisions about expansion and intervention, alongside economic, political, and military motivations.[33] So too, the desire of leaders, such as Theodore Roosevelt, to demonstrate their manhood through the use of military force played a role in shaping a hyperinterventionist U.S. imperialism. As for other imperial powers, the sense of mission—in the U.S. case, based around assumptions of white, Christian, U.S. American, and male supremacy—was helpful in rationalizing violence, intervention, and war. "Ottoman, Russian, and Chinese empires, like the French, Dutch, and US," Ann Stoler and David Bond explain, "have all insisted at different moments that their *raison d'être* was different, that their violences were temporary, and that their humanitarian visions excused or distinguished their interventions as ad hoc measures, not sustained excesses."[34]

✪

In the early twentieth century, periods of intervention, occupation, and base creation in new lands were lengthy at times but eventually came to an end. Occupation in Nicaragua, Haiti, Cuba, and the Dominican Republic lasted for many years or even decades, but, with the exception of Guantánamo Bay, the military packed up and left them for home at the end of each occupation period. The same was true after World War I in Europe. During the war hundreds of thousands of U.S. troops deployed to the continent and helped change the course of a war that killed tens of millions. After the war ended approximately fifteen thousand U.S. soldiers occupied parts of Germany between Luxembourg and the Rhine River; troops from Belgium, France, and Great Britain occupied other parts of Germany. For four months U.S. troops briefly occupied Austria. By early 1923 the entire occupation force had returned home.[35]

Less often remembered was the occupation of Russia. Toward the end of World War I, Wilson and the War Department deployed around fifteen thousand U.S. forces to both western and eastern Russia as part of a multinational invasion attempting, unsuccessfully, to support anti-Bolshevik forces during the Russian Revolution. With U.S. leaders also hoping to check growing Japanese power in East Asia, U.S. troops occupied Vladivostok from August 1918 until April 1920. They returned home when it became clear the Bolsheviks were firmly in control of the soon renamed Soviet Union.[36]

The only occupying troops that did not return home were in the Danish Virgin Islands. U.S. administrations had tried to buy the Dutch-colonized islands since the mid-nineteenth century. The Wilson administration finally purchased the soon renamed colony, the U.S. Virgin Islands, for

$25 million during the war. U.S. officials had worried Germany would overrun Denmark and create a base of its own in the Caribbean.[37]

During the Great Depression and the presidency of Franklin Delano Roosevelt, U.S. policy toward Latin America shifted, with a move away from the long series of U.S. invasions. Under Roosevelt's "Good Neighbor" policy, U.S. political and economic power and influence persisted in the hemisphere. With the onset of World War II and the "Cold War" that followed, the cessation of invasions and occupations would prove to be merely a pause.

Cuba was one country that faced renewed intervention after the war, of various kinds: military and political, economic and ideological. In 1934, however, the Cuban government would finally win the annulment of the Platt Amendment, which had cemented its colony-like status. Still, U.S. officials insisted on a new treaty to hold on to Guantánamo Bay. It contained the stipulation that Cuba could never force the United States to leave. Before World War II the military briefly considered giving Guantánamo Bay back to Cuba. A group of U.S. foreign policy experts pointed out that there were enough bases on the U.S. Gulf Coast and in Puerto Rico to ensure U.S security. They recommended the government "seriously consider whether the retention of Guantánamo will not cost more in political misunderstanding than it is worth in military strategy."[38]

The Roosevelt administration decided to hold on to Guantánamo, as it did Guam and the other colonies hosting military installations. By the end of the 1930s, before the start of World War II, the United States had a consolidated collection of bases across North America and a sizable but still comparably small collection of extraterritorial bases in the colonies. Most U.S. leaders called the colonies *territories* by this point, given growing global opposition to colonialism, but they were still colonies, without democratic incorporation into the United States. In addition to Guam and Guantánamo, they included Hawai'i, Alaska, the Philippines, Panama, Puerto Rico, the U.S. Virgin Islands, American Samoa, Wake Island, Midway Island, and Johnston Atoll (among other "guano islands").

During World War II, Guam, the Philippines, Wake Island, and some of Alaska's Aleutian Islands would be the only parts of the United States occupied by a foreign power, Japan. The skin color and limited rights of the colonies' inhabitants explain why these periods of brutal occupation are largely unknown in the rest of the United States. Few know that far more Filipinos died than any other U.S. nationals during the war: 1,111,938 Filipinos, compared to 407,316 U.S. military personnel. Many Filipinos were slaughtered by Japanese forces. Many died during a U.S. campaign to take back the Philippines that shelled and bombed Manila and other parts of the archipelago into rubble. The military's near-complete disregard for civilian casualties would have been unthinkable if Japanese forces had occupied one of the forty-eight states.[39]

By the end of World War II, after the defeat of Japan, the Philippines, Guam, and many of the other colonies would become major hubs in a globe-spanning network of foreign bases that rapidly became the largest in world history. While prewar U.S. leaders developed new economic and political tools of Open Door imperialism—backed as they were by military bases, invasions, and other demonstrations of force—bases would become foundational to the U.S. Empire in the post–World War II era.

8 REOPENING THE FRONTIER

I'm not exactly sure why for years I overlooked the importance of the Destroyers-for-Bases deal. This was President Franklin Roosevelt's agreement with Prime Minister Winston Churchill to exchange fifty World War I–era U.S. naval destroyers for ninety-nine-year leases for U.S. military bases in eight British colonies in the Western Hemisphere. In my work I tended to mention the deal as part of the history of U.S. bases abroad, but I spent little time investigating it or the bases involved. I, like others, at times confused the agreement with Lend-Lease, another World War II program, under which the United States provided military aid to Britain and dozens of other allies. I probably didn't pay the deal much attention because the United States would build and occupy thousands of other bases during World War II. A handful of bases in eight colonies were the first in the new collection, but they were just a handful. Plus, almost all of them were now closed. How important could these bases be?

As I looked more carefully, I began to realize that when President Roosevelt called the Destroyers-for-Bases deal "epochal," he was not simply engaging in presidential hyperbole or self-aggrandizement.[1] Even if most of these bases are now closed, one journalist proved prophetic in suggesting that "bases once established on a ninety-nine-year lease are . . .

to all intents and purposes permanent affairs which will affect policy long after present policy makers have left the stage."[2] Or, as another journalist said of the agreement signed September 2, 1940, "A new chapter in world history was written last week—perhaps the most important chapter of our time."[3]

At first, President Roosevelt said he actually didn't have big news. But the smile on his face belied the secret he was about to share. Shortly before noon on September 3, 1940, riding along the rails outside Charleston, West Virginia, Roosevelt called the traveling press corps of reporters to join him in his private railcar on the Presidential Special. The train was the Air Force One presidential plane of the day. Around twenty journalists crammed around Roosevelt at the back of the train. Some sat at his feet. He was dressed in a lightweight blue suit and "flourishing" his iconic, long-stemmed ivory cigarette holder. A *Time* magazine reporter described Roosevelt as "professorial" and "relishing the historicity of the scene." The reporters grew silent amid the sounds of the train's wheels rolling on the tracks and the swaying of the cars.[4]

The president said that his news was nothing less than "the most important action in the reinforcement of our national security since the Louisiana Purchase."[5] At noon that day, he said, his government would inform Congress that the United States had acquired the right to lease air and naval bases for periods of ninety-nine years in eight British colonies in the Western Hemisphere. In exchange the United States would give Britain fifty aging Navy destroyers, built at the end of World War I.[6] The "base colonies," as they would soon be known, stretched from Newfoundland (the British colony became part of Canada in 1949) in the north to Bermuda in the mid-Atlantic to the Caribbean islands of the Bahamas, Jamaica, Antigua, Saint Lucia, and Trinidad to British Guiana (today's Guyana) at the top of South America.[7] Roosevelt compared himself to Thomas Jefferson, whose purchase of the Louisiana Territory had similarly come without congressional approval.

"What electrified the crowded roomful of correspondents," wrote one reporter, "was the audacity with which the deal was consummated: it would not be presented to Congress for approval. A congressional veto was out of the question. Congress was being told about it as a *fait accompli*."[8] The *New York Times* said the deal marked "a new chapter of world

Alaska

Newfoundland

UNITED STATES
OF AMERICA

Bermuda

Hawai'i

Bahamas
Jamaica

Guantánamo Bay, Cuba

Antigua
St. Lucia

Puerto Rico
U.S. Virgin Islands

Trinidad

Panama

Philippines Guam Wake Island

British Guiana

★ New U.S. Base Site
in U.K. Colony

● Existing U.S. Base(s)
as of 1940

Map 13. Bases from Britain: The Destroyers-for-Bases Deal.
On September 2, 1940, President Franklin Roosevelt agreed to exchange fifty World
War I–era naval destroyers for ninety-nine-year leases for military bases in eight U.K.
colonies in the Western Hemisphere. These were the first of thousands of bases the U.S.
military would occupy during World War II. See, for example, High, *Base Colonies.*

history."[9] One journalist described the scene as worthy of a historical canvas capturing "the American story."[10]

U.S. and U.K. officials signed the deal a day before Roosevelt's announcement, which was exactly one year and one day after Nazi Germany invaded Poland, starting World War II. In May 1940 Adolf Hitler's armies had blitzed their way through Western Europe. Since July the German Air Force had been raining bombs on Britain; an invasion appeared imminent. Although the United States would not officially enter the war for another fifteen months, President Roosevelt's approval of the Destroyers-for-Bases deal marked the first major U.S. move toward formally joining the Allies' war against the Axis powers. As important for the United States and the world, the deal marked the beginning of a transformation of the United States from one of the world's most powerful empires into not just an empire of unparalleled military might but also a new kind of empire defined significantly by its global collection of military bases.

Compared to the other empires of the day—especially Britain and France—the United States had, in 1940, a sizable but still "rather insignificant overseas basing system."[11] By the end of World War II, in less than five years' time, the United States would build and occupy some thirty thousand installations at two thousand base sites worldwide.[12] While large numbers of bases would close at war's end, what remained was a global base network larger than any in human history. The United States would become a global empire defined to a significant extent by its historically unprecedented collection of bases. These bases would represent a quantitative and qualitative shift in the nature of U.S. power, the U.S. military presence abroad, and the country's relationship with the rest of the world. What would seem to some to be a prized source of power and stability deriving from World War II would lay the foundation for a long series of wars that have yet to end.

✪

The day of Roosevelt's announcement, a U.S. military survey team departed for the first of the eight British colonies to develop base-construction plans.[13] In less than five months, one thousand soldiers (notably all white, in the still-segregated U.S. military) would deploy from

Brooklyn's Army Terminal to Saint John's, Newfoundland. The Navy would follow with a base of its own in nearby Argentia. Soon a group of smiling sailors was posing on the seaside with a sign reading, "Navy property."[14] Other troops and construction teams rapidly began deploying to the other colonies. Throughout 1941 small ritual ceremonies marked the transfer of base sites to the United States. U.S. officials raised the U.S. flag over territory previously claimed by the British Empire for the first time since the Revolutionary and 1812–1814 wars. In Jamaica a local newspaper remarked, "The raising of the Stars and Stripes over any portion of British territory must have a solemn signification for the people of the country in which it takes place." A colonial officer in British Guiana similarly understood that a U.S. base in British Guiana or another British colony "is in effect a [U.S.] colony, an off-shoot of its own country, run upon lines peculiar to and dictated by the Government of that country."[15]

Acquiring new bases in the Atlantic was not a shocking development to many U.S. Americans. Buying entire European colonies in the Caribbean was a recurring public debate in the 1930s, largely because of the colonies' military value. "Strategic key to the Western Hemisphere" is how *Life* magazine described the Caribbean on a 1938 map of naval bases and sea routes. "From the strategist['s] viewpoint, America's long soul-searchings over 'imperialism' in the Caribbean are sentimental twaddle. America *must* control the Caribbean or some other power may control America."[16] With a new world war seemingly imminent in 1939, the War Department developed plans to create a defensive perimeter that included new bases in the Dominican Republic, Colombia, Venezuela, Brazil, Chile's Easter Island, and Ecuador's Galápagos. By 1940, 81 percent of U.S. respondents to a Gallup Poll supported buying British-, French-, and Dutch-controlled islands.[17]

Roosevelt was interested in obtaining new island bases in the Caribbean at least as early as 1939. Prior to the deal with Churchill's government, U.S. and U.K. officials signed a secret 1939 agreement giving the U.S. military access to seaplane base sites in three of the eventual "base colonies": Trinidad, Bermuda, and Saint Lucia. The military never needed to use the small sites. Soon it had much larger base-construction plans for these and the other colonies.[18]

Beyond the Caribbean Roosevelt had an early sense for the importance of island territories globally. Even the smallest and most isolated uninhabited islands were growing in significance as potential sites for landing strips, radio transmission, and cable and meteorological stations. As the 1930s unfolded, Roosevelt increasingly focused on the importance of air power and the need for bases to support a growing air force. Since the 1920s, Army Air Corps planners and other air war strategists had been arguing that "strategic air power would decide future conflicts." "The airplane was not considered just another weapon," writes historian Michael Sherry. For many strategists "it was the ultimate weapon" for preventing aggression and policing the world.[19]

Roosevelt's commitment to air power grew in 1938, after he watched France and Britain capitulate to Hitler's demand to annex Czechoslovakia in no small part because of their fear of the Luftwaffe, the German Air Force. Previously, most U.S. military planners had long thought of the Pacific and Atlantic Oceans as "unbridgeable moats" protecting the country. Increasingly, Roosevelt and others worried that the oceans were becoming bridgeable, given the rapidly growing flight ranges of modern aircraft. In public speeches the commander in chief warned about the danger of "lightning strikes" by enemies against the United States; he illustrated the danger by listing with "almost monotonous repetition" flight times from possible enemy bases to targets in the Americas.[20]

In November 1938 Roosevelt announced plans to build a dramatically expanded Army air force of ten thousand modern warplanes.[21] Soon thereafter he met some of the Navy's top admirals in Puerto Rico to discuss boosting naval defenses in the Caribbean. After Germany invaded Poland on September 1, 1939, the government accelerated a military buildup in Puerto Rico (which involved land expropriations to enable the expansion).[22] The aim of adding U.S. air bases in the region would be, as the president said, to "render inviolate" the entire hemisphere from enemy attack. With an enlarged and expanded collection of bases farther from U.S. shores, Roosevelt believed that "this country and this hemisphere" would once more "lie behind the 'moats' of the oceans."[23]

Roosevelt's interest in island bases extended beyond appreciating their *military* value. He and other officials saw that airfields scattered about the world's major oceans were critical for the infrastructure of the rapidly growing international air travel industry.[24] The president realized that investing in bases also would be a way to support U.S. airlines and ensure

Figure 2. America's Outposts of Security and Defense . . . and Trade. Before World War II, Pan Am secretly began developing forty-eight airfields throughout Latin America for the U.S. military and commercial airlines. "Vital as is Pan American Airways' role in furthering national defense," this advertisement from 1941 says, "the Flying Clipper Ships are even more vital as Uncle Sam's strong right arm in furthering U.S. trade and good will." Maps depict flight routes connecting major bases, indicated by flag symbols. Courtesy of David M. Rubenstein Rare Book and Manuscript Library, Duke University.

access to the natural resources, international markets, and investment opportunities that air travel was opening. Commercial and military interests frequently went hand in hand. Before the war Pan American Airways secretly began acquiring basing rights for the military throughout Latin America under the cover of developing an infrastructure of commercial airfields in the region. Pan Am eventually built and improved forty-eight land and seaplane bases from the Dominican Republic to Paraguay.[25] This gave the military the foundation for rapidly expandable military bases in the event of war. It also gave Pan Am and other U.S. air carriers a significant competitive advantage after the war.

France actually requested the destroyers first. Four days after Germany began its invasions of the Netherlands, Belgium, Luxembourg, and France, the French government asked to buy or lease U.S. destroyers. A day later, on May 15, with the German Army advancing rapidly toward the English Channel, Winston Churchill asked Roosevelt for "the loan of forty or fifty of your older destroyers."[26]

Roosevelt worried that a majority in Congress opposed entering the war and would reject such a deal; the next month members would pass a bill restricting the president's ability to transfer military equipment to another country. Roosevelt was particularly worried about publicly aiding France or Britain in a year when he was seeking to become the first-ever three-term president. There were also concerns that the destroyers might end up in Nazi hands if the recipient military capitulated. Roosevelt refused both requests.

France fell within six weeks. British officials badly wanted the United States to enter the war and hoped for U.S. material support. Churchill returned to Roosevelt to offer leased base sites in the eight colonies in exchange for fifty destroyers.[27] Roosevelt deliberated. By the end of July, Britain faced near-continuous German bombing and the possibility of a land invasion. "Mr. President," Churchill wrote Roosevelt, "with great respect I must tell you that in the long history of the world this is a thing to do NOW."[28]

Within days Roosevelt agreed to the deal. He and his cabinet decided "the survival of the British Isles under German attack might very possibly depend on their getting these destroyers."[29] Still, Roosevelt feared Congress would reject the leasing of base sites or the outright purchase of colonies. For a range of reasons ranging from pacifism to isolationism, many politicians and members of the public alike did not want to get involved in another European war. As a result, many would see the agreement as another step toward the United States' formally entering the conflict. Roosevelt realized he had to avoid seeking congressional approval. He got a legal brief from his attorney general providing some legal foundation for bypassing Congress and aimed to present a deal to the U.S. public that would look so good it would be safe from popular critique. He hoped that swapping decades-old destroyers for bases with ninety-nine-year leases in eight strategically located colonies would do the trick.[30]

The deal indeed proved widely popular with journalists, pundits, and the public. The *New York Times* editorialized that the base sites would "enormously strengthen our capacity for hemispheral and hence for national defense," given added protection for the Panama Canal and the Atlantic coastline. The bases were also a way to prevent Germany or any other enemy from establishing their own bases in the Caribbean or North Atlantic. This was a real possibility, given that Nazi armies were occupying France and the Netherlands, which had Caribbean colonies, and Denmark, which controlled Iceland and Greenland. The *Times* even proposed adding a few more "desirable though not quite so important" bases, at the easternmost point of Brazil and in Venezuela, Colombia, and Ecuador's Galápagos Islands.[31]

Some questioned the deal and the legality of Roosevelt's signing the agreement without congressional approval. Republican presidential nominee Wendell Willkie was one critic, although he noted "the country will undoubtedly approve." Three days later Willkie called the deal "the most arbitrary and dictatorial action ever taken by any president in the history of the United States."[32] While the heated rhetoric was clearly motivated by the looming election, Willkie's and others' concerns about unilateral executive action were prescient: a series of post–World War II presidents would repeatedly sidestep Congress to enable the expansion of the overseas bases network. Other critics of the Destroyers-for-Bases deal, especially in the colonies in question, felt that a de facto transfer of sovereignty was underway and that the islands had been traded without the consent of the islands' inhabitants. Years later the first prime minister of independent Trinidad and Tobago, Eric Williams, said of the deal for the destroyers, "We never consented to be sold for scrap."[33] (Williams was speaking metaphorically; however, British officials indeed found that only nine destroyers were operational, and "they were in a sorry state.")[34]

Despite the concerns, Congress effectively blessed the deal by year's end by appropriating tens of millions of dollars for new base construction.[35] Within months troops were operating from the bases. Within a year the bases were fully operational. Across the base colonies, the military built at least nineteen Army Air Forces, Army, and Navy installations, complete with all the trappings of U.S. suburbia (including segregation).[36] By October 1941 there were nearly forty-five thousand construction workers on the bases. Most were locals, who were often paid considerably less for their work compared to U.S. citizens (unsurprisingly, this created significant labor tensions). Total construction costs for Army and Army Air Forces bases alone reached almost $243 million. Most of the money went to the largest and most important of base locations: Trinidad ($82 million), Newfoundland ($62 million), and Bermuda ($41 million).[37]

Trinidad was called the "southern keystone" of "hemispheric defense." The naval base would soon play an especially important role in countering German submarine attacks in the Caribbean, which began to rise after the United States entered the war in December 1941. With the aid of more land expropriations, the military expanded the naval station from 7,940 to almost 12,000 acres. By 1943 there would be around twenty-one thousand soldiers and sailors on the island.[38]

Beyond any defensive role, the main function of the new bases was as an "air funnel," shipping desperately needed military materiel to allies. With airplanes transforming military strategy, tactics, and the course of empire, air bases would be "stepping stones" for planes hopping from the East Coast of the United States to Europe, Africa, and beyond. After the war, planners predicted, long-range bombers would be able to reach Europe directly from Bermuda.

The quantity and pace of U.S. supplies flowing to the war's battlefields increased significantly after Roosevelt signed the Lend-Lease program in March 1941. Lend-Lease allowed the United States to provide military aid to Britain in exchange for deferred payments and later economic "considerations." Additional Lend-Lease pacts with other allies followed. Over the course of the war, the United States sent around $50 billion in aid to at least thirty countries, including the Soviet Union, China, Greece, and Norway.[39] Bases in Newfoundland became a key part of the North Atlantic Air Bridge sending bombers, fighters, and other weapons and supplies through Greenland and Iceland to the British Isles. Bermuda similarly provided an air link to the Portuguese Azores, which was within range of bases in North and West Africa. Smaller seaplane bases appeared in Antigua, Saint Lucia, British Guiana, Jamaica, and the Bahamas. Each had only a few hundred marines and sailors, who primarily helped patrol sea lanes, monitor Vichy France's naval presence in nearby Martinique, and engage in other intelligence gathering and antisubmarine warfare.[40] The military now had a chain of bases in the Atlantic, much like its chain of Pacific bases in Hawai'i, Alaska, Guam, Midway Atoll, Wake Island, American Samoa, and the Philippines.[41]

☮

Even with the increased significance of air bases, President Roosevelt's comparison of acquiring a handful of military bases to Jefferson acquiring 530 million acres in the Louisiana Purchase does seem to be pure political hyperbole. In terms of the land physically occupied, there's no comparison. However, if we begin to think of territory not just as the surface of the Earth covered by land but also as the surface of the Earth covered by the oceans and the air above it, the picture changes. "The meaning of these new American bases is apparent from the most cursory glance at the map," reporter Hanson Baldwin wrote the day after Roosevelt announced the deal. "The American frontier," Baldwin continued, "will be extended to the Amazon River and the Grand Banks off Newfoundland; the United States will exercise virtually unchallengeable domination of the Caribbean area, and our outer bastions of defense will be emplaced in blue water 700 to 1,000 miles to the east of our coastlines."[42] In terms of the total acreage controlled by the United States, the Destroyers-for-Bases deal represented a dramatic expansion in territory under U.S. control: the newly added de facto territorial waters were roughly twice the size of the Louisiana Purchase.[43]

The United States was not the first empire to control (oceanic) territory in this fashion. "In the past, the British empire, knit by sea power, was built upon the stepping stones of fueling stations and naval bases,"

Baldwin observed. Given British naval dominance, other states needed at least Britain's "tacit consent" to trade and operate on the seas, historian Paul Kennedy explains.[44]

The Destroyers-for-Bases deal was, then, a sign of an imperial shift from the dominance of naval power to air power. Because of the rapid development of aviation technology, the United States would be the first empire to dominate the skies as well as the oceans below. What coaling stations and naval bases had been to the British Empire, air force bases were to the transforming U.S. Empire.[45] (Sea power and naval bases also would remain important to U.S. imperialism.)

In 1893 historian Frederick Jackson Turner first shared his "frontier thesis" in a speech at the Chicago World's Fair, which celebrated, tellingly, the four-hundredth anniversary of Cristóbal Colón's arrival in the Americas. Turner's thesis attempted to explain the significance of the declaration in 1890 by the superintendent of the U.S. Census Bureau—that the U.S. frontier had closed.[46]

Half a century later Roosevelt and his advisers had discovered a way to reopen the frontier and extend it beyond U.S. shores, following years of advocacy by a cohort of elites in military, political, and journalistic circles. The ninety-nine-year leases for the bases reflected U.S. leaders' grand ambitions: the intent was to cement U.S. global power for at least a century to come. During negotiations over the base colonies, U.S. officials aggressively pressed their desperate British counterparts to ensure the United States achieved not just the maximum military benefits but economic and political benefits as well.[47]

The U.S. government's control of new oceanic territory and airspace as a result of the Destroyer's-for-Bases agreement was not the same as U.S. control over colonies in the North American west or European empires' rule over large colonies in Africa and Asia. However, in military and geopolitical terms, the newly claimed oceanic and aerial territory was similarly significant. Observers at the time saw the deal in precisely these terms. At least one also saw the long-term imperial continuity: "Territorial expansion has been an American habit since the first settlers went ashore at Jamestown," wrote reporter Francis Brown shortly after the president's announcement. "The lure of land drew men into the forest valleys away from the sea, drew them across the Appalachians, drew them westward to the Pacific. In the nineteenth century, government policy and the voices of orators and editors urged on the movement. It was the nation's 'manifest destiny' to expand, men said."[48]

During the rest of World War II, government officials, as well as orators and editors, planned for and urged further expansion, although generally it was the kind characterized by the control of oceans, airspace, and bases rather than the direct control of large swaths of land and colonies. When it came to further expansion of this sort, U.S. officials largely got their wish. The British base colonies and the territory whose domination the bases enabled were just the start of this new expansion of U.S. frontiers and U.S. power during World War II. By war's end Roosevelt would oversee the largest expansion of bases, territory, and imperial power in U.S. history—arguably far exceeding the power of Jefferson's purchase.

PART IV **GLOBAL EMPIRE**

9 EMPIRE OF BASES

The person who probably taught me most about seeing the world and bases geographically was, appropriately enough, a geographer.[1] The late Neil Smith was one of my graduate school advisers. I knew Smith's work years before I met him in person. He had made a name for himself explaining the process of gentrification in the 1970s and 1980s, when the term was still relatively new and unfamiliar to most. Smith showed how the investment of financial capital in cities could be traced on a map block by block and how real estate investment often moved like a wave through neighborhoods, extending the "frontier" of gentrification as it went.[2]

When I met Smith, he was applying his critical geography to understanding the development of the United States as an empire in the twentieth century. In his book *American Empire*, Smith showed me (and others) that the Roosevelt administration's treatment of European allies' colonies revealed much about postwar U.S. imperial strategies and the transformation of imperialism in the twentieth century. Smith pointed to Franklin D. Roosevelt and Winston Churchill signing the Atlantic Charter in August 1941 as emblematic.[3] The United States was still not formally involved in the war. The Japanese surprise attack on Pearl Harbor, Hawai'i, would not happen for almost four months. It was almost exactly a year after the signing of the Destroyers-for-Bases agreement. Surely aware of the symbolism involved, Roosevelt and Churchill met to hash out the Atlantic Charter aboard U.S. and British naval vessels off the coast of one of the "base colonies": Newfoundland.

Together Roosevelt and Churchill made an explicit commitment to the right to self-determination at a time when around 40 percent of the world's inhabited continents was still colonized. They declared the "right of all peoples to choose the form of government under which they will live" and their "wish to see sovereign rights and self government restored to those who have been forcibly deprived of them." This was a powerful anti-colonial and democratic vision that colonial independence movements around the world would take as inspiration and support for their decolonization demands. Roosevelt and Churchill went further to affirm their countries' "desire to see no territorial changes that do not accord with the freely expressed wishes of the peoples concerned." They agreed that "their countries seek no aggrandizement, territorial or other," from the war.[4]

There were obvious contradictions here for Britain, which then ruled more than 350 million people as colonial subjects in India alone. There were contradictions, too, for the United States with its conquered territories in North America and its colonies in the Philippines, Hawai'i, Alaska, Puerto Rico, Guam, and beyond. And what of the ninety-nine-year leases for the bases in the eight British colonies? Were these colonies to get independence? If they did, would the leases not violate the principle of self-determination? And what were the bases themselves, if not colonies? As a colonial officer in British Guiana said, a U.S. base "is in effect a [U.S.] colony, an off-shoot of its own country, run upon lines peculiar to and dictated by the Government of that country."[5]

Privately, the president also saw no contradiction between the Atlantic Charter's principles and a belief that the "minor children among the peoples of the world" should be placed under the "trusteeship" of "adult nations."[6] The contradictions in Roosevelt's stance on colonialism would only deepen when he later chided Churchill for his imperialist instincts. Churchill scoffed when Chinese leader Chiang Kai-shek expressed no interest in controlling Indochina after the war; Churchill believed no one leaves territory on the table when it's offered. "You have 400 years of acquisitive blood in your veins," Roosevelt told Churchill. A "new period has opened in the world's history. You have to adjust yourself to it."[7]

As with the significance of the Destroyers-for-Bases deal, Roosevelt was right that the world was entering a new period in history, no longer marked by the acquisition and control of large swaths of territory. But the history of World War II would show that the president and other U.S. officials would be just as acquisitive as four hundred years of English officials when it came to bases, if not large formal colonies.

✪

After the Japanese attack on the Pearl Harbor naval station and other U.S. colonies, and the U.S. declaration of war against Japan, Germany, Italy, and the other Axis powers, the bases in Britain's eight colonies proved just a small start to the acquisition of bases abroad. The question for the U.S. military was how to add as many bases as possible as quickly as possible in as many places as possible around the world, while also accelerating U.S. weapons-production capacity and drafting men and women into the war effort. The government signed deals or otherwise stationed U.S. forces in one location after another: Northern Ireland in April 1941, Iceland in July, new bases in Alaska and Australia after Japan's military defeated U.S. forces to occupy the Philippines and Guam. Elsewhere there were bases on Britain's Ascension Island in the South Atlantic and in Haiti, the Portuguese Azores, Kenya, free Senegal, Palmyra Island near Hawai'i, the northern reaches of Canada, Mexico's Acapulco, Recife and Fortaleza in Brazil, Ecuador's Galápagos Islands, Dutch Suriname, and later French Guyana.[8] In Panama, in 1941, the War Department tried to pressure the Panamanian government into giving it, not 99-year, but 999-year leases on seventy small plots of land to be used for air defense installations for the canal.[9] There would eventually be thirteen Army bases and four Navy bases in Greenland. In the British Isles 1.65 million U.S. military personnel would occupy dozens of bases by 1943.[10]

Historian Daniel Immerwahr explains how "strings of bases functioned as arteries, carrying [cargo] to the battlefronts." The forty-eight states functioned "as a giant heart pumping out materiel"—planes, bombs, weapons, supplies—to send to Britain, Russia, China, and other allies. "The bases were where planes landed and ships docked, where spare parts, fuel, and food were stored, where wounded men and damaged things were repaired." In Egypt and elsewhere across the Middle East, the U.S. military carried out a "massive" campaign to build the piers, cranes, railways, roads, airfields, repair shops, factories, hospitals, and other infrastructure necessary to supply Allied forces battling German and Italian armies. While tanks and other heavy equipment arrived by ship around the southern tip of Africa, lighter cargo arrived by an air route stretching from Miami to Puerto Rico to Brazil to Ascension Island in the South Atlantic to West Africa, the Sahara Desert, and finally Cairo.[11] Iran and other parts of the Persian Gulf saw as many as sixty-five thousand U.S. GIs and civilians, who primarily transported war materiel to the Soviet Union as it battled Germany on the eastern front.[12] Cargo traveling to China continued through a series of bases and airfields in India and over the Himalayas—known to pilots as "the Hump"—to a landing point in Kunming, China. In late 1943 planes were landing, on average, every eleven minutes. At one point in 1945, the pace reached a rate of one landing every seventy-two seconds.[13]

In the Pacific Ocean the military built hundreds upon hundreds of small island bases to battle Japan. The Navy alone built 195 bases in and around the Pacific (along with 288 in the Atlantic and 11 in the Indian Ocean).[14] After the shock of the Pearl Harbor attack and the loss of bases in the Philippines, Guam, and Wake Island, U.S. military leaders breathed new life into Adm. Alfred Mahan's doctrine: island bases would win the war and ultimately control the peace. The military subsequently fought its way across the Pacific in a series of deadly and costly battles. In this "island hopping" campaign, U.S. forces retook lost islands and fought from island chain to island chain toward mainland Japan. Most of the Pacific islands and the people living on them faced devastation as their homes became battlegrounds.[15] Hundreds of thousands of Japanese and U.S. military personnel and local civilians died across the smaller islands of the Pacific alone. Between 100,000 and 140,000 Okinawans—up to one-third of the prewar population—died in the U.S. invasion; most were civilians.[16] Rapid construction followed each battle as the military built yet more bases to launch assaults on other Japanese-controlled islands and on Japan itself.

By war's end the U.S. military was building base facilities around the world at an average rate of 112 a month.[17] A single naval base on Manus, in the Admiralty Islands, for example, cost $156 million (about $2.3 billion in today's dollars).[18] "The number of bases" built in so little time "to mount the offensives against Germany and Japan defies the imagination," wrote one international relations scholar shortly after the war.[19] How'd the country do it? The wealth of the nation, its unmatched industrial capacity and war-making powers, its technical and logistical expertise, and the work of its people played a big role. So too did the labor of tens of thousands of mostly colonized peoples.

U.S. and other colonial bosses tended to call the people doing the labor "natives," no matter where they came from (even in predominantly white Newfoundland).[20] Often they received wages of as little as fifty, thirty, or even ten cents a day. Some worked for food rations. Conditions were often brutal. In captured Japanese territories, U.S. troops forced some Okinawans and Koreans to work.[21] "Native" laborers in the base colonies of the Western Hemisphere were paid better than most, even though wages were generally a fraction of those paid to U.S. laborers often working side by side. Historian Andrew Friedman provides examples of "this system of labour extraction":

> French colonial plantation labour sweated for US projects in New Caledonia, the New Hebrides, Dakar, Bizerte and Agadir. In Dutch Guiana, the Netherlands' colonial labour and equipment did the work. . . . In Liberia, Guam, the Philippines, Panama and Hawaii, US colonial labour did the job, including a group of Metlakatla Indians in Alaska. British colonial labourers worked for Americans throughout the system, in Trinidad, Jamaica, Barbados and Bermuda, in Accra, Kano, Khartoum, Cairo, Aden, Karachi, Calcutta and Assam, and in the Solomon and Gilbert Islands. In Papua New Guinea, Australia's colonial labourers did the work.[22]

The often extraordinarily low pay allowed U.S. and other colonial bosses to apply armies of local workers to build airfields, docks, roads, barracks, and other immense installations that would have involved mechanization and other recent construction methods in the United States or Britain. In Maiduguri, Nigeria, for example, "natives" leveled and surfaced mile-long runways with metal pans and shovels. In Chabua, India,

Alaska

Greenland

Iceland

Canada

Newfoundland

Midway French
Island Frigate
       Shoals

UNITED STATES
OF AMERICA

Bahamas
Guantánamo Bay, Cuba

Haiti   Bermuda
Dominican Republic
Puerto Rico

Mexico   Jamaica

Hawai'i   British Honduras
                 Guatemala
Palmyra Atoll   Honduras
Johnston Atoll
        Clipperton Island

Antigua & Barbuda
U.S. Virgin Islands
St. Lucia

Nicaragua
Costa Rica
Panama Canal Zone
Ecuador
Peru

Kiribati   Line Islands

British
Guiana

Dutch
Guiana

French
Guiana

Trinidad
& Tobago

Brazil

Society Islands
Cook Islands
American Samoa
Western Samoa
Wallis & Futuna
Tuvalu

Colombia
Aruba
Venezuela

Bolivia

Uruguay
Paraguay

U.S. War(s)

U.S. Base(s)

U.S. Bases (>25)

U.S. Small Base(s) Only

U.S. Naval Fleet

U.S. Colonies in Italics

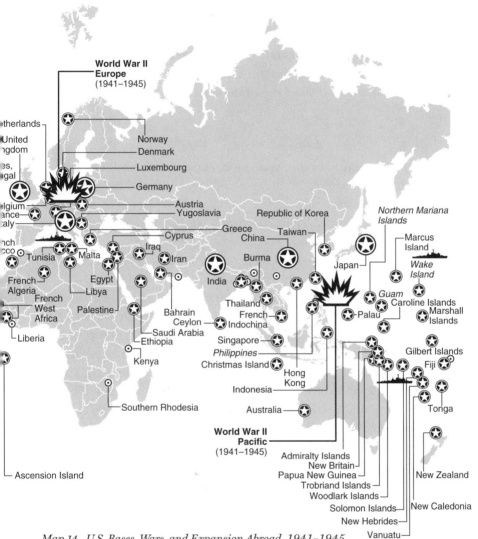

Map 14. *U.S. Bases, Wars, and Expansion Abroad, 1941–1945.*
Significant bases, combat, and expansion outside U.S. states are shown. At World War II's
height, the United States controlled approximately thirty thousand installations at two
thousand base sites abroad. The map reflects the relative number and positioning of bases
around 1945. Oceans not to scale. Key sources: Blaker, *United States Overseas Basing;*
United States Bureau of Yards and Docks, *Building the Navy's Bases in World War II:
History of the Bureau of Yards and Docks and the Civil Engineer Corps, 1940–1946,* vol. 2,
pt. 3, *The Advance Bases* (Washington, DC: Government Printing Office, 1947); Robert E.
Harkavy, *Strategic Basing and the Great Powers, 1200–2000* (London: Routledge, 2007);
John W. McDonald and Diane Bendahmane, eds., *U.S. Bases Overseas: Negotiations with
Spain, Greece, and the Philippines* (Boulder, CO: Westview, 1990); Stacie L. Pettyjohn, *U.S.
Global Defense Posture, 1783–2011* (Santa Monica, CA: RAND Corporation, 2012).

thousands of "Indian natives" used hammers to break large into small stones to fill and smooth runways. In Assam, India, long lines of women and men carried baskets on their heads to move wet cement from cement mixers to the airfields.[23] Without this huge supply of cheap labor often working under coercive conditions, the U.S. base network could never have expanded as broadly and rapidly as it did.

✪

One year to the day after the Japanese military's attack on Pearl Harbor, President Roosevelt asked his highest-ranking military officials, the Joint Chiefs of Staff, to study what overseas military bases would be needed to ensure postwar security. Their conclusion was unambiguous about the importance of overseas bases: "adequate bases, owned or controlled by the United States, are essential and their acquisition and development must be considered as amongst our primary war aims."[24]

Roosevelt's instructions to the Joint Chiefs of Staff asked them to study how to support a postwar multilateral defense system—an international police force—with U.S. overseas bases. In his instructions Roosevelt told the chiefs to identify desired base locations for such an international police force without regard to national sovereignty. The Joint Chiefs immediately expanded their inquiry beyond Roosevelt's request. Beyond planning for a multilateral security system, they would include airfields they considered necessary for postwar "national defense." They would consider the needs of the commercial aviation industry as well.

Some of the chiefs and other military and civilian leaders were skeptical that an international police force could succeed. Army Air Forces planners, for example, were generally ambivalent about such an idea. But they saw that planning for an international police force would be helpful in justifying a large and well-funded postwar Air Force (which they hoped would be an independent branch of the military). "There seems to be little doubt," retired Air Force general Perry McCoy Smith explained, "that if the international organization was looked upon with any favor by the postwar planners, it was not out of any great faith in collective security but out of a desire to justify a large postwar United States Air Force with world-wide base facilities."[25] Eventually, the Joint Chiefs concluded that any bases they considered necessary to defend the nation could also be used by an international military. "The requirements for national security and international peacekeeping appeared complementary to many military leaders because they equated the interests of the United States with those of the rest of the world," writes Michael Sherry.[26]

Through the rest of the war, the Joint Chiefs produced an array of memos, plans, maps, charts, tables, and official reports as they studied and deliberated what they considered to be the country's postwar basing needs. In a seminal paper that became known as the "Base Bible," military leaders outlined the creation of a network of bases that would provide a protective ring around the United States.[27] Beyond defending in any traditional sense of the term, the Joint Chiefs embraced a policy that we would today know as *preemption* and that they generally called "active defense" and "defense in depth." They, like some analysts outside the government, believed the U.S. military needed to be able to "strike the first blow."[28] "The United States must be capable of applying armed force at a distance," wrote one Joint Chiefs study. "This is turn requires a widespread system of bases beyond which lies a region which may be considered as constituting the United States strategic frontier."[29]

This hyperaggressive approach to defending the country aimed to use overseas air and naval bases to extend the frontiers of U.S. defenses as far from the East and West Coasts as possible. Bases would encircle most of the Western Hemisphere, reaching as far as the west coast of Africa, the borders of Asia, the Arctic Sea, and off the coasts of South America. "Overseas bases," Melvyn Leffler says about the strategy, "would enable the United States to interdict an attack from *any* source far from American shores." "If we are to keep America safe from the horror and destruction of war," Secretary of the Navy James Forrestal said, "we must hit our enemies at great distances from our shores." According to this strategy, the country would also need a newly expanded "intelligence apparatus" to warn of dangers (this became the CIA), as well as the world's dominant air force, the ability to rapidly mobilize an enlarged military to fight at any time, and, soon, a U.S. nuclear arsenal.[30]

The attack on Pearl Harbor, coupled with rapid developments in the lethality of weapons and the reach of strategic bombers, had created an "enormous sense of vulnerability" for U.S. officials. The idea that "there

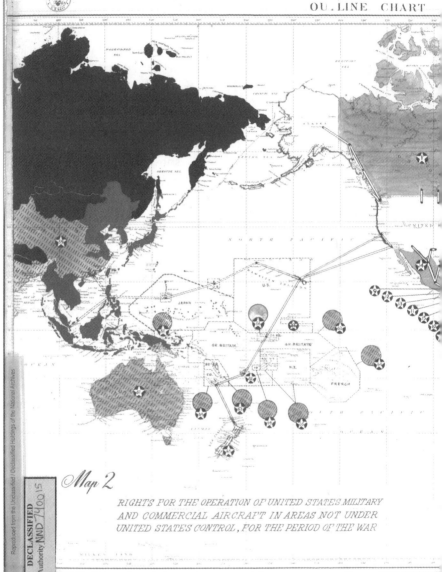

Map 2

RIGHTS FOR THE OPERATION OF UNITED STATES MILITARY
AND COMMERCIAL AIRCRAFT IN AREAS NOT UNDER
UNITED STATES CONTROL, FOR THE PERIOD OF THE WAR

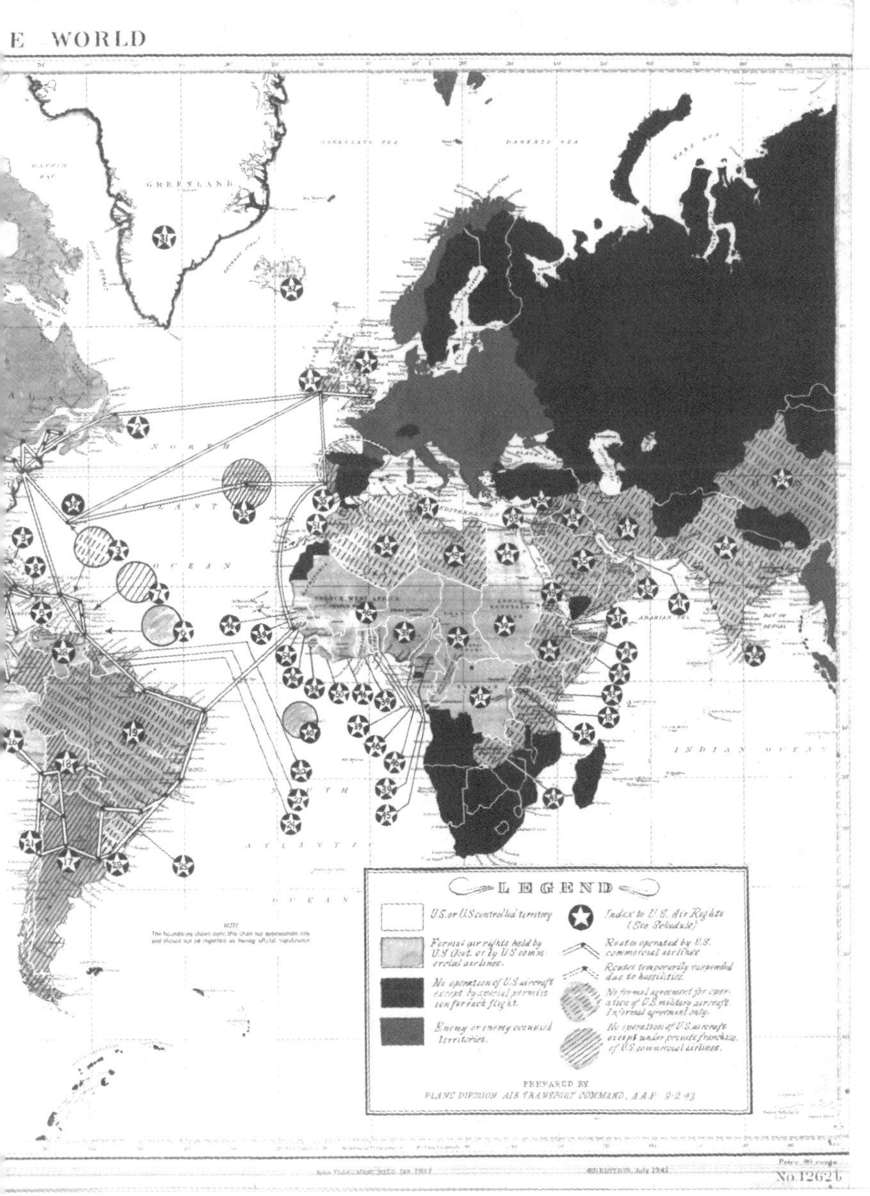

Map 15. U.S. Military and Commercial Air Rights Abroad: Postwar Planning Map.
Joint Chiefs of Staff, September 2, 1943. Stars indicate the territories where air rights
were desired or secured. Parallel lines indicate the routes operated by U.S. commercial airlines. Black dots along routes indicate airfields, airports, and landing strips.
Iceland, Greenland, and Saudi Arabia would be prominent base additions by the war's
end. Courtesy of NARA (A1 219/390/10/8/3–, box 199, Former TS Plans, Policies,
and Agreements, RG 107).

must never be another Pearl Harbor" became a guiding obsession for military and civilian leaders. After Pearl Harbor they tended to see threat as existing anywhere and everywhere on the planet. Most of the male policy makers concluded that the military weakness of the United States and its European allies had invited German and Japanese aggression. Rather than fearing any specific threat looming beyond Germany and Japan, officials feared the possibility of another future surprise attack against the contiguous forty-eight states by a future power. Military strength and aggression, they believed, were required to protect the country from *all* threats and to prepare for what almost all the men assumed would be a future war against a new and more dangerous military power.[31]

"To insure against any part of the United States mainland being visited by a sudden devastation beyond any 'Pearl Harbor' experience or our present power of imagination to conceive," wrote the Joint Chiefs, "we must meet such an attack as far from our own borders as possible."[32] Meeting an attack far from U.S. shores meant, in the minds of most military leaders, a large collection of distant bases. This meant the government had to take advantage of the opportunity provided by the war. The country had to snap up basing rights in wartime or else risk losing out on a chance to acquire bases in the future when a threat might emerge in peacetime. "The present is the most appropriate and most favorable time for obtaining the desired [base] rights," declared a Joint Chiefs study.[33]

In late 1943 and early 1944, President Roosevelt approved the Joint Chiefs' "US Requirements for Post War Air Bases." He called the "Base Bible" a "very clear and excellent" plan. Roosevelt requested minor changes: in the Pacific he ordered an expansion of the proposed U.S. "sphere of influence" to include the Marquesas—likely because of its importance for air travel rather than its military significance. In West Africa the president ordered the addition of basing rights in the Portuguese-controlled Cape Verde islands.[34] With Roosevelt's changes the Joint Chiefs' list of recommendations for the acquisition of "sole or joint" basing rights involved fifty-seven separate countries and territories.[35] A more comprehensive "List of Air Bases in Foreign Territory Required by the United States" included more than seventy base sites.[36]

There were dozens of other studies, and many involved even more detailed lists including additional information about facilities and local specifications. In January 1944 Roosevelt instructed the Secretary of State "as a matter of high priority, [to] initiate negotiations with the governments concerned to acquire permanent or long-term benefit of the bases, facilities and rights required, at the earliest possible moment." While air bases were the initial focus for the Joint Chiefs and Roosevelt, they soon expanded their plans to all types of military bases.[37] Concerned in no small part about the rising power of the Army Air Forces, the Navy began its own detailed postwar bases planning. By war's end the Navy sought bases, or at least the right to maintain bases, in at least forty-one foreign countries and colonies worldwide.[38]

In addition to bases officials prioritized securing air transit and landing rights from other countries globally. They wanted the ability for U.S. aircraft to be able to fly over and land at airfields from the Americas to Africa and the Middle East to South and Southeast Asia. Particularly desirable was an air transit route from Casablanca through Algiers, Tripoli, Cairo, Dhahran (Saudi Arabia), Karachi, Delhi, Calcutta, Rangoon, Bangkok, Saigon, and Manila. Toward the end of the war, the Secretary of War ordered efforts to ensure permanent rights to use seven airfields in North Africa and the Middle East.[39] Air transit rights were important in addition to actual bases because they could, as a Joint Chiefs study stated, "provide access to and familiarity with bases from which offensive and defensive action might be conducted in the event of a major war." Air flight rights were likewise helpful because they deepened military and diplomatic connections with the countries granting such rights. This, officials realized, could yield deeper relations, including the creation of permanent bases in the future.[40]

✪

Military preparedness was never the only consideration for the Joint Chiefs and other military and civilian planners interested in obtaining new bases. As with President Roosevelt, the economic implications of overseas bases were prominent. The chiefs, for example, saw that investments in overseas bases, as well as air transit and landing rights, would provide powerful bargaining chips to obtain postwar rights for U.S. commercial airlines. As Roosevelt had realized, air bases could double as airports and support U.S. airlines after the war.[41] Military and civilian planners pursued bases and air rights given their ability to serve "international military and commercial purposes" simultaneously. In 1943, the president sent a survey team to French-controlled islands in Polynesia to make plans for both postwar bases and commercial airports connecting North America and Australia.[42]

In addition to attending to the economic interests of U.S. corporations, Army Air Forces planners were also focused on their own interests. They understood that maintaining a large number of air bases in peacetime would require the maintenance of a large number of aircraft to station at the bases, which in turn would justify a large Air Forces budget: if you get the bases, you get the planes; if you get the planes, you get the budget. "Although the identity of the short-term enemy, Japan, and the long-term enemy, Russia, had a direct effect on the planning for bases, the principal concern of the postwar planners was their need to justify a large postwar air force," explains retired Air Force general Perry McCoy Smith. "The Army Air Forces' desire to obtain overseas bases had a direct relationship to its wish for a large portion of the defense budget. If a requirement for many overseas bases could be justified, then half the battle for funds would be won."[43]

A well-funded air force with a large number of aircraft would also "require continual replacement of aircraft" and thus "the ongoing operation of the aircraft industry, and the uninterrupted development of new weapons systems," Smith writes. Planners feared the end of the war would debilitate the capacity of the aircraft industry. They worried that restarting the industry would be difficult in case of another war. According to Smith, "The maintenance of a modern aircraft industrial plant was probably the most important single factor" in justifying a large Air Force featuring plentiful bases and planes after the war. The overlapping economic, political, and military interests shaping the base-planning process meant that, for example, Latin American bases "had very little strategic value" even if Army Air Forces officials may have genuinely believed that they needed bases in Latin America to protect the Panama Canal and defend the country against attack from the south.[44]

A partially completed base with little immediate strategic value in another part of the world illustrates how bases reflected an even more complicated intersection of economic and military interests. The base under construction was in Dhahran, Saudi Arabia, which had become a regional headquarters for U.S. oil firms. The base had been planned for use against Germany, but by June 1945, Germany had surrendered. Military leaders determined there was no need to use Dhahran for the war against Japan. Although there was no military need for the installation, the Secretaries of War, State, and the Navy pushed to complete the base. In a memo to President Harry Truman, Secretary of State Joseph C. Grew wrote that the three secretaries agreed that building the base was "in the national interest." Completion of an air base that would transition to civilian use (but retain military capabilities) after the war "would be a strong showing of American interest in Saudi Arabia and thus tend to strengthen the political integrity of that country whose vast oil reserves now are in American hands." U.S. officials were particularly interested in maintaining a presence in Dhahran because the neighboring oil fields were controlled by a consortium of Standard Oil Company–descended U.S. oil firms operating in a partnership with the Kingdom of Saudi Arabia as the Arabian American Oil Company, or Aramco (now Saudi Aramco, possibly the world's most profitable company). Commercial use of the airfield after the war would also be a "major asset to American civil aviation," Grew added.[45]

During the war U.S. oil company officials feared Italian and German attacks on prolific and lucrative oil fields in Saudi Arabia and Bahrain. They pleaded for U.S. antiaircraft defenses and other military protection. Initially, U.S. leaders were hesitant to boost U.S. forces in the region because military control over the oil-rich Middle East had been a British responsibility since before World War I.[46] State Department officials, however, realized that Saudi Arabian oil was, as they would later tell President Truman, "a stupendous source of strategic power, and one of the greatest material prizes in world history."[47]

Completing the base at Dhahran was an early sign of growing, direct U.S. military involvement in the Middle East, foreshadowing decades of intervention to come. It also reflected the "tacit alliance" between the United States and Saudi Arabia, forged by Roosevelt and Saudi King Ibn Saud. When it came to oil (among other industries), the U.S. government became "deeply involved in maintaining an international environment in which private companies could operate with security and profit," writes David S. Painter.[48] The decision to build the base in Dhahran indicates how important overseas bases were to postwar imperial strategies. Bases would help safeguard alliances, profit-making opportunities for U.S. corporations, and access to natural resources, such as the petroleum supplies that were critical to the daily functioning of capitalism and the military itself.

U.S. bases and well-armed troops had long provided a protection service to businesses and entrepreneurs since forts helped protect trappers, miners, land speculators, and other settler emigrants. After World War II, overseas bases and troops would play an even more substantial role as bodyguards and insurance policies for U.S. corporations and investors. In Saudi Arabia and around the world, overseas bases would become an important source of political power in support of U.S. business interests. Bases would allow U.S. military and diplomatic officials to deepen political, economic, and military ties with local leaders and elites to the benefit of U.S. corporations, including by providing a source of leverage over host nations' political, economic, and military decision making. Even during the Destroyers-for-Bases negotiations, when a Nazi invasion of Britain looked like a real possibility, "the US Government sought to extract political—even economic—as well as military advantages from its ally in what was an hour of most desperate need," writes historian Charlie Whitham.[49]

The decision to continue construction of the base in Dhahran reflects the importance of overseas bases to the new version of the U.S. Empire that was born during World War II, as well as a larger shift in the history of imperialism. Earlier territorial empires generally would have tried to claim any available territory, as suggested by Churchill's rejoinder to Chiang Kai-shek that no one turns down territory. Most earlier empires would have been especially interested in claiming any territory bearing a natural resource that was as profitable and significant as oil.

By World War II anticolonial movements made any thought of traditional large-scale colonial occupation a nonstarter. Beginning with the Atlantic Charter, President Roosevelt had framed the war as an anticolonial struggle and pledged to assist with decolonization at the war's end. The creation of the United Nations would further enshrine the decolonization process and the right of nations and peoples to self-determination and self-government. Whether or not they may have believed in the rights of colo-

nized peoples, many U.S. leaders believed colonies to be financially unprof-
itable and the source of what Roosevelt described as a "million headaches,"
much as European and U.S. predecessors had found. Roosevelt's administration's reaction to questions about buying all the base colonies from
Britain was typical. "Trinidad? No thanks. What a problem you have
there—what a scrambled population," Roosevelt was quoted as saying in
racially loaded terms. "What an ethnic potpourri you have there! No thank
you." The president didn't want overwhelmingly white Newfoundland
either. He called it a "bankrupt colony." Nor did he want Bermuda, "because
it was already an American resort whose wealthy visitors enjoyed vacation-
ing under a different flag."[50]

Senator William H. King's assessment of the World War I–era purchase
of the U.S. Virgin Islands applied well to most U.S. leaders' attitudes about
the possibility of acquiring new colonies: "It is only the military base
which gives this territory any value to us."[51] To take over more colonies
would have meant acquiring unwanted problems. The Destroyers-for-
Bases deal was a model in providing the military benefits of acquiring
colonies—that is, the bases—without most of the financial and other costs
of colonial rule.[52]

"Shaking loose the colonies" by pressing allies to decolonize was central
to U.S. officials' postwar economic strategy, explains Neil Smith. Roosevelt
administration officials aimed to ensure that the postwar world would feature a kind of "global open door." The strategy was to use economic tools
rather than colonial occupation to gain access to natural resources and
markets.[53] As Roosevelt and Churchill declared in the Atlantic Charter, all
nations should have "access, on equal terms, to the trade and to the raw
materials of the world which are needed for their economic prosperity."
Using state power to help open up markets was the basis for the new imperialism.[54] In this light newly independent postcolonial states could provide
critical new markets for U.S. businesses without the protectionist trade
restrictions that colonial rulers had imposed previously. Decolonization
would help create the global Open Door for U.S. corporations and investors
in large parts of the world where colonial powers had previously restricted
economic competition.

While bases rather than colonies symbolized the new version of empire, U.S. imperialism still remained rooted in colonialism and deeply reliant on colonies in important ways. The U.S. Empire was still one founded in the era of territorial empires. It still occupied huge territories seized during its conquests in North America, as well as a smaller collection of colonies outside the continental mainland. The power the United States amassed prior to World War II and that it collectively exercised during the war derived from the control of tremendous natural resources in North America, from the wealth generated by that land and the enslaved and free labor that worked it, and from the industrial economy and military might built with that wealth.

After the war the U.S. government would grant independence to the Philippines in 1946 but maintained its former colony as a neocolonial client state. Other "territories" remained colonies without democratic incorporation into the United States. They included Hawai'i, Alaska, Puerto Rico, the U.S. Virgin Islands, Guam, American Samoa, Guantánamo Bay, and the Panama Canal Zone. Hawai'i and Alaska would win statehood only in 1959. Puerto Rico and Guam received marginally improved rights, but their residents remain third-class U.S. citizens to this day. As postwar developments made clear, U.S. officials were generally determined to hold on to the colonies as colonies rather than grant them independence or statehood because of their base-hosting roles.

When it came to other countries' colonies, the Roosevelt administration's commitment to decolonization began to wane toward the end of the war. The desire for overseas bases and global military control played a critical role in this waning of support. The president's instructions to a State Department negotiating team headed to London in early 1944 were telling: military desires were more important than pushing Britain and France too hard on decolonization. With bases secured in the Caribbean thanks to the Destroyers-for-Bases deal, Roosevelt said, the United States still needed installations in colonial West Africa and in the French-controlled Polynesian islands of New Caledonia. The president instructed his team to "press the colonial question persistently" during meetings in London. But, he said, there was room for "ultimate sovereignty" in the colonies to remain unchanged provided some form of international inspection was in place.[55] Early in the war Roosevelt chided Churchill for his imperialist attitude about no one leaving territory on the table. By the end of the war, U.S. military and diplomatic officials were determined not to leave foreign bases on the table. Military officials in particular wanted to maintain control over as many bases as possible, in as many places as possible, with as much unilateral freedom to operate as possible.

After Roosevelt's death President Truman was even clearer that base access trumped commitments to decolonization and the right to self-determination, refuting Roosevelt's Atlantic Charter pledge to "seek no aggrandizement, territorial or other," from the war. "Though the United States wants no profit or selfish advantage out of this war," Truman said during the "Big Three" meeting in Potsdam, Germany, in July 1945, "we are going to maintain the military bases necessary for the complete protection of our interests and of world peace." In a grammatically tortured and marginally disguised declaration of imperial intent, Truman added, "Bases which our military experts deem to be essential for our protection we will acquire."[56]

And so they did. By the end of World War II, the United States commanded unparalleled military power and an unparalleled global military presence, with a collection of bases unmatched by any prior people, nation, or empire in history. The war resulted in a quantitative and qualitative shift in the nature of U.S. power—when it came to bases, broader military might, and intertwined economic and political forms of power—transforming forever the relationship between the United States and the rest of the world, as well as life in the United States, in the process.

Never before had so many U.S. troops been permanently stationed overseas. Never before had U.S. leaders thought about "national defense" as requiring the permanent deployment of military force so far from U.S. borders. While a significant number of the thousands of bases would close and while millions of troops would demobilize and come home after the war, U.S. officials had developed a new form of imperial power, revolving to a significant degree around foreign bases rather than foreign colonies, working in tandem with economic, political, and other military forms of power. "After the war," writes Sherry, "the United States possessed the power to destroy entire nations, positioned its forces throughout the globe, used them repeatedly . . . and allowed [the military] a commanding position in American government and economy."[57]

To say that World War II marked the transformation of U.S. imperialism or the invention of a new kind of U.S. Empire is not to suggest that this was a single, coherent, or smooth process. Roosevelt and his administration did not have a single vision for controlling the world or advancing what they perceived as "U.S. interests." They did not consciously orchestrate the creation of a new U.S. imperialism, and they did not see themselves as imperialists. Instead, the development of a new U.S. imperialism came about as the result of the actions of competing actors within and beyond government struggling to shape U.S. policy amid a war and the other constraints and forces of history and their time.

The outcome of the war could have been different in many ways. Some, for example, had other ideas about the role foreign bases would play in the postwar world. There were other options than the false choice often presented in foreign policy debates between isolationism or the hypermilitarized garrisoning of the globe that emerged from the war. Perhaps if the Joint Chiefs had more seriously supported the creation of an International Police Force, or if Roosevelt had pushed them to do so, multilateral overseas bases might have had more of a chance at success. Roosevelt's initial instructions to the chiefs were, after all, to plan for such an international force—not for a largely nationalist, unilateral base structure.

The man who nearly followed Roosevelt as president, Secretary of Agriculture Henry Wallace, offers another example of a different vision for bases and the postwar world. Wallace was by far the most popular choice among Democrats to serve as Roosevelt's vice presidential candidate in 1944 and as the Democratic presidential nominee if Roosevelt had chosen not to run for a fourth term. Democratic Party bosses and other elites, however, were adamantly opposed to Wallace, given his support for the "emancipation" of "colonial subjects," as well as for unions, women, and African Americans. The party bosses blocked Wallace's nomination for vice president, instead manufacturing the selection of little-known and little-supported Harry Truman.[58] As early as 1942, Wallace wrote in his diary that the future of air bases "is one of the most important of all the peace problems."[59] In a September 12, 1946, speech at New York's Madison Square Garden, Wallace elaborated a different vision than Truman's unilateral declaration that "bases which our military experts deem to be essential for our protection we will acquire." Wallace insisted that "the United

Nations should have . . . control of the strategically located air bases with which the United States and Britain have encircled the globe."[60]

By war's end, turning foreign bases over to the United Nations or another multilateral force was inconceivable to most high-ranking U.S. officials. Many resisted returning bases to host nation governments. During the war the Allied powers agreed to remove their bases and troops from most foreign nations soon after the fighting stopped. After the war U.S. officials resisted doing precisely that, especially in Iceland, Greenland, and the Azores. Soviet leaders likewise resisted withdrawing their bases and troops from Iran.[61]

Neil Smith described the general postwar strategy as "global economic access without colonies," with "necessary bases around the globe both to protect global economic interests and to restrain any future military belligerence."[62] In this new version of the Open Door, decolonization would be used to destroy European powers' economic monopolies in their colonies, opening new markets to U.S. corporations. A large collection of bases around the globe and the world's most powerful military would provide a powerful protection service for U.S. businesses to ensure that the Open Door stayed open worldwide.

U.S. officials further used the nation's unchallenged military superiority at the end of World War II to dictate much of the postwar international economic system, on which U.S. geoeconomic power would be based.[63] New global institutions such as the World Bank, the International Monetary Fund, and the United Nations became important economic and political tools to open and dominate markets and maintain other countries in subordinate relationships. In this context U.S. officials would deploy bases, other forms of military intervention, and periodic displays of military might to help enforce general compliance with the rules of an economic and political system shaped by U.S. policy makers.[64] Overseas bases and other military tools of empire would increasingly work in tandem with and undergird political-economic tools of imperial power.

The hundreds of U.S. bases abroad were thus a critical part of the invention of a new form of empire. In the eighteenth and nineteenth centuries, the U.S. Empire followed the example of Britain, France, and other European empires by tying its expansionist success to the direct control of foreign lands. World War II and the decolonization process that followed the war made this no longer an option for U.S. officials—at least on a large scale. At the end of World War II, the United States controlled large new territories and populations. In Germany, Japan, Italy, and Austria, the United States ruled more than 150 million acres of land and tens of millions of people. In addition to its colonies, there were more people living in territories occupied by the United States overseas—135 million—than the 132 million inhabiting the forty-eight contiguous states.[65] Many empires of the past would have maintained direct colonial occupation of conquered territories. Given the overwhelming power of the United States after the war, U.S. officials likely could have continued the occupation of Germany, Japan, Italy, Austria, and other countries. As we will see, in the case of some smaller territories, U.S. officials indeed made occupation permanent. In other cases, some military leaders wanted to continue formal occupation but failed due to opposition by locals (as well as by others in the U.S. government). For the most part, U.S. leaders pursued this new kind of empire symbolized by bases, not colonies.

The Philippines and Dhahran, Saudi Arabia, further illustrate the shift in the history of empire. The Philippines, then with more than eighteen million people, was too large for U.S. officials not to grant its independence after the war. But U.S. leaders found a way to ensure neocolonial control with the help of a ninety-nine-year rent-free lease on twenty-three bases and military installations. Clark Air Base and Subic Bay Naval Base became two of the largest U.S. bases outside the United States, playing critical roles in waging U.S.-led wars in Korea and Southeast Asia. Building a base in Dhahran after it was no longer needed militarily reflected the growing use of bases to support U.S. oil companies and to establish dominance over the Middle East and its natural resources.

With a "chain of military bases and staging areas around the globe," the editors of the *Monthly Review* explain, the U.S. government developed the ability to deploy air and naval forces nearly anywhere worldwide "on a moment's notice—all in the interest of maintaining its political and economic hegemony."[66] A large collection of overseas bases thus became a major mechanism of U.S. imperial control, allowing the control of territory vastly disproportionate to the land actually occupied. While the total acreage occupied by bases has been relatively slight, in the ability to rapidly deploy the U.S. military nearly anywhere on the globe, the basing system represented a dramatic expansion of U.S. power and a significant way in which the United States came to maintain its postwar dominance. "The United States," Daniel Immerwahr writes in his book *How to Hide an Empire*, "did not abandon empire after the Second World War. Rather, it reshuffled its imperial portfolio, . . . investing in military bases, tiny specks of semi-sovereignty strewn around the globe."[67]

✪

At war's end the United States was in a much stronger position economically, politically, and militarily compared to any of its allies or the vanquished powers. Germany, Japan, and Italy were in ruins. Respectively, they lost an estimated 6.6–8.8 million, 2.6–3.1 million, and 457,000 people to combat and other wartime violence. Britain and France were badly weakened, although they had not yet relinquished their colonies. They counted 451,000 and 567,000 dead at home, plus 1.5–2.5 million deaths in India and 1.0–1.5 million in French-controlled Indochina. The Soviet Union bore the brunt of the war's fighting against Germany: an estimated 24 million civilians and soldiers perished. Approximately 6 million Jews and another 5 to 6 million Roma, Poles, Soviet civilians, prisoners of war, sexual minorities, the disabled, and others were murdered in Nazi concentration camps and other parts of its Holocaust killing machine. Worldwide, an estimated 60 million died.[68]

Among U.S. forces from the then forty-eight states, around 407,000 died. By far the worst U.S. casualties were in the Philippines, where more than 1 million Filipino soldiers and civilians perished. On Guam CHamorus experienced a brutal Japanese occupation and thousands of deaths. Hawai'i and a small part of Alaska also experienced Japanese attacks.[69] Stateside civilians never saw combat reach their shores. The country's military and economy were by far the world's most powerful, and the nation's leaders held unmatched diplomatic sway to shape the postwar world system.

Even if the United States experienced a relatively small number of deaths in the war, suffering is relative. The military saw terrible losses and brutal fighting. This made U.S. leaders especially reluctant to give up the overseas bases for which U.S. troops had fought and died. Bases have also long been considered war trophies of a kind—a monument to a military's victory. Given the growing significance of bases in the world, U.S. political and military leaders, like the leaders of empires past, wanted to hang on to what most considered the "spoils of war."

10 THE SPOILS OF WAR

"YANKEE GO HOME"

Someone had spray-painted the iconic phrase next to my hotel near Pisa's iconic Leaning Tower. The international tourist attraction is a short drive from Camp Darby, a major U.S. weapons storage facility and logistical hub along Italy's west coast. Beyond Italy I saw or heard "Yankee go home" from Honduras to Germany to South Korea. Many in the United States have trouble understanding such "Yankee go home" sentiment. Why wouldn't a country want U.S. bases and troops? They provide security, not to mention jobs and other economic benefits, right? Why wouldn't their presence be welcomed? Many assume that any "Yankee go home" sentiment must reflect a seething anti-Americanism. With bases in Europe and Asia, some might go so far as to invoke the old sarcastic joke that if it weren't for the United States, they'd probably be speaking German or Japanese right now.

Since World War II the phrase "Yankee go home" has almost always referred to U.S. military personnel and not to all U.S. citizens or everything "American." Protesters have often gone to great lengths to emphasize that their opposition is *not* motivated by anti-Americanism. While many allies welcomed the U.S. military to bases on their soil during World War II, many, such as Iceland, began requesting the removal of U.S. forces and the return of their bases soon after the fighting stopped.[1] Generally, U.S. officials had promised to remove military forces at the end of hostilities or at the more ambiguous "termination of the present international emergency." Labor unions and left-wing political parties, especially in Europe and Latin America, generally opposed the existence of any foreign bases. Leftists in France soon complained about U.S. "occupiers" and—somewhat ironically, given the history of French colonialism—"Coca-Colonization."[2]

Demands to send the Yankees home also came from some of the Yankees themselves. Unsurprisingly, at the end of the war, most U.S. military personnel wanted to go home as quickly as possible after years of often horrific fighting. In 1945 and 1946 protesting soldiers, sailors, and marines in Manila, London, Paris, Guam, Honolulu, and Frankfurt pressured the Truman administration to demobilize. Millions of family members likewise wanted their sons, husbands, boyfriends, and brothers to come home. Hundreds of Bring Back Daddy clubs formed across the United States.[3]

In Latin America leaders had been willing to host bases during the war because of the opportunities to develop national infrastructure at the expense of Uncle Sam. Given the history of the U.S. intervention in the region and broad anti-imperial sentiment, most in the region were ready to see U.S. forces depart. In Panama, where there were as many as 134 U.S. bases during the war, public protests broke out by 1947. Signs read, "DOWN WITH YANKEE IMPERIALISM," and "NOT ONE MORE INCH OF PANAMANIAN TERRITORY."[4] Panama's National Assembly unanimously rejected a postwar base agreement. President Harry Truman asked, "Why don't we get out of Panama gracefully before we get kicked out?"[5]

❂

Despite opposition in Panama, U.S. bases would remain for another half century. This was typical. After World War II, U.S. leaders, like the leaders of empires past, were reluctant to give up the "spoils of war." Military leaders were especially adamant about retaining "their" bases overseas. Even if the military had little interest in using a base or a territory, most generals and admirals felt the United States should almost never cede its acquisitions. As justification, they generally invoked two military principles. The first, "redundancy," says the more bases, the better. The idea is that it's always good to have backups. The second, "strategic denial," says that it's advantageous to hold on to bases and territories simply to prevent enemies from using them.

In October 1945, two months after the end of the war, the Secretary of War, Secretary of the Navy, Secretary of State, and Joint Chiefs of Staff approved a plan for a permanent peacetime global system of bases.[6] Notably, the focus was on bases on islands in the Pacific and Atlantic Oceans. No basing presence was planned for the Eurasian landmass, with the exception of bases occupying Germany; most assumed they were temporary.[7] Gen. Leslie Groves gave instructions to acquire base rights rights quickly, even though there was no direct threat to the United States "and plan not for ten years but for 50–100 years ahead." Melvyn Leffler writes, "[Military] officials regarded overseas bases as one of the keys to retaining US strategic air superiority and its world leadership role."[8]

At the direction of the military hierarchy, State Department officials pursued diplomatic agreements that would allow U.S. bases and troops to remain in other countries. Officials understood that the immediate development of bases wouldn't be possible everywhere they desired, given domestic pressure to cut the postwar military budget and international pressure to remove foreign military forces. Instead, writes Leffler, the plan was to negotiate for and secure base *rights* that would allow base construction and base use when needed in the future.[9] The military would monitor other potential base locations to ensure they didn't fall into the hands of the Soviet Union or other competitors. U.S. officials prioritized securing long-term access to bases in Iceland, Greenland, the Azores, and Ecuador's Galápagos Islands, among others. Military officials considered Iceland and Greenland increasingly important because of their proximity to the Soviet Union over the North Pole. The Azores provided a critical transit point between the Western Hemisphere and Europe, Africa, and Asia. The Galápagos offered protection for the western entrance to the Panama Canal.

In most cases U.S. negotiators faced opposition from local officials wary of allowing a foreign base presence amid heightened nationalist sentiment in most of the world. In the case of the Azores and Iceland, Secretary of State James F. Byrnes asked British Foreign Secretary Ernest Bevin for help in advancing negotiations.[10] In the case of Danish Greenland, the State Department appears to have offered to buy the world's largest island for $100 million. The Danish government rejected the deal but allowed a U.S. base presence, which continues to this day.[11] (Nearly seventy-five years later, President Donald Trump again proposed buying Greenland. Some thought the proposal was a joke. Danish Prime Minister Mette Frederiksen immediately rejected it, saying, "Greenland is not for sale. Greenland is not Danish. Greenland belongs to Greenland.")[12]

Facing host nation resistance, Congress funded bases for fiscal year 1946 primarily in places where there was little question about U.S. control and no diplomatic agreements were needed: Hawai'i, Alaska, the Philippines, Guam, Wake, Midway, Johnston, Christmas, Manus, Espiritu Santu, Okinawa, and the other previously Japanese-occupied islands of Ogasawara (Bonins), Saipan, Tinian, Eniwetok, Majuro, Kwajalein, Truk, and Palau.[13]

The maintenance of a permanent collection of U.S. bases overseas reflected a profound change in how U.S. elites thought about the world, warfare, threats to the country, and even the very ideas of "defense" and a newly expansive concept of "national security." During World War II President Franklin D. Roosevelt and other leaders inside and outside of government developed a vision of the world as intrinsically threatening. Instability, no matter how far removed from the United States, was seen as a threat. The military needed to be a "permanently mobilized force" ready to confront threats wherever they might appear.[14]

This threatening view of the world developed even before the United States entered World War II. "No attack is so unlikely or impossible that it may be ignored," argued Roosevelt in 1939.[15] "If the United States is to have any defense," Roosevelt and others believed, "it must have total defense." In this way, Michael Sherry explains, the mentality of the U.S.-Soviet "Cold War" started to take hold long before the "Cold War" had even begun.[16]

After World War II the role of the U.S. military transformed into a force that would patrol the world and protect against any and all perceived threats twenty-four hours a day.[17] The result was a machinery of war cen-

tered on a perpetually mobilized military and an expanding "national security bureaucracy." That the country needed a large collection of bases and
hundreds of thousands of troops constantly stationed overseas, as close as
possible to any potential enemies, became a major tenet of U.S. strategy.
"Experience in the recent war," the Joint Chiefs of Staff wrote in March
1946, "demonstrated conclusively that the defense of a nation, if it is to be
effective, must begin beyond its frontiers. The advent of the atomic bomb
reemphasizes this requirement. The farther away from our own vital areas
we can hold our enemy through the possession of advanced bases . . . the
greater are our chances of surviving successfully an attack by atomic weapons and of destroying the enemy which employs them against us."[18]

In the minds of policy makers, patrolling the world and protecting
against threats meant maintaining a large collection of overseas bases where
hundreds of thousands of troops could be stationed and from which they
could be deployed at any moment. The overseas base infrastructure became
an unquestioned keystone of the U.S. government's approach to the "Cold
War." This policy emphasized defending the United States and the West as
close as possible to the enemy—initially the Soviet Union and later China,
after the communist takeover. U.S. (and allied) forces, the strategy held,
needed to create a line of defense against any future Nazi Germany–like
expansion. This strategy of "offensive defense" was akin to the military (and
now sports) principle that "the best defense is a good offense."

As a result, one scholar explains, "the security of the United States, in
the minds of policymakers, lost much of its former inseparability from the
concept of the territory of the United States." With the national government increasingly organized around preparations for war and permanent,
intervention-ready military mobilization on a global basis, U.S. officials
"did not wait to be invited" virtually anywhere on Earth.[19] Especially in the
Pacific Ocean, military leaders pursued the creation of a large collection of
island bases that would enable the use of air power to control East Asia
without large ground forces. This strategy was rooted in a widely held
strategic belief that the security of the nation and the prevention of future
wars depended on dominating the ocean through an Alfred Thayer
Mahan–inspired combination of unparalleled naval and air forces and
island bases. "This imperial solution to American anxieties about strategic
security in the postwar Pacific exhibited itself," writes bases expert Hal

Friedman, "in a bureaucratic consensus about turning the Pacific Basin into an 'American lake.'"[20]

For Gen. Douglas MacArthur, the Supreme Commander of Allied Forces in Japan, and other military leaders, securing the Pacific meant creating an "offshore island perimeter." The perimeter was to be a line of island bases stretching from north to south across the western Pacific. It would be like a giant wall protecting the United States, yet with thousands of miles of moat before reaching U.S. shores. "Our line of defense," MacArthur explained, "runs through the chain of islands fringing the coast of Asia. It starts from the Philippines and continues through the Ryukyu Archipelago, which includes its main bastion, Okinawa. Then it bends back through Japan and the Aleutian Island chain, to Alaska."[21]

Military leaders demanded complete sovereignty over Guam and the other islands in the Marianas and in Micronesia, along with the retention of Okinawa and other captured Japanese islands. Some suggested making Guam and other Pacific islands into new states or including them in an anticipated new state of Hawai'i. The military felt especially justified in retaining captured Pacific islands because of the financial costs and "sacrifice of American blood" involved.[22] "Having defeated or subordinated its former imperial rivals in the Pacific," a group of bases experts explain, "the United States military was in no mood to hand back occupied real estate."[23] In many cases the armed services pressed for full annexation of former Japanese-controlled islands. Many in Congress "shared the feeling that no one had the right to give away land which had been bought and paid for with American lives." Louisiana Representative F. Edward Hébert explained the imperial logic prevalent after the war: "We fought for them, we've got them, we should keep them. They are necessary to our safety. I see no other course."[24]

Others in Congress, the State Department, and the media differed. Many State Department officials opposed full U.S. sovereignty over any island except Guam. With the decolonization process gaining momentum at the United Nations and pressure growing for Britain and France to give up their colonies, U.S. diplomats were sensitive to being attacked as colonialists. Amid congressional and public pressure to cut the military budget and demobilize, President Truman ultimately opposed the formal annexation of conquered islands. His administration struck a compromise. It ensured that the former Japanese-controlled islands of Micronesia and other Pacific islands became a U.S.-administered UN "strategic trust territory." Like League of Nations "mandates," the Trust Territory of the Pacific Islands was a paternalistic, racist, and de facto colonial system based on the supposed inferiority of Pacific islanders. With the blessing of the United Nations, the United States gained control over the islands, including the right to maintain bases, in exchange for ensuring inhabitants' well-being and eventual right to self-determination. The Navy assumed direct administrative control of the islands, which it retained until the Department of the Interior took over in 1951. As one observer put it, the trusteeship was "de facto annexation, papered over with the thinnest of disguises."[25]

✪

By the time Winston Churchill gave his Iron Curtain speech in early 1946, tensions between the United States and Soviet Union were growing amid public signs of a "Cold War" between the wartime allies. For a time a war between the two remaining world powers, the two empires, appeared possible, even likely in the minds of some people. U.S. officials, on the other hand, shared a "widespread assumption" that the Soviets had no interest in military aggression and would "seek to avoid war" with the United States for at least five to ten years. Although the Soviet Army had millions of men who had defeated Nazi armies in Eastern Europe, overall Soviet military capabilities were quite limited: the country essentially had no strategic air force, no real navy, and no atomic bomb. "Nonetheless," writes Leffler, "US officials felt threatened." They felt threatened not because of Soviet military power but because of a "growing apprehension about the vulnerability of American strategic and economic interests in a world of unprecedented turmoil and upheaval." They also feared the possibility of an accidental conflict set off by Soviet attempts to expand control of territory or resources in Eurasia.[26]

Amid the fears a globe-encircling collection of overseas bases became an important part of U.S. officials' conception of security. Roosevelt and Joseph Stalin had agreed at the Allies' 1944 meeting in Yalta to withdraw their forces from foreign lands. U.S. officials now insisted on staying in the Galápagos, Iceland, Greenland, and the Azores, among other locations, while insisting equally that Soviet forces leave Iran and gain no basing rights in the Dardanelles. Army officials and other leaders understood the "logical illogicality" of this position but persisted nonetheless. U.S. intentions were pure and defensive in nature, they thought, while they did not trust what they believed to be the expansionist ambitions of Russia and international communism. Military and State Department leaders agreed that U.S. forces "could not withdraw from critical locations."[27]

U.S. leaders saw access to British bases in the Middle East as particularly significant in the event of war with the Soviet Union. Installations in the region would be critical to attacking Soviet oil refineries and industrial regions and to protecting U.S.- and U.K.-controlled oil supplies. The base complex between Cairo and the Suez Canal, for example, hosted two hundred thousand British troops in 1945 and one hundred thousand in the first years after the war. As early as the summer of 1946, secret meetings with U.K. officials included discussions about using Middle East bases to launch U.S. atomic bombers in the event of a new war. Negotiators reached an agreement to build infrastructure at five British bases to allow their use by U.S. B-29 nuclear-capable bombers. Within a few years B-29s at Cairo-Suez were a threat to 94 percent of Soviet oil refineries.[28]

The Soviet military maintained foreign bases after the war's conclusion. Most were in neighboring countries that came under Soviet occupation or influence, as well as in East Germany, Kaliningrad, and North Korea. In total the number and scope paled in comparison to the entrenched U.S. base network, which was more expansive still, given U.S. access to the "intertwined" bases of British and French allies in their remaining colonial possessions and in the metropoles. By September 1946 a Russian Navy admiral was publicly describing U.S. basing policy as "clearly offensive in nature." According to a contemporaneous account, the admiral "declared that [U.S.] far-flung peacetime naval bases cannot be intended for the defense of the American continent, since some of them are situated at the close approaches to the Asiatic continent (Okinawa) and of Europe (Iceland and Greenland)."[29]

Former Roosevelt vice president Henry Wallace was similarly concerned. "How would it look to us if Russia had the atomic bomb and we did not," he wrote in a July 1946 memo to Truman. How would it look "if Russia had 10,000-mile bombers and air bases within a thousand miles of our coastlines and we did not?" Wallace warned that an arms race was most likely to bring about war rather than ensure peace. He ticked off major elements of this aggressive U.S. policy, including "the effort to secure air bases spread over half the globe from which the other half can be bombed"; $13 billion in military spending since war's end; atomic bomb tests in the Marshall Islands' Bikini Atoll and the production of additional bombs; plans to arm Latin America with U.S. weapons; the continued production of B-29 bombers and plans to build newer B-36 bombers. All these steps, Wallace said, "make it appear either 1) that we are preparing ourselves to win the war which we regard inevitable, or 2) that we are trying to build up a predominance of force to intimidate the rest of mankind." Although Wallace had been one of the most popular Democratic Party politicians in the country during his time as Roosevelt's vice president, his views on military policy were clearly in the minority.[30] Wallace's 1948 Progressive Party presidential campaign failed to pose a serious challenge to Truman, securing less than 3 percent of the national vote.

❂

The military's grandest plans for postwar bases were ultimately trumped by concerns about costs, demands for demilitarization, and local opposition. The calls to bring GIs home were especially difficult for the Truman administration to ignore. The government shrunk the military from over 12 million men and women in 1945 to just 1.5 million by June 1947. In the same period military spending decreased from 83 percent of federal expenditures to 38 percent.[31]

Less than a year after the war's end, as a result of the slow pace of negotiations for base rights and "budgetary trends," the military had reduced its desired base locations to seventy bases, with six deemed "essential"— Iceland, the Azores, Greenland, the Galápagos, Panama, and Casablanca, or the Canary Islands. By September 1947 the Joint Chiefs of Staff reduced their "requirements" to fifty-three bases.[32] To the disappointment of military leaders, the nation ultimately returned about half its foreign bases after the war.[33] In the Pacific, for example, the military abandoned plans for an offshore island perimeter. Instead, to keep the Pacific an "American

Greenland
(Denmark)

Alaska

Icela

Canada

Newfoundland

UNITED STATES
OF AMERICA

Bermuda

Midway Island

Bahamas

Hawai'i

Puerto Rico

Guantánamo Bay,
Cuba

U.S. Virgin Islands
St. Lucia

Johnston Atoll

Jamaica

Antigua

Panama
Canal Zone

British Guiana

Trinidad

American Samoa

U.S. War(s)

Other U.S. Combat Actions

U.S. Base(s)

U.S. Bases (>25)

U.S. Small Base(s)

U.S. Naval Fleet

U.S. Colonies, Military Occupations in Italics

Antarctic

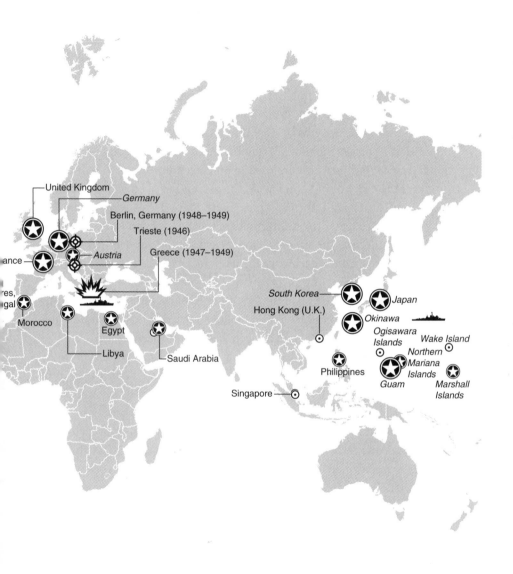

Map 16. U.S. Bases, Wars, and Expansion Abroad, 1946–1949.
Significant bases, combat, and expansion outside U.S. states are shown. The map
reflects the relative number and positioning of bases, which totaled just under six
hundred, in 1949. Oceans not to scale. Key sources: Blaker, *United States Overseas
Basing;* Robert E. Harkavy, *Strategic Basing and the Great Powers, 1200–2000*
(London: Routledge, 2007).

lake," the military relied on key bases in Okinawa and mainland Japan, Guam, Hawai'i, and the UN Trust Territory of the Pacific Islands.

Despite the significant cutbacks, U.S. leaders found a range of ways to ensure the country entrenched a "permanent institution" of bases in peacetime.[34] The budget cuts may have "limited the depth of the base system," writes Leffler, "but not the breadth of American ambitions."[35] Increasingly, economic aid, diplomatic support, and military assistance became tools and incentives to acquire base rights. In response to local opposition in places including Ecuador, Denmark, Portugal, France, and Saudi Arabia, military and diplomatic officials found ways to reduce the profile of the U.S. presence and avoid the perception of an ongoing foreign occupation. In Iceland, for example, where many locals were clamoring for U.S. forces to leave, the military shrunk its forces from forty-five thousand to around one thousand personnel who could service U.S. aircraft but were barred from wearing uniforms.[36] In 1948 the two governments agreed on the removal of U.S. forces and the appearance of a "U.S. base" by having a civilian company run the U.S.-built Keflavik airfield. U.S. officials complained that the country had a "jealous regard for its absolute independence and sovereignty" and a "deep fear of 'Americanization.'"[37]

In the Azores U.S. officials ensured a Portuguese flag continued to fly over what the U.S. military considered a critical base. With the help of agreements signed in 1946, 1948, and 1951, Portuguese personnel ran the base in Lajes, while U.S. personnel serviced aircraft transiting between the United States and Europe, North Africa, and beyond. In French colonial Morocco U.S. Navy personnel secretly serviced aircraft at the Port Lyautey naval airfield, which officially remained under the command of the French Navy.[38] In Japan U.S. officials, reportedly at the suggestion of Emperor Hirohito, insisted on retaining full control of Okinawa and other small islands, such as Iwo Jima, after the end of the occupation of Japan's main islands.[39] The U.S. government asserted the right to establish military facilities and to govern the islands effectively as part of the United States. Neither the new U.S.-imposed Japanese Constitution nor the U.S. Constitution applied. To avoid accusations of colonialism, U.S. officials described Japan as maintaining "residual sovereignty" over Okinawa and the other islands.[40]

Elsewhere there was little effort made to disguise the U.S. presence. In the rest of Japan and in Germany, U.S. forces occupied bases under the terms of armistice agreements made with the defeated nations, although they were initially considered temporary. The military kept facilities in most of the British territories occupied under the Destroyers-for-Bases agreement and gained further access to British facilities in Ascension, Bahrain, Libya, Guadalcanal, and Tarawa. When Britain wanted to grant complete independence to India and Burma, the U.S. State Department asked its ally to maintain control of three airfields in the former and one in the latter. There were so many U.S. bases in the British isles that many began referring to Britain as the U.S. Air Force's "unsinkable aircraft carrier" (the phrase has been used to describe other hosts, from Honduras to Okinawa).

Among its own colonial possessions, the United States retained important bases in Guam, Puerto Rico, and Wake Island, as well as Guantánamo Bay. During talks that led to independence for the Philippines in 1946, U.S. negotiators threatened to withhold military assistance when Philippines government representatives opposed some U.S. basing demands. At Subic Bay Naval Base, Clark Air Base, and elsewhere, the United States effectively continued formal colonial rule, maintaining sovereignty over the city of Olongapo, adjacent to Subic Bay, as well as control over Filipino workers, criminal prosecutions, and taxation. In return the Truman administration sent limited aid and some military advisers. As in other countries, the interests of U.S. officials and Filipino elites converged; the latter wanted economic aid, access to U.S. markets, and U.S. military help repressing the Huk Rebellion.[41]

✪

Diplomat George Kennan was one of the chief architects of early "Cold War" strategy. His views were typical of policy makers and other elites of the day. "We have about 50% of the world's wealth but only 6.3% of its population," Kennan wrote in a memo drafted when he was part of the State Department's Policy Planning Staff. "Our real task in the coming period is to devise a pattern of relationships which will permit us to maintain this position of disparity without positive detriment to our national security. To do so, we will have to dispense with all sentimentality and day-dreaming; and our attention will have to be concentrated everywhere on our immediate national objectives. We need not deceive ourselves that we can afford today the luxury of altruism and world-benefaction." Kennan added, "The day is not far off when we are going to have to deal in straight power concepts. The less we are then hampered by idealistic slogans, the better."[42] Like most other elites, Kennan believed that the exercise of sheer military and economic power was critical to ensuring U.S. dominance globally. Guided by such beliefs, U.S. leaders entrenched a global system of military bases abroad in the first years after World War II, despite the calls to send the Yankees home coming from many allies and U.S. citizens alike.

Kennan called his policy "containment." It quickly came to guide "national security" strategy. In the eyes of Kennan and other government officials, the aim of containment was to establish a worldwide balance of power favorable to the United States. For Kennan this meant the use of not just military force but also political, economic, and psychological power as well. Economic aid, such as the Marshall Plan, came to be a primary tool of Truman administration foreign policy in an attempt to rebuild Japan and the nations of Western Europe as strong anti-Soviet allies and markets for U.S. businesses. The North Atlantic Treaty Organization (NATO) and other treaty organizations played an equally important political-military role as part of Kennan's vision for a selective approach of using the military to defend key strategic strongpoints.[43]

A set of "interlocking interests" supported this kind of expansive and expensive containment policy, Sherry explains. These interests included the military branches, military industries, and powerful individuals in both settings. All faced contraction or economic slowdown after the war. Collectively, they advocated for the maintenance of hundreds of bases abroad and a historically large military. While self-interest at bureaucratic, corporate, and individual levels continued to shape leaders' thinking and planning, Sherry points out that policy makers' fears did as well. "Real and frightening changes in the technology of war and the conduct of international diplomacy" meant that "the makers of postwar policy would have been derelict in their duty had they failed to incorporate those changes into their strategic thinking."[44]

"Obsessed by the pattern of Axis aggrandizement" in the last war, U.S. officials "were primed to see that pattern in the activities of other nations"— namely, in the Soviet Union. Unfortunately for the United States, the Soviet Union, and the world, the strategy of U.S. leaders remained, as Sherry says, "simplistic." They "overrated the usefulness of military solutions for postwar policy problems." They maintained a "misguided faith" in U.S. air power, nuclear weapons, and bases "to deter or check future aggressors" by failing to see how, from the Soviet perspective, their actions were threatening and encouraged the Soviets to build up their own military forces to counter the U.S. threat.[45] To this day, writes Andrew Bacevich, U.S. leadership "expects others to view US military power, the Pentagon's global footprint, and an American penchant for intervention not as a matter of concern but as a source of comfort and reassurance."[46] In the 1960s, when Soviet leader Nikita Khrushchev spent time at a vacation home on the Black Sea, he would ask visiting guests what they saw. Referring to the threat just over the horizon, Khrushchev would say, "*I* see US missiles in Turkey, aimed at *my dacha.*"[47]

⊛

After the Soviet Union successfully tested its first atomic weapon in 1949, a new iteration of the containment policy emerged with the drafting of National Security Council Report 68 of 1950 (NSC-68). The report was written in large part by Paul H. Nitze, a powerful foreign policy official whose influence would extend into the 1980s. Unlike Kennan's strategy, NSC-68 emphasized the military aspects of containment. Instead of defending key strategic strongpoints, NSC-68 saw danger everywhere and emphasized defending the United States and the West at every point on its "perimeter."[48]

The "forward strategy," as this policy became known, insisted that the United States maintain bases and military forces as close as possible to the Soviet Union to block any possibility of Soviet expansion or any other threat.[49] Both NSC-68 and Kennan's containment strategy shared an almost limitless global vision of U.S. foreign policy and an aim of encir-cling perceived enemies with offensive nuclear and nonnuclear military power. Although there are precedents for such a policy dating to the nineteenth-century acquisition of naval and coaling stations in the Pacific, the postwar policies of Kennan and Nitze represented a shift in U.S. for-eign policy. At a time when the "national security state" itself became entrenched in the fabric of U.S. life, the entrenchment of the global basing system embedded the forward strategy in the minds of policy makers, other elites, and the institutions in which they were located. The idea that the country should have a large collection of bases and hundreds of thou-sands of troops permanently stationed overseas became one of the most fundamental and unquestioned precepts of U.S. foreign and "national security" policy throughout the "Cold War" and beyond it as well. Members of this foreign policy establishment, as well as many others, came to treat as gospel, as common sense, the idea that bases overseas provide forward lines of defense against potential threats; allow the nation to intervene in world crises by quickly deploying military forces most anywhere on the planet; make the world and regions of the globe safer and more peaceful by maintaining global and regional balances of power; protect and pro-mote U.S. economic and political interests; and spread democracy.

Nearly three-quarters of a century after the war, base expert Kent Calder observed that "a strong bias toward [the] forward deployment" of bases and troops remained "clearly embedded in twenty-first-century America's political-military institutions" and even "in much of our tradi-tional psychology."[50] The policy has been shared by both major political parties, as well as by most of the U.S. media, think tank analysts, academ-ics, and many others. As a result, U.S. citizens "have long since become accustomed to the stationing of US troops in far-off lands," writes Bacevich. To many "this global military presence is ostensibly essential to the definition of American freedom even in places where the actual threat is oblique or imaginary."[51]

✪

With so many bases maintained as "spoils of war" in so many places world-wide, U.S. policy makers were more likely to use them. Bases abroad became a tempting policy solution to problems that generally had no military solutions. Overseas bases appeared to provide protection, safety, and security. They appeared to hold out the promise of never having to fight a world war again. But by making it simpler to wage foreign wars, they made military action an even more attractive option among the foreign policy tools available to U.S. policy makers. As Catherine Lutz and others remind us, when all you have in your foreign policy toolbox are hammers, everything starts looking like a nail.[52] Overseas installations made overseas wars not just easier but also more likely. The spoils of war came to significantly shape U.S. foreign policy.

With overseas bases framed as a pillar of U.S. security, the acquisition of new bases and the buildup of existing bases became a seemingly logical and relatively easy solution to growing U.S.-Soviet tensions and U.S. citizens' fears. In Japan, for example, the Navy began discussing the possibility of maintaining bases there after the signing of a peace treaty and the end of the formal occupation period. When the State Department was negotiating the eventual 1951 U.S.-Japan peace treaty, John Foster Dulles, adviser to Secretary of State Dean Acheson, noted that carefully crafted language in the draft "gave the United States the right to maintain in Japan as much force as we wanted, anywhere we wanted, for as long as we wanted."[53]

While some officials' broadest desires for overseas bases after World War II were stymied, a still-massive, entrenched collection of bases laid the foundation for a rapid expansion of the base network within a few years. While the Yankees actually closed their bases and left Italy (among other locations) after the signing of a peace treaty in 1947, they would return after Italy joined NATO in 1949, amid communist forces' seizure of power in China and escalating East-West tensions. After the start of the war on the Korean peninsula in 1950, an unprecedented buildup of installations and troops followed in Italy, Germany, and other parts of Europe and Asia. Rather than going home for good, the Yankees were coming back in unprecedented numbers in "peacetime."

11 NORMALIZING OCCUPATION

In 1950 the United States was again at war, this time in Korea. Planes flying from air bases in Japan, Okinawa, Guam, and the Philippines were transporting material to U.S. and allied forces and carrying out bombing raids on North Korean troops, industrial centers, and supply lines. Under the auspices of the United Nations and with a coalition of around twenty other nations, the U.S. military led an effort to come to the aid of South Korea after North Korea's 1950 invasion. The conflict would see U.S. forces march into North Korea and toward the Chinese border, bringing the world to the brink of an even larger conflict and a possible nuclear exchange involving the United States and its allies facing China, the Soviet Union, and North Korea. Three to four million are estimated to have died in a war that left the peninsula devastated.[1]

During the conflict an Air Force–led U.S. negotiating team traveled to Lisbon, Portugal, in the fall of 1951. They were authorized to bring with them a silver cigarette box, a double-pedestal Parker 51 fountain pen desk set, and a Winchester Model 70 rifle with a Lyman Alaskan Sight and two hundred rounds of .30-06-caliber ammunition. Each was a gift, engraved for the Portuguese Minister of National Defense and the chiefs of the Portuguese Armed Forces and Portuguese Air Force. The gifts were intended as "tokens of appreciation" from Secretary of Defense George Marshall to thank the Portuguese government for signing an agreement giving U.S. forces expanded rights to operate from and build bases in the Azores.[2]

President Harry Truman, with the support of Congress, was in the process of sending hundreds of thousands of troops back to Asia and Western Europe, including Portugal, to contain "communist aggression" and pursue the war in Korea. After a period of significant base closures during post–World War II demobilization, the Korean War led to a 40 percent increase in the number of overseas bases.[3] For military and civilian leaders, the war cemented the importance of maintaining large bases in the eastern Pacific Ocean, including on Okinawa and elsewhere in Japan, on Guam, and in South Korea itself.[4] By 1952 U.S. negotiators had secured long-term postoccupation access to bases in Japan, as well as continued U.S. rule in Okinawa. U.S. officials soon signed mutual security pacts with the Philippines, New Zealand, and Australia. Chinese nationalist Taiwan, countries in Southeast Asia, and South Korea would follow. U.S. bases would appear in most of these allied nations.[5]

Across the globe U.S. forces occupied and built bases in Europe, Latin America, and the Middle East. The government of Iceland allowed the Air Force to officially return, although with a strict ban on dating or marrying local women. U.K. officials provided access to twenty-six new air bases. In Morocco the Air Force built a base nearly as large as almost anything that had existed during World War II. By 1952 the Air Force alone was supervising the construction of almost one hundred bases abroad.[6]

"The sun never sets on American bases—army, navy and air—around the world," stated the *Chicago Daily Tribune* in 1955. "American military installations now girdle the globe with more outposts than ever known to any nation in history. . . . The American overseas commitment ranges from a handful of men at lonely outposts in arctic wilds to huge bases in Africa, Europe, and the Pacific. The American flag flies in every continent and over every sea."[7] By decade's end the United States had entered into eight mutual defense pacts with forty-two nations and executive security agreements with more than thirty others, most of which provided various kinds of basing access.[8]

"In geopolitical terms," writes historian Alfred McCoy, the United States "became history's most powerful empire because it was the first, after a millennium of incessant struggle, to control 'both ends of Eurasia,'" with bases from the British Isles through Southeast Asia to Japan. To guard the empire, the U.S. military had 2.6 million active duty troops; 2,650 ships and 7,195 Navy combat aircraft; 15,000 Air Force fighters, bombers, and transport aircraft; and nuclear weapons ready for launch from the air, the land, and the sea.[9] The growing nuclear weapons arsenal of the Soviet Union played some role in the base proliferation: more U.S. bases meant more targets and dispersed forces. The growing fear of a nuclear-armed Soviet Union likewise played an important role in governments agreeing to a U.S. presence. "Viewed from one perspective, this was an act of [U.S.] benevolence," writes foreign bases expert Amy Holmes. The United States was providing protection. On the other hand, other nations were ceding a significant degree of sovereignty to the United States (while also turning themselves into targets for Soviet missiles).[10]

In Portugal "the supersensitive question of Portuguese sovereignty was constantly being raised before our negotiators," reported Col. Lawrence C. Coddington, Air Force Deputy Assistant for Air Bases. "Every point of issue revolved around the question of sovereignty and were [sic] resolved only after lengthy discussions on many proposed drafts." Coddington acknowledged that "the agreement as written does not meet the ultimate in Air Force desires." But, he continued, "it must be kept in mind that the Air Force cannot hope to achieve its desired ultimate in operating rights in small foreign countries purely because of that country's jealousy over its sovereignty."[11]

The sensitivity of the Portuguese government about its loss of sovereignty was common among countries hosting U.S. bases. The rapid requests for the Yankees to leave after World War II revealed this. Even with growing fears of a clash between East and West, base negotiations were often difficult. Generally, they revolved around the degree to which U.S. forces would enjoy "extraterritoriality"—that is, the extent to which U.S. forces would be free from local laws, free from local prosecution for committing any crimes, and free to conduct military operations without restraint or consultation with the host nation. In other words, negotiations focused on how much effective sovereignty the U.S. military would have on foreign soil and thus how much sovereignty a host country would give up. Even with the United States' closest allies, such as Great Britain, sovereignty would long remain a "focus of tension," especially when it came to crimes committed by troops.[12]

The perceived "supersensitivity" of the Portuguese government and other countries about allowing U.S. bases on their soil was understandable. For centuries foreign bases were generally the product of empires' imposing bases in occupied foreign lands. Portugal had plenty of its own experience imposing its bases in Brazil, during the colonization of the Americas, and those still occupying colonial Mozambique, Angola, Cape Verde, and East Timor during the 1951 negotiations. Foreign bases and foreign troops on another country's soil likewise runs counter to the modern Westphalian nation-state system that enshrined sovereignty and self-determination as major international norms since the seventeenth century.

A cigarette box, a couple of pens, and a rifle were obviously not what convinced Portuguese dictator António de Oliveira Salazar and his top military aides to cede some of Portugal's sovereignty to the United States. The real gifts offered by U.S. officials in exchange for Azores basing agreements in 1946, 1948, and 1951 were U.S. support for (1) ongoing Portuguese colonialism, (2) Portugal's wars to suppress independence movements in Africa, and (3) its entry as a founding member of the North Atlantic Treaty Organization (NATO) (the only fully undemocratic member country).[13]

✪

The Portuguese government's agreement to allow U.S. forces to operate from bases in the Azores reflects a significant transformation in the history of empire generally and U.S. Empire in particular. While U.S. officials entrenched an unprecedented collection of foreign bases globally after World War II, U.S. leaders had to negotiate for extraterritorial rights to a greater extent than most prior empires during their colonization of foreign lands. Imperial negotiation was nothing new. The image of empires as all-powerful forces imposing their will completely on conquered territories has always been misleading. Most empires through history have dealt with varying degrees of local acquiescence and complicity, incomplete imperial sovereignty, and negotiation to maintain rule and avoid local rebellions.[14]

Changing international political norms related to the decolonization movement, resistance to Nazi and Japanese imperialism, and the creation of the United Nations forced U.S. officials to negotiate with host nations more than most prior empires had needed to.[15] After World War II U.S. officials had to work harder to establish and ensure extraterritorial, undemocratic sovereignty on foreign soil—an encouraging development from the perspective of efforts to build greater democracy. This meant that while some countries hosting U.S. bases remained in a fundamentally imperial relation with the United States, some maintained relatively greater sovereignty than imperial dependencies of the past. It also meant that, unlike in many previous imperial relationships, the national governments of many—but far from all—countries hosting U.S. bases were consenting, to varying degrees, to the foreign U.S. presence. The term *consent* is misleading, however, given both the significant power imbalances between the U.S. Empire and base hosts and the pressure U.S officials inflicted on potential hosts amid fearmongering about the Soviet threat. Agreeing to the presence of U.S. bases and troops was never a matter of simple free choice. (Even the word *host* is inaccurate, given the degree of coercion involved in a government's—let alone an entire citizenry's—agreeing to allow this unusual type of "guest" on its territory.)

There were significant exceptions to the bases secured by some degree of consent, including bases in the territories of World War II's vanquished powers (Germany, Japan, Italy, and Austria), Cuba's Guantánamo Bay, U.S. colonies, UN-sanctioned Trust Territory colonies, and European-controlled colonies hosting U.S. bases. Still, across Western Europe and beyond, governments were agreeing to forfeit what sociologist Max Weber called a state's "monopoly on the legitimate use of force" by allowing U.S. bases and troops on their territory.[16] When U.S. bases remained in Germany, Japan, and Italy following the end of formal occupation, these governments also forfeited the monopoly on the use of violence. Of course, this forfeiture came in a context of gaping power disparities, in which U.S. officials used U.S. dominance, political-economic coercion, and fears about the Soviet Union to ensure national governments agreed to a base presence.

During the "Cold War" U.S. officials developed a range of tools to ensure other countries acquiesced to U.S. basing demands. Just as when they supported Portuguese colonialism and NATO membership, U.S. officials often struck political and diplomatic deals in exchange for basing access. Locating bases in dictatorships and other undemocratic countries, such as Portugal, the Kingdom of Saudi Arabia, and soon fascist Spain, greatly eased the challenges of gaining and maintaining popular support for a U.S. presence. Undemocratic rulers simplified the maintenance of an imperial basing relationship by preventing or severely limiting the possibility of protest or opposition of any kind.

Elsewhere economic assistance, in the form of preferential trade deals, development funds, and military aid, provided sweeteners to secure the consent of local officials. "Unlike Portugal," writes António José Telo, "Spain wanted direct, clear and extensive compensation from the United States" in exchange for a 1953 agreement that allowed the U.S. military to create bases anywhere on Spanish territory. "Spain accepted everything demanded of it, even the establishment of nuclear bomber bases close to Madrid." The Spanish economy grew with the help of U.S. capital and technical assistance, "while the Portuguese economy grew much more modestly."[17]

Spain and Portugal show how the imperial relationship was rarely one-way. Given the desires of U.S. leaders for foreign installations, potential or existing base hosts were in a position to negotiate benefits from the U.S. government. Publicly, U.S. officials "denied a direct relationship between" base rights and any form of payment or "rent." However, Gretchen Heefner explains, "nearly everyone understood that bases equaled money. And the money flowed." It flowed in the form of loans and grants to purchase U.S. weapons and equipment; as education, training, and infrastructure projects; as new highways, air defense systems, and runways; and as disaster relief, food aid, M60 machine guns, and tens of thousands of pairs of military-grade boots. Technically, all allies were eligible for this sort of assistance. In practice "countries [that had] U.S. installations received far more generous terms and goods than those that did not."[18]

By 1963, after the Kennedy administration reversed its anticolonial policy in Africa to support Portugal at the United Nations and in other international forums, the CIA noted that Portuguese dictator Salazar considered the Azores bases to be his "bargaining chip": "The threat of expulsion from the Azores base [w]as a valuable instrument for muting United States criticism of Portuguese colonial policies."[19]

The two-way nature of imperial relationships was again nothing new. Empires have depended for centuries on buying off, bribing, and otherwise assisting local elites as part of the maintenance of rule in conquered lands. As the "Cold War" progressed, and the economic strength of allies increased and the strength of the U.S. dollar declined, the balance of these relationships changed. In many countries—notably Germany and Japan—U.S. officials pressured host governments to make cash and in-kind payments and purchases of various types to support a U.S. military presence.[20] The West German government, for example, agreed to buy large quantities of U.S.-made arms and supplies to "offset" U.S. military spending. Between 1961 and 1967 these purchases totaled $4.71 billion. The West German Army soon had more U.S. weaponry than it could use. The offsets led to the fall of Chancellor Ludwig Erhard's government. By the mid-1970s the government and many citizens had had enough of what they saw as "occupation costs" similar to those paid immediately after the war. Both governments agreed to end the offset agreement in exchange for a one-time payment of about half the total costs for a new U.S. base in northern Germany.[21]

✪

In 1948, national elections in Italy had U.S. political, military, economic, and even Catholic religious leaders fearful that Italy's favored communist and socialist parties would come to power. Military and diplomatic officials were particularly concerned, because of left-wing opposition to any foreign military presence and Euro-American military cooperation more broadly. In the lead-up to the election, the CIA, the State Department, the military, and other parts of the U.S. government used propaganda, smear campaigns, and threats to withdraw economic aid, among other tactics, to help the right-wing Christian Democratic Party secure victory. Shortly before the election the military stationed warships off Italy's coasts to demonstrate its concern about and opposition to a left-wing victory.[22]

The electoral meddling is a reminder that bases were always an imperial tool used in tandem with other tools, including covert CIA efforts to influence elections and to encourage and support coups in Iran, Guatemala, and the Dominican Republic in the 1950s alone. Underlining the paramilitary nature of the CIA and the military base–intelligence nexus, the CIA used a Honduran banana plantation belonging to United Fruit (today Chiquita Brands International) as a military base to help train and finance the rebel army that overthrew the democratically elected government in Guatemala in 1954. The Guatemalan government became a U.S. target after President Jacobo Árbenz Guzmán dared to threaten the near-monopoly powers of United Fruit in Guatemala.[23]

In some ways this was a continuation of U.S. imperial patterns of gunboat-style intervention found mostly in Latin America, dating to the nineteenth century. The difference was that in the post–World War II era, in the era of decolonization, the interventions and meddling were generally covert and less brazen. "In the 1950s era of decolonization," writes anthropologist Carole McGranahan, "empires did not go away, but went underground." Indeed, the U.S. and Soviet Empires "fiercely guarded themselves against any accusations of empire or imperialism."[24]

U.S. and Soviet officials were always in a high-profile competition for the loyalties of publics and governments around the world, in places like Guatemala and Italy. Votes in democratic elections were at stake, as were the political, economic, and military loyalties of whole nations. U.S. leaders decided that too much was at stake to leave the outcome of this competition to chance, especially when, for example, democratic elections didn't go their way. Covert methods became a favored imperial tool. They ranged from coups and assassinations to the recruitment of paid local agents and informers to secret funding for political parties and for U.S. artists, novelists, musicians, and academics.[25]

Between 1949 and 1952, CIA "stations" overseas—bases of a kind—expanded from seven to forty-two. The CIA's budget increased from $4.7 million to $82 million. Personnel jumped from 302 to over 6,000. Between 1951 and 1953 alone, CIA covert operations increased by a factor of sixteen. These included propaganda campaigns, psychological warfare, support for insurgent groups, and paramilitary operations against communist China and North Korea and communist-aligned groups in Southeast Asia.[26] In a single year, 1958, the CIA led the government's efforts to train more than five hundred thousand police officers in twenty-five nations, creating secret police units in nearly half and "strengthening the repressive capacity" of undemocratic governments in particular. The CIA supported a string of right-wing military juntas in South America with military assistance, covert infusions of cash, and intelligence. Other forms of military aid strengthened the armed forces of friendly, often undemocratic, nations worldwide. U.S. advisers would train more than three hundred thousand soldiers in seventy countries between 1945 and 1970.[27]

"In effect," writes McCoy, "clandestine manipulation became Washington's preferred mode of exercising old-fashioned imperial hegemony in a new world of nominally sovereign nations." During his eight years in office, President Dwight D. Eisenhower authorized 170 major covert operations in forty-eight nations.[28] "Intervention, even in the domestic affairs of other nations, became an accepted governmental and military practice," writes John Lukacs. To the limited extent that citizens knew anything about such covert actions, most "largely approved of and seldom opposed" them.[29] "The sum of these policies," McCoy says, was a "'reverse wave' away from democracy, as military coups succeeded in more than three dozen nations, a full quarter of the world's sovereign states."[30] Today, when many in the United States have decried Russian interference in U.S. elections, few note that between just 1946 and 2000, the CIA intervened in an estimated eighty-one national elections, using cash and media disinformation campaigns, as well as paramilitary action in some cases. In this period the CIA intervened in at least five elections in Japan and eight in Italy, beginning in the latter country's fateful 1948 election.[31]

In 1948 Italy's Christian Democratic Party won a surprise victory. Although historians debate how much the U.S. government influenced the outcome, the election became the foundation for a stable U.S. base presence in Italy during the "Cold War" and to this day. In other words, the Christian Democrats repaid the favor. U.S. troops had departed Italy in 1947, following the signing of a formal peace treaty with the Allies. In 1949 the new Italian government allowed U.S. troops to return. Like Portugal, Italy joined NATO.

Italian and U.S. officials agreed to call U.S. bases in the country "NATO bases." They hoped to avoid the perception of foreign military occupation and deflect left-wing critiques of the U.S. presence. Officials used the terminology thanks to a NATO-wide agreement that calls the bases occupied by U.S. troops "NATO bases." Ever since, many locals have referred to the bases this way. In practice, U.S. facilities, weaponry, and personnel dominate almost every "NATO base" in Italy.

Beyond linguistic creativity, U.S. and Christian Democratic officials used secret negotiations to pen the 1954 Italian-American Bilateral Infrastructure Agreement. The agreement secured the foundation for a larger U.S. military presence by allowing more U.S. troops to move to Italy after withdrawing from Austria in 1955. (Austria's declaration of neutrality in the confrontation between East and West included a constitutional ban on foreign bases and meant the removal of U.S., Soviet, and other foreign forces.) The conditions governing U.S. bases and forces in the Italian-American agreement remain classified to this day. A former Italian Ministry of Defense official has suggested that the secrecy is because parts of the agreement violate the Italian Constitution.[32]

Following the 1954 agreement, ten thousand U.S. Army troops deployed to bases in the north of Italy alone. Elsewhere Army, Air Force, and Navy bases grew in places including Naples, Sicily, Aviano, and Sardinia.[33] For most of the "Cold War," the United States maintained well over one hundred military installations on thousands of acres of Italian territory.[34] There have been (and there still are) more U.S. bases in Italy than in any other country in the world, outside an active war zone, except Germany, Japan, South Korea, and the United States itself.* After the 1948 elections the Christian Democrats maintained a client relationship with the U.S. government. This gave U.S. officials a stable partner agreeable to most requests about bases and other military matters. Thanks to this relationship and the 1954 Bilateral Infrastructure Agreement, the U.S. military has enjoyed what one Italian analyst has called a "permissive environment" in Italy, offering significant freedom of operation.[35]

The ability of U.S. government officials to do what they want with the U.S. military in Italy and elsewhere has depended on a legal architecture in the post–World War II era.[36] Most countries hosting U.S. bases have had a status of forces agreement, like Italy's Bilateral Infrastructure Agreement, allowing U.S. forces to occupy their territory and governing the rights and freedom of the U.S. military. These agreements have given U.S. forces *extraterritorial* privileges in many countries—meaning that they are governed by U.S. military law rather than local laws. SOFAs, as status of forces agreements are called, determine everything from taxation to driving

---

* At times during the "Cold War," there were more in the United Kingdom.

permits to what happens if a GI breaks a host country's laws. Each SOFA is different. Each is subject to negotiation. SOFAs often allow U.S. troops to escape host nation prosecution entirely.[37] Base expert Joseph Gerson has noted that the length of a SOFA usually bears an inverse relationship to the power differential between the United States and the host country: the greater the power of the United States relative to the host, the shorter the SOFA, meaning fewer restrictions on the military.[38]

Regardless of length, most SOFAs (or significant parts of SOFAs) and related basing agreements are almost always highly secretive. Many of a string of agreements signed during the renewed buildup of U.S. bases and forces abroad between 1950 and 1955 remain classified today. As in Italy, U.S. officials have frequently employed secret basing agreements, often struck between executive branches, to avoid the involvement and over-sight of legislatures, media, and the public. Secrecy has helped protect host governments from critique by obscuring the extraterritoriality inher-ent in a foreign military presence.

✪

One surprising thing that helped legitimize the U.S. military's presence across much of the globe wasn't hidden: for the first time the U.S. govern-ment allowed families to accompany deployed military personnel in many countries, including Italy, Japan, and Germany. This was the moment when the military began transforming bases into "Little Americas" to sup-port the lives of family members and troops abroad with schools, housing, entertainment, and much more. The presence of families and Little Americas helped normalize the peacetime deployment of hundreds of thousands of U.S. troops abroad and the long-term occupation of sover-eign countries. In Germany, for example, "the success of the domesticat-ing reforms," writes economist John Willoughby, "permitted President Truman to double the troop presence during the Korean War crisis with few complaints from the German state [or its people]."[39]

Reform was necessary in Germany and elsewhere because of growing complaints about U.S. troops in the years following World War II. In the nations conquered during the war, relations between occupiers and occu-pied were mixed. Tensions emerged particularly in Germany and Japan.

Although some Germans have fond memories of smiling GIs, Hershey's bars, jazz, and big U.S. cars from the early years of occupation, local complaints quickly multiplied.[40] After years of deadly fighting, the first year of postwar U.S. occupation in particular was characterized by an aggressive campaign to seize homes, automobiles, bicycles, wine, and other property. GIs called this "liberating." This led to an ugly euphemism for rape: "liberating a blond."[41] Tensions grew between occupiers and occupied amid rampant survival prostitution and sexually transmitted infections, GI theft and violence, and racial tensions within a still-segregated military and among Germans who feared relationships between black GIs and German women. One of the few things to help the U.S. image was the comparison to Soviet occupation in East Germany.

News of the Army's "disarray" in West Germany began filtering back to the United States. *Life* magazine and other news outlets published articles with titles such as "Failure in Germany" and "Heels among the Heroes." Writer John Dos Passos reported in *Life*, "Never has American prestige in Europe been lower. People never tire of telling you of the ignorance and rowdyism of American troops."[42] Army and civilian leadership decided something had to be done. To reassert control and ease the tensions of the occupation, the Army employed a combination of harsh discipline and "wholesome" educational and recreational activities. In the words of Willoughby, a lifestyle emerged somewhere "between boot camp and summer camp."[43]

At the heart of this lifestyle was the Army's decision, in 1945, to allow small numbers of family members to join GIs on bases in West Germany and elsewhere overseas. It now seems natural for spouses and children to join members of the military at bases worldwide. At the time this was a radical decision. Traditionally, men in the U.S. military—as in most other militaries—deployed overseas alone. Until 1913 the Army actively discouraged its soldiers from marrying. This helped popularize the line that if the Army wanted you to have a wife, it would have issued you one.[44] Allowing family members to join troops abroad only became more radical as families found themselves literally near the front lines of the "Cold War" and the growing nuclear standoff between East and West.

U.S. officials hoped the family decision would help improve morale and alleviate "problems involved in fraternization" between U.S. troops and

German women. The hope was that the presence of wives would shame or otherwise encourage GIs to improve their behavior. Beyond improving conditions in West Germany, the family decision was a response to growing demands in the United States to reunite families by bringing troops home.[45] Military leaders hoped that allowing family members to join GIs would quiet these protests and keep personnel in the military. As an added benefit, officials believed, family members could serve as "unofficial ambassadors," modeling democratic values in occupied countries.[46]

The number of wives and children in West Germany jumped from around 4,000 in 1946 to around 30,000 in 1950; globally there were 90,000. When President Truman and Congress sent massive army reinforcements to both Asia and Western Europe in late 1950 and early 1951, U.S. troops in West Germany soon numbered 176,000. By 1955 there were more than 260,000. The number of family members climbed accordingly in West Germany and worldwide. By 1960 there were almost half a million family members outside the United States. For the first time family members outnumbered GIs overseas.[47] Hundreds of thousands of U.S. troops and family members would remain for almost four decades across West Germany's south, where military planners thought any Soviet invasion was most likely.[48]

As the family population quickly grew, a massive building campaign followed in Germany and worldwide. The aim was to create replicas of U.S. towns so GIs and their families would feel at home overseas. The military built housing, commissaries and shopping centers, recreational facilities, and hospitals on a global basis. It created an entire overseas school system and established a Family Services Program and other family support systems. The result was the creation of the suburban-style Little Americas that are still sprinkled around the world today.

In West Germany's poor, rural state of Rheinland-Pfalz, more than 100,000 GIs and family members arrived between 1950 and 1951. Rapid construction followed. Millions of dollars in local base construction and other spending flowed into the economy, improving relations with locals in the process. Thousands of new jobs were created. Unemployment, which had been over 10 percent in the region and over 22 percent in the major base town of Baumholder, "simply vanished" amid a gold rush atmosphere, writes Maria Höhn.[49] With a strong dollar U.S. Americans splashed money around the West German economy. Baumholder's roughly 2,500 residents came to live with an average of 30,000 U.S. troops and family members. As in other parts of the world, an underground economy flourished. Bases became a source for cheap and desirable consumption items like cigarettes and, later, blue jeans, further normalizing the U.S. presence.[50]

People in Rheinland-Pfalz now recall the 1950s as the "Golden Years" and the "Fabulous Fifties." The decade is "fondly remembered," Höhn writes, "as a time when Americans drove large, shiny cars and Germans marveled at the extraordinary wealth that the dollar's favorable exchange rate created for the American GIs." Exposed to a world of jazz, rock and roll, and consumer goods, people mostly overlooked problems like airplane noise and damage caused by frequent military exercises that took place on local streets and in farmers' fields. The damage was so much a part of ordinary operations that in Baumholder, for example, a permanent office paid compensation.[51]

Amid growing fears about the possibility of a Soviet invasion of Western Europe and broader U.S.-Soviet conflict, most in West Germany saw the U.S. presence as protection. Relatively few described it as an "occupation," even as U.S. troops continued to enjoy many of the same extraterritorial privileges after the end of formal occupation in 1955. To many the presence of wives and children living on the front lines of the "Cold War" in West Germany, Italy, Japan, and elsewhere was a powerful sign of the U.S. commitment to defending its allies. (Although officials did not publicize the fact, the military had detailed plans to evacuate families—but not locals—from bases abroad during any threat of war.)[52] GIs' wives also helped improve relations when they began forming volunteer organizations to help civilians trying to recover from the war's devastation. This oft-overlooked unpaid labor eased tensions and increased the military's freedom of operation in West Germany.[53] Five years into Truman's buildup in Europe, a government survey indicated that a majority of Germans felt troop conduct and German-American rapport had improved.[54]

The construction of Little Americas in Western Europe, in Japan, and later in South Korea and other parts of the world was critical to making the U.S. occupation of other lands a permanent and seemingly normal feature of "Cold War" life. Despite the popular reputation of the United

Greenland
(Denmark)

Iceland

Canada

UNITED STATES
OF AMERICA

Bermuda

Midway Island

Bahamas

Cuba (1962)
Guantánamo Bay

Puerto Rico
U.S. Virgin Islands

Johnston Atoll

Honduras

Antigua & Barbuda
Dominican Republic
(1965)

Nicaragua

Panama Canal Zone

American Samoa

Brazil

Antarctic

U.S. War(s)

Other U.S. Combat Actions

U.S. Base(s)

U.S. Bases (>25)

U.S. Small Base(s)

U.S. Naval Fleet

U.S. Colonies in Italics

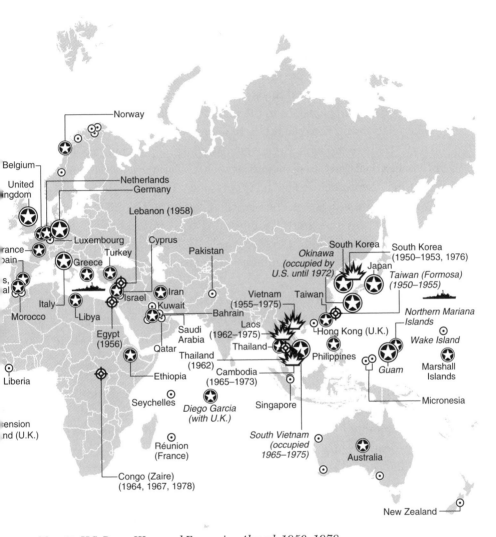

Map 17. *U.S. Bases, Wars, and Expansion Abroad, 1950–1978.*
Significant bases, combat, and expansion outside U.S. states are shown. By the 1960s
the total number of bases exceeded one thousand, roughly doubling since 1949, after
expansion during U.S. wars in Korea and Southeast Asia. Oceans not to scale. Key
sources: Blaker, *United States Overseas Basing;* Robert E. Harkavy, *Strategic Basing and
the Great Powers, 1200-2000* (London: Routledge, 2007); Stacie L. Pettyjohn, *U.S.
Global Defense Posture, 1783-2011* (Santa Monica, CA: RAND Corporation, 2012);
Barbara Salazar Torreon and Sofia Plagakis, *Instances of Use of United States Armed
Forces Abroad, 1798-2018* (Washington, DC: Congressional Research Service, 2018).

States as the liberator in World War II and, for some, the protector in the confrontation between East and West, "opposition to the US military presence arose both when and where it was least expected," writes Amy Holmes.[55] Crimes and accidents, racism, and geopolitical tensions at times undermined the goodwill bought by U.S. spending and the military's efforts to improve the image of the GI. In West Germany growing crime, drug use, and general chaos in the U.S. military during the Vietnam War era led to rising tensions in the years that followed.

The relationship between a U.S. base and locals "is inherently contradictory," Holmes explains. Even when "the host population may be fully enfranchised citizens" in democracies such as Germany, locals "are at the same time disenfranchised by the US presence. They have virtually no say in what the United States does on their territory, US officials are not elected, and only rarely are US personnel tried in local courts for any crimes they may commit." In other words, Holmes explains, locals were "being subjected to a foreign military presence that operated outside the realm of democra[cy]."[56]

There's good reason to believe that nearly everywhere where foreign bases have existed across history they have generated anger, opposition, and protest of some kind. Foreign bases, by definition, "involve the presence of one nation's military on another nation's soil," writes bases expert Kent Calder. They "are almost invariably unpopular for that reason."[57] Other sources of anger and opposition are similarly unsurprising around the globe and across time: the displacement of locals from their lands; crimes committed by military personnel; traffic and training accidents causing death, injury, and property damage; sex work and red-light-district bars aimed at military personnel outside bases' gates; the support bases provide for dictators and undemocratic regimes; and environmental damage caused by everyday military operations.[58]

The stationing of foreign troops in Britain's thirteen American colonies was, after all, one of the abuses listed in the U.S. Declaration of Independence. The lists of Redcoats' crimes that locals kept in Boston resemble those of Okinawan activists today. It's little surprise, then, that U.S. bases abroad have generated anger and opposition since U.S. forts occupying Native Americans' lands provoked anger and violent resistance across the continent. In the Philippines after 1898, the U.S. military faced opposition and an insurgency seeking independence. Cuban leaders protested the terms of the 1903 lease for Guantánamo Bay from the moment U.S. officials imposed it.[59] Latin American governments and peoples developed lasting antagonisms toward the United States as a result of decades of U.S. occupation in countries including Haiti, Honduras, Mexico, Nicaragua, Panama, Guatemala, Costa Rica, El Salvador, and the Dominican Republic.

Protests broke out in Okinawa against land seizures and U.S. occupation within months of the end of World War II.[60] Tensions burst into public consciousness across the whole of Japan in 1956 at Tachikawa Air Base in the Tokyo suburb of Sunagawa. The Japanese government's announcement that it would be expropriating local land to expand Tachikawa on behalf of the U.S. Air Force led to years of large protests featuring "pitched battles" between protestors and Japanese police in "bloody Sunagawa." The protests "very nearly upended the US-Japan military relationship" and "threatened the heart of American military policy in East Asia," writes a scholar of base protests.[61]

By 1958 even Britain, probably the most accommodating of hosts, saw growing protests against the presence of bases and nuclear weapons on British soil. In London's Trafalgar Square, five thousand demonstrators gathered for a four-day march to the Aldermaston base. The protest doubled in size along the way. "NO MISSILE BASES HERE" and "NUCLEAR DISARMAMENT," their banners proclaimed. Another sign depicted for the first time the soon-to-be internationally recognized symbol for peace: ⊕.[62]

Over time U.S. officials became concerned about such opposition. They shaped basing policy accordingly. The "thank you" gifts that Air Force leaders brought to their Portuguese counterparts in 1951 were small symbols of the degree to which U.S. military and diplomatic officials would shape policy to hold on to bases abroad, in Portugal and around the world. Bases trumped commitments to decolonization, to democracy, to peace. Backing Portugal's dictatorship and its colonial wars in Africa was one example of the many gifts U.S. leaders handed out to help smooth and normalize the occupation of foreign lands and foreign bases in the post–World War II era.[63]

★

Opposition to the U.S. military presence was nowhere greater than in South Vietnam. The presence of what came to be more than half a million U.S. troops in the country and in neighboring Laos and Cambodia represented another significant shift in imperial strategy. Overseas bases played a key role in the shift. By the end of World War II, U.S. support for the decolonization of European colonies had waned. U.S. officials looked to Britain and France to ensure Western control over large parts of the world still under their colonial control. In places such as French Indochina (Vietnam), this policy meant providing tens of millions of dollars' worth of cash and weapons to support European efforts to quash communist-linked or communist-influenced independence movements. By the time of France's final defeat in Vietnam, at the 1954 battle of Dien Bien Phu, the U.S. government was providing 75 percent of the funding for France's war.[64] The French military's defeat coupled with Britain's disastrous handling of the 1956 Suez Canal crisis led to a change in strategy, from supporting the crumbling colonial powers to a growing reliance on direct military action and colonial occupation.

In Vietnam, after 1954, U.S. funding and U.S. military advisers replaced the French rulers. The U.S. government would soon dominate South Vietnam as a de facto colony, just as France had, but with far more destructive power. In another part of the former French Empire, Lebanon, thousands of U.S. troops invaded in 1958 to support a pro-Western government. U.S. forces saw almost no combat and stayed in and around Beirut for only a matter of months. The invasion, however, marked the first significant U.S. incursion into the Middle East, setting a precedent in the region and globally.

President John F. Kennedy followed President Eisenhower in office, determined to expand the U.S. military's presence and its intervention capabilities globally.[65] Politically, he wanted to stave off accusations that he was "soft" or "weak" on communism and military matters more broadly. Such highly gendered political attacks became a regular part of "Cold War" politics in the United States. Male leaders were susceptible to such rhetoric and frequently resorted to the use of military force as a policy solution in no small part to prove their manhood.

These dynamics played out in Vietnam and Southeast Asia—first with Kennedy and then with President Lyndon B. Johnson building up the U.S.

military presence in South Vietnam. By late 1964 and early 1965, the U.S. military had bases in South Vietnam and some 20,000 military advisers and support personnel. After U.S. bases came under attack by communist forces in South Vietnam, President Johnson ordered the start of what would become a massive bombing campaign against North Vietnam and the deployment of 3,500 marines—no longer "advisers"—to South Vietnam. This was just the start of a gradual buildup of troops and dozens of bases to support their operations throughout South Vietnam. By 1969 U.S. troops in Vietnam would number almost 550,000.[66]

When the U.S. military, backed by the CIA, the State Department, and other government agencies, went to war in Vietnam and neighboring Laos and Cambodia, it "had the infrastructure for large-scale overseas combat in place." The U.S. Pacific Fleet was on its own the largest navy in the world. Hundreds of bases in Japan, Okinawa, the Philippines, and Guam, among other locations, enabled the deployment and regular resupply of U.S. forces in Southeast Asia and continual attacks by sea and air. Thanks to a military buildup by the Kennedy and Johnson administrations, the United States had military alliances with 43 nations, as well as 375 "major" foreign military bases and 3,000 "minor" military facilities world-wide by the mid-1960s.[67] "Two decades of militarism and imperial planning made the path to war in Vietnam an easy one to take," writes historian Joshua Freeman. "Explaining it was harder"—as was explaining the numbers of dead and wounded: the death toll of civilians and military forces on all sides is estimated at 3.8 million.[68] Amid the destruction, U.S. officials were increasingly fearful about decolonization. As colonized peoples were rapidly winning their independence, U.S. leaders started worrying increasingly that they would get booted from bases abroad.

12 ISLANDS OF IMPERIALISM

Stuart Barber was one of many U.S. government officials in the 1950s and 1960s who were growing concerned that decolonization would mean getting evicted from bases in newly independent countries. "Within the next 5 to 10 years," Barber wrote as the leading figure in a Navy long-range planning office, "virtually all of Africa, and certain Middle Eastern and Far Eastern territories presently under Western control, will gain either complete independence or a high degree of autonomy."[1] The inevitable result, Barber told his superiors, would be "the withdrawal . . . denial or restriction" of U.S. and Western European military bases across the decolonizing world.[2] Put plainly, Barber worried that at the very least U.S. bases would face restrictions on their operations or demands for higher "rent" payments.

I learned about Barber because he was the first to suggest building a U.S. base on the Indian Ocean island of Diego Garcia, the subject of my first book. Barber had been dead for years by the time I learned of him, but, given his central role in the base's history, I tried several times, unsuccessfully, to find one of his family members. A week before my first book was due to the publisher, a research assistant, Naomi Jagers, made a breakthrough. She helped me find one of Barber's sons, Richard, who was living in Brooklyn. It was after eight o'clock on a Friday night, but, with the impending deadline, I rushed to call.

With the sounds of dishes being washed in the background, Richard said he remembered his father talking about the base. Our phone call became the first of many conversations about Richard's father's contributions to the base on Diego Garcia. Over the next two days, Richard emailed several remarkable typewritten letters his father had written about the subject. I quickly incorporated the contents into my book. They were so revealing, and surprising, that the letters spawned a last-minute epilogue.

I learned that, as a child, Stuart Barber, or Stu, as he was known, had a passion for collecting the stamps of far-flung island colonies. While the Falkland Islands off the coast of Argentina in the South Atlantic became his favorite, Stu noticed that the Indian Ocean was dotted with many small islands claimed by Britain.[3] Thirty-six years later, in 1958, Barber was working as a civilian for the Navy and drawing up lists of small, isolated colonial islands from every map, atlas, and nautical chart he could find. Barber feared that in the era of decolonization, European allies were in the process of losing their colonies (like losing stamps from a stamp collection), including many of the world's small, strategically located islands. For the U.S. military, this would mean the loss of base access across the potentially unstable decolonizing world. At a time when the power of the Soviet Union and the Eastern Bloc was growing relative to that of the United States and its Western European allies, this was disturbing to men such as Barber.

Barber's answer to this perceived problem was what he called the "Strategic Island Concept": a plan to purchase or otherwise ensure long-term access to small, strategically located colonial islands on which the U.S. military could build bases in the future whenever it so desired. The concept, and its embrace by much of the U.S. military and diplomatic bureaucracy, shows how the U.S. Empire continued to rely on imperial tools of overseas bases and military power to maintain U.S. dominance. Clearly, the Strategic Island Concept was not the only reaction to the relative decline in U.S. power during the 1950s and 1960s—there were economic, political, and other military reactions as well. But the Strategic Island Concept was an important part of a militarized response to the challenges of decolonization and the growing power of the Soviet Bloc.

While the early post–World War II period showed U.S. officials largely forsaking traditional forms of imperialism, occupation, and colonial rule in favor of indirect forms of imperial control, influence, and rule, islands proved a significant exception to this pattern. U.S. officials maintained numerous islands, most relatively small, as colonies for one reason: because the islands hosted or had the potential to host U.S. bases. Despite the transformations in empire, U.S. officials never fully abandoned traditional imperialism in the decolonization era. While large-scale colonial rule was no longer an option given the political power of the decolonization movement, U.S. leaders found a range of "underground" ways to hang on to smaller colonies and especially to islands such as Diego Garcia. In this new era, Daniel Immerwahr explains, "tiny islands . . . and other small pockets of land became the mainstays" of the U.S. Empire.[4]

This shouldn't be surprising. Islands have been instruments of imperial power for centuries because of their ability to host bases to control sea lanes, guard coastlines, and protect surrounding landmasses. For more than two millennia, the leaders of empires and other powers saw Malta as the key to controlling the Mediterranean. Two hundred years before Stuart Barber, in 1769, a French lieutenant saw Diego Garcia's strategic, military potential, given its position in the Indian Ocean and ability to safely harbor a "great number of vessels."[5]

Since the expansion of the United States into a truly global empire during and after World War II, some of the most significant U.S. bases abroad have been on islands. To this day many have been critical to launching and sustaining U.S. wars: Iceland, Greenland, Puerto Rico, Cuba, the British Isles, Crete, and Sardinia amid "Cold War" competition; the Philippines, Guam, Japan, Okinawa, and Hawai'i during the wars in Korea and Southeast Asia; the Azores to resupply Israel during its 1973 war with a coalition of Arab nations; and Bahrain, Sicily, Ireland, Ascension, and Diego Garcia during the post-2001 wars. Soviet leaders also understood the importance of island bases. When the Soviet military developed a missile base in Cuba in 1962, U.S. officials reacted fearfully and aggressively. The "Cuban Missile Crisis" that followed was the most dangerous moment of the U.S.-Soviet conflict and the closest the world has come to nuclear Armageddon.

★

If the people of the Philippines at least got a neocolonial kind of formal independence, many other peoples wouldn't get independence at all. Bases were the main the reason why. Hawai'i, for example, was on the UN decolonization committee's list of territories that were not self-governing, given its colonial status since the overthrow of the indigenous Hawaiian Kingdom and annexation by the U.S. government. U.S. officials could not contemplate Hawaiian independence as an option; the Pearl Harbor naval base remained too important to risk losing. They gave voters two choices during a 1959 vote: statehood or continued "territorial" status. Military personnel and other settlers were allowed to vote, outnumbering indigenous Hawaiians. Alaska and Hawai'i became the forty-ninth and fiftieth states added to the union.[6] Many indigenous Alaskans and Hawaiians still consider themselves colonized.

Government officials also maintained bases in the UN Trust Territory of the Pacific, where the United States had de facto sovereignty over hundreds of small islands, including base-construction rights. The U.S. military wasted little time before taking advantage. Beginning in 1946, the Bikini Atoll and other atolls in the Marshall Islands became U.S. nuclear weapons test sites. The Marshalls' Kwajalein Atoll saw a growing base and missile-testing infrastructure.

In parts of occupied Japan, the question of whether occupation would be temporary or permanent was unclear for decades. When the occupation of Japan ended in 1952, Okinawa, Iwo Jima, and other small Japanese islands remained de facto U.S. colonies.[7] This arrangement was politically palatable to Japanese leaders because concentrating U.S. bases and troops on islands previously colonized by Japan meant reducing the U.S. military's impact on the main Japanese islands. The U.S. ambassador to Japan openly called Okinawa "a colony of one million Japanese."[8] Some U.S. military officials argued for holding on to Okinawa permanently.

In Okinawa neither the new (U.S.-imposed) Constitution of Japan nor the Constitution of the United States applied. The occupation government required Okinawans to obtain a U.S.-issued travel pass to visit Japan and controlled the movement of Japanese visitors to Okinawa. By the mid-1950s the military had seized more than 40 percent of Okinawa's farmland and displaced a similar proportion of its people.[9] A Navy officer would later say to high-ranking Pentagon official Morton Halperin, "The military doesn't have bases in Okinawa. The island itself is the base."[10]

U.S. leaders continued to support fading European empires in holding on to some of their last colonies, in no small part to maintain bases and base access. Among the colonies of the United Kingdom, the military kept bases in the Destroyers-for-Bases islands, including Bermuda, Trinidad, Newfoundland, and the Bahamas; on Ascension Island, off the east coast of Africa; and in Bahrain and Libya. Additional installations and access could be found in Danish Greenland and the French colonies of Morocco and Réunion.[11] In Portugal U.S. officials' desire to hold on to bases in the Azores meant that a succession of presidential administrations helped keep one of Europe's last dictators in power until 1974, thus helping keep the peoples of Angola, Mozambique, and Cape Verde colonized.[12]

❂

Most postwar decolonization movements were opposed to the presence of foreign military facilities after independence, given fears about bases perpetuating forms of neocolonialism. As a result, U.S. officials grew increasingly fearful that they were losing control of the world. These fears reflected a decline in the relative supremacy of the United States. Despite unparalleled U.S. power at the end of World War II, the Soviet Union had acquired its own nuclear arsenal, rebuilt from the ravages of war, and become another global superpower. China was emerging as a regional competitor. With the decolonization movement gaining momentum, Britain, France, and other Western European nations were clearly in their last days of empire. In the confrontation between East and West, the alignment of newly independent nations was up for grabs. A perception was building that many of the new nations and the world were tilting toward the East. In reality, the erosion of U.S. power and influence was less significant than it was in perception. U.S. military and economic power remained unparalleled. Soviet military strength was often exaggerated by U.S. politicians and military leaders for political and economic purposes. Still, the perception of decline, of supremacy challenged, was significant among some U.S. officials. Stuart Barber's solution to this *perceived* threat of losing bases and global control had its roots in the days when he was collecting stamps from the world's small colonial islands.[13]

According to Barber's Strategic Island Concept, the Navy needed to ensure it would have bases without the kind of "political complications" that might lead to eviction in the decolonizing world. Traditional base sites located in populous mainland areas would likely face local protest and opposition. Instead, Barber thought, "only relatively small, lightly populated islands, separated from major population masses, could be safely held under full control of the West."[14] Having island bases near hotspots in the so-called Third World, he argued, would increase the nation's ability to rapidly deploy military force wherever and whenever officials pleased. Island bases would help maintain U.S. dominance for decades to come. But if the United States wanted to protect its "future freedom of military action," government officials would have to act fast to "stockpile" future basing rights by buying or otherwise ensuring that Western allies maintained sovereignty over as many small, little-noticed colonial islands as possible. Otherwise, the islands could be lost to decolonization forever.[15]

After considering hundreds of possibilities from the Galápagos in the Atlantic to the Marshalls in the Pacific, Barber remembered those small British-controlled islands in the Indian Ocean that he noticed as a child. There, Barber later recounted, he found "that beautiful atoll of Diego Garcia, right in the middle of the ocean."[16] The island was isolated but within striking distance of a wide swath of the globe, from southern Africa to the Persian Gulf to Southeast Asia. There was enough room for a runway, and the lagoon would be perfect to host entire naval strike forces. Plus, Barber noted, Diego Garcia had "unquestioned UK sovereignty" and a population "measured only in the hundreds."[17]

Barber's numbers were not entirely correct. There were around 1,000 people on Diego Garcia alone in the 1960s. With the other islands of the surrounding British-controlled Chagos Archipelago, the population numbered between 1,500 and 2,000. The people were then called *Ilois*—the Islanders. Now called Chagossians, they were the descendants of enslaved African and indentured Indian laborers who had been living in Chagos since around the time of the American Revolution.[18]

Others in the "national security bureaucracy"—who were almost without exception considered white and of Euro-American ancestry—

embraced Barber's idea and the selection of Diego Garcia as the most important target for acquisition. Navy officials approached their British counterparts in 1960 and began secret negotiations for the Chagos Islands. U.S. negotiators emphasized that they wanted Diego Garcia, as they wrote in a secret memo, under their "exclusive control (without local inhabitants)."[19] Officials wanted the Chagossians gone. Or, as another document said more forthrightly, they wanted the islands "swept" and "sanitized."[20] British officials agreed to the plan. Under a secret 1966 agreement, the Pentagon transferred $14 million to the British military without telling Congress or Parliament. In exchange Britain provided basing rights and promised to carry out the removal of the Chagossians.[21]

When the Navy asked Congress for base-construction funds, officials said Diego Garcia's population was "negligible . . . for all practical purposes . . . uninhabited."[22] U.S. and British officials had agreed to, as one document explains, "maintain the fiction that the inhabitants of Chagos are not a permanent or semi-permanent population." A British diplomat was blunt: "We are able to make up the rules as we go along." If anyone bothered to ask, they would call the Chagossians a "floating population" of "transient contract workers" with no connection to the islands.[23]

Navy and Pentagon officials told Congress that the base would be an "austere communications facility." They knew this was what Congress members wanted to hear. Facing concerns about military spending during the war in Vietnam, the Navy's Office of Communications and Cryptology admitted, "The communications requirements cited as justification [for funding] are fiction."[24] The Navy was really asking for the nucleus of a base that could be expanded rapidly with already planned future budget requests.[25]

The Strategic Island Concept revolved around a realization that despite overseas bases' advantages, they involve significant risks. Especially in the decolonization era, bases abroad faced the risks of local protest, operational restrictions, rent demands by host governments, and eviction from strategic locations where large sums had been invested.[26] With the Chagossians deported, military planners were thrilled at the idea of a base with no civilian population within almost five hundred miles. Given the "special relationship" between the United States and the United Kingdom, the U.S. military would have near carte blanche (pun intended, given the racism underlying the U.S.-U.K. plan). With any British role reduced to a few token functionaries and the right to be consulted before major U.S. deployment shifts, Diego Garcia definitively became a U.S. base and practically became U.S. sovereign territory (the island is, along with Gibraltar, the only place in the United Kingdom where cars drive on the right side of the road). With the British doing the dirty work of the expulsion for just $14 million, the United States would also have the legal and political alibi that Great Britain was the sovereign and thus responsible for the local population. U.S. officials saw Diego Garcia as almost the perfect base. With near free rein over an idyllic and strategically located atoll, it's no wonder the Navy calls Diego Garcia "Fantasy Island."[27]

❂

The history of Diego Garcia shows that much of the "national security bureaucracy" adopted Barber's Strategic Island Concept as an important strategic framework. At the request of the Joint Chiefs of Staff, the Navy made plans for scores of strategic island bases around the globe. Ultimately, the costs of the wars in Southeast Asia meant that Diego Garcia was the only major base formally created under Barber's concept. Still, the strategy became an important argument for the retention and expansion of major preexisting island bases, including those in Guam, Micronesia, Ascension, Bahrain, the Azores, Okinawa, and Japan's Ogasawara Islands.

The U.S. government finally returned Okinawa and Ogasawara to formal Japanese sovereignty in the late 1960s and early 1970s. The United States used this as an opportunity to move even more bases to Okinawa after the prefecture's 1972 "reversion" to Japan. Although Okinawa makes up just 0.6 percent of Japan's land area, it is now home to around 75 percent of all the military installations in Japan used exclusively by U.S. forces—more than thirty bases altogether. U.S. bases take up almost 20 percent of the main Okinawa island today, in addition to expansive sea and airspace for training. Many Okinawans feel occupation never ended.[28]

After the Philippines' independence and Hawaiian and Alaskan statehood, the remaining U.S. colonies were also "Fantasy Islands" for the military. The U.S. government maintained Puerto Rico, Guam, American Samoa,

Thule, Greenland[4]

Iceland

UNITED STATES
OF AMERICA

Puerto Rico[1]

Hawai'i[1]

British Virgin Island

Little Cayman[2]

Barbuda[2]

Kanton Island[2,3]   Guantánamo Bay[1]

Grenadines[2]

Oneata Island, Fiji[2]

Key Colonized Island Bases

Other Key Island Bases

Sample of Islands Considered
under the U.S. Navy's
Strategic Island Concept

Colonial power, c. 1960:

[1] = U.S.   [2] = U.K.   [3] = Australia

[4] = Denmark   [5] = Portugal   [6] = Spain

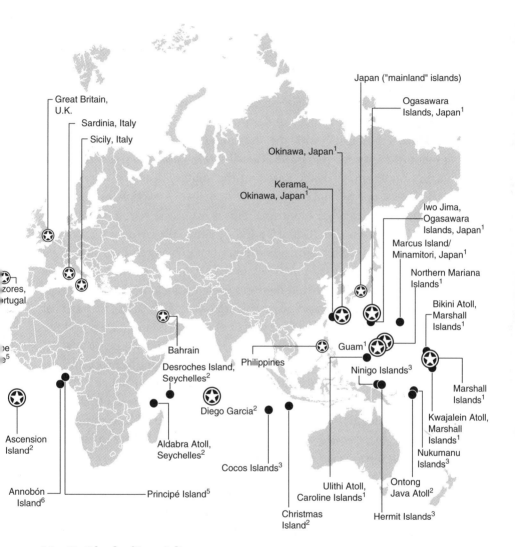

Map 18. Islands of Imperialism.
While U.S. leaders have generally favored indirect imperial control since World War II, islands have been a prominent exception because of their ability to host some of the most significant U.S. bases abroad. The Strategic Island Concept formalized this strategy. Oceans not to scale. Source: R. Johnson to Deputy Chief of Naval Operations, U.S. Navy Archives, 2–3.

the U.S. Virgin Islands, and Wake, Midway, and Johnston Islands, as well as smaller uninhabited islands under its control. U.S. officials may have called them "territories," but these islands remained in a colonial relationship with the rest of the United States. Guantánamo Bay and the Panama Canal Zone also remained de facto colonies.

The colonies show how the U.S. Empire has relied on the perpetuation of colonial relationships under new guises and with new vocabulary. From the perspective of the military and the rest of the government, maintaining a colonial relationship with the "territories" offers unmatched military autonomy. In recent years Maj. Gen. Dennis Larsen told a reporter at Guam's Andersen Air Force Base that the military need not worry about local protest, operational restrictions, or the fear of eviction, as it must at bases in other sovereign countries. "This is American soil in the midst of the Pacific," Larsen said. "Guam is a U.S. territory. We can do what we want here, and make huge investments without fear of being thrown out."[29]

The military also has more freedom than it does in the fifty U.S. states because the colonies have few democratic rights, including no voting representation in Congress and no presidential vote. With voting members of Congress, governors, and the full weight of U.S. law, states have power the colonies don't have to monitor and restrict military operations. "If California says they want to do this or that," one blunt Air Force officer explained, "it is like my wife saying that she wants to move here or there: I'll have to respect her wish and at least discuss it with her. If Guam says they want to do this or that, it is as if this cup here," he said, pointing to his coffee mug, "expresses a wish: the answer will be, you belong to me, and I can do with you as best I please." The officer explained, "They are a possession, and not an equal partner."[30]

The fantasy-like ability to have near-total control and operational freedom in the U.S. colonies and in a few other places held by close U.S. allies helped accelerate a shift of bases from locations near crowded population centers to isolated locations insulated from any potentially antagonistic locals. (More than half a century later, this model can be seen in today's "lily pad" basing strategy, creating isolated bases protected from protest.)[31] Diego Garcia and the Strategic Island Concept were part of the continued development of a new, more discreet form of empire, relying increasingly on isolated, often island bases to exert power.

Beyond bases on islands, all foreign bases have become islands of imperialism in the post–World War II era. No matter where they're located, bases abroad are islands of extraterritorial rule, enclaves of exceptionality, "specks of semi-sovereignty."[32] Even in largely democratic countries, U.S. officials have used bases as levers of power and sources of control over hosts. Increasingly, U.S. leaders have used bases and troops abroad "to influence and limit the political, diplomatic, and economic initiatives of host nations," explains Joseph Gerson.[33]

The Philippines—perhaps the most prominent example of the United States publicly forsaking empire after World War II—illustrates how U.S. leaders used bases, combined with other political, economic, and military tools, to keep nations in various kinds of colonial relationships with the United States. U.S. officials used military, economic, and political assistance to extract not only base access from the Philippines government but also favorable terms of trade, and exert ongoing political influence.[34] The Bell Trade Act of 1946, for example, "required that the newly 'independent' Philippines grant the United States preferential tariffs and Americans 'parity rights' in the exploitation of Philippine natural resources."[35] U.S. leaders "heralded Philippine independence as a sign of [the United States'] benevolent, anti-imperial credentials," writes historian Gretchen Heefner, while they "essentially tied the islands to the United States as a quasi-military colony."[36] Much like Cuba after 1898, the Philippines remained (and remains to a great extent) politically, economically, and militarily dependent on the United States.

U.S. officials in the decolonization era thus never abandoned traditional forms of imperial and colonial rule. There were significant changes in empire, such as the degree to which negotiation and political-economic forms of imperialism became important features of the U.S. Empire after World War II. Nonetheless, the treatment assigned to the exiled Chagossians and to other similarly vulnerable peoples shows how maintaining colonies and what can only be described as the colonial treatment of the colonized have remained fundamental parts of the U.S. Empire and its expanding global base network. For the Chagossians and others, the effects have often been catastrophic. Few, however, have accepted their fates passively. Many, including the Chagossians, are resisting to this day.

13 THE COLONIAL PRESENT

The expulsion of the Chagossians during the creation of the base on Diego Garcia is no aberration. Their experiences of displacement and exile are helpful in understanding the fate of at least seventeen other peoples displaced during the creation or expansion of U.S. bases abroad since World War II. Most of the displaced have been indigenous. In most cases the displaced have ended up, like the Chagossians, deeply impoverished.

There are more than superficial connections between these cases of "base displacement" and earlier examples of bases displacing and dispossessing people in Hawai'i, the Philippines, and Panama at the turn of the twentieth century and the Army-led displacement of Native American peoples in the eighteenth and nineteenth centuries.[1] "Following the examples of earlier empires, the United States has adroitly practiced displacement and demolition" of others' land, writes former Air Force officer and bases scholar Mark Gillem. "Displacements and demolitions are the norm."[2]

Marie Rita Bancoult was one of the displaced. Aunt Rita, as most called her before her death in 2016, was one of the first Chagossians exiled in a multistage expulsion process between 1967 and 1973. Beginning in late 1967, she and others who left Diego Garcia and the other Chagos Islands for regular vacations or medical care in Mauritius were barred from returning home and marooned in Mauritius.[3] When I interviewed her in 2004, I asked Rita how she felt that day in 1968 when she heard she could not return to her homeland. She said she felt like she'd been sliced open and all the blood spilled from her body. She said that for an hour she couldn't open her mouth to tell her family. Her heart was too "swollen" with emotion. Finally, Rita told her family what the man at the steamship company had said: "Your island has been sold. You will never go there again."

Rita; her husband, Julien; and their five children found themselves exiled, separated from their home, their land, their animals, their possessions, their jobs, their community, and the graves of their ancestors. The Bancoults had been, as Chagossians say in their Bantu- and French-based Kreol language, *derasine*—deracinated, uprooted, torn from their natal lands. Upon hearing the news, Rita's husband suffered a stroke and increasing paralysis. Within a year, Rita spent several weeks in a psychiatric hospital, where she told me she received "shocks"—electroshock therapy.

In January 1971, with the Bancoults and other Chagossians already in exile, the Navy began construction on Diego Garcia. The highest-ranking admiral in the U.S. Navy, Chief of Naval Operations Adm. Elmo Russell Zumwalt, issued the final expulsion order for the remaining Chagossians. The order came in a three-word inter-office note: "Absolutely must go."[4]

Between 1971 and 1973 British agents forced the Chagossians on Diego Garcia and the other Chagos Islands to board overcrowded cargo ships. As Chagossians awaited their deportation, British agents and U.S. Navy personnel herded the Chagossians' pet dogs into sealed sheds, gassed them with exhaust from U.S. Navy jeeps, and burned the dogs' carcasses.[5]

The ships deposited the Chagossians 1,200 miles away, on the docks of the western Indian Ocean islands of Mauritius and the Seychelles. They were left homeless and jobless and without almost all of their possessions. Most Chagossians had little money. The people effectively received no resettlement assistance and quickly became impoverished. In 1975 the *Washington Post* found Chagossians in Mauritius living in "abject poverty." The editorial page called their expulsion an "act of mass kidnapping."[6]

In 1973, five years after suffering his stroke, Julien Bancoult died. Rita said the cause of death was *sagren*—profound sorrow. In their half century in exile, many Chagossians have reported deaths from *sagren.* Sagren is a form of dying from a broken heart, which is not just a metaphor but a syndrome supported by a growing body of medical evidence among forcibly displaced peoples and others experiencing acute incidents of trauma.[7] After Julien's death the Bancoults' son Alex lost his job as a dockworker. He died at thirty-eight, addicted to drugs and alcohol. Their son Eddy died at thirty-six of a heroin overdose. Another son, Rénault, died suddenly at age ten, for reasons still mysterious to the family, after selling water and begging for money at a cemetery near their home.

"My life has been buried," Rita told me before her death, sitting on a torn brown vinyl couch in her small sitting room in Mauritius. The only compensation Rita and some (but not all) Chagossians received came five and ten years after the last deportations. It totaled about $6,000 per recipient. Rita and some families received what were generally their first proper homes after more than a decade in exile: small concrete-block houses. "What do I think about it?" Rita said of her expulsion. "It's as if I was pulled from my paradise to put me in hell." The Chagossians number several thousand people today, including at least four generations born in exile, and most remain impoverished. Most remain marginalized outsiders in exile, still struggling to win proper compensation and the right of return. A sign at the base on Diego Garcia reads, "Welcome to the Footprint of Freedom."

✪

Similar histories have unfolded for those who suffered through other cases of base displacement. In Hawai'i during World War II, the Navy turned the entire island of Kaho'olawe into a weapons-testing range and forced its inhabitants to leave.[8] In colonial Alaska the military displaced Aleutian islanders from their homelands in 1942, fearing a Japanese attack on Alaska. The government forced the Aleuts to live in abandoned canneries and mines. They lived there for three years, even after Japan no longer posed a threat. The government also removed the Aleutian people of Attu Island for their protection but prevented them from returning in peacetime when the government built a Coast Guard station and designated Attu a wilderness area. In 1988 Congress provided limited restitution and acknowledged, "The United States failed to provide reasonable care for the Aleuts, resulting in illness, disease, and death."[9]

Before the U.S. entrance into World War II, the military displaced thousands in Trinidad, Newfoundland, and Puerto Rico. On Puerto Rico's Vieques the Navy displaced thousands in the 1940s, seizing three-quarters of the small island. Productive local economies gave way to economic stagnation, poverty, unemployment, prostitution, and violence.[10] On the smaller neighboring island of Culebra, the Navy took over one-third of the land and the entire coastline by 1950, encircling civilians with a bombing range and a mined harbor. The Navy halted plans for a full expulsion only after protests by locals and the Puerto Rican independence movement. In 1953 the U.S. Air Force and the Danish government gave an entire community of 150 indigenous Inughuit (Inuit) people four days' notice before displacing them from their homeland in Thule, Greenland, to expand a nuclear weapons base.[11]

Indigenous CHamorus on Guam suffered through thirty-one months of brutal Japanese occupation during World War II, including internment in concentration camps, widespread rape, forced prostitution and other forced labor, and hundreds murdered by machine gun, grenade, and sword.[12] CHamorus expected their bravery and loyalty to the United States to be rewarded with U.S. citizenship and self-rule. Instead, the Navy reestablished military rule and took around 60 percent of their land after the war.[13] Civil disobedience and threats of a general strike forced the Truman administration to transfer control of Guam from the Navy to the Department of the Interior in 1951.[14] Congress made Guam an "unincorporated territory" with limited rights to self-governance. The Department of the Interior described Guam as an "area in which the United States Congress has determined that only selected parts of the United States Constitution apply."[15]

Guam is still on the United Nations' list of territories that are not self-governing, along with American Samoa and the U.S. Virgin Islands. The military still controls almost one-third of the island. To this day the people of Guam and the other colonies have third-class U.S. citizenship: they have neither a presidential vote nor voting representation in Congress (residents of Washington, DC, have had second-class citizenship since gaining the presidential vote in 1961). The people of American Samoa have fourth-class citizenship because they don't even get automatic U.S. citizenship.

Greenland
*Thule (1953,
with Denmark)*

Alaska
*Aleutian and
Attu Islands
(1942)*

Newfoundland
(1940–1941)

Puerto Rico
*Vieques
(1941–1961)*

Hawai'i
*Pearl Harbor
(1898)*

UNITED STATES
OF AMERICA

Puerto Rico
*Culebra
(1941–1970)*

Hawai'i
*Kaho'olawe
(1941–1942)*

Panama Canal Zone
(1908–1931)

Puerto Rico
(1939–1942)

Trinidad
(1940–1942)

U.S. Base(s)

U.S. Nuclear
Testing Facilities

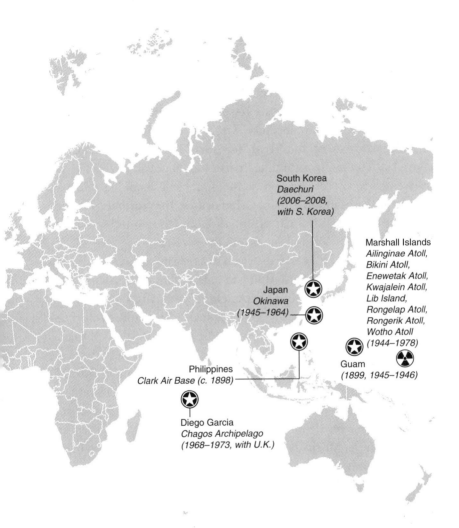

South Korea
Daechuri
(2006–2008,
with S. Korea)

Marshall Islands
Ailinginae Atoll,
Bikini Atoll,
Enewetak Atoll,
Kwajalein Atoll,
Lib Island,
Rongelap Atoll,
Rongerik Atoll,
Wotho Atoll
(1944–1978)

Japan
Okinawa
(1945–1964)

Guam
(1899, 1945–1946)

Philippines
Clark Air Base (c. 1898)

Diego Garcia
Chagos Archipelago
(1968–1973, with U.K.)

Map 19. Base Displacement since 1898.
Bases and other military facilities whose creation or expansion displaced locals
outside U.S. states are shown. During the eighteenth and nineteenth centuries,
bases in North America also helped enable the displacement, dispossession, and
deaths of millions of Native American people. Oceans not to scale. See Vine, *Base
Nation,* chap. 3.

The base buildup on Okinawa displaced around 250,000 Okinawans, or nearly half the island's population; amid growing overcrowding, U.S. authorities sent 3,218 "volunteers" about eleven thousand miles across the Pacific Ocean to jungled-covered land in Bolivia.[16] Elsewhere in the Pacific, the UN Trust Territory of the Pacific Islands system provided a new colonial mechanism to hold on to more land and more islands, complete with basing rights, even as the Territory was dissolving. In the 1970s representatives from the Northern Mariana Islands negotiated their islands' departure from the Trust Territory. The Northern Marianas became a U.S. commonwealth (like Puerto Rico) but had to give the military the entire island of Farallon de Medinilla as a bombing range and two-thirds of the island of Tinian. CHamorus in the Northern Marianas got the same third-class U.S. citizenship as fellow CHamorus in Guam and the people of the U.S. Virgin Islands and Puerto Rico.

In other Trust Territory islands, years of nuclear weapons testing displaced the people of the Bikini Atoll and at least four other island groups in the Marshall Islands. Bikini experienced complete contamination. Hundreds were irradiated across the Marshalls. The military displaced hundreds more to create a missile-testing base in the Marshalls' Kwajalein Atoll. In addition to deaths and disease directly linked to radiation exposure, the deportations led to similar effects as those suffered by others displaced: declining social, cultural, physical, and economic conditions; high rates of suicide; poor infant health; and the proliferation of slum housing, among other debilitating effects.[17] Most of the displaced have ended up on Ebeye, which observers have called the "ghetto of the Pacific" and "the most congested, unhealthful, and socially demoralized community in Micronesia."[18]

The Marshall Islands, along with Palau and the Federated States of Micronesia, eventually left the Trust Territory and gained formal independence. U.S. government officials found a way to retain military control over the islands by signing "compacts of free association" with the new nations. The compacts gave responsibilities for defense to the United States, which allowed the military to retain bases, training areas, and wartime base-construction rights in exchange for yearly aid packages and greater immigration to the United States.[19] As recently as 2008, displacement continued when South Korean authorities displaced villagers south of Seoul to help U.S. officials expand Camp Humphreys, now the largest U.S. base overseas.[20]

◉

"The fact is," former Pentagon official Gary Sick said of the Chagossians, "nobody cared very much about these populations." Sick testified to Congress about the Chagossians' expulsion in 1975, on the one day Congress has ever examined the issue. "It was more of a nineteenth-century decision—thought process—than a twentieth- or twenty-first-century thought process," Sick said. "I think that was the bind they got caught in. That this was sort of colonial thinking after the fact, about what you could do."[21]

The displacement of the Chagossians, of the Bikinians and other Marshallese, of Okinawans, of Inguhuit, of Viequenses, and of others like them demonstrates the vulnerability of isolated, mostly indigenous, non-European peoples who have suffered the effects of U.S. imperialism. In her study of Vieques, Katherine McCaffrey notes that "bases are frequently established on the political margins of national territory, on lands occupied by ethnic or cultural minorities or otherwise disadvantaged populations."[22] While strategic geographic considerations generally shape decisions about which regions should have bases, within a region the selection of specific base locations is heavily influenced by the ease of land acquisition. The ease with which the military can acquire land tends to be strongly linked to the relative power or powerlessness of that land's inhabitants. This, in turn, is usually linked to factors such as the people's nationality, economic power, population size, and skin color.

In the minds of many U.S. officials, the supposed gains to be realized from a base justified what they saw as the limited impact of removing what they considered to be an insignificant number of people. Removing locals promised the ultimate in stability and freedom from what government officials considered "local problems." U.S. officials displaced the Chagossians, the Bikinians, the CHamorus, and others because the military prefers not to be bothered by local populations and because government officials have the power to enforce that preference. Sociologist Frances Fox Piven put it to me simply: U.S. officials displaced the Chagossians "because they could."[23]

Despite the supposed end of colonialism, despite the decolonization process, despite changing public attitudes about race in the United States, the displaced were easy targets for removal. The pattern of who was displaced strongly suggests that high-ranking U.S. officials saw the displaced as insignificant and "negligible" in no small part because U.S. officials were almost exclusively Euro-American white men and the displaced were non-European peoples of color. The five hundred people displaced from Argentia, Newfoundland, before the official U.S. entrance into World War II is the only case I have found outside formal wartime of a white, European-descended people displaced by a base abroad.[24]

In 1946, in Japan's Ogasawara (or Bonin) Islands, U.S. officials actually helped around 130 displaced Euro-American islander families return to live next to a naval base. The Japanese government had removed the families and other islanders of Japanese descent for protection during World War II. While the Navy allowed the descendants of nineteenth-century Euro-American immigrants to return home, they barred those of Japanese ancestry from returning.[25]

That the Chagossians and others displaced were generally small in number, economically poor, and living on isolated islands contributed to U.S. officials' attitudes. But race played a fundamental role. Because they were Africans, Asians, or indigenous Americans, planners could regard them as insignificant, as people whose existence and concerns could be overlooked entirely. U.K. Foreign Office official Denis Greenhill revealed some of the racism of officials on both sides of the Atlantic when he described the Chagossians in a memo as "some few Tarzans" and, using a racist *Robinson Crusoe* reference, "Men Fridays."[26]

✪

Since the invention of the idea of race in the seventeenth century, racism was fundamental to European empires' colonial conquest in the Americas. It was fundamental to the colonial conquest of the U.S. Empire that followed in North America. Racism has continued to play a fundamental role in the U.S. Empire in ways that connect the displacement and dispossession of the Cherokee, the Crow, and other Native American peoples in the eighteenth and nineteenth centuries to the displacement and dispossession of the Chagossians, the CHamorus, and others in the twentieth century.

Racism, however, played a different role in older forms of empire than in the displacement of the Chagossians and others like them. Racism was the explicit ideology of eighteenth- and nineteenth-century European and U.S. imperialism.[27] In more recent history racism has played a prominent role in structuring the vulnerability of those displaced. It has also served as a more subtle, internal ideological influence, allowing officials to "assume the license" to displace those racialized as "non-white" and thus, according to the racialized worldview (that remains endemic today), inherently *less than*.[28]

Racism has played a similar role in almost all of the United States' post–World War II wars. Racism was, for example, a pervasive feature of the U.S. war in Southeast Asia, which was waged at the same time as U.S. officials were orchestrating the expulsion of the Chagossians. The frequent use of racial slurs, such as "gooks," to describe the Vietnamese followed a long history of racializing enemies in wartime. Racist propaganda targeted "Japs" during World War II, while U.S. troops called Filipinos "n****rs" and "gugus" during the war in the Philippines at the turn of the twentieth century. Long-standing racist ideas about a Chinese or Asian "yellow peril" shaped U.S. and European responses to the Chinese "Boxer" Rebellion around the same period.

The racist, savage targeting of supposed Indian "savages" during the wars of the eighteenth and nineteenth centuries reverberates to this day in the military's appropriation of Native American peoples' names as celebrations of the killing prowess of military weaponry, such as the Apache helicopter and Tomahawk cruise missile. (Widespread anti-indigenous racism also surfaces in the racist names, mascots, and rituals of U.S. professional sports teams, such as the Washington "R******s," the Cleveland Indians' "Chief Wahoo," and the "tomahawk chop" of the Atlanta Braves, Florida State Seminoles, and Kansas City Chiefs.) The widespread use of racist slurs for Iraqis and Afghans ("towel heads," "Hajjis," "camel jockeys," "sand monkeys," "sand n****rs") reflects how central racism has remained in U.S. imperialism.[29]

The violence of U.S. wars and the violence that displaced the Chagossians and others like them are connected by what anthropologists Nancy Scheper-Hughes and Philippe Bourgois call a "continuum of violence." The violence continuum links the most extreme forms of violence in war with a range of daily humiliations and degradations, dehumanization and social exclusion, and assault and rape inflicted on those deemed inferior and "less than" in a society. The violence continuum draws inspiration from Franco Basaglia's idea of "peacetime crimes" that "imagines a direct relationship between wartime and peacetime violence. Peacetime crimes suggests that war crimes are merely ordinary, everyday crimes of public consent applied systematically and dramatically in the extreme context of war."[30] The idea of peacetime crimes shows how the distinction between wartime and peacetime is, in many ways, artificial and often causes us to overlook the violence of everyday life, of supposed peacetime, that's committed against the most vulnerable and that makes wartime violence possible.

The displacement of local peoples during the creation or expansion of U.S. bases abroad is one such peacetime crime—a crime that generally has taken place outside officially declared wartime but that has direct connections along a continuum of violence with the violence of war. Locals living near U.S. bases abroad have consistently experienced a range of other well-documented peacetime crimes. Just a few include cases of robbery, assault, rape, and murder regularly committed by military personnel; support for illegal and exploitative sex work industries; and widespread environmental damage caused by everyday military operations and the intentional disposal of toxic materials in other people's soil and water.[31]

The violence continuum connecting these peacetime crimes to the violence of war shapes the violence that humans can inflict on others. The violence continuum "refers to the ease with which humans are capable of reducing the socially vulnerable into expendable nonpersons and assuming the license—even the duty—to kill, maim, or soul murder," write Scheper-Hughes and Bourgois.[32] Importantly, the men who made the decision to displace the Chagossians and others were, in many cases, the same men making decisions about waging war in Vietnam, Laos, and Cambodia. The men in the offices of the Pentagon, the Navy, the State Department, the National Security Council, the Joint Chiefs of Staff, and the CIA were the same men who made decisions about forcibly displacing South Vietnamese villagers into "strategic hamlets", about assassinating tens of thousands of accused South Vietnamese communists with little or no evidence as part of the Phoenix Program, about destroying forests and bodies with napalm and Agent Orange, and about dropping millions of tons of bombs on soldiers and civilians alike in North Vietnam, Laos, and Cambodia.

Former Nixon administration military officials Anthony Lake and Roger Morris describe the geographic and "spiritual" distance between the government offices in Washington, DC, where "affable, authoritative and always urbane men" made decisions about war and the "piles of decomposing bodies in a ditch outside Hue or a village bombed in Laos, the burn ward of a children's hospital in Saigon, or even a cemetery or veteran's hospital here."[33] This "spiritual" distance—which is shaped by ideas about race, nationality, religion, class—between the lives of decision makers and those affected by their decisions makes it easier for humans to inflict violence on other humans. So too, how much easier does it become to deploy the violence of war when you have deployed violence outside a war zone or during supposed peacetime? Does this not lower the bar on what you can do to another human being? If officials can see it as their duty to displace people from their homes to build a base without the justification of a hot war, how much easier is it for officials to justify displacing people from their homes during wartime or targeting them with bullets, bombs, and napalm?

Of course, the violence continuum flows in both directions: how much easier must it have been to displace the Chagossians and others like them when U.S. officials had participated in so much violence in Southeast Asia or the war in Korea or World War II and when U.S. officials had the justification of the supposedly "Cold War" with the Soviet Union? The violence continuum extends in many ways to people of color in the United States, including, for example, the displacement, dispossession, and incarceration of Japanese Americans during World War II, the systemic torture of African Americans in, for example, Chicago by former Vietnam military police interrogator Jon Burge, or the extrajudicial killing of African Americans and other people of color.[34]

The pattern of forcibly displacing "not white," non-European, numerically small, colonized peoples to build bases is connected to many forms of violence that tend to afflict the darker, the poorer, and the less powerful. Scheper-Hughes and Bourgois explain that processes of dehumanization lead whole societies to treat entire groups as "rubbish people." Erik Eriksen, they note, called it "pseudo-speciation": the "human tendency to classify some individuals or social groups as less than fully human."[35]

Across history and geography the Chagossians and others displaced by U.S. bases abroad are thus linked along a continuum of violence to the victims of war in Southeast Asia, Iraq, and Afghanistan; to Native American peoples displaced, dispossessed, and murdered; to Angolans and Mozambicans kept under Portuguese colonial rule for decades with U.S. aid exchanged for Azores basing rights; to Indonesians slaughtered in a U.S.-supported genocide; to Cubans and Haitians and many others killed during dozens of U.S. invasions in Latin America; to Guatemalans and Chileans tortured, assassinated, and disappeared during U.S.-backed coups; to the enslavement, murder, and disenfranchisement of African Americans over centuries; to attacks on immigrants and religious and sexual minorities in the United States; and to the poor in the United States whose bodies are so often ground up by the workings of everyday capitalism and the U.S. wars they are so often sent to fight.

✪

"Inexcusably inhuman wrongs" is how one observer described the treatment of the Chagossians when he learned of their fate years later. Thanks to the letters that Stuart Barber's son shared with me, I learned that the author of those words was none other than Stuart Barber. In another letter, written in 1975, Barber admitted the expulsion of the Chagossians "wasn't necessary militarily." He called for providing as much as $40–$50 million in compensation and allowing them to return home.[36]

To this day Chagossians and many others among the displaced are struggling to return home, to win some justice and recompense for what they have suffered. "We are reclaiming our rights, our rights like every other human being who lives on the Earth has rights," Rita's son Olivier Bancoult, a prominent Chagossian leader, told me at his home in exile. "A right to liberty, a right—I was born on that land; my umbilical cord is buried on that land; I have a right to live on that land," said Olivier.[37]

Rita, Olivier, and other Chagossians have tried petitions, protests, hunger strikes, negotiations, and lawsuits against both the U.S. and U.K. governments. They have won three suits against the British government, pressured the United Kingdom into giving them full U.K. citizenship, and had the International Court of Justice and UN General Assembly rule and vote overwhelmingly in their favor in 2019.[38] They are still not home. While the Chagossians have endured more than fifty years of impoverished exile, their island, Diego Garcia, has been at the center of a multibillion-dollar base buildup across the Greater Middle East. The deadly consequences of this buildup for the region and the world are still being felt today in ways that are difficult to exaggerate.

14 BUILDING BLOWBACK

The Pentagon and the Navy actually needed several years to convince Congress to provide funding for a new base on Diego Garcia. As the 1960s ended and U.S. involvement in the wars in Southeast Asia reached high points in terms of troops deployed, there was considerable opposition in Congress to expanding military commitments and spending. An unprecedented Senate investigation reflected the concern at the time. "Once an American overseas base is established, it takes on a life of its own," concluded the investigation's final 1971 report. "Original missions may become outdated, but new missions are developed, not only with the intent of keeping the facility going, but often to actually enlarge it."[1]

In 2012 I visited one of the authors of the investigation at the *Washington Post,* where he worked. Walter Pincus left his position as a staffer for the Subcommittee on U.S. Security Agreements and Commitments Abroad to become a Pulitzer Prize–winning reporter and columnist writing about military, intelligence, and foreign policy issues. Brooklyn-born Pincus walked out of the *Post* building looking like a Hollywood vision of an old-school reporter. Pincus wore gray flannel pants, a tie, and a slightly frayed white-striped shirt, its collar splayed open past the lapels of a blue blazer. His hair was stark white, his eyebrows bushy. Only a fedora with a "Press" card in the hatband was missing.

Over coffee Pincus told me that his Senate research took him to twenty-five countries hosting U.S. troops in Europe, Asia, and Africa. The subcommittee represented the first major investigation of the expansion of U.S. military bases and commitments around the globe since World War II. The final report totaled 2,442 pages. "We took away that we had bases *all over* the place," he said. After some overseas base closures following the end of combat in Korea, the number of U.S. bases had grown again by 20 percent, as U.S. combat in Vietnam and Southeast Asia deepened.[2] Despite the war context, Pincus's subcommittee found that many bases abroad had little purpose and remained open mainly due to bureaucratic inertia.

The result was that the military, backed by the State Department, was maintaining and even expanding a large number of decades-old bases thanks to a series of rotating rationales and vague or dubious justifications for their continued existence. "Arguments can always be raised to justify keeping almost any facility open," the subcommittee concluded, in language Pincus helped draft. "To the military, a contingency use can always be found. To the diplomat, a base closing or reduction can always be at the wrong time in terms of relations with the host country and other nations." The report noted that in the Pentagon and State Department there was "little initiative to reduce or eliminate any of these overseas facilities." Some of the explanation lay in the tendency of bureaucracies to want to perpetuate themselves: "It is only to be expected that those in embassies abroad, and also at overseas military facilities, would seek to justify continued operations in their particular areas," explained the subcommittee. "Otherwise, they recommend a reduction in their own position."[3]

Some of the patterns of inertia and expansion were the result of making "commitments," official guarantees, to ruling governments to ensure base access. Especially in authoritarian states, Pincus told me, establishing bases meant "we will also defend the regime that got us in there," because the regime's removal would threaten a base's existence. In the case of Gen. Francisco Franco's Spain, Pincus said, "I kept asking, 'Why do we keep Morón [Air Base]?'" The answer, military representatives told him, was that it was a "key base" for exercises.

Greenland
(Denmark) (3)

Iceland (8)

Canada (18)

Midway
Island

UNITED STATES
OF AMERICA

Bermuda (4)

Bahamas (12)

Guantánamo Bay, Cuba

Honduras (9)

Puerto Rico (40)
U.S. Virgin Islands (6
Antigua & Barbuda

El Salvador (1981)
Nicaragua (1981–1989)

Panama Canal Zone (15)
Panama (1988, 1989–1990)
Colombia (1989)

Grenada (1983)

Johnston Atoll

Peru (1989)

American Samoa

Bolivia (1986, 1989)

U.S. War(s)

Other U.S. Combat Actions

U.S. Base(s)

U.S. Bases (>25)

Argentina

Antarcti

U.S. Small Base(s)

U.S. Naval Fleet

U.S. Colonies in Italics

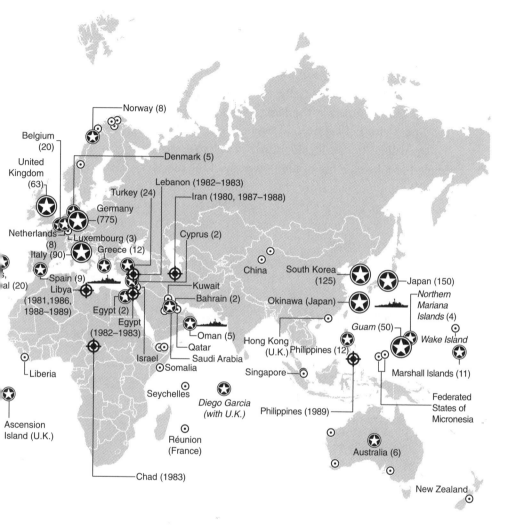

Map 20. *U.S. Bases, Wars, and Expansion Abroad, 1979–1989.*
Significant bases, combat, and expansion outside U.S. states are shown. Some bases
were occupied for only part of this period. By 1989, near the end of the "Cold War,"
bases abroad totaled around 1,600. Oceans not to scale. Key sources: *Base Structure
Report for Fiscal Year 1989* (Washington, DC: U.S. Department of Defense, 1988);
Blaker, *United States Overseas Basing;* Robert E. Harkavy, *Strategic Basing and the
Great Powers, 1200-2000* (London: Routledge, 2007); Barbara Salazar Torreon and
Sofia Plagakis, *Instances of Use of United States Armed Forces Abroad, 1798-2018*
(Washington, DC: Congressional Research Service, 2018); David Vine, "Lists of U.S.
Military Bases Abroad, 1776–2020," American University Digital Research Archive,
April 27, 2020, https://doi.org/10.17606/bbxc-4368.

"So what the hell are we exercising with Spain?" he asked. The yearly exercises practiced saving the dictatorial government from any forces that might seek to unseat Franco, Pincus was told. The justification for bases at times became circular: we need to protect the regime to protect the base; we need the base to protect the regime. Pincus realized, too, that the exercises were, not coincidentally, timed to end around the start of one of Spain's biggest festivals, the Feria de Sevilla. The good weather in southern Spain also helped explain why the military was still in Spain. What Pincus called the "perk side" of overseas bases was another reason bases tended to take on a life of their own. Even the military's post exchange—the "PX" commissary store where military and State Department personnel buy cheap, tax-free goods on base—played a role in dulling the critical faculties of State Department embassy officials who came to enjoy this perk of overseas duty.

"The Pentagon also takes care of Congress," Pincus added, when it should be playing an oversight role for bases abroad. When members visit overseas bases, he explained, the military tends to orchestrate everything, including a light schedule of three meetings a day plus "dinner and shopping and all that shit." These are the people who "are supposed to be doing oversight," he said. "And it's infectious."

✪

Bases' tendencies toward inertia and expansion were on full display with Diego Garcia. In 1972, before the base was even operational, Chief of Naval Operations Adm. Elmo Zumwalt was asking others in the Navy about expansion plans: "What do we do in [fiscal years] 74, 75, and 76 for Diego Garcia?"[4] By Christmas Day Bob Hope and Red Foxx were cracking jokes for the troops on Diego Garcia as part of a USO show, like those performed at bases worldwide.[5] Shortly before the final deportations of Chagossians in 1973, a Navy Seabee construction battalion completed an eight-thousand-foot runway. Within months the Navy was using the base to support Israel in its 1973 war with Arab countries.

As top Navy officials and others in the U.S. government had hoped, what they sold to Congress as an "austere communications facility" served as the nucleus for a rapidly expanding base. In 1973 the Navy submitted a request to the Pentagon for an almost $32 million expansion between 1974 and 1976. The "communications facility" would now include ship support and air surveillance capabilities. Just days after the Navy's submission, the Chair of the Joint Chiefs of Staff, Adm. Thomas Moorer, sent a recommendation to Secretary of Defense James Schlesinger to expand the base further. Moorer wanted a runway extension to accommodate huge B-52 bombers.[6] Diego Garcia soon proved to be the leading edge of a far larger base presence throughout the Greater Middle East and a decades-long strategy to use military force to control Middle Eastern oil and natural gas supplies.

Attempts to create a significant U.S. military presence in the Greater Middle East started decades earlier; however, decolonization, the Arab-Israeli conflict, and the wars in Southeast Asia had rolled back these efforts significantly. Continuing to build a base in Dhahran, Saudi Arabia, after it was no longer needed to fight World War II was an early sign of the strategy. After the war, U.S. officials used arms sales to Saudi Arabia and Egypt, as well as other countries, to ensure basing access rights. Planners negotiated with British officials for access to their bases and encouraged Britain to maintain a powerful presence in the region. They made an agreement for air facilities in newly independent Libya and struck a secret deal with France for vast basing rights in North Africa. U.S. officials created a small naval force in Bahrain in 1949 and tried unsuccessfully to get Congress to fund a U.S. basing presence alongside the British between Cairo and the Suez Canal.[7]

Maintaining bases in Turkey became particularly important in the eyes of U.S. officials. The country was near Middle East oil fields and along the Soviet Union's southern border, straddling Europe and Asia. Although U.S. planners understood that any immediate Soviet threat to the United States and its allies was exaggerated, they believed bases in Turkey were important to guarding against a Soviet invasion of Western Europe or the Middle East and, in the event of war, to attacking Soviet oil assets.[8] To secure access to bases in Turkey, U.S. officials included Turkey in the Marshall Plan and the North Atlantic Treaty Organization (NATO) and provided additional economic and military aid under the Truman Doctrine.

When "Cold War" tensions with the Soviet Union deepened, U.S. leaders saw the Middle East as even more important to war plans. U.S.

officials, writes Melvyn Leffler, aimed to bring nations in the region "into a U.S.-led orbit in order to insure that they would cooperate strategically in wartime and allow Western corporations to develop and control their petroleum resources in peacetime."[9] Many U.S. leaders were so concerned about Middle East basing access that they favored backing Arab countries in the Arab-Israeli conflict. Ultimately, growing U.S. support for Israel resulted in the Saudi Arabian government evicting the United States from Dhahran. The Middle East buildup was rolled back further as the commitment of U.S. troops and funds skyrocketed in Southeast Asia. U.S. officials, particularly after the enunciation of the Nixon Doctrine, moved to maintain U.S. influence in the Middle East through proxies rather than through a direct U.S. military presence. This meant backing and arming regional powers, beginning with the authoritarian states of Saudi Arabia and Iran under the shah, as well as, increasingly over time, Israel. This relatively hands-off approach ended within months of the Soviet Union's 1979 invasion of Afghanistan and Iran's 1979 revolution overthrowing the shah—which resulted in the eviction of the U.S. military from Iran.

In his January 1980 State of the Union address, President Jimmy Carter announced a profound transformation of U.S. policy. The new policy would become known as the Carter Doctrine. It has continued to shape—and destabilize—the Middle East and the United States to this day. In his speech Carter warned of the potential loss of a region "containing more than two-thirds of the world's exportable oil" and "now threatened by Soviet troops" in Afghanistan. In a threat aimed at Soviet leaders, Carter warned that "an attempt by any outside force to gain control of the Persian Gulf region will be regarded as an assault on the vital interests of the United States of America." He added pointedly, "Such an assault will be repelled by any means necessary, including military force."[10]

If Carter's words sound a bit like macho bluster, there's a reason. During his reelection campaign, Carter was facing economic stagnation, Iranians holding U.S. hostages in Tehran, and the perception of being weak in the wake of the Iranian Revolution and the Soviet invasion of Afghanistan. "To impress the US public in an election year that" he was "doing something," Carter launched one of the greatest base-construction efforts in history.[11] As an election strategy, it wasn't enough to win in 1980, but Carter's successor, Ronald Reagan, continued the expansion of bases in

Diego Garcia, Egypt, Oman, Saudi Arabia, and other countries in the region. Diego Garcia expanded faster than any other base since the war in Vietnam. By 1986 more than $500 million had been invested. Before long the total ran into the billions.[12] What began in no small part as an election-year public relations campaign has become de facto U.S. policy in the Middle East to this day. The Middle East buildup is particularly ironic, given that it was publicly a response to the Soviet invasion of Afghanistan; Carter's "national security" adviser Zbigniew Brzezinski later claimed to have lured the Soviet Union into the invasion by backing Islamic fundamentalist militants in Afghanistan, the mujahideen, to give the Soviets a taste of their own Vietnam.[13]

Carter's and Reagan's new Middle East bases soon hosted a Rapid Deployment Force, which was to stand permanent guard over Middle Eastern petroleum supplies. The Rapid Deployment Force would expand into the U.S. Central Command, the regional command that has led a long series of wars and invasions across the region in the decades since its creation.

In addition to the base buildup, U.S. officials continued to support a group of largely authoritarian Middle East allies with billions in military and financial aid and diplomatic support. Most prominent among them were Israel, Saudi Arabia, Egypt, and Turkey. In Afghanistan the CIA continued to orchestrate shipments of weapons and other aid to mujahideen, seeking to end Soviet occupation and remove the Soviet-backed Afghan government from power. The Reagan administration also backed Saddam Hussein's Iraq during its 1980–88 war with the new revolutionary regime in Iran. In 1987 and 1988 the military became involved in the "tanker war" in the Persian Gulf between Iraq and Iran. U.S. Navy vessels protected Kuwaiti oil tankers carrying Kuwaiti and Iraqi oil. The tense standoff led to a U.S. Navy vessel accidentally shooting down an Iranian civilian airliner, killing 290 passengers. An Iraqi jet accidentally struck a U.S. vessel with two missiles, killing 37 and wounding 21.

Reagan administration officials ultimately backed both sides. In the biggest presidential scandal since Watergate, reporters and Congress revealed that U.S. officials, with the help of Israel, had secretly sold overpriced weaponry to Iran. The administration used the proceeds of the weapons sales to secretly and illegally ship money and weapons to the

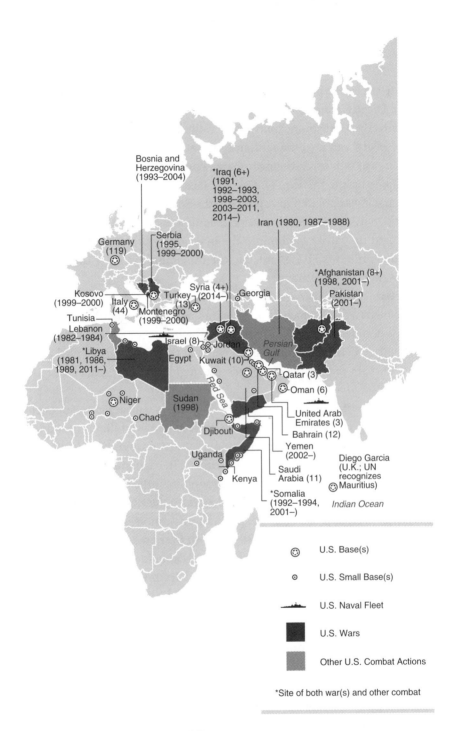

Bosnia and
Herzegovina
(1993–2004)

*Iraq (6+)
(1991,
1992–1993,
1998–2003,
2003–2011,
2014–)

Iran (1980, 1987–1988)

Germany
(119)

Serbia
(1995,
1999–2000)

*Afghanistan (8+)
(1998, 2001–)

Kosovo
(1999–2000)

Italy
(44)

Turkey
(13)

Syria (4+)
(2014–)

Georgia

Pakistan
(2001–)

Montenegro
(1999–2000)

Tunisia

Lebanon
(1982–1984)

Israel (8)

Jordan

Persian
Gulf

*Libya
(1981, 1986,
1989, 2011–)

Egypt

Kuwait (10)

Qatar (3)

Oman (6)

Niger

Sudan
(1998)

Red Sea

Chad

United Arab
Emirates (3)

Djibouti

Bahrain (12)

Uganda

Yemen
(2002–)

Diego Garcia
(U.K.; UN
recognizes
Mauritius)

Kenya

Saudi
Arabia (11)

*Somalia
(1992–1994,
2001–)

Indian Ocean

	U.S. Base(s)
	U.S. Small Base(s)
	U.S. Naval Fleet
	U.S. Wars
	Other U.S. Combat Actions

*Site of both war(s) and other combat

Map 21. Enabling Wars in the Middle East.
Bases in the Greater Middle East helped launch U.S. wars and other combat actions
in at least fifteen countries in the region between 1980 and 2020. Inspired by
Andrew J. Bacevich, "Even If We Defeat the Islamic State, We'll Still Lose the Bigger
War," *Washington Post,* October 3, 2014.

Nicaraguan Contra rebels seeking to overthrow Nicaragua's leftist Sandinista government. The scandal deepened when reporters uncovered evidence of the Contras' involvement in drug trafficking. Congress's Iran-Contra hearings showed that the Contras' main benefactor, the CIA, had known since at least 1984 that the rebels were smuggling drugs.[14] CIA, military, and diplomatic officials showed little concern for the drug trafficking and for the atrocious human rights record of the fighting force that was at the center of the decade's other base buildup, in Central America.

❂

The Central American buildup focused on Honduras, strategically located on the borders of three terrible civil wars, in Nicaragua, El Salvador, and Guatemala. The creation of dozens of bases in the country earned Honduras the nickname the USS *Honduras:* for the Reagan administration, the entire country was like a static, unsinkable aircraft carrier.[15] The Reagan administration used Honduras to support the Contras and to orchestrate support for brutal right-wing regimes in El Salvador and Guatemala. Shortly before Ronald Reagan took office, the leftist Sandinista Revolution had deposed Nicaraguan dictator Anastasio Somoza Debayle. Despite the disaster of the U.S. war in Vietnam, many on the U.S. Right, among others, still believed in the "domino theory": the idea that any leftist government coming to power risked spreading communism to neighboring countries and advancing communist desires for global domination. According to these domino-theory true believers, the U.S. government had to help remove any leftist government that came to power.

In the case of Nicaragua, the shadow of Vietnam made a U.S. military invasion politically impossible. Reagan administration officials saw a proxy army, in the form of the Contras, as a second-best option. The Reagan administration's much-hyped 1983 invasion of Grenada, an island nation smaller than Portland, Oregon, was actually a sign of the constraints on U.S. military activity at the time. The brief war the U.S. military waged against Grenada's tiny military and a contingent of one hundred or fewer Cuban military advisers reflected attempts by the Reagan administration to expand latitude for the use of military force in the post-Vietnam era.

To support the Contras and the governments in El Salvador and Guatemala, U.S. officials more than tripled military aid to Honduras between 1981 and 1982, from $8.9 million to $31.3 million. Aid more than doubled again to $77.4 million in 1984.[16] The Reagan administration flooded Honduras with weapons and military equipment, U.S. military personnel, CIA operatives, and bases. In exchange for the increased aid, Honduras agreed "to loan its territory and provide essential sanctuary for the Contras."[17]

The Contras and the governments of El Salvador and Guatemala received tens of millions more in military and economic aid, special forces training, weapons, and other military materiel. In El Salvador, for example, U.S. aid grew from $42.2 million in 1982 to $704.7 million in 1987. The Salvadoran military grew from twenty thousand to fifty-six thousand over the same period.[18] The support for authoritarian regimes in El Salvador and Guatemala was part of a larger imperial strategy, spanning Africa, Asia, Europe, and Latin America, to fund and provide arms to repressive governments and other proxy armies combating political movements and insurgencies in any way linked to the political Left or the Communist Bloc.

The Contras never became powerful enough to hope to overthrow the Sandinistas. They were, in the words of former Foreign Service officer Todd Greentree, "a classic guerilla counterweight who could harass and bleed the Sandinistas and who[m] the Sandinistas could not defeat." The Contras had no real political platform. They were almost exclusively a military force run by the CIA. President Reagan infamously described the group as the "moral equivalent of the founding fathers." Greentree more accurately described them as a group led by "petty warlords" with "the reputation of being brigands and brutes who raped women, executed prisoners, and enjoyed murdering civilians."[19]

The CIA set up six bases for the Contras in Honduras in the first year of support alone. CIA operatives, Argentine military advisers, Israelis, and Chileans started training the rebels. A C-130 cargo plane landed with the first twenty-five-ton delivery of CIA-supplied weapons. The CIA secretly provided other weaponry to the Contras with the help of the Honduran military: as the Honduran military got new U.S. weapons, it transferred its older weapons to the rebels.[20] Soon the Contras had "virtually taken over [entire Honduran] provinces along the Nicaraguan border."[21]

The centerpiece of the Central American buildup was the creation of a major U.S. military base in Palmerola, which the U.S. military calls Soto Cano. On the site of a tiny Honduran Air Force base, U.S. troops first built a runway and assembled some tents and other basic living facilities. Soon there was an airplane ramp, hangars, and more facilities. Next came a runway capable of accommodating F-16 fighter jets and C-5 cargo planes, along with offices and recreational facilities, twenty-two miles of roads, and extensive water, sewer, and electrical systems.[22] U.S. and Honduran officials insisted the base was "temporary." The base, which remains open today, would host as many as five thousand troops. It launched military operations involved in all three Central American civil wars. By decade's end, analysts described Honduras as "little more than a vast US military base" and a "virtual US protectorate."[23]

Beyond Soto Cano the Reagan administration engaged in a massive base-building campaign, constructing or expanding dozens of Contra, Honduran, and U.S. bases and other facilities to support the Contras and back the governments in El Salvador and Guatemala. Most were relatively spartan. The Contras alone eventually enjoyed at least thirty-two of their own bases in Honduras as well as in Nicaragua, Panama, Costa Rica, El Salvador, Florida, and Texas.[24] On Honduras's Tiger Island the CIA coordinated a mercenary contractor force, absurdly named Unilaterally Controlled Latino Assets.[25]

In some cases the Pentagon asked for and Congress appropriated funds for the bases, as required by most military construction projects worldwide. When Congress began to limit and cut funding for the Contras, the Pentagon used military exercises as a cover for unauthorized base construction. "When Congress refused to fund the construction of new military bases in Honduras, the Pentagon built them anyway," explains historian William LeoGrande. The exercises involved thousands of troops and implicitly threatened a U.S. invasion of Nicaragua. At the end of the exercises, newly constructed buildings and other facilities and leftover supplies were simply given to the Hondurans and the Contras. Reagan administration officials thus avoided the challenges of seeking congressional approval.[26] Elsewhere officials used Honduran military bases to supply the Contras and simply told Congress otherwise.[27]

In the background of the U.S.-backed wars, Honduras saw a decade of death squads, extrajudicial killings, and torture. U.S. advisers gave the Honduras military an Army counterinsurgency manual later dubbed by the *Washington Post* the "murder manual" for its advocacy of assassination and other violent tactics. Between 1980 and 1984 alone, there were 274 unsolved killings and disappearances of leftists and other dissidents in Honduras.[28]

Elsewhere the toll was far higher: 50,000 dead in Nicaragua, 75,000 dead in El Salvador, and 200,000 dead in Guatemala, in what's widely considered a genocide. The majority in each case were civilians and poor peasants. They died, as a former Foreign Service officer put it, in "large and indiscriminate numbers, families, clans, entire villages, the victims of torture, of bombardment, of massacre, of crossfire."[29] Eric Haney, an original member of the Army's elite Delta Force, who participated in combat operations with the Contras, commented, "Mr. Reagan's secret wars in Central America were always merciless affairs."[30] Hundreds of thousands of refugees flooded to neighboring countries and, when they could, to the United States. The toll extended far beyond, to the injured and orphaned and entire nations of traumatized survivors.

✪

The end of the "Cold War" effectively ended the wars in Central America, as it did U.S.-Soviet competition in the Middle East. With U.S. funding for the Contras withdrawn, a Government Accounting Office report declared, "The original reasons for the establishment of U.S. presence at Soto Cano no longer exist." Many U.S. military and diplomatic officials agreed that there was "not reason enough to maintain the presence" of the "expensive, semi-permanent logistics base."[31] Officials saw that any counternarcotics or disaster relief operations in the region could be conducted just as effectively from domestic bases.

Likewise in the Middle East, the end of the "Cold War" and the Soviet Union itself removed any possibility of a supposed Soviet threat to oil supplies—a threat that was always exaggerated. The reason for the Carter

Doctrine's Middle East base buildup had disappeared. With peace in both Central America and the Middle East, the U.S. military could have packed up and gone home. Some bases in Europe and Asia did close with the end of the "Cold War." Many, like Soto Cano in Honduras and Diego Garcia, did not.

U.S. government support for repressive forces in Central America and for dictators in the Middle East and its continued basing of troops in both regions would become telling examples of what the CIA calls "blowback."[32] Popularized by former CIA analyst–turned-scholar Chalmers Johnson, *blowback* describes the unintended consequences of covert operations whose causes the public cannot understand because the precipitating operations were covert. Put simply, the United States reaps what it secretly sows.[33]

In the case of the U.S. taxpayer–funded dirty wars in Central America, many of the refugees from these conflicts ended up in poor neighborhoods of cities like Los Angeles. Once there many impoverished boys and young men (and, to a lesser extent, girls and young women) found themselves joining U.S. gangs. In addition to terrorizing U.S. neighborhoods, these refugee–gang members were often arrested and deported to their home countries. In El Salvador, Honduras, and Guatemala, they soon established new branches of their U.S.-based gangs.[34] The gangs became central players in the growth of drug trafficking in Central America—which the CIA-backed Contras helped kick-start. Drug traffickers took advantage of the region's poverty and the glut of weapons and men with military training from the wars to create a new transshipment hub between South American producers and North American points of sale.[35] In recent years an estimated 90 percent of the cocaine shipped from Colombia and Venezuela to the United States has gone through Central America. More than one-third of that total has gone through Honduras.[36]

The drug trade's violence and the proliferation of gangs have been mutually reinforcing amid the violence of life in three of the poorest countries in the hemisphere. There should be little wonder that the murder rates in Honduras, El Salvador, and Guatemala have consistently ranked among the world's highest. In 2013, for example, Honduras had the world's highest murder rate—higher than those in Afghanistan and Iraq, more than four times that of Mexico, roughly twenty times the U.S. rate, and ninety times greater than Western Europe's.[37] Deteriorating and increasingly desperate conditions in the three countries have pushed thousands of Central

American migrants to flee for safety in the United States. Like the Central American refugees who arrived at U.S. borders fleeing violence in the 1980s, these new refugees are in part blowback from decades of overt and covert support for repressive governments and rebel groups in the region.

The United States was not responsible for all the problems in Central America in the 1980s, and it is not today. But the violence and insecurity today are directly linked to the violence and insecurity produced by more than a century of continuous U.S. domination and the transformation of Honduras into a base for U.S. military, paramilitary, and intelligence-gathering operations in the 1980s.

Covert CIA support for the mujahideen war against the Soviet Union in Afghanistan would similarly produce blowback that's still being felt today: CIA backing helped fuel the rise of Islamist rebels pledging allegiance to the son of a Saudi construction magnate with Yemeni roots. That Saudi magnate, ironically enough, helped build the U.S. base in Dhahran at the end of World War II; his construction equipment later helped build some of the mujahideen's fortified cave complexes in Afghanistan.[38] The irony deepens: the name of the construction firm is Bin Laden. The name of the son is Osama. The name of his soon-to-be global rebel group, al-Qaeda—the base.

PART V **HYPERIMPERIALISM**

15 DID THE "COLD WAR" END?

Andrew "Andy" Hoehn was a leading Pentagon strategist in the presidential administrations of Bill Clinton and George W. Bush. Toward the end of his tenure in the Pentagon, he was responsible for reviewing and repositioning U.S. bases worldwide. When we met, Hoehn was a senior vice president at the RAND Corporation, the powerful government-funded think tank a short walk from the Pentagon in northern Virginia. A squeeze ball in the shape of planet Earth sat next to his computer. Hoehn said that, despite what one might have expected after the end of the "Cold War," there wasn't a major change in the global base collection. "We shrank in place. But we really didn't reposition," he said. There was "a lot of hedging at that moment."[1]

The end of the "Cold War" meant significant reductions in the size of U.S. military deployments worldwide, but the underlying base structure changed little. Beginning in 1989 with the fall of the Berlin Wall and the reunification of Germany, the world changed radically. Globally, hundreds of foreign bases belonging to several nations closed and tens of thousands of foreign troops returned home. Soviet troops began leaving Eastern Europe. The dissolution of the United States' only imperial competitor led to the end of many of the world's civil wars, including those in Afghanistan and Central America. By 1995 Russia removed former Soviet forces from the former East Germany. Britain and the other occupying nations withdrew many, but not all, of their forces from the reunified Germany. In the first half of the 1990s, the U.S. government returned or closed around 60 percent of its foreign bases worldwide and brought almost three hundred thousand troops back to the United States. Hundreds of domestic bases also closed.[2] Between 1991 and 1995 the U.S. military returned tens of thousands of acres of land to the German government alone.[3]

But U.S. base and troop reductions stopped. In Germany hundreds of bases and around fifty thousand U.S. troops remained despite the disappearance of the Eastern Bloc. Worldwide the U.S. military continued to deploy over two hundred thousand troops outside the fifty states and Washington, DC. Total forces declined from just over 2 million in 1990 to no lower than 1.38 million in the decade that followed.[4] The U.S. Congress and Presidents George H. W. Bush and Bill Clinton presided over large cuts to military spending. Still, U.S. military spending remained prodigious relative to the rest of the federal budget and the rest of the world. In 1989, the year the Berlin Wall fell, the U.S. military represented 26 percent of federal spending. By 1992, the year Bill Clinton was elected, military spending was 21 percent of the federal budget. By 2000, Clinton's last year in office, military spending had declined to 16 percent.[5] (These percentages were significantly higher each year if you include spending on nuclear weapons and veterans, the CIA, and military expenditures by other government agencies.) After the reductions, the United States still had nearly 1.5 million troops under arms and more than seven hundred bases abroad, plus thousands of additional installations in the fifty states and Washington, DC. The number of troops in China's military exceeded the U.S. total, but, by every other indicator, the U.S. military operated on a scale and with a war-making capacity far beyond all other nations.[6]

Despite the disappearance of the Soviet Empire, writes historian Joshua Freeman, "the American military empire remained gigantic." U.S. leaders continued to act "on a set of assumptions about the relationship between the United States and the rest of the world that did not radically differ from prior administrations and still owed a great deal to the Cold War."[7] The "givens" of post–World War II foreign policy, including the forward strategy, remained unquestioned.

I asked Hoehn why he thought there was, relatively speaking, little change after the end of the "Cold War." "There's this funny phenomenon called *habit*, and a lot of this was habitual. *And*," Hoehn added,

> there were important voices in the American community that didn't want to leave. It was comfortable. . . . It was comfortable for a young soldier or airman to move to Europe. Culturally, it was a fairly easy transition. There wasn't a lot of tension in that relationship. In fact, there were a lot of benefits, in terms of living abroad: comfortable life, nice facilities—it was exciting. There were a lot of reasons of habit that led us to that and why people didn't necessarily want to change. *Habit.* I think it was habit.

The habit and comfort of U.S. military personnel were part of why the overseas basing structure and military spending levels remained relatively unchanged. But some of the habit ran deeper. Some of the habit lay in the deeply held belief that bases abroad advance the economic interests of U.S. corporations and investors. In 1997 and 1998 Clinton administration Pentagon Secretary William S. Cohen talked frequently about the military's post–"Cold War" mission. The strategy, said Cohen, was "to shape the environment" and "events that will affect our livelihood and our security."[8]

"How do we do that?" Cohen asked. "We have to be forward deployed." He left no room for debate: "We're going to keep 100,000 people in the Asia Pacific region, so that's off the table; and we're going to keep 100,000 people in Europe [so] that's off the table. We have to be forward deployed . . . to shape people's opinions about us in ways that are favorable to us." In using the collective "us," Cohen made the long-standing conflation of U.S. corporate and elite interests with the interests of all U.S. citizens. Forward deployment, Cohen and other elites believed, was essential to advancing U.S. business interests overseas.

At the same time, some of the *habit* stemmed from decades of habitually huge military spending. After World War II, military spending became, as Catherine Lutz explains, the country's "largest public works project."[9] Whereas other wealthy nations created welfare states after the war to provide an array of health care, education, and other services to their citizens, U.S. leaders created a "permanent war economy," or, as some have called it, a "warfare state."[10]

Greenland
(Denmark) (2)

Iceland

Canada

UNITED STATES
OF AMERICA

Midway
Island

Bermuda (4)

Bahamas (12)

Puerto Rico (40)

U.S. Virgin Islands (6)

Guantánamo Bay

Antigua & Barbuda

Johnston
Atoll

Honduras (2)

Haiti
(1993–199

Panama Canal Zone (15)

Venezuela (2)

Colombia (4)

American Samoa

Peru (3)

U.S. War(s)

Other U.S. Combat Actions

Argentina

Antarctica

U.S. Base(s)

U.S. Bases (>25)

U.S. Small Base(s) Only

U.S. Naval Fleet

U.S. Colonies in Italics

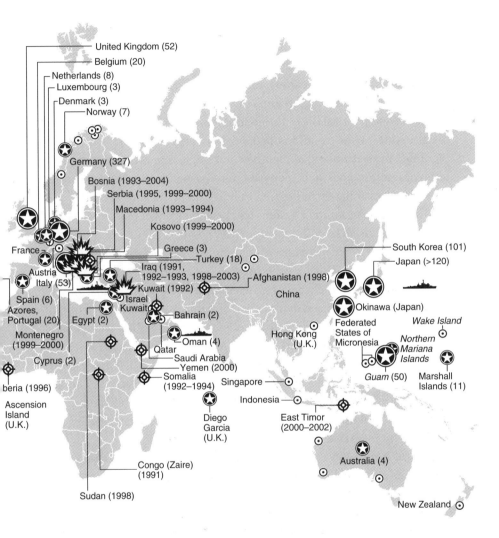

United Kingdom (52)
Belgium (20)
Netherlands (8)
Luxembourg (3)
Denmark (3)
Norway (7)

Germany (327)

Bosnia (1993–2004)
Serbia (1995, 1999–2000)
Macedonia (1993–1994)
Kosovo (1999–2000)

France
Austria
Italy (53)
Spain (6)
Azores,
Portugal (20)
Montenegro
(1999–2000)
Cyprus (2)

Greece (3)
Turkey (18)
Iraq (1991,
1992–1993, 1998–2003)
Kuwait (1992)
Israel
Kuwait
Egypt (2)
Bahrain (2)
Oman (4)
Qatar
Saudi Arabia
Yemen (2000)
Somalia
(1992–1994)

Afghanistan (1998)

China

Hong Kong
(U.K.)

South Korea (101)
Japan (>120)

Okinawa (Japan)

Federated
States of
Micronesia

Wake Island

Northern
Mariana
Islands

Guam (50)

Marshall
Islands (11)

beria (1996)

Ascension
Island
(U.K.)

Diego
Garcia
(U.K.)

Singapore

Indonesia

East Timor
(2000–2002)

Australia (4)

Congo (Zaire)
(1991)

Sudan (1998)

New Zealand

Map 22. U.S. Bases, Wars, and Expansion Abroad, 1990–2000.
Significant bases, combat, and expansion outside U.S. states are shown. Some bases
were occupied for only part of this period. Approximately 60 percent of bases abroad
closed after the end of the "Cold War." Oceans not to scale. Key sources: *Base Structure
Report: Fiscal Year 2001 Baseline (A Summary of DoD's Real Property Inventory)*
(Washington, DC: U.S. Department of Defense, 2001); Robert E. Harkavy, *Strategic
Basing and the Great Powers, 1200–2000* (London: Routledge, 2007); Barbara
Salazar Torreon and Sofia Plagakis, *Instances of Use of United States Armed Forces
Abroad, 1798–2018* (Washington, DC: Congressional Research Service, 2018); David
Vine, "Lists of U.S. Military Bases Abroad, 1776–2020," American University Digital
Research Archive, April 27, 2020, https://doi.org/10.17606/bbxc-4368.

During World War II the U.S. government turned on a faucet of military spending unlike any the world had ever seen. Spending dropped after the war, but shutting off the faucet was difficult. When the government turned the faucet up higher during the Truman and Eisenhower administrations, shutting it off became harder still. By this point years of funding a Military Industrial Congressional Complex had become ingrained in the economic and political life of the country. It had also become ingrained in the thinking of the country's people. Most significant, it had become ingrained in the thinking of members of Congress, military leaders, military contractors and their lobbyists, foreign policy pundits, and others who disproportionately influenced military spending and policy.

"The American military system had become its own reason for being," writes Freeman. "The military-industrial complex that Eisenhower had warned about remained an important influence on government policy and spending priorities. Having been in place for a half century or more, the defense industries, intelligence agencies, secret weapons systems, massive army, widespread overseas deployment of military personnel, web of military alliances, and economic burden of maintaining global military superiority were taken for granted by most Americans and [were] rarely the subject of serious debate. The majority of the population had never known a time when the United States was not mobilized for war."[11] The U.S. Empire rolled on, unchecked. Before the end of the 1990s, the military would start building new bases. The imperial expansion would be even larger in the years that followed.

Central America was one of the regions where U.S. troops remained, despite the end of the region's civil wars. Many inside and outside the government agreed that there was little reason to keep the main base in Honduras, Soto Cano, open. Among those calling for the base's closure were members of Congress, the Government Accounting Office (GAO), and many U.S. military and diplomatic officials. The GAO found that, beyond being unnecessary, Soto Cano's continued existence was counterproductive to U.S. policy. The GAO recommended closing the base.[12] A study supported by the military's National Defense University agreed. It concluded that the base "does not have a significant impact on regional stability, is potentially a political problem between [the] US and Honduran governments, and unnecessarily costs the US taxpayer millions of dollars."[13]

Soto Cano didn't close. Overall U.S. military spending in Honduras declined significantly, but military activities and "exercises were continuing through sheer bureaucratic inertia," one former Army and Foreign Service officer explains. "Even though the original rationale for the base was disappearing, no one seemed to be considering packing up and going home."[14] The seeming permanence of the "temporary" base wasn't just the result of the bureaucratic inertia identified by the Senate investigation two decades prior. High-ranking military officials made concerted efforts to create new missions and justifications for the supposedly temporary base and for the military's entire Southern Command. Without the "Cold War," the combatant command responsible for patrolling Latin America had found itself marginalized and with little to do. Southcom (in military lingo) discovered its salvation in disaster and drugs.[15]

The first opportunity came in 1998 in response to damage caused by a major hurricane in, of all places, Nicaragua. The command coordinated a $30 million relief effort for its former enemy and used the opportunity to expand its operations in the region. The following year the command used the closing of bases in Panama as a pretext to set up four new U.S. air bases in Ecuador, El Salvador, and the Dutch colonies of Aruba and Curaçao. The "war on drugs" provided an even more successful public rationale for broadening U.S. military activities in Latin America. By the end of the 1990s, Southcom saw its budget expand more than any of the other regional commands.[16]

Early in the new century, the U.S. military again would be building bases and expanding its presence in Honduras, for the first time since the end of Central America's civil wars. Shortly after the start of the George W. Bush/Richard Cheney administration, the U.S. government began spending tens of millions to upgrade Soto Cano, to build or expand at least five small bases along Honduras's violent northern coast, and to fund the Honduran armed forces and national police.[17] In 2009 Soto Cano was the refueling point when the Honduran military launched a coup, kidnapping President Manuel Zelaya and sending him into exile. By 2012 the Pentagon would spend a record $67.4 million on military contracts in

Honduras and authorize a remarkable $1.3 billion in military electronics exports to the country, among other spending.[18] The Pentagon and State Department describe these developments and the U.S. military presence in Honduras as promoting Honduran, U.S., and regional security through counternarcotics, disaster relief, and humanitarian missions. There's little evidence of success.[19]

✪

If it had been entirely up to many locals, U.S. troops, U.S. bases, and other foreign troops would have gone home. U.S. installations remained controversial in most of the world through the end of the "Cold War." Protests in Okinawa continued amid ongoing crimes and accidents involving military personnel. In Turkey U.S. bases were the source of intense national controversy throughout the 1960s and 1970s, prompting protests drawing thousands, strikes by base employees, extremist bombings and kidnappings, and the withdrawal of U.S. troops from all but two bases in 1975.[20] Elsewhere in these turbulent decades, the U.S. military was forced to vacate bases in countries including Trinidad and Tobago, Libya, Taiwan, Ethiopia, Morocco, and France.[21]

During the 1980s the deployment of U.S. nuclear-tipped cruise missiles in Europe gave birth to a large and vibrant antinuclear movement. A Women's Peace Camp grew at the U.S. base in Greenham Common, England. Starting in 1981 and continuing for two decades, women regularly blocked the base's gates, slowed military operations, and cut through the fence line to interrupt military exercises. Tens of thousands of women, supported by men, participated in protests.[22] In Madrid, Rota, and Zaragoza, Spain, movements helped push the national government to negotiate for the withdrawal of U.S. forces from Zaragoza and Madrid's Torrejón suburb.[23] The removal of Soviet bases and troops from Afghanistan, Mongolia, the former East Germany, and Eastern Europe inspired yet more activists to call for the closure of U.S. bases in their countries.[24]

Within a few months of the official dissolution of the Soviet Union at the end of 1991, an antibase movement in the Philippines forced the former colonial ruler to leave the country and the two largest U.S. bases overseas, Clark Air Base and Subic Bay Naval Base. The country's new constitution banned foreign military bases. By decade's end the military would be forced to vacate its bases in the Panama Canal Zone, as part of the termination of the canal treaty. First, however, U.S. forces would launch an invasion of their host.

Just over a month after residents of East and West Germany were allowed to cross the wall that had divided their city for almost thirty years, around 26,000 U.S. troops invaded Panama from bases in the Canal Zone and the United States. The U.S. invasion quickly forced the small Panama Defense Force to surrender and captured Panama's leader, Gen. Manuel Antonio Noriega. U.S. leaders accused Noriega of involvement in drug trafficking, among other sins. Not long before, Noriega was working for the CIA to support the Contras and target Salvadoran leftist guerillas. The fighting caused the deaths of more than 300 Panamanian forces and more than 200 unarmed civilians, wounding thousands more. U.S. forces suffered 26 deaths and 325 wounded.[25]

Within a year U.S. forces were again deploying, this time to the Middle East. U.S. soldiers were the first to arrive in Saudi Arabia six days after Saddam Hussein's Iraqi Army invaded and overwhelmed Kuwait. Seven days later prepositioning ships, usually anchored in Diego Garcia's lagoon, arrived in Saudi Arabia to outfit fifteen thousand marines flown to the country from California. The prepositioning ships brought 123 M-60 battle tanks, 425 heavy weapons, 124 fixed-wing and rotary aircraft, and enough fuel, ammunition, water, food, and other supplies to support the marines for thirty days. Another brigade of fifteen thousand marines soon met up with weaponry and supplies stored in prepositioning ships deploying from Guam.[26] In total, hundreds of thousands of U.S. and allied troops arrived in Saudi Arabia from bases in Turkey, Qatar, Diego Garcia, Germany, the United States, and beyond. The 1991 war against Iraqi autocrat and former U.S. ally Hussein lasted forty-two days. More than 20,000 Iraqi troops lost their lives, with more than 50,000 wounded or captured. Thousands of Iraqi and Kuwaiti civilians died. U.S. troops and their allies suffered 247 battle deaths.[27]

Before the decade ended, U.S. forces would fight again, in Somalia, Haiti, and the Balkans. During interventions led by the North Atlantic Treaty Organization (NATO) in the former Yugoslavia, the Pentagon built up a

Greenland
(Denmark)*

Iceland (194

UNITED STATES
OF AMERICA

Puerto Rico
Vieques
(2003)

Hawai'i
(2003, 2006)

Puerto Rico
Culebra (1970)

Cuba

Barbados (1979)

Honduras

Trinidad & Tobago
(1963)

Panama (1999)

Colombia (2010)

Ecuador
(2009)

U.S. Base(s) Closed
or Blocked by Locals

Major Contemporary
Antibase Protest(s)

(XXXX)   Year U.S. Base(s)
         Closed or Blocked

*Movement by displaced people
demanding the right of return but
not necessarily base closure

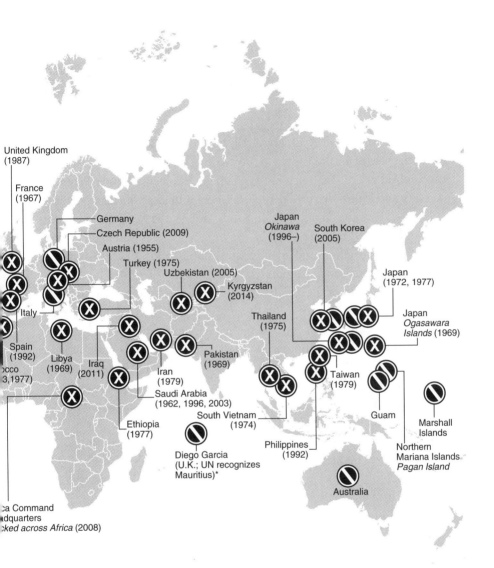

United Kingdom
(1987)

France
(1967)

Germany
Czech Republic (2009)
Austria (1955)
Turkey (1975)
Uzbekistan (2005)
Kyrgyzstan
(2014)

Japan
Okinawa
(1996–)

South Korea
(2005)

Japan
(1972, 1977)

Italy

Thailand
(1975)

Japan
Ogasawara
Islands (1969)

Spain
(1992)
Libya
)cco   (1969)
3,1977)

Iraq
(2011)

Iran
(1979)

Pakistan
(1969)

Taiwan
(1979)

Saudi Arabia
(1962, 1996, 2003)

Ethiopia
(1977)

South Vietnam
(1974)

Guam

Marshall
Islands

Diego Garcia
(U.K.; UN recognizes
Mauritius)*

Philippines
(1992)

Northern
Mariana Islands
Pagan Island

Australia

:a Command
dquarters
:ked across Africa (2008)

Map 23. Protests and Evictions at U.S. Bases Abroad, 1950–2020.
Local social movements and national governments have forced the closure or blocked
the creation of bases worldwide. Antibase protests represent particularly large and
prominent contemporary examples. Oceans not to scale. Key sources: Cooley, *Base
Politics;* Catherine Lutz, ed., *Bases of Empire: The Global Struggle against U.S. Military
Posts* (New York: New York University Press, 2009); Stacie L. Pettyjohn and Jennifer
Kavanagh, *Access Granted: Political Challenges to the U.S. Overseas Military Presence,
1945–2014* (Santa Monica, CA: RAND Corporation, 2016); David Vine, "Social
Movements Related to U.S. Foreign Military Bases Crowdsourced List," Google Sheet
spreadsheet, accessed March 1, 2020, https://bit.ly/2CUMcUg.

significant base infrastructure. The largest, Camp Bondsteel in Kosovo, covered 955 acres. It included two gyms, two movie theaters, extensive dining and entertainment facilities, coffee bars, and a PX for shopping. By contrast, military personnel from other NATO countries lived in existing apartments and factories.[28] To a degree far exceeding those of past conflicts, the military used private contractors to build, supply, and maintain U.S. forces. Contractor Brown and Root, above all, built Camp Bondsteel and thirty-three other bases for the Pentagon. Brown and Root (later known as KBR) was a subsidiary of Halliburton, the company headed by former Pentagon secretary and future vice president Dick Cheney. In total, during operations in Somalia, Rwanda, Haiti, Kuwait, Saudi Arabia, and the Balkans, Brown and Root received more than $2 billion in base support and logistics contracts for construction and maintenance, food services, waste removal, water production, transportation services, and more.[29]

In the aftermath of the 1991 Gulf War, U.S. forces continued to patrol the skies of Iraq to enforce a "no-fly zone" preventing Iraqi aircraft from attacking Shi'a and Kurds opposed to the Hussein regime. The no-fly zone coupled with sanctions imposed on the country effectively maintained a state of war. By 2020 the U.S. military had been bombing Iraq for twenty-nine consecutive years.[30] Throughout the region the military dramatically expanded its presence. Thousands of troops and an expanded base infrastructure remained in Saudi Arabia and Kuwait. Elsewhere in the Gulf, the military expanded its naval presence at a former British base in Bahrain, which became the headquarters for the Navy's Fifth Fleet. The Air Force built major installations in Qatar. Other U.S. installations expanded in the United Arab Emirates and Oman.

The buildup in Saudi Arabia caused particular ire. In 1996 militants bombed Khobar Towers, an Air Force housing complex near the first prominent U.S. base in the country, Dhahran, built with the help of Mohammed bin Laden's construction firm. Nineteen Air Force personnel died and hundreds more were wounded in the bombing. Attacks on two U.S. embassies in East Africa and on the USS *Cole* in Yemen followed. Investigators linked the four attacks to Mohammed bin Laden's son Osama and al-Qaeda.

The maintenance of U.S. bases and troops in the Muslim Holy Land proved to be a major recruiting tool for al-Qaeda. Saudi-born Bin Laden repeatedly railed against the presence of non-Muslim U.S. troops in Saudi Arabia. He called their presence "the greatest of these aggressions incurred by the Muslims since the death of the Prophet."[31] Subsequent research has suggested that U.S. bases and troops in the Middle East have been a "major catalyst for anti-Americanism and radicalization," at least since a suicide bombing killed 241 U.S. marines in Lebanon in 1983. Other research indicates a strong correlation between a U.S. basing presence and al-Qaeda recruitment.[32]

When al-Qaeda operatives downed four airliners and destroyed the World Trade Center towers and part of the Pentagon, killing around three thousand, the U.S. government could have responded in many ways. The Bush/Cheney administration, supported by Congress, could have pursued the perpetrators of the attacks as criminals and responded with criminal-justice and intelligence tools. The U.S. government responded this way to other terrorist attacks, including the 1993 bombing of the World Trade Center. Other governments had done much the same. Research shows that responses to terrorist acts based in policing and intelligence gathering are more successful than war-based approaches. Surveying cases globally, Matthew Evangelista finds that approaches treating terrorist acts as crimes rather than war "are likely to be more successful, because they avoid the backlash that can breed further terrorism."[33]

The Bush/Cheney administration chose war. The administration went further to declare a "global war on terrorism." Bush described the war as a "crusade," inflaming radicals and angering many in the Islamic world. The administration launched an invasion of Afghanistan in October 2001 and quickly began planning another war in Iraq. The people and governments of both countries had no involvement in al-Qaeda's attacks (which were carried out by Saudis and Egyptians). The only connection was that the Taliban government had allowed al-Qaeda to maintain training bases in remote parts of Afghanistan.

U.S. and allied forces invaded Afghanistan from bases in Diego Garcia, Oman, Pakistan, and other parts of central Asia, as well as with special operations and CIA teams on the ground, long-distance bombers flying from the United States, and jets based on five aircraft carriers in the Persian Gulf and the Indian Ocean. By November 2001 the U.S. military was establishing major bases in Afghanistan and occupying Afghan and former Soviet bases. With the help of allied Afghan forces, the U.S. government soon completed the removal of the Taliban from power.[34]

The invasion and fighting that overthrew the Taliban government inflicted new damage on a country that already had been torn apart by more than twenty years of near-continuous war. The new war left roads pockmarked, bridges destroyed, and the land scattered with unexploded ordnance in a country with more landmines per square mile than any other in the world.[35] Civilian casualties were widespread. In one of the worst incidents, a B-52 and two B-1B bombers repeatedly bombed a wedding party (possibly as a result of bad intelligence). According to a British media report, the attacks "vapourised" five buildings as well as rescuers who arrived to dig through the rubble an hour after the first bombs hit. The bombing killed 110 people at the wedding, leaving only 2 survivors.[36] A reporter for London's *Guardian* newspaper found forty-foot craters, scraps of human flesh, and "bloodied children's shoes and skirts, bloodied school books, the scalp of a woman with braided grey hair, butter toffees in red wrappers, wedding decorations."[37]

In a small, brightly lit hospital in northern Afghanistan's Panjshir Valley, the metallic clanking of gurneys rang out as doctors and nurses wheeled in the wounded from another attack early in the war. The high-pitched screams and heaving wails of children filled the room. In one corner a man sat against the surgical center's stark white wall, cradling a child in his arms. Thick white bandages were wrapped around the whole of the child's head. His face was marked with dark shrapnel wounds. "It was an aircraft," the man said. "They've hit the people. The people."[38]

Doctors were scrubbing their hands and arms at sinks and tying green surgical masks on their faces. "Give me just a small dressing," said one doctor. The doctor laid his hand carefully on the chest of a boy no more than six years old. Staff wiped soot and debris from the face and hair of another crying child, bearing a bandaged head and an intravenous line. A woman sat with an improvised white head covering balanced tenuously on her tangled hair, holding up an exposed arm pocked with shrapnel marks. Several staff members held another scared child on his side as they shaved his head to expose a shrapnel wound for treatment.

"Was it a rocket?" someone asked a man lying on a gurney. On his thin, bare chest, staff had penned the number 2.

"Bomb," he replied, before saying quickly, "Air force, air force, air force. The American air force. . . . My mother died," he said, slowly now. The cries of children and adults and the rapid chatter of hospital staff filled the room. "Alikhan's mother died. . . . My father died. . . . My brother . . . ," he said, as he looked toward the ceiling, his eyes filling with tears.[39]

For members of the Bush/Cheney administration and their supporters in the Republican and Democratic Parties, the media, and other segments of the United States, the choice to go to war was a relatively easy one. The choice was an easy one in part because the United States had been building a permanent infrastructure of bases in the Greater Middle East for more than half a century. The buildup of U.S. bases in the Greater Middle East began in World War II and the early days of the "Cold War," continued with the development of Diego Garcia, accelerated dramatically following President Jimmy Carter's enunciation of the Carter Doctrine, and expanded significantly after the "Cold War" ended.

A Congressional Research Service report presciently pointed out in 1979 that "essentially, Diego Garcia makes periodic military operations in the . . . Arabian Sea more convenient."[40] This was just one base. By 2001, the existence of an entire network of U.S. bases in the Middle East, coupled with bases in Europe and East Asia, made it look easy to wage war far from home. Prominent neoconservative and Pentagon adviser Ken Adelman infamously predicted in 2002 that "demolishing Hussein's military power and liberating Iraq would be a cakewalk."[41] In both Iraq and Afghanistan, the Bush/Cheney administration proved profoundly unprepared for what followed the initial invasions. Two subsequent administrations, led by presidents Barack Obama and Donald Trump, have fared little better. The outcome of these wars for the Greater Middle East, for the United States, and for the world has been so catastrophic that there's no way to describe the horror of the situation.

16 OUT-OF-CONTROL WAR

On March 20, 2003, little more than a year after beginning the occupation of Afghanistan, U.S.-led forces invaded Iraq. Land, air, and naval forces attacked Iraq from bases in Kuwait, Diego Garcia, Jordan, Qatar, Oman, Bahrain, elsewhere in the Middle East, and the United States. Bases in Germany, Italy, and other countries in Europe and as far off as Japan and Thailand were critical logistical hubs, shuttling troops and supplies in preparation for the invasion and throughout the subsequent occupation. Installations as distant as Australia played command and control roles in orchestrating the coordination of U.S. and allied military forces. The Turkish government quietly permitted U.S. forces to use some Turkish territory and airspace before and during the invasion (after having bowed to large protests and publicly refused to allow the use of U.S. bases in the country).[1] Once in Iraq, U.S. and allied forces quickly began building bases on Iraqi soil and taking over Iraqi military installations.

Removing Saddam Hussein from power had been a long-term goal for many in the Bush/Cheney administration, following the failure to topple Hussein during the 1991 first Gulf War. Shortly before the 2000 presidential election, a prominent group of neoconservatives, organized as the Project for a New American Century, articulated this goal. They also declared their dream of ensuring complete U.S. geopolitical-economic domination for, as their name suggested, another century.[2] Al-Qaeda's attacks on the United States provided an opportunity to pursue these goals. Vice President Cheney led administration efforts to find evidence tying Hussein to al-Qaeda to provide justification for an invasion. When such evidence couldn't be found, Cheney and other administration officials sold the war with threads of false intelligence, anti-Saddam Iraqi exile propaganda, and fearmongering about nonexistent chemical weapons and the "mushroom cloud" of an equally nonexistent Iraqi nuclear stockpile.

While the administration may not have been prepared for the aftermath of the initial invasions of Afghanistan and Iraq, officials were prepared to oversee a new expansion of bases in the Middle East that made the buildups after the Carter Doctrine and the first Gulf War look small. At the same time, to the surprise of many, the Bush/Cheney administration also closed more bases, mostly in Europe, than had been closed since the early 1990s. Despite the closures, however, spending on bases abroad reached record highs. New construction actually appeared in some of the same places where bases were closing. Unraveling these contradictions helps reveal the economic and political foundations of the global network of bases and the war system itself.

✪

At the height of the wars in Afghanistan and Iraq, there were more than 1,200 U.S. checkpoints, outposts, and major bases in the two countries.[3] The extensive amenities, sheer size, and construction plans for many of the largest bases indicated that the military intended to occupy the countries for a decade or more to come.[4] Balad Air Base near Baghdad was one of five "mega bases" in Iraq. It housed some thirty thousand troops and ten thousand contractors in facilities complete with fortified Pizza Hut, Burger King, and Subway outlets and two Walmart-sized shopping centers. "The base is one giant construction project, with new roads, sidewalks, and structures going up across this 16-square-mile fortress in the center of Iraq, all with an eye toward the next few decades," National Public Radio (NPR) reported. "Seen from the sky at night, the base resembles Las Vegas: While the surrounding Iraqi villages get about 10 hours of electricity a day, the lights never go out at Balad Air Base."[5]

Beyond Afghanistan and Iraq, scores more bases dotted the region. They were and mostly still are in nearly every country in the Greater Middle East, including every Persian Gulf nation except Iran. Globally, extraterritorial U.S. bases totaled two thousand or more—perhaps more bases than at any time since World War II.

The buildup started almost immediately after al-Qaeda's September 2001 attacks. The Air Force sent around two thousand personnel to Diego Garcia, where it built a new thirty-acre housing facility, "Camp Justice." Flying from the atoll, B-1 bombers, B-2 "stealth" bombers, and B-52 nuclear-capable bombers dropped more ordnance on Afghanistan than any other flying squadron in the Afghan war.[6] In central Asia the Pentagon used several countries as logistical pipelines to supply troops in Afghanistan. The military built new bases in Uzbekistan and Kyrgyzstan and explored installations in Tajikistan and Kazakhstan. (In 2005 the military left Uzbekistan due to the Uzbek government's egregious record of human rights abuses; in 2013 the Kyrgyz government, under pressure from the Russian government, evicted U.S. forces. Despite the departures, U.S. bases are today in around forty countries—about half the total—ruled by authoritarian or otherwise undemocratic governments.)[7]

Elsewhere the military expanded a critical base in Djibouti at the strategic chokepoint between the Suez Canal and the Indian Ocean. In East Africa the Pentagon created or gained access to small bases in Kenya, Ethiopia, and the Seychelles. Along the northwestern edge of the Middle East and the western side of the gas-rich Black Sea, new bases appeared in Bulgaria and Romania. The military and the CIA quietly established at least five drone bases in Pakistan; the U.S. war in Afghanistan really has been a war in Afghanistan and Pakistan ever since al-Qaeda and Taliban fighters fled across the border shortly after the war started.[8]

Kuwait has remained an equally important hub for thousands of U.S. troops and sprawling military infrastructure ever since the first U.S.-led Gulf War forced occupying Iraqi forces to leave Kuwait. The country served as the main staging area and logistical center for ground troops in the 2003 invasion and occupation of Iraq. Weaponry and supplies prepositioned in Diego Garcia's lagoon were also among the first to arrive at staging areas near Iraq's borders. Bombers from Diego Garcia launched some of the first attacks.

By the summer of 2003, with the occupation of Iraq underway, the Pentagon removed most of its forces from Saudi Arabia. The departure was a response to the 1996 bombing of Khobar Towers near Dhahran, as well as other al-Qaeda attacks in the region and mounting anger about non-Muslim troops in the Muslim Holy Land (one of Osama bin Laden's justifications for attacking the United States). A small U.S. military contingent quietly remained to train Saudi personnel and keep bases "warm" as backups for future wars. The military later established a secret drone base in the kingdom.

The Central Command moved its air operations center for the Middle East from Saudi Arabia to Qatar. Al Udeid Air Base now hosts a fifteen-thousand-foot runway, large munitions stocks, and thousands of troops and contractors. The base has coordinated much of the newest war, against the so-called Islamic State in Iraq and Syria. Qatar's neighbor, competitor, and recent antagonist, the United Arab Emirates (UAE), is home to Al Dhafra Air Base, which hosts five thousand troops and appears to have launched more attack aircraft against the Islamic State than any other base. Bahrain is headquarters for the Navy's Middle Eastern operations, whose primary mission is to ensure the free flow of oil and other resources though the Persian Gulf and surrounding sea lanes.[9]

Toward the end of the Bush/Cheney administration, officials began planning to withdraw large numbers of U.S. troops from Iraq while

Map 24. U.S. Bases, Wars, and Expansion Abroad, 2001–2020. (Map appears on following pages.)
Significant bases, combat, and expansion outside U.S. states are shown. Some bases were occupied for only part of this period. The range in the approximate number of bases across the period is provided for countries that saw significant changes. At the height of U.S. wars in Afghanistan and Iraq, there were over two thousand bases abroad. By 2020 there were around eight hundred. Oceans not to scale. Key sources: *Base Structure Report: Fiscal Year 2002 Baseline; A Summary of DoD's Real Property Inventory Data* (Washington, DC: U.S. Department of Defense, 2002); Barbara Salazar Torreon and Sofia Plagakis, *Instances of Use of United States Armed Forces Abroad, 1798–2018* (Washington, DC: Congressional Research Service, 2018); David Vine, "Lists of U.S. Military Bases Abroad, 1776–2020," American University Digital Research Archive, April 27, 2020, https://doi.org/10.17606/bbxc-4368.

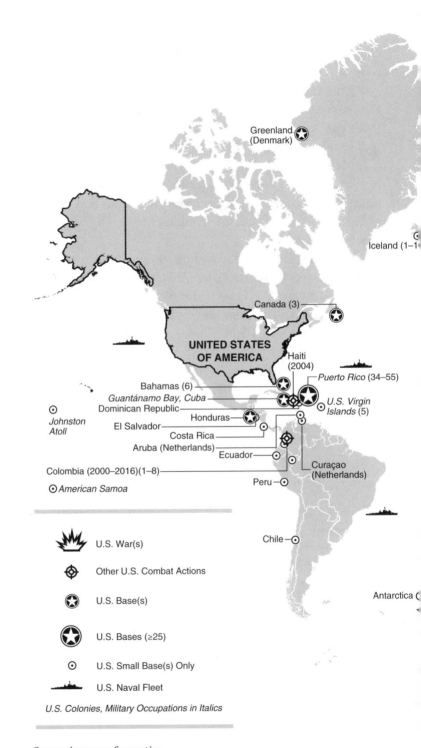

Greenland (Denmark)

Iceland (1–1

Canada (3)

UNITED STATES OF AMERICA

Haiti (2004)

Puerto Rico (34–55)

Bahamas (6)

Guantánamo Bay, Cuba

Dominican Republic

U.S. Virgin Islands (5)

Johnston Atoll

Honduras

El Salvador

Costa Rica

Aruba (Netherlands)

Ecuador

Curaçao (Netherlands)

Colombia (2000–2016)(1–8)

Peru

American Samoa

Chile

Antarctica

💥	U.S. War(s)
◉	Other U.S. Combat Actions
✪	U.S. Base(s)
✪	U.S. Bases (≥25)
⊙	U.S. Small Base(s) Only
⚓	U.S. Naval Fleet

U.S. Colonies, Military Occupations in Italics

See previous page for caption.

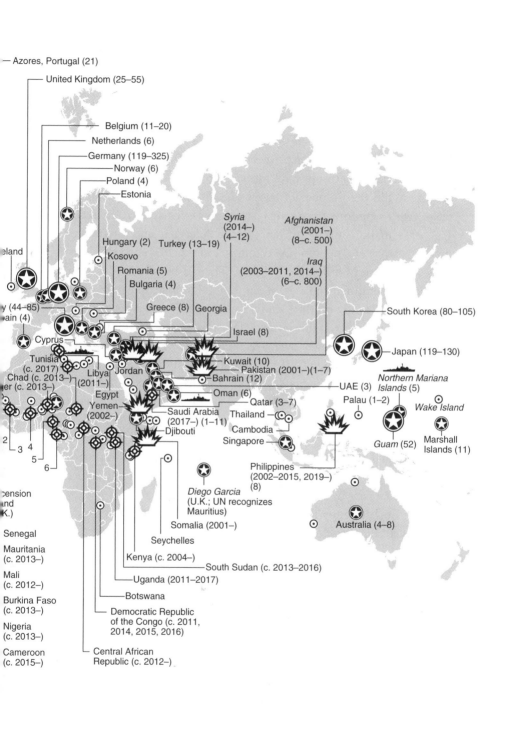

Azores, Portugal (21)

United Kingdom (25–55)

Belgium (11–20)

Netherlands (6)

Germany (119–325)

Norway (6)

Poland (4)

Estonia

eland

Hungary (2)   Kosovo   Turkey (13–19)

Romania (5)

Bulgaria (4)

Greece (8)   Georgia

y (44–85)

ain (4)

Cyprus

Tunisia
(c. 2017)

Chad (c. 2013–)   Libya   Jordan
er (c. 2013–)   (2011–)

Egypt

Yemen
(2002–)

2

3   4

5

6

cension
nd
K.)

Senegal

Mauritania
(c. 2013–)

Mali
(c. 2012–)

Burkina Faso
(c. 2013–)

Nigeria
(c. 2013–)

Cameroon
(c. 2015–)

Syria
(2014–)
(4–12)

Afghanistan
(2001–)
(8–c. 500)

Iraq
(2003–2011, 2014–)
(6–c. 800)

Israel (8)

Kuwait (10)

Pakistan (2001–)(1–7)

Bahrain (12)

Oman (6)

Qatar (3–7)

Saudi Arabia   Thailand
(2017–) (1–11)

Djibouti   Cambodia

Singapore

Philippines
(2002–2015, 2019–)
(8)

Diego Garcia
(U.K.; UN recognizes
Mauritius)

Somalia (2001–)

Seychelles

Kenya (c. 2004–)

South Sudan (c. 2013–2016)

Uganda (2011–2017)

Botswana

Democratic Republic
of the Congo (c. 2011,
2014, 2015, 2016)

Central African
Republic (c. 2012–)

South Korea (80–105)

Japan (119–130)

*Northern Mariana
Islands* (5)

UAE (3)

Palau (1–2)

Wake Island

Guam (52)   Marshall
Islands (11)

Australia (4–8)

keeping fifty-eight "enduring bases" in the country, much as bases have remained in South Korea for decades after the end of active Korean War hostilities.[10] To the surprise of many, the Iraqi parliament rejected the proposed deal. Following the 2011 withdrawal of most U.S. troops from Iraq, the Obama administration signed an agreement with Afghanistan permitting U.S. troops to stay in that country until 2024, with access to at least nine major installations. Since the start of the new war with ISIS in 2014, thousands of troops have returned to Iraq. As troop numbers have grown, so did the number of bases. U.S. forces now occupy around six bases. They withdrew from four installations in early 2020 following the U.S. assassination of Iranian Gen. Qassim Suleimani and the Iraqi parliament's passage of a nonbinding resolution to expel U.S. troops.

Near the Iraqi border, F-16 fighter jets and hundreds of U.S. troops have been operating from at least one Jordanian base. The military has six base sites in Oman and thirteen in Turkey. The Turkish government has restricted their use but allowed some logistical operations and the launching of surveillance drones over Syria and Iraq.[11] The Navy has no such constraints in the Persian Gulf, given that it maintains at least one aircraft carrier—a massive floating base—on an effectively permanent basis in the Gulf. Other naval vessels in the Gulf and the Red Sea have launched cruise missiles into Iraq and, more recently, Syria. Nearby in the Mediterranean, there's a de facto U.S. naval base in Haifa, Israel. For years there have been as many as six secret U.S. bases in Israel that can be used to preposition weaponry and equipment. Recently, the Pentagon acknowledged the existence of a base in Israel's Negev Desert.[12]

Some Bush/Cheney Pentagon officials actually took office wanting to close bases. Pentagon Secretary Donald Rumsfeld wanted to initiate a new round of Base Realignment and Closure. BRAC, as it's known, is the process Congress created in 1990 to close domestic bases after the end of the "Cold War." Since then Congress had closed hundreds through four separate multiyear BRAC processes. Congress had never considered base closures abroad as part of BRAC, and there was no BRAC-like process for bases overseas. Rumsfeld's staff convinced him to make overseas base closures a priority.[13] As senior Pentagon official Ray DuBois explained to me, Rumsfeld began a Global Defense Posture Review, by asking the regional combatant commands to answer one question: "In a post–Cold War environment, what do we really need and why?" Weeks later the combatant commanders responded. In effect, according to DuBois, each said, "We need everything that we already have."[14]

Rumsfeld was not pleased. Rumsfeld and his staff issued more specific directions, firmly telling the commanders to revisit the issue. Rumsfeld and his staff soon made progress. In late 2003, amid intensifying insurgencies in Iraq and Afghanistan, Bush surprised many by declaring plans to "realign the global posture" of the U.S. military. The goal, Bush said, was to "ensure that we place the right capabilities in the most appropriate locations to best address" the world's security threats.[15] The administration said it would eliminate more than a third of the nation's "Cold War"–era bases in Europe, South Korea, and Japan. The Pentagon would shift troops east and south, away from Europe, to be closer to current and predicted conflict zones, from the Middle East and the Black Sea to Asia, Africa, and South America. The administration said it would return as many as seventy thousand troops stationed abroad—about 20 percent of the overseas total—as well as one hundred thousand family members to the United States. The military would concentrate most of its remaining forces overseas (still numbering in the hundreds of thousands) at about two dozen very large bases, called "main operating bases" (or "MOBs," in Pentagon speak). These included installations such as Ramstein Air Base in Germany and Kadena Air Base in Okinawa.

The Pentagon would focus on creating smaller, more flexible bases, called "forward operating sites." They would also build even smaller installations, "cooperative security locations," or, as some called them, "lily pad" bases. Andy Hoehn's boss, the Pentagon Under Secretary for Policy, Douglas Feith, wrote in an op-ed, "The standard comment of those briefed on the realignment has been: The United States should have done this a long time ago."[16]

The global transformation plans succeeded in closing more bases than at any time since the first four years after the end of the "Cold War." Most of the closures were in Europe, where hundreds of bases closed and tens of thousands of troops returned to the United States, mostly from Germany and Britain.[17] The Army consolidated most of its forces at eight "enduring communities" (each consisting of multiple base sites) in Germany; Vicenza, Italy; and a group of installations in Belgium, the Netherlands, and Luxembourg.[18] Meanwhile, the Army started building smaller bases in central and eastern Europe, to the increasing concern of Russian leaders.

At the same time the military was closing bases and returning them to host nations, the Pentagon began a construction boom in Asia and Europe. There were already construction projects all over Iraq and Afghanistan to house U.S. troops. Others appeared in central Asia and in every Persian Gulf nation, bar Iran. More surprising were major construction projects in Italy and Germany, where many of the base closures took place. There was also new construction in South Korea, Japan, Guam, Australia, and East Asia; in the Marshall Islands; across much of Africa; and in Latin America. Between 2001 and 2009 military construction funding expanded to highs not seen since World War II. "MilCon," as it's called, almost tripled in constant dollar terms from $13.6 billion in fiscal year 2002 to $33.6 billion in fiscal year 2009.[19] The $33.6 billion is almost double the previous post–World War II high, reached during the military buildup in Vietnam in 1966.[20]

One of the most illustrative, and galling, projects was in Vicenza, Italy. In 2006 the Army told Congress it needed more than $600 million for a new base that would consolidate an airborne brigade moving from Germany to Vicenza. In 2013, just weeks after moving into the base, the Army said it wouldn't be putting the entire brigade in Vicenza after all. One-third of the brigade would stay in Germany. Roughly half of the planned number of soldiers and family members would relocate to Vicenza. A Senate Committee on Appropriations report expressed its "concern," stating, "This decision is in direct contravention of the [consolidation's] original purpose."[21]

Andy Hoehn's Global Defense Posture Review envisioned billions in construction and other spending to carry out the base transformation. Such spending doesn't explain the scale of the construction spending spree that followed October 2001. The construction spree in part reflects overall war spending and skyrocketing military budgets that followed the invasions of Afghanistan and Iraq. Bush/Cheney administration officials repeatedly lowballed the costs of the wars. Most members of Congress and the mainstream media supported the wars and the military budget increases that followed. Even members of Congress opposed to the wars were fearful of opposing Pentagon budget increases, because opponents might accuse them of "not supporting the troops." They likewise feared the economic and voting-booth consequences of military budget cuts in their districts and states.

Annual Pentagon budgets increased rapidly to around the same level (in constant dollar terms) reached at the height of the "Cold War." Prior to the invasion of Afghanistan, in fiscal year 2001, the Pentagon budget was $316 billion. By 2007 the total, including war budgets, was $600 billion. It was $690 billion by 2010. A decade later the total neared $750 billion. For several years military spending nearly equaled the rest of the world's military spending combined, despite the absence of another superpower and an al-Qaeda threat numbering only in the thousands of militants. (The United States still spends around three times what China spends and exceeds the combined military spending of the next seven countries, most of whom are U.S. allies.)[22] The cost of nuclear weapons and additional military spending in the Departments of Homeland Security, State, and Veterans Affairs brought annual totals to around $1.25 trillion in 2019.[23] Total costs for the post–October 7, 2001, wars, including obligated future spending on interest and veterans care, will soon reach $6.4 trillion.[24]

Some of the spending on bases, like the overall military budget, reflects the inflation of budgets, outright fraud, and profiteering in a wartime context, with even laxer levels of oversight for a military already known for negligent, incompetent, and dysfunctional bookkeeping.[25] In 2011 the Commission on Wartime Contracting, which Congress established to investigate waste and abuse, estimated there had been $31–$60 billion in contracting fraud in the wars. Most of the waste, fraud, and abuse involved contracts on bases in and around Afghanistan and Iraq.[26] Nearly a decade later the total is likely many billions higher, despite some improved efforts to prevent fraud.

My examination of government-spending data and contracts showed that from late 2001 (when the war in Afghanistan began) to 2013, the Pentagon dispersed around $385 billion in taxpayer-funded contracts to private companies for work outside the United States.[27] Most of this money has gone to overseas bases. Overall, base spending has been marked by spiraling expenditures, outright fraud, and the growing use of uncompetitive contracts and contracts lacking incentives to control costs. Companies with well-established histories of fraud and abuse repeatedly won noncompetitive sweetheart contracts. Financial irregularities have been so common that any attempt to document the total misappropriation of taxpayer funds at overseas bases would be a mammoth effort. Almost a third of the total—more than $115 billion in my 2001–13 calculation—was concentrated among the top ten corporate recipients alone. The largest single recipient was the major base-construction and maintenance contractor KBR, the former subsidiary of Dick Cheney's old company Halliburton.[28]

Over time the Pentagon used war budgets as a financial trick to evade spending restrictions placed on its regular "base" budget. War budgets were a way to get additional funds from Congress for construction, operations and maintenance, and other spending.[29] To keep the funding flowing, base contractors have made millions in campaign contributions to Congress members. According to the Center for Responsive Politics, individuals and Political Action Committees (PACs) linked to military contractors gave more than $30 million in election donations in the 2018 election cycle alone and have donated more than $300 million between 1990 and 2020.[30] Contractors pay lobbyists and industry associations millions more to sway military budgeteers and policy makers. Kellogg Brown and Root and Halliburton spent nearly $5.5 million on lobbying between 2002 and 2012—a large sum, but one that's incredibly modest given the payoff of tens of billions in Pentagon contracts over the same period. Fluor, another top-ten recipient of Pentagon contracts abroad, racked up nearly $9.5 million in lobbying fees from 2002 to 2012. Even German states hoping to stop U.S. base closures paid lobbyists on Capitol Hill. This foreign lobbying illustrates how politicians and business leaders in many countries, as well as foreign weapons manufacturers, food-service contractors, oil companies, and many, many others who supply the U.S. military, are deeply invested in maintaining the base status quo.[31]

✪

While some of the out-of-control spending is the result of profiteering, corruption, and fraud, some is the result of the Pentagon and the military branches simply not caring about costs. Operating in a context with astounding amounts of money, where tens of millions of dollars can be a

rounding error, leaders generally have had the license to make policy decisions with massive financial implications without regard to cost. If the
same things happened in any other government agency, it usually would
be a national scandal. In the Pentagon such misuse of funds tends to generate little notice or outrage.

Repeatedly one sees the Pentagon making decisions to spend hundreds
of millions of taxpayer dollars based on incomplete data, shoddy math,
little or no attempt to consider cheaper alternatives, and cost analyses that
appear to be either incompetent or intentionally manipulated. A long,
regular stream of Government Accountability Office (GAO formerly
General Accounting Office) reports provides abundant evidence of the
problems. Unfortunately, each report appears in isolation, and they generally portray the problems as unrelated incidents. Rarely does anyone point
out the larger pattern: the Pentagon, the armed services, and many of
their component parts are spending tens of billions on overseas military
construction with what frequently appears to be a willful disregard for
costs and, often, the law. For its part, Congress has provided little or no
oversight.[32]

These are symptoms of the profligacy in the military budget as a whole
and the Military Industrial Congressional Complex about which President
Dwight Eisenhower warned. In his famous farewell address of 1961,
Eisenhower alerted U.S. citizens that the "conjunction of an immense
military establishment and a large arms industry" was wielding "economic, political, even spiritual" influence "in every city, every State house,
every office of the Federal government." He warned of the "grave implications" of this new development and the need to "guard against the acquisition of unwarranted influence" and "the potential for the disastrous rise of
misplaced power." Failing to do so, he said, would "endanger our liberties
or democratic processes" and the "very structure of society."[33]

Overseas bases have become, in even more complicated ways than
major weapons systems, Eisenhower's worst nightmare about the Military
Industrial Complex.[34] The establishment of overseas bases has created
entire social worlds with corporations and thousands of people economically, socially, institutionally, and psychologically dependent on the continued operation of those worlds. Bases abroad are a perfect, if horrifying,
microcosm of how the Military Industrial Congressional Complex can

be like Frankenstein's monster, taking on a life of its own thanks to the spending it commands. This has been true since the days of Eisenhower, but the wars in Afghanistan and Iraq and twenty-one other countries since 2001 have taken the Complex to new levels of profligacy.

More worryingly, the Military Industrial Congressional Complex has broader and deeper influence than it had in 1961. The result is what investigative reporter Gareth Porter calls a "permanent-war complex." Porter writes that out-of-control military spending on the post-2001 wars, coupled with the dramatic privatization of the military in recent decades, has made the Military Industrial Congressional Complex a "much more serious menace" than ever before.[35] After the invasion of Afghanistan, thousands of new contracted employees began working in the Pentagon, the CIA, and other parts of the national military bureaucracy. Pentagon Secretary Robert M. Gates admitted in 2010 that he couldn't determine how many contractors worked in his own Office of the Secretary. Contractors soon outnumbered soldiers in Afghanistan. By the end of the Obama presidency, there were nearly three contractors for every soldier.[36]

For the highest-ranking military leaders, the "revolving door" to jobs with weapons manufacturers and other contractors is spinning faster than ever. In 1993, 45 percent of three- and four-star Army generals took such jobs as consultants or executives. By 2005 it was 80 percent. Two *Washington Post* reporters rightly asked whether these military contractors were now "obligated to shareholders rather than the public interest."[37] Today the Military Industrial Congressional Complex might be more accurately called the *Industrial Military* Congressional Complex—such is the power of private, profit-seeking corporations in this government-corporate entity. With millions of dollars spent on lobbyists and campaign contributions to members of Congress and the ability to spread contract dollars to as many congressional districts as possible, contractors have secured billions in government contracts and repeatedly demonstrated their power to force the military to buy weaponry that the military doesn't even want. "It just hits you like a ton of bricks when you think about it," said one high-ranking officer with almost thirty years of experience in the military. "The Department of Defense is no longer a war-fighting organization, it's a business enterprise."[38]

The wars that the Bush/Cheney administration launched in Afghanistan, in Iraq, and far beyond spawned out-of-control military budgets completely out of proportion to the threats facing the United States. The out-of-control military budgets, in turn, enabled a base buildup, first in the Greater Middle East, and then in regions far from the war zones. As we'll see, the new buildups included proliferating bases in Africa, among other regions that had previously seen little U.S. military presence. In Africa especially, there's a risk that building bases will again sow blowback, making future conflicts more likely and further entrenching a self-perpetuating system of permanent war.

17 WAR IS THE MISSION

The first thing I saw when I walked into the belly of the dark gray C-17 Air Force cargo plane was a void—something missing: a missing left arm, gone, severed at the shoulder, temporarily patched and held together. All that remained was thick, pale flesh, flecked with bright red at the edges. It looked like meat sliced open. The face and what remained of the rest of the man were obscured by bandages, blankets, a U.S. flag quilt, and a jumble of tubes and syringes, drip bags, wires, and medical monitors. A tattoo on the soldier's surviving arm read, "DEATH BEFORE DISHONOR."[1]

That man and two other critically wounded soldiers—one with two stumps where legs had been, the other missing a leg below the thigh—were intubated, unconscious, and lying on litters hooked to the walls of the plane that had just landed at Ramstein Air Base in Germany. It was June 2012. A fourth critically injured patient was sitting motionless, his head in his hand. I asked a member of the Air Force medical team about the casualties they were seeing. Many, like those on this flight, were coming from Afghanistan, he told me. "A lot from the Horn of Africa," he added.

"Where in Africa?" I asked. He said he didn't know exactly, but generally from the Horn, often with critical injuries. "A lot out of Djibouti," he added, referring to Camp Lemonnier, the main U.S. base in Africa, but from "elsewhere" in the region too. "You don't really hear about that in the media." With little attention in recent years, there has been a growing number of U.S. combat injuries and deaths in Africa: three special operations commandos and three women (whom U.S. military sources called "Moroccan prostitutes") killed in an unexplained car accident in Mali; at least four troops wounded in South Sudan in 2013; four soldiers dead in Niger in 2017; at least one Navy SEAL and one Green Beret killed and two military personnel wounded in Somalia in 2017 and 2018; and a soldier and two contractors killed in Kenya in January 2020.[2]

In a 2018 interview Brig. Gen. Donald Bolduc, retired former commander of the Special Operations Command Africa between 2015 and 2017, acknowledged the casualties: "We had them in Somalia and Kenya. . . . We had them in Tunisia. We had them in Mali. We had them in Niger, Nigeria, Cameroon, and Chad. But those were kept as quiet as possible. Nobody talked about it."[3] These casualties reflect a dramatic but little-noticed U.S. military expansion in Africa. Since around the turn of the century, and with little public debate, the Pentagon has been spending tens of billions of dollars to build a large and unprecedented U.S. military presence across Africa. For nearly two decades the military has discreetly built dozens of lily-pad bases and larger installations, fuel depots, and other facilities in almost every country on the continent. For most of those same two decades, military officials in the newly created Africa Command consistently denied the existence of *any* U.S. bases in Africa other than Camp Lemonnier. With news slowly emerging U.S. Army Africa Commander Maj. Gen. Darryl Williams admitted in 2016, "We have very austere, lean, lily pads, if you will, all over Africa now."[4] On any given day there are now at least six thousand and likely more U.S. troops on the continent—more than anywhere outside the United States, except Europe and Asia. As of 2016 there were more special operations troops in Africa—1,700—than anywhere other than the Middle East.[5]

U.S. forces have played active roles in both overt and covert warfare in Somalia and the 2011 U.S. and European war in Libya that overthrew the Muammar Gaddafi regime and plunged the country into civil war. Since that time the military has launched drone strikes and other operations in Libya on an ongoing basis. Elsewhere U.S. special operations forces have been engaged in reconnaissance and combat missions in countries including Cameroon, the Central African Republic, Kenya, Mali, Mauritania, Niger, and Tunisia.[6] U.S. forces operating out of Djibouti have launched deadly drone strikes into Yemen since 2002 and provided support for the brutal Saudi-led war in Yemen since 2015. In total, U.S. forces in Africa now represent a foreign military presence not seen since the last days of European colonial rule.

At a time of growing global competition with China, European nations, Russia, and other rising powers, the growing U.S. military presence on the continent has become a testing ground for the newest incarnation of aggressive U.S. imperial strategies. So far, the track record has not been good. The extent of the human damage is still emerging. There is a grave risk that U.S. imperial strategies will trigger future blowback or, more catastrophically still, war with China, Russia, or another major power.

✪

Until the twenty-first century, the Pentagon paid relatively little attention to Africa. Before the creation of the Africa Command in 2007, there was no command strictly responsible for the continent. Africa was mostly an afterthought overseen by the European Command. During World War II North Africa was a major battlefield. After the war U.S. officials maintained bases in parts of North Africa before decolonized, newly independent governments evicted most U.S. bases and troops (a small presence remained in Morocco). In the 1990s twenty-five thousand troops deployed to Somalia as part of UN humanitarian operations. After soldiers took heavy casualties in 1993, during the "Black Hawk Down" incident in Mogadishu, U.S. forces retreated rapidly from the country; U.S. leaders retreated from any thought of sending more troops into African combat.

Just nine days after the attacks of September 11, 2001, attitudes changed. U.S. officials began inquiring about creating a base in Djibouti. The country is near the strategic entrance to the Gulf of Arabia and within striking distance of the Middle East and much of Africa. A little more than a year later, hundreds of troops started arriving at Camp Lemonnier. The initial cost was just $30 million a year and a Voice of America radio transmitter.[7] Within a few years there were more than four thousand troops at the six-hundred-acre base and hundreds of millions of dollars in construction and annual spending.[8]

The Pentagon described Camp Lemonnier as an important tool in the Bush administration's global war on terrorism. Almost immediately after its creation, the military began searching for more bases and lily pads and negotiating agreements with a string of African governments for basing rights. The pace of U.S. military activity in Africa accelerated in 2007 after the Bush/Cheney administration established the Africa Command. Bush said the new geographic command, known as Africom, would "enhance our efforts to bring peace and security to the people of Africa and promote our common goals of development, health, education, democracy, and economic growth."[9]

Many in Africa and elsewhere were skeptical. No African country would host the command. Its headquarters remained with those of the European Command, in Stuttgart, Germany. Many saw Africom as a new incarnation of nineteenth-century Western colonialism. Cloaked in the language of humanitarianism was a thirst for the domination of African oil and other resources. Many U.S. critics likewise feared the command represented the militarization of foreign policy and development aid, with Africom planned to usurp roles played by the State Department and the U.S. Agency for International Development.[10]

Africom's official line that Camp Lemonnier was the only U.S. base in Africa was always hard to believe, given multiple news reports to the contrary. A 2014 article in the U.S. Army's own *Army Sustainment* magazine identified nine "forward operating locations" in the Horn of Africa alone.[11] "A fiction" is what investigative journalist Nick Turse called the "one base" claim.[12] As of late 2018, Turse found that the military had at least thirty-four base sites in Africa. In addition to Camp Lemonnier, a Pentagon list mentioned twelve "cooperative security locations," twenty "contingency locations," and another major "forward operating site" on Ascension Island, off Africa's west coast. There are likely even more bases.[13] In 2017 a military spokesperson said there were forty-six outposts across the continent, including fifteen "enduring locations."[14]

The lack of transparency and pattern of misleading statements in the Africa Command and the Pentagon leave considerable uncertainty about the U.S. presence. But it's clear the expansion of bases has been rapid and

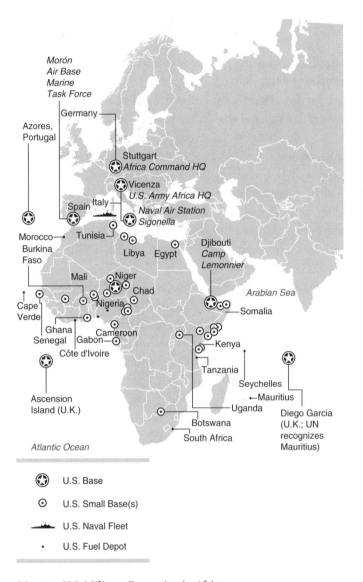

Morón
Air Base
Marine
Task Force

Germany

Azores,
Portugal

Stuttgart
Africa Command HQ

Vicenza
U.S. Army Africa HQ

Spain Italy
Naval Air Station
Sigonella

Morocco   Tunisia

Burkina   Libya Egypt
Faso   Djibouti
                                Camp
                                Lemonnier

Mali   Niger

          Chad   Arabian Sea

Cape   Nigeria
Verde   Somalia

Ghana   Cameroon
Senegal Gabon   Kenya

Côte d'Ivoire

                        Tanzania

                        Seychelles

Ascension   Mauritius
Island (U.K.)   Uganda
                Botswana   Diego Garcia
                South Africa (U.K.; UN
                              recognizes
Atlantic Ocean   Mauritius)

⊛   U.S. Base

⊙   U.S. Small Base(s)

⥤   U.S. Naval Fleet

·   U.S. Fuel Depot

Map 25. U.S. Military Expansion in Africa.
The U.S. military presence in Africa is especially difficult to determine given
secrecy and limited transparency. This map reflects the best data as of 2020.
Fuel bunkers are indicated only in countries *without* a confirmed base pres-
ence; most countries hosting lily pads also host U.S. fuel. Key sources: Ploch,
Africa Command; Stephanie Savell and 5W Infographics, "This Map Shows
Where in the World the U.S. Military Is Combatting Terrorism," *Smithsonian
Magazine,* January 2019, www.smithsonianmag.com/history/map-shows
-places-world-where-us-military-operates-180970997/; David Vine, "Lists
of U.S. Military Bases Abroad, 1776–2020," American University Digital
Research Archive, April 27, 2020, https://doi.org/10.17606/bbxc-4368.

broad. It's easier to list the African countries that have not had a U.S. presence: they number fewer than fifteen of the fifty-four. Djibouti has the largest presence. In addition to Camp Lemonnier, the military has built what's "perhaps the largest drone complex in the world" in Chabelley.[15] The base has played a major role in launching drone strikes in Yemen and Somalia. For operations in both countries, the military has an "afloat forward staging base"—a floating base—off Djibouti's coast.[16] U.S. forces have targeted al-Qaeda and al-Shabaab militants in Somalia since shortly after al-Qaeda's 2001 attacks. In 2007 the military backed an Ethiopian government–led invasion that helped generate renewed anger at the presence of foreign military forces in Somalia and fueled the al-Shabaab movement. With fighting ongoing, there are now around five installations and at least one CIA base supporting a UN-recognized government. In neighboring Kenya, the military appears to have three bases; one was the target of a 2020 al-Shabaab attack that killed three U.S. military personnel, wounding several others.[17]

There appear to be two facilities near Libya's Mediterranean coastline, after the 2011 U.S.- and European-led overthrow of the government of Muammar Gaddafi resulted in tens of thousands of deaths, failed state or "near-failed-state" status, and a civil war that has never ended.[18] In neighboring Tunisia there's at least one base, where the military has launched drones. In Cameroon the U.S. occupies or has regularly used as many as five bases to support the Cameroonian military's fight against Boko Haram. In Burkina Faso there's a lily pad at the Ouagadougou International Airport for operations targeting Boko Haram and other militants in Africa's Sahel. There are additional lily pads for drones, surveillance aircraft, special operations troops, and other forces in Chad, Uganda, Botswana, Gabon, Ghana, Mali, and Senegal.[19]

The expansion is continuing in Niger, where the military now has at least six base sites. A new drone base in Agadez was the largest construction project ever undertaken by Air Force personnel.[20] As of 2018 the Air Force was working on nearly thirty construction projects in four countries alone: Kenya, Tunisia, Djibouti, and Niger. That year, the Navy named six companies the recipients of a contract worth up to $240 million over five years to design and build naval facilities in Djibouti and potentially across Africa.[21] Africom has also built local Coast Guard and maritime operations facilities in at least Liberia, Senegal, and the Ivory Coast, where U.S. forces will have access.[22]

Beyond bases the Pentagon has installed fuel bunkers for U.S. aircraft and naval vessels in countries including Cameroon, Cape Verde, Côte d'Ivoire, Mauritius, Nigeria, South Africa, and Tanzania. U.S. forces have twenty-nine "gas and go" refueling agreements in at least nineteen countries. The military also has or has had access to shared lily pads in Algeria, Namibia, Sierra Leone, and Zambia. Previously there were additional drone bases, surveillance sites, and other installations in Ethiopia, Liberia, Mauritania, the Seychelles, the Central African Republic, the Democratic Republic of the Congo, and South Sudan; some of these locations may still be in use or may soon be in use again.[23]

The force dedicated to Africa is larger when one considers bases surrounding the continent that provide logistical support and aerial and naval firepower, from Italy, Spain, Britain's Ascension and Diego Garcia, Greece, and Germany.[24] Sicily has become a major node for U.S. military operations in Africa, which is less than one hundred miles away across the Mediterranean. The Sigonella naval station has become a major drone base to patrol the northern half of Africa continuously and reach anywhere on the continent at virtually any time. A force of eight hundred marines is located less than one hundred miles from Africa at a base in Morón, Spain, ready for deployment to conduct training, exercises, and combat operations.[25] Off the coast of West Africa a floating base has allowed the Navy to provide training and other "engagement" activities to local forces.[26]

The military has been conducting a variety of operations regularly in at least forty-nine African countries. It may be operating in every single one.[27] Worldwide, training, exercises, and other forms of military engagement have become a key way to establish a de facto U.S. presence without the potential bad publicity of building a "base." As of 2018, the military was carrying out an annual total of about 3,500 exercises, programs, and other activities in Africa—about ten every day.[28] Throughout the continent the U.S. military's presence has spread quietly, minimizing opposition locally and in the United States. The ability of U.S. leaders to use military force with few constraints on the continent and in surrounding regions has expanded accordingly.

✪

Understanding why the U.S. military has been in Djibouti since shortly after October 2001 and now has relatively small, secretive bases across much of Africa requires a return to the 1992 eviction of U.S. bases from the Philippines. After getting kicked out of Subic Bay Naval Base and Clark Air Base, the military began developing new strategies to broaden its presence around the world while preventing future evictions and restrictions at bases abroad. The Philippines was one of the first places where these strategies were put into action. Less than five years after leaving the country, the military began finding ways to return. In 1996 U.S. negotiators signed a "visiting forces agreement" with the government of the Philippines that allowed U.S. troops back into the country for military exercises and training. Within months of the U.S. invasion of Afghanistan and President Bush's declaration of a global war on terrorism, hundreds of U.S. special forces troops started operating in the country's south, near where U.S. forces had fought an anticolonial insurgency one hundred years earlier, following the U.S. conquest of the Philippines.

Thousands of troops started appearing for regular military exercises that were a way to establish a de facto large-scale troop presence. By 2003 there were eighteen exercises a year. Soon there were more than thirty annually. By 2008 there were six thousand U.S. troops involved in a single exercise—three times the number of Filipinos.[29] The exercises had become a way to hide the near-permanent deployment of large numbers of U.S. troops involved in counterinsurgency operations in the Philippines' south.[30] The other major tool for hiding the U.S. troop presence was the creation of flowery-sounding lily-pad bases: U.S. special forces troops began operating from as many as seven lily pads despite the Philippines' constitutional ban on foreign bases.[31]

Lily-pad bases are relatively small, secretive, strategically located military installations. The name suggests a frog jumping from lily pad to lily pad toward its prey. Much like Stuart Barber's Strategic Island Concept, the lily-pad strategy seeks to insulate bases from local protest by finding remote, isolated base locations away from major population centers. The aim is to "lighten US foreign footprints to reduce friction with host nations."[32] Lily pads thus have limited numbers of troops, no families, and few amenities. Sometimes they rely mostly or entirely on private military contractors, whose actions the U.S. government can more easily disown if necessary.

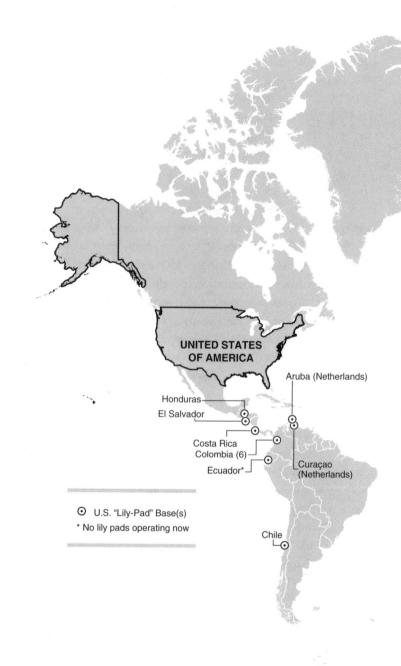

UNITED STATES
OF AMERICA

Aruba (Netherlands)

Honduras
El Salvador

Costa Rica
Colombia (6)
Ecuador*

Curaçao
(Netherlands)

⊙ U.S. "Lily-Pad" Base(s)
* No lily pads operating now

Chile

Map 26. *The Global Proliferation of "Lily-Pad" Bases.*
Small lily-pad bases ("cooperative security locations") built since around 2000 are
shown. By design lily-pad bases are secretive in nature and difficult to distinguish
from host-nation facilities, making an authoritative list nearly impossible. Some
installations are now closed, although the U.S. military may retain base access agree-
ments in some previously occupied locations. Oceans not to scale. Key sources:
Michael J. Lostumbo et al., *Overseas Basing of U.S. Military Forces: An Assessment of
Relative Costs and Strategic Benefits* (Santa Monica, CA: RAND Corporation, 2013);
Ploch, *Africa Command;* Savell and 5W Infographics, "This Map Shows Where";
Vine, "Lists of U.S. Military Bases."

To further maintain a low profile and preempt accusations about building "new US bases," the Pentagon has often hidden lily pads within existing host nation bases or on the margins of civilian airports. Most lily pads in the Philippines, for example, have been hidden within Philippines military installations. In Pakistan the military leased a base technically owned by the United Arab Emirates so the Pakistani government could deny (flimsily) the presence of a "US base" on its territory.[33] To disguise their presence further, U.S. officials strenuously avoid calling lily pads "bases." Formally, they call them "cooperative security locations." Like *forward operating site*, the terms *cooperative security location* and *lily pad* seek to minimize the perceived size and significance of a base.

Just as Barber envisioned in the 1950s and 1960s, the military's aim has been to acquire as many lily pads as possible in places that previously had little U.S. military presence, creating a constellation of installations—like lily pads on a pond—in places such as Latin America, parts of Asia, eastern and central Europe, and especially Africa. With the Philippines eviction, followed by the loss of bases in Panama in 1999, Bill Clinton's Pentagon began creating lily-pad bases and other small installations in places such as Ecuador, Aruba, Curaçao, and El Salvador. Although statistics are hard to assemble given the often secretive nature of such bases, it is clear that since the late 1990s the Pentagon has built upward of fifty lily pads and other bases, while exploring the construction of dozens more.[34] In yet more countries access agreements have given U.S. forces regular-use rights at airfields, ports, and bases. "Access not bases" has become a mantra to some—although sometimes, as in the Philippines since 2001, "access" can become just another euphemism for a base.[35]

Compared to the construction of massive bases in the Middle East and the ongoing operation of city-sized bases in Europe and East Asia, the buildup of lily pads can sound smarter and more cost-effective than maintaining huge installations, which have often caused anger, as in the Philippines. The *lily pad* language, however, can be misleading. Most lily pads and other small bases are designed for rapid expansion and "surge capacity" to accommodate much larger numbers of troops and weaponry. In 2017 U.S. troops in Gabon carried out an exercise to test their ability to expand a lily-pad-style base into a forward command post capable of receiving a large number of troops.[36] Navy officials likewise presented

Diego Garcia to Congress as an "austere communications facility"—a lily pad of its day—but knew it would be the nucleus of a major base, which has since grown into a multibillion-dollar facility.[37]

Like other bases, lily pads can also lead to snowballing costs, taking on lives of their own through bureaucratic tendencies toward inertia and expansion.[38] The Pentagon originally announced that the drone base in Chabelley, Djibouti, had a planned lifespan of two years; within a few months the military named it an "enduring" location.[39] The drone base in Agadez, Niger, originally had a $50 million price tag; the total more than doubled to $110 million by the time it became operational in 2019. With operating costs the Pentagon expects the total to reach $280 million by 2024.[40]

Lily pads also can be a slippery slope to a larger U.S. military presence in a country. Building on the lily pads and exercises established under Bush/Cheney, the Obama administration signed an agreement with the Philippines government to allow U.S. troops—quite remarkably—to return to Clark and Subic Bay. U.S. troops also gained access to Philippines airspace, airfields, sea lanes, and harbors, as well as repair and supply bases from the Vietnam War era. A 2014 agreement allows an even larger U.S. presence. Both governments insist the agreement will respect Filipino sovereignty and create no U.S. "bases."[41] The U.S. military now has "everything—and arguably more than—it had" before 1992, according to Herbert Docena. Only now, it has this presence "without the economic and political costs of maintaining large garrison-like bases that can serve as visible symbols for the opposition."[42]

✪

The developments in the Philippines have been replicated worldwide, with U.S. lily pads spreading around the globe. The result appears to be a case of back to the future, with the creation of what military analyst Robert Work likens to a "global coaling-station network" last seen in the nineteenth century and the days of Adm. Alfred Thayer Mahan.[43] While the collection of giant bases from the "Cold War" has shrunk, the proliferation of new lily pads and other relatively small bases in recent years has meant that the global collection of bases has actually grown in geographic scope. Between 1991 and 2007 the number of agreements permitting the presence of U.S. troops on foreign soil more than doubled, from forty-five to over ninety.[44]

The aggressive, interventionist approach of U.S. foreign policy in Africa and beyond represents a logical extreme of the basing strategies developed during World War II and the early years of the "Cold War." During the war military leaders in the Joint Chiefs of Staff embraced the hyperaggressive policy of "active defense." The U.S. military needed to be able to "strike the first blow" by "applying armed force at a distance." To do so the military "require[d] a widespread system of bases" to attack any perceived threat virtually anywhere on Earth.[45]

The "forward strategy" that came to dominate U.S. foreign policy after the war and ensure that U.S. bases would continue to encircle the globe was somewhat more restrained. Bases and troops far from U.S. shores and as close as possible to the Soviet Union would hem in Soviet expansion and allow rapid military deployment to respond to any perceived threat. This was aggressive and threatening to the Soviet Union, to be sure, just as it would have been to the United States if the roles were reversed. (When Soviet leaders dared place a single missile base in Cuba, the response of U.S. leaders brought the world closer to nuclear war than at any other time during the U.S.-Soviet conflict.) However, given that U.S. officials faced another nuclear-armed empire, their approach was less aggressive than the earlier active defense strategy of "striking the first blow" and "hitting" enemies far from U.S. shores. Given the potential consequences of miscalculating and triggering a war with the Soviet Union, U.S. officials were somewhat constrained in their ability to use military forces wherever and whenever they wished, even if they could deploy their forces to bases worldwide. After the dissolution of the Soviet Union, U.S. leaders suddenly faced few, if any, constraints. Many officials moved quickly to demonstrate this fact with the 1991 war against Iraq, the war in Panama, and the series of military interventions that followed.

After al-Qaeda's 2001 attacks, the United States enjoyed unparalleled support worldwide, and the Bush/Cheney administration could have responded in many ways. Bush and Cheney chose to respond with a war on terrorism that channeled the hyperaggressive World War II–era approach of "active defense," now articulated as the Bush Doctrine of "preemptive war." The doctrine held that the United States could and should preemptively launch wars to remove any perceived threat to the nation *before the threat was imminent* (which was the typical standard in international law governing the legitimacy of an offensive attack on another nation). The idea of preemptive war became a key part of the justification for invading Iraq, which relied on soon-to-be-proven-false allegations that Saddam Hussein's regime possessed chemical, nuclear, or other weapons of mass destruction (there were none).

"The war on terror will not be won on the defensive," President Bush proclaimed in 2002. "We must take the battle to the enemy, disrupt his plans and confront the worst threats before they emerge. In the world we have entered, the only path to safety is the path of action. And this nation will act." Bush laid out an expansive vision of "uncover[ing] terrorist cells in 60 or more countries" and "transforming the military" into one "ready to strike at a moment's notice in any dark corner of the world."[46]

This vision of deploying U.S. military power to strike in every "dark corner" of the world has shaped U.S. foreign policy ever since, no more so than in Africa. The expansion of bases and troops as a permanently mobilized, rapidly deployable force throughout the continent is a realization of this vision in a part of the globe that had been mostly untouched by U.S. military power prior to the twenty-first century. Bush/Cheney and subsequently Obama and Trump administration officials sought to create a presence in as many countries as possible in Africa to be able to respond— militarily—to any threat officials might perceive.

"The forces that have drawn the US military to Djibouti will draw it many other places, as well," wrote two leading neoconservatives, Thomas Donnelly and Vance Serchuk, in the summer of 2003. Emboldened by the seeming victory of overthrowing Saddam Hussein, they proclaimed, "American power is on the move." Indeed it was, as the proliferation of lily pads shows. Donnelly and Serchuk tellingly likened these lily pads to "frontier forts." Employing language of the West is no coincidence. The lily-pad strategy is an unabashedly imperial attempt to ensure U.S. global domination. "The realignment of our network of overseas bases into a system of frontier stockades is necessary to win a long-term struggle against an amorphous enemy across the arc of instability," Donnelly and Serchuk write. "Patrolling the perimeter of the Pax Americana is transforming the US military . . . into the cavalry of a global, liberal international order. Like the cavalry of the Old West, their job is one part warrior and one part policeman."[47]

Donnelly and Serchuk airbrush the role of the U.S. cavalry in ethnic cleansing and genocide and overlook the fact that militaries are not police forces. Generally, military forces serve as undemocratic judge, jury, and executioner. On the other hand, the U.S. cavalry's role in helping Euro-American settlers seize land and natural resources and pursue profit-making opportunities in the West is revealing about some of the economic forces and, for some, racist ideology underlying the buildup of lily pads and other U.S. military presence in Africa.

Bush's racialized language describing the military as "ready to strike at a moment's notice in any dark corner of the world" is telling. The president was largely referring to the Middle East, Africa, and Muslim parts of Asia in a global war on terrorism that he described initially as a "crusade" and that was shaped from the start by centuries-old racist tropes about West and East; Occident and Orient; Christians and Muslims; Crusaders and infidels; cowboys and Indians; civilization and barbarism; "enlightened" Europe and "darkest" Africa; white and black, brown, red, and yellow.

Racism has been a fundamental structuring force in U.S. imperialism from independence to today. When journalist Robert D. Kaplan visited lily pads and other small bases around the world in the first years after the declaration of a war on terrorism, he repeatedly heard the refrain "Welcome to Injun Country."[48] The "Indian Country" metaphor has been a recurring one "in the rhetoric of US militarism overseas," notes Nikhil Pal Singh, from the Philippines after 1898 to World War II in the Pacific to the war in Vietnam, Laos, and Cambodia to Afghanistan and Iraq since 2001. Chickasaw scholar Jodi Byrd explains that anyone who is "made Indian" becomes easier to kill.[49]

U.S. troops' use of ugly, racist slurs for Iraqis and Afghans, such as "sand n****rs," is another sign of the effective recruitment of racist ideas by U.S. leaders in support of imperial wars.[50] That some of the terms derive from slurs aimed at African Americans points to the long-standing export of North American racism to demean other peoples of color around the world, just as soldiers called Filipinos the *n*-word during the U.S. 1898–1913 war in the Philippines.

✪

In addition to being shaped by ideas about race and racism, U.S. imperialism and its military strategy today are being driven by the economic challenge posed to the U.S. Empire by an increasingly intense global competition with China and to a lesser extent the European Union, Russia, and rising powers, such as India and Brazil. U.S. military activity in Africa reflects this competition for economic and geopolitical supremacy, which has also spread to resource-rich lands and markets in Asia, Latin America, and the Pacific, Indian, and Arctic Oceans. The greatest challenger to U.S. geopolitical-economic dominance, China, has generally pursued this competition and the challenge of trying to dominate markets and secure oil, minerals, and other important natural resources with its economic might: the Chinese government has dotted the globe with strategic investments and development projects, from roads in Africa to ports in Pakistan and Australia.

By contrast, the U.S. government has relied heavily on the U.S. military, regionally and globally: it has dotted the planet with bases, like those in Africa, as well as with troops and other forms of military power, including training, arms sales, and exercises. The commander of the African Command has described such activities as a "distinct U.S. advantage that our competitors cannot match." Testifying to Congress in early 2020, Gen. Stephen J. Townsend explicitly justified the large military presence in Africa and efforts to counter militant organizations as a "key component of global power competition" with both China and Russia. Pentagon Secretary Mark Esper was blunt about Africa: "Mission number one is compete with Russia and China."[51]

One base that the military appears *not* to have built helps illustrate the dynamics at play. Within months of the U.S. invasion of Afghanistan, high-ranking U.S. military officials and senators started visiting São Tomé and Príncipe, the tiny island nation off the oil-rich coast of West Africa. U.S. officials said São Tomé might make a good location for a lily pad.[52] The sudden interest in a lily pad in one of the smallest and poorest countries in the world stemmed not from terrorism but from the petroleum found beneath the Gulf of Guinea and elsewhere in West Africa.[53] Beginning around the turn of the century, the region became an important source of global energy supplies. U.S. companies, including ExxonMobil and Noble Energy, won oil-exploration concessions in the Gulf. The Pentagon may not have a base in São Tomé yet, but it has created lily pads along the Gulf of Guinea. They include installations in Cameroon, Gabon, and Ghana's "oil city," Takoradi, home to U.S. firms ExxonMobil, Halliburton, Hess, and Kosmos Energy, among others in the oil and gas industry.[54]

Although the recent boom in U.S. oil production caused a drop in imports from West Africa, a few years ago the Council on Foreign Relations was suggesting that sub-Saharan Africa was "likely to become as important a source of US energy imports as the Middle East."[55] Despite the drop, ExxonMobil, for example, recently increased its exploration activities and investments in Ghana and Equatorial Guinea. On the other side of the continent, East Africa has grown in importance as a source of oil and gas. North Africa continues to be a large supplier. In all, five of the globe's top thirty oil producers are in Africa. Just as in the nineteenth century's scramble for Africa's resources, the continent remains a source for gold, diamonds, coltan, copper, cobalt, platinum, nickel, titanium, uranium, and other strategic natural resources. An estimated 30 percent of Earth's remaining mineral resources are on the continent.[56]

Africa also represents a vast and largely untapped consumer market—one of the few remaining over which corporations can compete. As a result, foreign direct investment is growing faster in Africa than in any other region. Six of the world's ten fastest-growing economies are in sub-Saharan Africa.[57] In short, a "new scramble for Africa" has begun, with the United States, China, the United Kingdom, France, Italy, India, Russia, and others eager to secure access to the continent's wealth and profit-making opportunities.

Amid the scramble, Africa appears to be following the basing trajectory of the Middle East and, more recently, the oil- and gas-rich Caspian Sea region, where the U.S. military has also tried to create a base infrastructure.[58] The difference is that because of political and financial constraints, the Pentagon can't build major new bases in Africa, as it did in Europe, Asia, and the Middle East. Without this freedom the Pentagon is using a growing collection of lily pads and other military operations in a bid for regional control. "U.S. Africa Command must continue to find ways to expand the competitive space," Africom Commander Townsend told Congress in early 2020, euphemistically suggesting plans for expansion to "outpace Chinese and Russian influence to maintain our strategic access to Africa."[59]

The U.S. military buildup in Africa is a major face of U.S. imperialism today and what many call the "new way of war" for the United States (although by now the strategy is more than a decade old). "Forget full-scale invasions and large-footprint occupations on the Eurasian mainland," military expert Nick Turse has written of the new way of war. "Instead, think: special operations forces working on their own but also training or fighting beside allied militaries (if not outright proxy armies) . . . the militarization of spying and intelligence, the use of drone aircraft, the launching of cyber-attacks, and joint Pentagon operations with increasingly militarized 'civilian' government agencies." Add to this list the expansion of joint military exercises; superficially "humanitarian" missions that clearly serve military intelligence, patrol, and public relations functions; the rotating deployment of U.S. forces around the globe; port visits and other long-standing "showing the flag" demonstrations of U.S. military might; and the growing use of private military contractors—plus lots and lots of bases.[60]

Beyond any military utility, the increased U.S. military presence in these countries and regions is a kind of back door to introduce a range of military tools, activities, and relationships into host countries in an attempt to hold on to geopolitical-economic dominance. "Africa is key terrain for competition with China and Russia," Africom Commander Townsend testified to Congress. "If the U.S. steps back from Africa too far, China and Russia will fill the void to our detriment." Noting that militant groups could also grow if Africom reduces its presence, Townsend emphasized, "We will lose opportunities for increased trade and investments with some of the fastest growing economies in the world."[61]

Bases have become a key mechanism of this new-way-of-war-cum-geopolitical-economic strategy: because of the contact and negotiations that maintaining bases in a foreign country generally requires, bases provide an opportunity to deepen ties between the U.S. and foreign militaries and foreign governments more broadly. A base of any size can thus lead to increased training and humanitarian-assistance activities, which can lead to military exercises, which can lead to arms sales, which can lead to other trade deals, and more.

These deepening military ties involve highly unequal relationships, in which U.S. leaders can offer their counterparts various "gifts"—including, for example, opportunities to buy sophisticated and expensive equipment and weaponry or what are perceived to be prestigious training opportunities in the United States. But, like most gifts, these come with obligations and a certain degree of expected loyalty. The obligation-laden relationships can later bear fruit for U.S. military leaders when, for example, they want to gain valuable intelligence from high-ranking counterparts or shape decisions about another country's arms purchases or military policy. These relationships "are sources of information," former Bush/Cheney Pentagon official Ray DuBois told me. So too, "you may be able to influence the country's procurement policies so they will buy US equipment."[62]

Anthropologist Lesley Gill shows how training foreign military personnel at the infamous School of the Americas "secured their collusion" and "bound them closer to the United States, opened them to greater manipulation . . . and preempted military assistance from other states that might challenge US dominance."[63] Relationships built around bases, exercises, and local training have done much the same. Even a relatively small lily-pad base "has an influence by virtue of its presence," DuBois said, "a political impact."[64] This frequently translates into economic impact: U.S. embassy officials and other diplomats enjoy more power and influence representing U.S. corporate interests in the country where a base is located. Much like U.S. and European patrol bases helped "open" China to trade in the nineteenth century, bases can help provide privileged U.S. access to overseas markets, resources, and investment opportunities.

Since World War II, overseas bases have been a major source of power through which the United States has asserted control in the world. As implicit threats and demonstrations of power, bases have provided U.S. officials with levers to help secure support overseas for all manner of economic agreements and diplomatic negotiations. In a variety of ways, bases have safeguarded U.S. political and economic dominance, supported U.S. corporate interests, opened markets, helped maintain alliances, and kept as many countries as possible within a U.S. sphere of influence. A State Department official once told me that he always likes walking into a negotiating room with the diplomats of another country "with a [U.S.] aircraft carrier off the coast."[65] Having bases and a permanent U.S. military presence across Africa offers a similar power, a similar ability to ensure U.S. influence and control.

At a time when a growing number of countries are asserting their independence or gravitating toward China and other rising powers, U.S. officials hope that the relationships built by bases and other military activities will bind governments as closely as possible to the U.S. military and the U.S. government—and so, to continued U.S. political-economic dominance. Often portrayed as gifts, bases frequently become something of a Trojan horse: once established, bases provide U.S. officials with a powerful tool to influence foreign governments' decisions about economics and politics far beyond bases and military policy. The threat of withdrawing a base alone becomes a way to bend the will of host governments and populations. Even if the economic benefits of foreign bases are much less significant than one might expect, the perceived economic damage of base closure provides a powerful diplomatic weapon.[66]

✪

While lily pads and other secretive forms of military presence have economic and political utility, they have also increased the ease and likelihood of using military force. As in the Middle East, they have increased the likelihood of war in Africa. A major part of lily pads' appeal for military officials is the flexibility they provide in applying military force without restriction. With the military maintaining some kind of a foothold in almost every country in Africa, U.S. officials increasingly see the military as the answer to anything perceived as a threat, no matter how remote or fanciful that threat might be.[67] By making it simpler to wage war, lily pads have made military action a more attractive option among the foreign policy tools available to U.S. policy makers.

Rarely, it seems, have leaders considered the possibility that military solutions might fail, as they have, often spectacularly, as in Libya. Rarely have leaders considered the possibility that there might not be military solutions to the problems they see. Rarely have leaders considered the possibility that using military force might be counterproductive, that it might make problems worse or create entirely new problems, as has been the case with foreign military forces fueling militant movements in Somalia. Rarely have leaders considered the possibility that other, non-military solutions might be available and more effective.

With the help of skyrocketing budgets after the invasion of Afghanistan in 2001, the military has been able to find and create new missions for itself. Tens of billions of dollars coupled with high levels of secrecy, compliant local regimes, and limited congressional, media, and public oversight have given birth to virtually unlimited missions shaped overwhelmingly by military leaders. Protecting the profit-making interests of U.S. corporations has shaped the broad contours of the missions and deployments—as the concentrations of bases in oil-rich areas of West and East Africa suggest.

But there need not always be a clear economic logic to the military's activities. With so much funding available after the launch of the post–October 2001 wars, the deployment of forces throughout the continent has taken on a life of its own. Africom leaders' decision to keep the command's headquarters in Germany rather than in the United States is one example of the profligacy of military spending; a Government Accountability Office report showed that moving the headquarters to the United States would save tens of millions of dollars a year and benefit the U.S. economy.[68] In addition to wasting money, the U.S. military's operations in Africa have frequently undermined peace and security and been beset by corruption and poor planning and performance, multiple researchers have found. The only clear case where the military appears to have met its stated goals has been in multinational antipiracy patrols in the Indian Ocean, which lowered hijackings significantly, to nine failed attempts in 2013.[69]

On the other hand, a 2013 Pentagon Inspector General's report found Africom's humanitarian activities to be poorly planned, executed, and monitored. This is unsurprising because the military's humanitarian operations in Africa and worldwide are not primarily aimed at providing humanitarian aid: Pentagon budget documents explain that humanitarian operations help "maintain a robust overseas presence" and "obtain . . . access to regions important to US interests."[70] Beyond the questionable value of the hundreds of millions of dollars invested in such programs, militarized humanitarianism also risks undermining the credibility and efficacy of future legitimate humanitarian work (the CIA's fake polio-vaccination campaign that helped find Osama bin Laden has had this effect).[71]

Several of the militaries recently trained by U.S. forces have gone on to overthrow or attempt coups against democratically elected governments, including in Mali, Mauritania, Niger, and Chad.[72] In other cases the U.S. military's growing base presence and broader relationships with African militaries and their governments appear to have strengthened repressive, undemocratic regimes and their militaries. At a base in Salak, Cameroon, where U.S. troops have trained local soldiers, there have been

documented cases of illegal imprisonment, torture, and extrajudicial killings by Cameroonian troops.[73]

There is "little acknowledgement of the toxic nature of these partner-
ships," the Oxford Research Group has found. "Governance and human
rights are considerably undermined by the current securitisation of policy
in the Sahel-Sahara."[74] Two experts on human rights in Africa agree, writing, "Counterterrorism assistance has a better track record reinforcing
bad government than rooting out extremists."[75] Strengthening the militaries of repressive regimes can encourage rulers to use their militaries
against opponents. It likewise encourages opponents to see military force
as the only way to claim a share of a country's wealth and political power,
increasing the possibility of coups and violence.[76] U.S. bases also provide
a powerful symbol for militants to use to rally nationalist sentiment and to
promote the use of violence against ruling regimes and the United States,
following the lead of Osama bin Laden and al-Qaeda. The presence of U.S.
bases and forces frequently appears to have been a boon to insurgent
groups, "increasing the[ir] profile and activity."[77] In the U.S. Army's own
Military Review journal, political scientist at Ohio Northern University
and former Ghanaian Air Force lieutenant Kofi Nsia-Pepra concludes,
"The US militarization policy [in Africa] has backfired, undermining the
attainment of its strategic objectives."[78]

The counterproductive effects of U.S. military activity targeting militant
groups in Africa are a microcosm of the abject failure of the entire war on
terror: according to military figures, the number of Islamist militant
organizations in Africa rose from five major groups in 2012 to twenty-one
"active militant Islamist groups" in 2017; another study suggests the total
may have topped fifty by 2015. Similarly, in Afghanistan the war on terrorism has increased the number of enemies from two—al-Qaeda and the
Taliban—in 2001 to what the Pentagon counts as more than twenty militant groups today. Worldwide there were almost four times as many Sunni
Islam–identified militants in 2018 compared to on September 11, 2001.[79]
Meanwhile, research has consistently shown that military action is rarely
effective in shutting down militant "terrorist" groups; policing, intelligence
gathering, and diplomacy tend to be far more effective tactics.[80]

✪

The proliferation of lily pads and other U.S. bases has accelerated the militarization of Africa and the militarization of an already profoundly militarized U.S. foreign policy. Like real lily pads—which are actually aquatic weeds—bases have a way of reproducing uncontrollably. The growing U.S. military presence and the spread of U.S. bases on the continent have encouraged other nations to create their own bases along the Horn of Africa and in the Sahel (most are small, relative to U.S. installations). Hosting foreign military bases belonging to at least seven nations, Djibouti now has more foreign militaries on its soil than any other country outside war zones such as Syria and perhaps Afghanistan and Iraq.[81]

Foreign governments have generally explained their bases and troops in Africa as ways to battle al-Qaeda-inspired militants, such as Boko Haram and Somalia's al-Shabaab, and to combat piracy and protect trade in the Indian Ocean. The underlying motivation behind the "base race" is largely the new scramble for resources and markets in Africa. This base race risks heightening regional military tensions, discouraging diplomatic solutions to conflicts, and potentially instigating a clash between the foreign powers or their proxies.[82]

For the United States, deploying lily pads and other surreptitious forms of military presence in Africa has deepened a system of permanent, endless war. Fueled by massive post-2001 budgets and a Military Industrial Congressional Complex that's been happy to support and profit off the militarization of a new part of the globe, U.S. imperialism today risks inflaming local conflicts and, with little public discussion, drawing U.S. forces into new wars.

With almost no public awareness, the military has been involved in wars and combat since 2001 in Somalia, Libya, Burkina Faso, Cameroon, the Central African Republic, Chad, the Democratic Republic of the Congo, Kenya, Mali, Mauritania, Niger, Nigeria, South Sudan, Tunisia, Uganda, and, across the Red Sea, Yemen. In Africa, war has been the mission. War has been the solution to nearly every perceived problem. War has been *the* foreign policy. Unless there is a fundamental change in policy, the list of wars in Africa in which U.S. forces are involved is likely to grow. The result could be unknown forms of blowback for generations to come. One ominous sign was a 2017 U.S. military war game envisioning a U.S. invasion of West Africa following a terrorist attack in New York City.[83]

Frighteningly, U.S. leaders' pursuit of a similar imperial strategy in East Asia is even more dangerous than in Africa. For well over a decade, U.S. leaders have responded to China's rise by adding to what were already hundreds of U.S. bases and tens of thousands of troops near China's borders. Guam, South Korea, and Japan have seen major new base construction. Australia has become an increasingly important node in the global base network, with a new Marine Corps base in Darwin and expanded war fighting, drone targeting, and espionage roles for a highly secretive base in Pine Gap.[84] On South Korea's Jeju Island, the South Korean military has built a controversial base that's part of a U.S. missile defense system and to which U.S. forces will have regular access. Since around 2000, the Pentagon has expanded the military's presence in Singapore and the Commonwealth of the Northern Marianas, as well as in the return to the Philippines. The Pentagon has also considered bases in Indonesia, Malaysia, Brunei, and even Vietnam, while pushing stronger military ties with India. Every year in the region, the military expands its presence by conducting hundreds of port visits and military exercises.[85]

As in Africa, the growing U.S. military presence in East Asia is part of a global effort to check China's growing power. But imagine how U.S. leaders or the U.S. public would respond if China (or Iran or North Korea or Russia) were to build even a single small base in Mexico, Canada, or the Caribbean. Just as during the 1962 Cuban Missile Crisis with the Soviet Union, large numbers of U.S. politicians and citizens would likely demand a military response. So too, building up bases near China's borders increases threats to Chinese security and encourages the Chinese government to respond by boosting its own military spending and activity.

Bases near the borders of China, as well as those near the borders of Russia, Iran, and North Korea, threaten to fuel tensions between militarized, nuclear-armed or near-nuclear powers. U.S. officials insist that building more bases in East Asia is a defensive act meant to ensure peace in the Pacific. Tell that to the Chinese. The country's leaders are undoubtedly not reassured by the creation of more bases encircling their borders. Given the record of U.S. wars and invasions, Chinese leaders have good reason to fear—and respond to—the growing U.S. presence. (For context, China has not fought outside its borders since a one-month war with Vietnam in 1979.)

Germany (119)
United Kingdom (25)
Italy (44)
RUSSIA
IRAN
CHINA
NORTH KOREA
Japan (119)
South Korea (80)
Guam (52)

⊛ U.S. Base(s)

⊛ U.S. Bases (≥ 25)

⊙ U.S. Small Base(s)

⎯ U.S. Naval Fleet

Map 27. Encircling "Enemies."
Hundreds of U.S. military bases surround China, Russia, Iran, and North Korea. Tens of thousands of U.S. troops occupy these bases, with large supplies of high-powered weaponry, including nuclear arms. Few in the U.S. consider how they would feel if surrounded by foreign bases designed to wage war against the United States. Key source: Vine, "Lists of U.S. Military Bases."

China

Iran

North Korea

Russia

Foreign Navy

Map 28. How Would We Feel? A Hypothetical Map.
The Chinese, Iranian, North Korean, and Russian bases shown here do not exist. This map is
designed to encourage U.S. Americans in particular to consider how it would feel—and how we
might react—if we were surrounded by foreign bases near our borders.

Just as the global war on terrorism has spread terror and exponentially expanded the number of militants willing to carry out terrorist acts, the creation of new U.S. bases to protect against imagined future Chinese or Russian threats risks becoming a self-fulfilling prophecy: the proliferation of U.S. bases in East Asia, coupled with aggressive naval and air patrols and military exercises, risks creating an ever-more-powerful Chinese military threat that the U.S. buildup is supposedly designed to protect against. Contrary to the claim that bases increase global security, they are ratcheting up an arms race and regional military tensions. This increases the risk of a military clash or war, accidental or otherwise, while also wasting vast sums of money that could be used to meet people's health, education, housing, infrastructure, and other needs. Some irresponsibly dangerous U.S. military leaders and pundits already appear to assume that a war with China is inevitable, reinforcing the self-fulfilling prophecy further. Far from making the world a safer place, U.S. bases and the military attitudes they reinforce are actually making war more likely and the world less secure.

CONCLUSION

ENDING "ENDLESS WARS"

During Barack Obama's presidency, there were promising signs that the long history of U.S. wars might be waning. On his second day as president, Obama promised to close the Guantanamo Bay prison. Soon after taking office he won the Nobel Peace Prize, in part for promoting the abolition of nuclear weapons. In late 2011 President Obama's administration closed the last U.S. bases in Iraq and officially removed the U.S. military from the country. The administration was beginning to remove tens of thousands of troops from Afghanistan. Meanwhile, Republican and Democratic congressional leaders were imposing mandatory budget caps on military and civilian spending and looking for ways to cut billions from the Pentagon budget with the national debt then nearing $20 trillion. Countries in the North Atlantic Treaty Organization (NATO) were likewise cutting their military budgets and removing many of their troops from Afghanistan.

Amid these developments military contractors were fearful that the military "market" was shrinking. This fear was the proverbial elephant in the room at two military industry conferences I attended in 2012, in London and Washington, DC. The London conference was for military contractors building, supplying, and running bases around the world. In a chic London hotel, Peter Eberle, a representative for the major weapons manufacturer and base contractor General Dynamics, asked the crowd, "What if we have peace break out?"

Maj. Tim Elliott, one of a few NATO military representatives on hand, blurted out in response, "God forbid!"

Elliott's retort was intended as an ironic joke. Others in the room laughed because the major and others knew the truth: peace would be bad for business, bad for them. Contractors would lose contracts; profits would shrink; stock prices would likely fall; some employees might face layoffs. For military officers, too, peace might see their careers stall, without opportunities to deploy and lead troops in combat. Lower levels of military spending would also mean fewer lucrative jobs after retirement from the military, in the military-contracting and weapons-manufacturing industries.

Eight years later it's clear the conference attendees needn't have worried. Troop reductions continued and some budget cuts occurred, but the U.S. war in Afghanistan continued and the Pentagon and its their allies in Congress found ways to circumvent the cuts. Presidents Obama and Donald Trump responded to the rise of that product of the U.S. war in Iraq the Islamic State by sending new U.S. troops to Iraq and Syria. The military began occupying territory in both countries and building new bases, which were soon hosting thousands of troops.[1] The Pentagon used bases around the region to launch what remains an ongoing bombing campaign against ISIS and other militants. The military also used these installations to provide refueling, logistical, and other support for the government of Saudi Arabia's war against the Houthi movement in Yemen, which seized power there in 2015.[2] The military and the CIA have continued drone missile attacks on suspected militants in Afghanistan, Pakistan, Libya, and Somalia, as well as in Syria, Iraq, and Yemen.[3] By the end of his presidency, Nobel Peace Prize winner Obama supported spending $1 trillion over thirty years to upgrade the U.S. nuclear weapons stockpile. By the last full year of his presidency, Obama's military was dropping an average of seventy-one bombs every day across at least seven countries.[4]

In the United States, some in Congress, the military, the media, and the think tank world began talking openly about cold and hot wars with Russia and China. This talk has helped fuel greater spending on expensive weapons systems. In President Donald Trump's first years in office, his administration pushed for and secured major increases to the military budget, including billions in additional funding for nuclear weapons and a new Space Command.

In 2024 the Army is scheduled to open a new military hospital in Germany, at a cost of what will likely be more than $1 billion. The new facility, located near Ramstein Air Base, is a replacement for the Landstuhl Regional Medical Center, which was built in the 1950s and has received thousands of casualties from Afghanistan, Iraq, and other war zones. When I visited the existing hospital in 2012, Landstuhl had a level-one trauma center rating—the highest possible grade, shared with elite hospitals such as Cedars-Sinai Medical Center in Los Angeles and Massachusetts General in Boston. I asked a surgeon who had been working at Landstuhl for a decade about the condition of the hospital and whether there was need for a replacement. The surgeon, who spoke on condition of anonymity, said he couldn't comment.

"Is the hospital deficient or suboptimal in any way?" I asked.

"No," the surgeon replied. If it were at all deficient, he explained, the military would have had to repair it immediately to maintain the hospital's level-one status.[5]

I asked *Washington Post* Pulitzer Prize–winning military reporter Walter Pincus what we should make of spending more than $1 billion to replace a world-class medical facility in Germany.

Without missing a beat, he said, "It implies we're going to keep fighting."[6]

Numerous signs suggest that unless there are significant changes in the United States, the wars that began in October 2001 won't be coming to an end soon. *Why?* is the question I asked at the start of this book. In many ways, that the United States has existed in a state of near-permanent war since its revolution is unsurprising. This book has shown that the newly independent country's embrace of a long string of wars and invasions followed nearly three hundred years of deadly colonizing warfare by European empires and European settlers in the Americas. After independence, the aim for many U.S. civilian and military leaders was expansion and conquest. The aim was empire. And the construction of bases on and beyond the borders of U.S.-claimed territory helped make wars for imperial expansion possible.

These dynamics, which developed in the eighteenth and nineteenth centuries, intensified and became more powerfully embedded in the economic, political, and social life of the United States in the twentieth and twenty-first centuries. During the earlier period, forts and the U.S. Army made land available and relatively safe for settlement and Euro-Americans' individual and familial enrichment. The Army protected major trading posts, trade routes, railroads, and eventually growing towns and cities to support Euro-American profit making and to ensure the smooth operation of capitalism in North America. After 1898 and especially after World War II, bases abroad continued to support individual and corporate profit making, but at a much larger, global scale.

In the post–World War II era, overseas bases have played an important role in the creation of a permanent war system in the United States. When the global base infrastructure remained in place after World War II, it became entrenched in tandem with the expansion of the Military Industrial Congressional Complex. The global base network became a microcosm of the Complex as it became embedded in local, national, and international political-economic and social systems, making it increasingly difficult to uproot.

The growth in the size and power of the Military Industrial Congressional Complex reflected the central role that military spending came to play in the U.S. economy after World War II. Weapons production and other military spending became the "largest public works project" in the postwar era, Catherine Lutz notes. While other wealthy industrialized nations created welfare states after World War II with investments in universal health care, education, child care, housing, and other social benefits, U.S. leaders and elites created a warfare state built around the construction and maintenance of military bases, the world's largest arms industry, a large standing military, and the wars that followed in their wake. U.S. leaders directed tax spending to create "the largest budget for the production of violence of any government, anywhere, ever."[7] It's no coincidence that the other major postwar public works project was created by former Army general President Dwight Eisenhower with military functions firmly in mind: the nationwide Interstate Highway System offered a way to move military forces quickly and reliably around the country. A global infrastructure of bases abroad was likewise helpful in advancing elite economic interests and the personal and professional interests of high-ranking military officers. A large collection of bases abroad provided justification for a large standing military and for high levels of spending to maintain the bases, all to the benefit of the Military Industrial Congressional Complex.

Following the start of the U.S. war in Afghanistan in 2001, this Complex and the system of permanent war have reached new levels of entrenched power and insidiousness. The intensification of power is the result of Congress's willingness to appropriate extraordinary levels of taxpayer funding for the military and war after October 2001 and the ability of the U.S. government to run up trillions in dollar-denominated debts (now around $23 trillion). Since 2006 military budgets have exceeded the highest spending levels of the "Cold War," when the United States confronted another empire in the form of the Soviet Union.[8] This more profound economic, political, and sociocultural power in turn has helped normalize permanent war. Indeed, military leaders, analysts, journalists, and others now can talk with a straight face about the United States existing in a state of "infinite war." Air Force General Mike Holmes explained "infinite war" in a 2018 speech. Infinite war, he said, is "not losing. It's staying in the game and getting a new plan and keeping pursuing your objectives."[9]

In other words, the Military Industrial Congressional Complex has become a Dr. Strangelove–like caricature of itself: a system transparently and perhaps exclusively dedicated to its own perpetuation and expansion, lacking any threat warranting these levels of profligate spending but producing catastrophic warfare that has created more militants, thus ensuring higher levels of funding and more war in a cycle that indeed appears infinite.

Journalist Andrew Cockburn compares the Complex to a "giant, malignant virus" with a "built-in self-defense reflex that reacts forcefully whenever a threat to its food supply—taxpayers' money—hits a particular trigger point." In another world, where the consequences weren't so wasteful and deadly, it might be humorous. Except it's not, because the waste and destruction have been so profound and because daily U.S. military operations risk triggering a new, even more catastrophic, potentially nuclear war, whether with Russia, China, Iran, or North Korea. The irony deepens given that the astronomically high military budgets have yielded a "very poor fighting force for our money."[10] People in the United States should pray the military never actually has to defend the United States.

With little public awareness or debate, war and military spending have become even more deeply rooted in the structure of U.S. politics and government as de facto U.S. economic policy and *the* major form of national economic investment. Today's collection of U.S. bases abroad has given military and other government leaders the ability to deploy and use military force almost anywhere in the world, whether it be with aerial bombing campaigns, ground troops, drone strikes, or proxy armies guided by special forces operators. This hyperinterventionist vision of deploying U.S. military power to strike in any and every "dark corner" of the world has shaped U.S. foreign policy and further entrenched the United States in a state of permanent, endless war. That many and perhaps most U.S. Americans think and feel little about these wars—if they're aware of them at all—is due to the absence of a national draft and the government's ability to put the costs of infinite war effectively on a credit card by running up trillions in debt.[11]

This book has shown some of the powerful forces that have shaped the permanent system of imperial war in which the United States is trapped today. As "God forbid [peace might break out]!" reveals, there are corporations, elements of the military and other government agencies, politicians, lobbyists, journalists, think tank analysts, academics, and many others who are literally invested in war—while also being professionally, psychologically, and socially invested. U.S. bases abroad and the near-continuous wars they have helped enable indeed have benefited some. I have been one of the beneficiaries as a Euro-American man growing up in a privileged upper-class home in and around Washington, DC, a city whose economy revolves to a significant degree around the Military Industrial Congressional Complex. (That much of my professional career has revolved around studying and writing about U.S. bases abroad is another ironic way I have benefited.) The people securing most of the benefits of this system have tended to be elites with direct economic interests tied to bases and to the markets and industries directly supported by bases and wars abroad.

Some will respond that the system creates jobs. It does. But the U.S. military should not be a jobs program. If the country needs a jobs program, Congress should invest in other sectors of the economy that create far more jobs per dollar spent than investments in the military: infrastructure and clean energy create 40 percent more jobs for every $1 million invested, health care creates 100 percent more jobs, and education creates 120 percent more.[12] Even if military investments created just as many jobs as other sectors, or even more, the military should be focused on defending the country. And it should defend the country's people at the lowest possible cost and not a cent more. As Eisenhower said, "Every arms dollar we spend above adequacy has a long-term weakening effect upon the nation and its security."[13]

Beyond the nation, we must of course face the full breadth of harm inflicted by the war system. As we've seen, the total dead from U.S. wars number in the tens of millions. The wars have left millions more injured and traumatized physically and mentally in the countries where the wars have been waged and in the homes of people who went to fight. The wars have displaced millions. They have torn apart neighborhoods, communities, and societies. They have impoverished people economically, politically, and even spiritually, as President Eisenhower suggested in his Military Industrial Complex speech. Others have suffered "peacetime crimes" as a result of U.S. bases abroad and other regular preparations for war.[14] The victims include people displaced by bases, such as the Chagossians. They include the people of the U.S. colonies, who still are colonized and live as third- and fourth-class U.S. Americans because of the freedom the military gets from having bases in their homes, while their freedoms are denied.[15]

In Afghanistan the Taliban is stronger than it's ever been since being evicted from power almost two decades ago. In 2001, when the Bush/Cheney administration launched its global war on terrorism, al-Qaeda was the only significant militant group in the country. There are now more than twenty, including the Islamic State. For most of two decades, U.S. officials have dedicated little energy to peace negotiations, although there are encouraging signs of some diplomatic progress as I finish this book in early 2020. Thousands of Afghans have continued to die on a yearly basis as a result of the ongoing war and attacks on civilians.[16] Around the world the war on terrorism has largely fueled terrorism, creating dozens of new militant groups willing to use attacks on civilians as a political tool, often with devastating effects.

Thousands of civilians have also died in the U.S.-led war against ISIS, which resulted in the reduction of ISIS-held territory from an area the size of Britain in 2015 to an area the size of Manhattan by 2018.[17] As of 2017, an estimated one in five U.S. bomb strikes resulted in civilian casualties, leading to more than 3,000 noncombatant deaths.[18] The U.S.-backed Saudi war in Yemen "has turned much of Yemen into a wasteland," states the *New York Times Magazine*. The world's worst modern cholera epidemic has broken out there. The United Nations estimates that 14 million Yemenis are at risk of starvation.[19] The most recent data suggests that, since 2015, more than 91,000 people have died in the war. More than 11,700 of the dead have been civilians, with the Saudi-U.S. coalition responsible for almost 70 percent of those deaths.[20]

The role of the U.S. government in the suffering is clear. As others have noted, U.S. forces have literally fueled the war by providing eighty-eight million pounds of in-air refueling (as of January 1, 2018) for the Saudi Air Force's bombing campaign in addition to providing intelligence and targeting assistance. In 2017 the Trump administration signed a deal to sell the Kingdom of Saudi Arabia tens of billions of dollars' worth of U.S. weapons, continuing a decades-old arms-sales relationship. When a Saudi air strike hit a school bus in 2018, killing forty-four children and ten adults, locals found bomb fragments indicating the ordnance had come from the United States. Nearby graffiti in English and Arabic read, "America Kills Yemeni Children."[21]

The toll of U.S. wars on U.S. citizens has also been grave. This damage includes the casualties suffered by U.S. military personnel as well as the suffering of their families, friends, and communities touched by such deaths, injuries, and impairment. I opened this book with the story of Peggy Madden Davitt, who lost her son Russell Madden to the war in Afghanistan. After Russell's death, Peggy suffered from severe depression for most of the rest of her life, before her death in 2018. "It doesn't stop" on the battlefield, Peggy told me, of the post-traumatic stress disorder (PTSD) she suffered after losing Russell. The secondary effects keep going, she said.

The domestic toll of endless fighting also includes the trillions of dollars spent on war and preparations for war. President Eisenhower famously described war spending as a "theft":

Every gun that is made, every warship launched, every rocket fired signifies, in the final sense, a theft from those who hunger and are not fed, those who are cold and are not clothed. This world in arms is not spending money alone. It is spending the sweat of its laborers, the genius of its scientists, the hopes of its children. The cost of one modern heavy bomber is this: A modern brick school in more than 30 cities. . . . We pay for a single fighter with a half million bushels of wheat. We pay for a single destroyer with new homes that could have housed more than 8,000 people.[22]

"Theft" is not a strong enough word. Consider the $6.4 trillion that Congress has spent and obligated to fund the post-2001 wars.[23] "Horror" seems a more appropriate word when we consider:

How many have died because the U.S. government has not spent even a small portion of this sum to provide universal health care or to improve U.S. public health infrastructure and pandemic preparedness?

How many children and adults have gone hungry?

How many students suffer every day going to deteriorating, delapitated, unhealthy schools where they get a substandard education?

How many college students have taken on tens of thousands of dollars in debt because the country lacks free higher education?

How many have suffered the pain of unemployment when the country could have put millions more to work in sectors such as education, housing, health care, and infrastructure that produce far more jobs per dollar spent than the military?[24]

How far could the country have gone to build a green-energy infrastructure to slow global warming and its catastrophic effects?

How many millions of preventable deaths could have been avoided worldwide with comparably small investments to stop epidemics of disease, malnutrition, and gender-based violence?

And this is just the beginning of a proper accounting of war's damage since October 2001, let alone since July 1776.

✪

Despite the depressing signs, there are reasons for optimism about the future of the U.S. Empire. Throughout U.S. history people within and beyond the borders of the United States have opposed, resisted, and protested U.S. wars. Frequently, the powers supporting war have succeeded. At other times opponents of war have prevented the United States from fighting anew. The mobilization of tens of millions worldwide to protest the 2003 war in Iraq—including the largest day of protest in human history, February 14, 2003—was not a failure. That movement and protests against the war in Afghanistan helped ensure that public opinion in the United States and beyond turned against the war in Iraq as fast as against perhaps any war in U.S. history. This movement and the catastrophic outcome of the wars have meant that, since George W. Bush's second term as president, U.S. leaders have not had the political freedom to launch a new large-scale ground war.

In 2013 public protest and opposition among Republicans and Democrats in Congress prevented a major new U.S. war against the government of Syria. This reflected what the late historian Marilyn Young called "a little break in the wall of war."[25] Some might object that the years of deadly violence that have followed in Syria's civil war are a sign that the Obama administration should have gone to war against the Bashar al-Asad government. This objection rests on an assumption that invading Syria would have made the situation better rather than making the situation worse. Attacking Syria could have resulted in a far broader war, potentially involving Russia, Iran, and other Gulf states. The experience of the U.S. war in Iraq, alone, should be a reminder of war's potential to generate violence and forces beyond the control and comprehension of any nation, no matter how militarily powerful some might believe it to be. The better questions about Syria are whether the Obama administration could have done more diplomatically to bring about an end to the war and whether U.S. leaders are doing enough now. The idea that a nation either "does something" and fights or "does nothing" is a false binary revolving around unsupported mythologies about the efficacy of war and the idea that there are military solutions to problems that actually can't be solved with bombs and bullets.

Thankfully, in 2019 more breaks in the wall of war appeared when both houses of Congress voted to end U.S. support for the Saudi-led war in Yemen and to bar arms sales to Saudi Arabia and its ally in the Yemen war, the United Arab Emirates. While President Trump vetoed both laws, the bipartisan votes were more evidence that members of Congress are increasingly trying to reclaim war-making powers from the executive branch. In early 2020, the House and Senate passed bills requiring the president to get congressional authorization before initiating any further military attacks on Iran. This followed Trump's assassination of Iranian Maj. Gen. Qassim Suleimani, which brought the two countries close to a war whose damage could have far eclipsed that of the U.S. wars in Afghanistan and Iraq combined. Trump again vetoed the legislation.

The opposition to war with Iran also followed the *Washington Post*'s 2019 publication of the "Afghanistan Papers"; the trove of government documents showed that, since the beginning of the war in Afghanistan in 2001, "senior U.S. officials failed to tell the truth about the war in Afghanistan . . . making rosy pronouncements [about progress] they knew to be false and hiding unmistakable evidence the war had become unwinnable." In some cases, the *Post* found "explicit and sustained efforts by the U.S. government to deliberately mislead the public."[26]

One Republican senator, Utah's Mike Lee, who joined Democrats in voting to require congressional authorization before there could be any further attacks on Iran, explained his vote: "We need congressional authorization. We've been lied to by the Pentagon for years regarding a war that has gone on two decades. That's long enough. . . . We don't want any more wars without the people's elected representatives being able to debate."[27] At least seven major Democratic presidential candidates signed a pledge to "end the forever wars."[28]

Growing bipartisan antiwar sentiment shows how opposition to U.S. war making and empire has spread across the political spectrum. A group of anti-interventionist Republicans has slowly begun to find common ground with antiwar activists on the Left, even if their motivations and broader politics differ considerably. Strange bedfellows Charles Koch and George Soros have helped launch a major new transpartisan foreign policy–focused think tank, the Quincy Institute. Pointing to a "once-in-a-generation opportunity to bring together like-minded progressives and conservatives," the institute says it "will lay the foundation for a new foreign policy" that moves "away from endless war and toward vigorous diplomacy in the pursuit of international peace."[29] Recent public-opinion polls show that a wide bipartisan majority supports such approaches: with a rare degree of agreement among Republicans, Democrats, and independents, 86 percent of U.S. respondents supported the use of the military only as a last resort.[30]

Clearly, the U.S. military has found increasingly surreptitious ways to fight and deploy its forces around the planet. But the fact that a significant majority of the U.S. public has turned against large-scale, publicly declared warfare is encouraging. It's also encouraging that the military has had to spend more money and work harder to camouflage its activities and that it has had to go further "underground" with the help of lily-pad bases and other disguised operations. These are signs that a majority in the United States and beyond wants to avoid war and that this sentiment is taking hold as a political and social norm.

President Trump is another surprising sign of the growing questioning of the status quo of war and empire. While Trump has unabashedly embraced old-school imperialism, torture, and war crimes in a range of contexts (among other vile views), he tends to be like a stopped clock: twice a day he's right on time. It's encouraging that he has worked toward a Korean peace agreement, taken some steps toward diplomacy and the removal of U.S. troops from Afghanistan, and questioned the existence of NATO when its reason for being (the Soviet Union) hasn't existed for three decades. Of the tens of billions spent on bases abroad, Trump has been one of a growing number to ask, "What are we getting out of this?"[31]

Trump's track record in following through on these issues has been inconsistent at best. At the very least, his public articulation of once-heretical views has opened new room for questioning the foreign policy status quo—and for changing it. Simultaneously, Trump's articulation of views associated with nineteenth-century imperialism—including taking Iraq's oil, condoning U.S. war criminals, and torturing terrorist suspects and killing their family members—is both dangerous in legitimizing such ideas and helpful in revealing ongoing racist imperialism in the twenty-first century.[32]

✪

Those concerned and hopefully angered by the U.S. record of war must find ways to demand and force change. Failing to do so out of an assumption that nothing will change is the worst kind of self-fulfilling prophecy. Not imagining and advancing alternatives to the war system and to existing U.S. foreign policy is the surest way to guarantee the continuation of the status quo, the continuation of endless, infinite war.

Giving up empire, or *deimperializing* the United States, must be at the heart of change. How can people initiate a process to deimperialize the United States? Beginning to close bases abroad is a critical part of that process. Unlike closing domestic bases, which usually generates understandable opposition from locals fearful about losing jobs and economic activity, closing overseas installations should be relatively easy. After all, U.S. politicians have few constituents abroad to whom they need to be beholden. For locals abroad, closures would provide opportunities to transform bases into schools, housing, parks, museums, shopping centers, offices, and more; research reveals that most communities bounce back quickly from base closures and often end up with healthier economies postclosure.[33]

Congress should create a regular review process to assess the need to maintain every base overseas. The Pentagon should be required to scrutinize every base annually as well. Congress could create incentives for the military to carry out closures abroad by ensuring that a proportion of savings would remain in the budget of each military branch responsible for closures, while also allocating funds to assist the transition of individuals and communities affected by closures.

As important as extraterritorial bases have been to making war more likely, even the closure of all U.S. bases abroad wouldn't guarantee a reduction in war. The United States and other nations can wage war from domestic bases. While closing significant numbers of bases abroad is a critical step toward deimperializing the United States, changing the economic, political, and ideological structures supporting the war system is also fundamental. This means reducing the power of the Military Industrial Congressional Complex. The interlocking and mutually reinforcing nature of this structure of power makes it particularly difficult to challenge. There are structural changes in U.S. law and the U.S. political system that could reduce some of the power of the Complex, and military contractors in particular. Dramatically increasing civilian oversight over contracts and every aspect of the operations of the military agencies responsible for more than half of discretionary spending is one important step to crack down on tens of billions of dollars in annual waste, fraud, and legalized profiteering.

Most in the United States have little idea of the vast sums of money or the percentage of total taxpayer funds that go to military operations, including bases abroad. Doing more to educate people about this diversion—this theft—of the country's wealth is an important step to advancing a movement demanding the transfer of money from the Military Industrial Congressional Complex to address the daily insecurity experienced by most U.S. Americans in their health, employment, housing, and education. While many proposals exist, cutting half of the *total* $1.25 trillion annual military budget would still leave the United States with the largest military budget in the world—larger than the budgets of China, Russia, Iran, and North Korea combined.[34]

Buying off the military contractors that form the core of the Complex is another approach. Given the breadth and depth of contractors' power, providing incentives for them to convert their operations and move into other industries, such as civilian infrastructure and green energy, may be more likely to succeed than attempts to cut the contracts of firms such as Lockheed Martin, Raytheon, and KBR entirely. Stymied attempts to shut down the production of shockingly wasteful and ineffective multibillion-dollar weapons systems, such as the F-35 Joint Strike Fighter, show how difficult it is to take on the Military Industrial Congressional Complex.[35]

U.S. citizens and others need to think even more boldly about broader structural changes necessary to deimperialize the United States and end the system of permanent war. For example, we should consider using anti-trust laws to break up or nationalize the major weapons manufacturers. This could help eliminate or reduce the conflict of interest that makes them literally invested in perpetuating war. The Pentagon likewise has become so powerful that it is now truly a fourth branch of government, such is its power to shape U.S. foreign policy over the desires of the president and Congress and its domination of more than half of the federal discretionary budget (which effectively shapes domestic policy too).[36] While there are many legislative changes that could help return power to Congress in particular, a constitutional amendment may be required to shift the balance of power. A paired constitutional amendment could return the authority to wage war to Congress, given how a long line of presidents has effectively seized this extraconstitutional power for the executive.

An initial step toward such radically needed transformation would be to *deprivatize* many contracted military services, which could save billions and improve outcomes dramatically (in contrast to proponents' claims, privatization has squandered massive sums in recent decades).[37] One of many possible legislative strategies to reduce the military's hold on the national budget would be to bar the Pentagon and the military branches from lobbying Congress for taxpayer funds.

Giving people in the U.S. colonies full constitutionally guaranteed citizenship rights, including the presidential vote and full democratic representation in Congress as well as the right to determine their political futures in accordance with international law, should not be a radical proposal. It's but one important step in a parallel process to *decolonize* the United States. This would require the U.S. government to fulfill indigenous peoples' land and treaty rights and take real steps to repair the damage inflicted since U.S. independence.

Making these kinds of structural changes would require a Reconstruction-like effort similar to the process after the U.S. Civil War. The horror of the death, the destruction, and the theft caused by the U.S. record of war should make it obvious that small changes alone will not suffice.

Without major structural transformation, the U.S. Empire and its Military Industrial Congressional Complex are likely to crumble only as the result of an epochal economic crisis or another calamity starving the system of the money that fuels it. After World War II, elites in Britain and France struggled futilely to maintain their empires. This led to terrible wars, whose effects are still being felt, and forced imperial decline.

The United States may be on a similar path, accelerated by the past two decades of disastrous war and by what looks to be the epochal economic crisis of COVID-19. There is still time for people in the United States and allies abroad to demand an end to endless wars and the closure of bases abroad, reclaiming money from the Military Industrial Congressional Complex and ending the imperial mission. Alternatively the United States will likely follow the British-French path, forced to give up bases and empire from a position of desperation. For all of China's flaws and long record of human rights violations, the Chinese government last fought a war outside its borders in 1979, for one month in Vietnam (in 1988 the two countries' militaries had a brief clash in the South China Sea). While there are now around eight hundred U.S. bases in some eighty-five countries and territories, the Chinese military has one foreign base, in Djibouti. There are five if we count reefs and shoals turned into bases in parts of the South China Sea where national sovereignty is disputed. Since 1979, rather than building bases abroad and fighting unnecessary wars, the Chinese government has focused its wealth and energies on building more wealth, infrastructure, and employment for its people.[38]

✪

President Eisenhower's warning about the Military Industrial Congressional Complex applies equally to this system of endless war and empire. It has militarized "the very structure of our society" (and our world) with "economic, political, even spiritual" effects "in every city, every statehouse, every office of the federal government" (and far beyond). As a result of what Eisenhower rightly called the "disastrous rise of misplaced power," endless war, empire, and the Military Industrial Congressional Complex have shredded many of our "democratic processes." They have shredded "our liberties" that grew in the United States and worldwide after World War II, thanks to decolonization struggles and other global social movements that demanded equality, justice, democracy, peace, and the extension of liberties to those denied them for far too long.[39]

Returning to the visions of these movements offers a foundation for a fundamentally new vision for U.S. foreign policy and for U.S. engagement in the world. In keeping with the best traditions in U.S. history, this would be a democratic vision embracing the equality and equal rights of all human beings. It should be obvious, but needs saying, that imperialism and war are antidemocratic. As an antidemocratic ideology and form of rule based on the fraudulent idea that some humans are superior to others, imperialism—like war—must be rejected in favor of a renewed commitment to ensuring universal democratic rights for all. "A nation that continues year after year to spend more money on military defense than on programs of social uplift is approaching spiritual death," Dr. Martin Luther King Jr. said in 1967, a year to the day before his assassination.[40]

Little has changed since 1967, when King rightly (if painfully for some of us) declared his own government "the greatest purveyor of violence in the world." So little has changed that I suspect King would rephrase his speech at New York's Riverside Church only slightly, replacing the word *communism*—the bogeyman of the day—with *terrorism:* today's bogeyman. King would thus urge us to undertake "a positive thrust for democracy, realizing that our greatest defense against *terrorism* is to take offensive action on behalf of justice. We must with positive action seek to remove those conditions of poverty, insecurity, and injustice, which are the fertile soil in which the seed of *terrorism* grows and develops." As King said simply, "war is not the answer."[41]

King pointed trenchantly to the "giant triplets of racism, extreme materialism, and militarism."[42] To this day they connect war and imperialism waged abroad with the war and imperialism waged at home against people of color, the poor, and other vulnerable, stigmatized peoples. Building justice abroad must be mirrored by building justice at home.

To do so, I follow King and others in believing that U.S. Americans need to reckon honestly with our history of war and with the tremendous suffering our country has caused. Beyond reckoning we must repair some of the damage. Here Germans provide a model, for reckoning with their history of war and genocide and for trying, however imperfectly, to repair some of the damage and ensure that such crimes cannot be repeated. The payment of billions in reparations as well as public education and memorialization programs have been critical to this work—so too have individual, community, and national efforts to build reconciliation with Nazi victims. Reckoning with the past and offering some measure of repair also requires exposing and documenting past crimes. Countries such as Argentina, South Africa, Guatemala, and Rwanda provide complicated, imperfect but useful models in the form of truth and reconciliation commissions, public hearings and investigations, and war-crimes trials.

There has been no such reckoning here. Without a reckoning with our history of war and its effects, we will likely continue to lurch from one war to the next, with war begetting more war. I hope this book helps contribute to such a reckoning. I hope this book provides some encouragement and ideas to those who would act on the basis of our knowledge of the past—to end wars funded with U.S. taxpayers' money and to help repair and heal some of the damage that U.S. wars have inflicted on victims from all nations, including victims in the United States.

Equal enjoyment of democratic rights globally. Justice for all. Global equity. Reckoning with past wars and violence. The pursuit of healing. Surely these are better foundations for the foreign policy of the United States and for engaging with other human beings in the world than a foreign policy and an entire society revolving around a state of permanent war?

As challenging as attaining these goals may be, we must try, or else we continue down a path of endless war that has long sowed destruction. "Perfectionists [often] hold that anything less than total victory is failure, a premise that makes it easy to give up at the start or to disparage the victories that are possible," Rebecca Solnit has written. "We cannot eliminate all devastation for all time, but we can reduce it, outlaw it, undermine its source and foundation: these are victories."[43]

For those who find such sentiments and perhaps all my suggestions naive or unrealistic, retired Army officer and historian Andrew Bacevich rightly asks, "How is it then that *peace* has essentially vanished as a US policy objective?"[44] Given the violence my country has wreaked, given the millions of deaths that U.S. wars have caused in the Middle East alone in the past two decades, how can the central U.S. foreign policy objective be anything except real efforts to build peace through diplomacy and other nonmilitary forms of international engagement and cooperation? How can war still be a legitimate policy option for the United States? To state the obvious that needs stating, the United States must become a United States of Peace, not a United States of War.

For those who would say the status quo of permanent war is the only realistic option or that small reforms are the only realistic change possible, I would ask, realistic for whom?

GRATITUDE AND THANKS

I am profoundly grateful to everyone who helped make this book possible. Given the book's breadth, I could not have written it without the help and generosity of hundreds of people. Thank you especially to everyone who spoke with me about my research, who hosted me during my travels, and who helped arrange visits, tours, meetings, interviews, interpretation and translation, access to research materials, meals, lodging, transportation, and other critical assistance. There is no way to appropriately thank the hundreds of people and organizations that deserve thanks. I wish I could thank everyone by name, and apologize in advance to anyone I have accidentally overlooked.

First, I must thank the Chagossian people for making so much of my work and career possible. A special thanks goes to the Chagos Refugees Group, Chagos Committee (Seychelles), Chagos Football Association, Olivier Bancoult, Marilyne Bancoult, the Bancoult family, Sabrina Marie Jean, Ghislain Jean, and the Jean family. Thank you as well to others who have been tremendous mentors, colleagues, and friends since I began this work in 2001, including Shirley Lindenbaum, Michael Tigar, Jane Tigar, Ali Beydoun, UNROW clinic members, Richard Gifford, Robin Mardemootoo, Phil Harvey, Wojtek Sokolowski, Laura Jeffery, Dick Kwan Tat, and Simon Winchester.

Thank you to friends in many other parts of the world: In Manta, Ecuador, thank you, Alberto Chonillo and the widows and other family members of those who tragically died on the *Jorge IV*. I am still trying to share your story as widely as possible. In Germany thank you to Barbara Danowski, Maria Höhn, Elsa Rassbach,

Sandra Archer, Kilian Bluemlein, DFG-VK, and the Ramstein Air Base and Land-stuhl Regional Medical Center Public Affairs Offices. In Guåhan/Guam and the Northern Mariana Islands, I send deep thanks and appreciation to Julian Aguon, Michael Bevacqua, Leevin Camacho, Hope Cristobal Sr., Hope Cristobal Jr., Cara Flores-Mayes, LisaLinda Natividad, James Oelke, the Hofschneiders, University of Guam, Vivian Dames, and We are Guåhan. For my work in Cuba, thank you, Jana Lipman and everyone I met at Naval Station Guantanamo Bay and Joint Task Force GTMO. In Honduras, thanks especially to COFADEH, Dana Frank, Bertha Oliva, Camille, Oscar, Simón, and the Soto Cano Air Base Public Affairs Office.

In Italy, there are many, many people to thank, including Laura Bettini, Michael Blim, Cinzia Bottene, Manuel Falsarella, Lindsay Harris, the late Olol Jackson, Antonio Mazzeo, Marco Palma, Francesco Pavin, Pizzeria da Michele, Gordon Poole, Angelica Romano, Philip Rushton, Sonia Salvini, and Stephanie Westbrook, as well as many more in Vicenza, including Anna, Caterina, Delfino, Diletta, Emanuele, Fede, Grappa, Janis, Jimi, La Billo, Lorena, Marta, Martina, Massimo, Monica, Moran, Nicoletta, Rosella, Ska, Umberto, Assemblea Perma-nente We Want Sex, Presidio Permanente No Dal Molin, Gruppo Donne No Dal Molin, and U.S. Army Garrison Vicenza PAO. A special thanks goes to Enzo Ciscato, Emily Ciscato, Martina Copiello, Guido Lanaro, Francesca Marin, Giulia Rampon, Annetta Reams, Luca Rigon, Chiara Spadaro, Katherine Wilson and Salvatore Avallone, Laura Zanardi, and Pietro.

My work in Japan would not have been possible without the help of Kozue Akibayashi, Mitzi Uehara Carter, Eiichiro Ishiyama, Chie Miyagi, Satoko Nori-matsu, the late Masahide Ota, Michael and Gretchen Robbins, Sayo Saruta, Suzuyo Takazato, Miyume Tanji, Sunao Tobaru, Ginowan City Hall, Kadena Air Base and Camp Smedley Butler PAOs, and many more friends in Tokyo, Iwakuni, Fukuoka, Naha, Takae, and Henoko. Thank you all. For my work in South Korea, thank you, Christine Ahn, Youngsil Kang, YouKyoung Ko, Seungsook Moon, Yunae Park, Emily Wang, Durebang, and all the inspiring friends I met in Jeju and elsewhere during my travels.

I am deeply thankful for the careful reading and feedback that many people provided during my writing process. They include Mary Amato, Andrew Bace-vich, Medea Benjamin, Annie Claus, Roxanne Dunbar-Ortiz, Cynthia Enloe, John Feffer, Max Paul Friedman, Greg Grandin, Brooke Kroeger, Peter Kuznick, Catherine Lutz, Adrienne Pine, Rob Rosenthal, Michael Sherry, Elly Truitt, Col. Lawrence Wilkerson, participants in the American University Ethnographies of Empire Research Cluster, and 2019–20 coordinators Marcelo Bohrt and Anthony Fontes. Special thanks go to Fred Appel, Jennifer Hammer, and Tom Engelhardt for supporting and encouraging my writing.

Thank you to many other wonderful colleagues and friends who have supported me in so many ways and who make the colleagues/friends distinction irrelevant: Phyllis Bennis, Catherine Besteman, Sarah Block, Michael Cernea, Peter Certo,

Paul Thomas Chamberlin, Nancy Chen, Lindsey Collen, Ted Conover, Abby Conrad, the Costs of War Project, Neta Crawford, Kelvin Crow, CUNY Graduate Center, Dave Davis, Mike Davitt, Ray DuBois, Daniel Else, Paul Farmer, Bruce Gagnon, Joseph Gerson, Harjant Gill, Lesley Gill, Roberto González, Zoltan Grossman, Hugh Gusterson, Matt Gutmann, Nell Haynes, Gretchen Heefner, Andrew Hoehn, Amy Holmes, Gustaaf Houtman, Sen. Kay Bailey Hutchison, Jean Jackson, Raed Jarrar, Barbara Rose Johnston, Kyle Kajihiro, Jennifer Kavanagh, Dylan Kerrigan, Elizabeth Kerrigan, Ragini Kistnasamy, Lalit de Klas, Louise Lennihan, Chuck Lewis, John Lindsay-Poland, Catherine Lutz, Julie Maldonado, Kate McCaffrey, Carole McGranahan, Devin Molina, Leith Mullings, Network of Concerned Anthropologists, Overseas Base Realignment and Closure Coalition, Miriam Pemberton, Lynne Perri, Stacie Pettyjohn, John Pike, Walter Pincus, David Price, Stephen Rossetti, Stephanie Savell, School of Advanced Research and the Biosecurity and Vulnerability Conference, Lesley Sharp, Service Women's Action Network, Rodolfo Tello Abanto, Temple University's U.S. Bases and the Construction of Hegemony symposium, Matt Thomann, Maureen Tong, Micah Trapp, Kalfani Turé, Nick Turse, John Willoughby, Emira Woods, Andrew Yeo, and Wilbert van der Zeijden.

Thank you to all my colleagues in American University's Department of Anthropology—undergraduates, graduates, faculty, staff—for creating such a supportive and enriching community. I wish I could name everyone here, but please know I feel grateful to everyone. Special thanks go to terrific research assistants (and friends): Mysara Abu-Hashem, Andrea Elganzoury, Francesca Emanuele, Aaron Howe, Laura Jung, Siobhán McGuirk, and Michel Tinguiri. Thanks also for the extremely helpful feedback from classes including Craft of Anthropology; the Public Anthropology Clinic; the Public Anthropology Seminar; Refugees, War, and Human Rights; the Violence Seminar; and Writing Ethnography for Social Change. Among many others, thank you, Candelaria, Hope Bastian, Geoff Burkhart, Ori Burton, Juana Castro Bonilla, Annie Claus, Audrey Cooper, Robert Craycraft, Joe Dent, Stacy Fagan, Kaelyn Forde, Sean Furmage, Nell Gabiam, Allie Gardner, Beth Geglia, Jeanne Hanna, Pawan Haulkory, Hoching Jiang, Katalina Khoury, Ben King, Dolores Koenig, Chap Kusimba, Sibel Kusimba, Bill Leap, Manissa Maharawal, Bryan McNeil, Hannah Opperman, Joowon Park, Chris Partridge, Becca Peixotto, Michael Polson, Marta Portillo, Sabiyha Prince, Kareem Rabie, Caroline Robertson, Joeva Rock, Alyssa Röhricht, Dan Sayers, Gretchen Schafft, Josh Schea, Nina Shapiro-Perl, Ed Smith, Emily Steinmetz, Keara Sullivan, Sue Taylor, Susanne Unger, John Villecco, Arvenita Washington-Cherry, Rachel Watkins, Julie Wesp, Brett Williams, Jeanie Wogaman, Buck Woodard, and our great work-study students, including Kayleigh Thompson, Abby Nix, and Jacob Sobel, who helped with this book.

A special, belated thanks goes to Adrienne Pine for getting me teargassed, for graciously putting up with my not crediting you with getting me teargassed, and for being a dear friend always.

Elsewhere at American University, thank you to so many who have been incredibly supportive and helpful, including Dean Peter Starr, Deputy Provost Mary Clark, Provost Dan Myers, former provost Scott Bass, Kelli South, and Mimi Fitig. Thanks also go to other wonderful friends and colleagues, including Akbar Ahmed, Fanta Aw, Kim Blankenship, Lauren Carruth, Erin Collins, DAC, Farhang Erfani, Eileen Findlay, Scott Freeman, Max Paul Friedman, Jolynn Gardner, Nikhat Ghouse, Garrett Graddy-Lovelace, IRB, Despina Kakoudaki, Carl LeVan, Chuck Lewis, Jordan Maidman, Elissa Margolin, Celine Marie-Pascale, Juliana Martinez, Jordanna Matlon, Mieke Meurs, Lynne Perri, Malini Ranganathan, Gwendolyn Reece, Rachel Sullivan Robinson, Theresa Runstedtler, Catherine Schaeff, Cathy Schneider, Courtney Schrader, Susan Shepler, U. J. Sofia, Lauren Tabbara, Katharina Vester, Salvador Vidal-Ortiz, Núria Vilanova and Quim Tres and FCB, Linda Voris, Brenda Werth, Barbara Wien, Lily Wong, Gay Young, and Matt Zembrzuski.

There are many other beloved friends and family who have supported, sustained, and assisted me through this long process. Thank you for all your patience with me and for helping in so many ways, from consulting on the smallest details of the book to sharing all the love that kept me going. Although I will surely forget some (sorry!), they include Mom, Dad, Joanne, Adam, Ana, Rachel, Max, Megan, Nolan, Colby, Brian, Todd, Roberto Abadie, Mireille Abelin, Sarah Kowal Alden, Hillary Angelo, Sunny Banwer and Emma Hunter and Annie and Rob and Sam Rosenthal, Barr Barkeem and Lori Lovell, Alisha Berry, Keane Bhatt, the Blumenthals, Leah Bolger, Lisa Braun, Sam Buckingham, Jean Campbell, Assis Castellanos and Lilia, Natalie Chwalisz, Patricia Cogley, Barra Cohen, Lindsay Davison and Sarah Rigney and Rowan and Ruthie, Le Caprice DC, Ellen and Ed and Jeremy and Jonathan and Campa Singer-Vine, the Dworkins, Andrew and Eliza Epstein, Colin Findlay, Jesse Franzblau, Eric Frater, Hilary Galland, the Gan, Susie Goldman, the Goobs, Sam Goodstein and Trisha Miller and Theo, Alex Goren, the Gottfrieds, Aunt Joan Greenbaum, Catherine Griffin and Ryan Benson, Josep Guardiola, Mamadou Gueye, Cory Hartquist, Claire and Dan and Sue and Rudy and Messi Hirsch, Joanne Hirsch and A. T. Stephens, Kate Horner, Amanda Huron, Paulette Hurwitz, the Isaacsons, Andrea Johnson, the Kanters, Lakshmi Kanter, David Keplinger, Josh Kletzkin, Lynn and Morris and David Kletzkin and Jessica Ferro, the Krupskys, Radha Kuppalli, Maia Kutchakaya, Peter and Simki Kuznick, Nicole Laborde, Brenna Lavelle, Randall Lavelle, Steve Lavelle, Willow Lawson and Dan and Max and Sonja Aibel, Kanhong Lin, Rae Linefsky, Malcolm Logan, the Lutzkers, Carola Mandelbaum and Dahn Warner and Olivia and Amalia, Nancy Markowitz, Michelle Marzulo, Jaime Masick, Khyrell and Kiara and Shaun McNeil, Lionel Andrés Messi Cuccittini, Derek and Shelly Musgrove, Meyer Treatment Center friends, Sarah Newman, Alix Olson and Zinn and Gray, Sascha Paladino and Erin Torneo and Cole and Gianluca and Liam, Roee Raz, Alison and Matt Rodgers and Vivian and Veronica and Eleanor,

D. J. Rosenthal, Cliff Rosky, Eric Ruben, Nancy Schoenfeld and Lee Weiner, Mara Silver and Frank Scaduto and Liv and Willa, Caroline Simmonds and Jon Cook and Gabriel, Mitzi Sinnott, Anna Stein, Mary Stephens, Shawn Greenbaum and Antonia Stout and Adelaide and Marlowe, Cathy Sulzberger and Joe Perpich, Maria Tonguino, Matthew Tripp, Elly Truitt and Tick Ahearn, Mauricio Tscherny, Dylan Turner, Ellis Turner, Hugh and Lydia Vine, Lee Ving, the Vises, Eirene Visvardi, Maria Amelia Viteri, Deb Yurow, Yan Zheng and Rae Rae, and Ari Zoe.

At University of California Press, thank you to everyone who made the production of this book possible. Thank you especially to Naomi Schneider, Alex Dahne, Summer Farah, Kate Hoffman, Benjy Malings, and Rob Borofsky for many months of support, guidance, and help. Thanks go to Lia Tjandra for your beautiful cover design and to Joan Shapiro for producing the index. Thank you to Susan Silver, for your excellent copyediting, and to Juliana Froggatt, for fine-grained proofreading, which caught so many of my errors and improved the book significantly. Thanks, too, for generously allowing some nonstandardized style choices in this part of the book and for your support and solidarity beyond the page.

Special thanks and appreciation go to Kelly Martin, the book's cartographer. You have again produced gorgeous maps that are an incredibly important part of this book and my work as a whole. Thank you for your endless patience and collaborative spirit throughout.

Thank you to American University and the College of Arts and Sciences for providing research funds and other support that helped me complete this book. I am grateful for a tremendously lucky (and productive) month spent at the Rockefeller Foundation's Bellagio Center. Thanks especially go to Pilar Palacio, Alice Luperto, and the entire Bellagio staff (from the kitchen to housekeeping to administration) and to the other friends in residence who enriched my writing and my life (Donald Byrd, Mary Coleman, Zhiyuan Guo, Saed Haddad, Santoshi Halder, Alice Hill, Ming Hu, Kati Marton, Sabrina McCormick, Diego Osorno, Søren Pors, Aparna Rao, and Kathleen Wynne). Thank you to the Stewart R. Mott Foundation's Fund for Constitutional Government for supporting research trips in 2011–12. Thanks also to the lovely people at the Baker Lane and Michigan Avenue writers' retreats for putting up with me on more than on occasion.

Love and special memories go to some of the many who are no longer with us, including Rita Elysée Bancoult, Doere Bernhard, Peggy Madden Davitt, Erwin Eichengrün, Joan Gero, Bob Greenbaum, Alan Hirsch, Vera Isenberg, Marty Pinson, Neil Smith, Erwin Stiefel, Tea Stiefel, Lisette Aurélie Talate, Neal Tonken, Gloria Vine, and Ted Vine.

APPENDIX

U.S. WARS, COMBAT, AND OTHER COMBAT ACTIONS ABROAD

This list documents U.S. wars (in italics), combat that cannot be characterized as war, and other actions involving combat forces beyond U.S. borders from 1776 to 2020. This list does not necessarily capture every conflict between U.S. forces and Native American peoples during near-continuous warfare between 1776 and 1890. The dates for conflicts are often debated. The key sources I've used are Barbara Salazar Torreon and Sofia Plagakis, *Instances of Use of United States Armed Forces Abroad, 1798-2018* (Washington, DC: Congressional Research Service, 2018); Roxanne Dunbar-Ortiz, *An Indigenous Peoples' History of the United States* (Boston: Beacon, 2014); and John Grenier, *The First Way of War: American War Making on the Frontier, 1607-1814* (Cambridge: Cambridge University Press, 2005). See also page 348, note 7.

Year(s)	Country/Nation/People
1774-1783	*Shawnee, Delaware*
1776	*Cherokee*
1777-1781	*Iroquois Confederacy (Haudenosaunee)*
1780-1794	*Chickamauga*
1790-1795	*Miami Confederacy*
1792-1793	*Muskogee (Creek)*
1798-1801	*France (undeclared war)*

1801–1805	*Tripoli*
1806	Mexico
1806–1810	Spanish, French privateers
1810	*Spanish West Florida*
1810–1813	*Shawnee Confederacy*
1812	Spanish Florida
1812–1815	*Canada (War of 1812 with Great Britain)*
1812–1815	*Dakota Sioux*
1812–1815	*Iroquois Confederacy (Haudenosaunee)*
1813	*Spanish West Florida*
1813–1814	Marquesas Islands
1813–1814	*Muskogee (Creek) Confederacy*
1814	*Spanish Florida*
1814–1825	Pirates
1815	Algiers
1815	Tripoli
1816	*Spanish Florida*
1817	Spanish Florida
1817–1819	*Seminole*
1818	Oregon (Russia, Spain)
1820–1861	African Slave Trade Patrol
1822–1825	Cuba (Spain)
1824	Puerto Rico (Spain)
1827	Greece
1831–1832	Falkland Islands
1832	*Sauk*
1832	Sumatra
1833	Argentina
1835–1836	Peru
1835–1842	*Seminole*
1836	Mexico
1836–1837	*Muskogee (Creek)*
1838–1839	Sumatra
1840	Fiji Islands

1841	Samoa
1841	Tabiteuea
1842	Mexico
1843	China
1844	Mexico
1846-1848	*Mexico*
1847-1850	*Cayuse*
1849	Turkey
1850-1886	*Apache*
1851	Johanna Island
1851	Turkey
1852-1853	Argentina
1853-1854	Japan
1853-1854	Nicaragua
1853-1854	Ryukyu, Ogasawara islands
1854-1856	China
1855	Fiji Islands
1855	Uruguay
1855-1856	*Rogue River Indigenous Peoples*
1855-1856	*Yakima, Walla Walla, Cayuse*
1855-1858	*Seminole*
1856	Panama (Colombia)
1856-1857	*Cheyenne*
1857	Nicaragua
1858	*Coeur d'Alene Alliance*
1858	Fiji Islands
1858	Uruguay
1858-1859	Turkey
1859	China
1859	Mexico
1859	Paraguay
1860	Angola
1860	Colombia
1862	*Sioux*

1863–1864	Japan
1864	Cheyenne
1865	Panama (Colombia)
1866	China
1866	Mexico
1866–1868	*Lakota Sioux, Northern Cheyenne, Northern Arapaho*
1867	Formosa (Taiwan)
1867	Nicaragua
1867–1875	*Comanche*
1868	Colombia
1868	Japan
1868	Uruguay
1870	Hawai'i
1870	Mexico
1871	Korea
1872–1873	*Modoc*
1873	Colombia (Panama)
1873–1896	Mexico
1874	Hawai'i
1874–1875	*Comanche, Apache, Arapaho, Cheyenne, Kiowa*
1876–1877	*Sioux*
1877	*Nez Perce*
1878	*Bannock (Bana'kwut)*
1878–1879	*Cheyenne*
1879–1880	*Utes*
1882	Egypt
1885	Panama (Colombia)
1888	Haiti
1888	Korea
1888–1889	Samoa
1889	Hawai'i
1890	Argentina
1890	*Lakota Sioux*

1891	Bering Strait
1891	Chile
1891	Haiti
1893	*Hawai'i*
1894	Brazil
1894	Nicaragua
1894–1895	China
1894–1896	Korea
1895	Panama (Colombia)
1896	Nicaragua
1898	*Cuba (Spain)*
1898	Nicaragua
1898	*Philippines (Spain)*
1898	*Puerto Rico (Spain)*
1898–1899	China
1899	Nicaragua
1899	Samoa
1899–1913	*Philippines*
1900	*China*
1901–1902	Colombia
1903	Dominican Republic
1903	Honduras
1903	Syria
1903–1904	Abyssinia (Ethiopia)
1903–1914	Panama
1904	Dominican Republic
1904	Tangier
1904–1905	Korea
1906–1909	Cuba
1907	Honduras
1909–1910	Nicaragua
1911–1912	Honduras
1911–1941	China

1912	Cuba
1912	Turkey
1912–1933	Nicaragua
1914	Dominican Republic
1914	Haiti
1914–1919	*Mexico*
1915–1934	Haiti
1916–1924	Dominican Republic
1917–1918	*World War I (Europe)*
1917–1922	Cuba
1918–1920	*Russia*
1918–1921	Panama
1919	Dalmatia
1919	Turkey
1919–1920	Honduras
1920	Guatemala
1921	Costa Rica, Panama
1922	Turkey
1924–1925	Honduras
1925	Panama
1932	El Salvador
1941–1945	*World War II (Europe, North Africa, Asia/Pacific)*
1946	Trieste
1947–1949	*Greece*
1948–1949	Berlin, Germany
1950	Formosa (Taiwan)
1950–1953	*Korea*
1953–1954	Formosa (Taiwan)
1955–1975	*Vietnam*
1956	Egypt
1958	Lebanon
1962	Cuba
1962	Thailand

1962–1975	*Laos*
1964	Congo (Zaire)
1965	*Dominican Republic*
1965–1973	*Cambodia*
1967	Congo (Zaire)
1976	Korea
1978	Congo (Zaire)
1980	Iran
1981	El Salvador
1981	Libya
1981–1989	*Nicaragua*
1982–1983	Egypt
1982–1983	Lebanon
1983	Chad
1983	*Grenada*
1986	Bolivia
1986	Libya
1987–1988	Iran
1988	Panama
1989	Bolivia
1989	Colombia
1989	Libya
1989	Peru
1989	Philippines
1989–1990	*Panama*
1990	Saudi Arabia
1991	Congo (Zaire)
1991–1992	*Kuwait*
1991–1993	*Iraq*
1992–1994	Somalia
1993–1994	Macedonia
1993–1996	Haiti
1993–2005	*Bosnia*

1995	*Serbia*
1996	Liberia
1996	Rwanda
1997–2003	Iraq
1998	Afghanistan
1998	Sudan
1999–2000	*Kosovo*
1999–2000	*Montenegro*
1999–2000	*Serbia*
2000	Yemen
2000–2002	East Timor
2000–2016	Colombia
2001–	*Afghanistan*
2001–	*Pakistan*
2001–	*Somalia*
2002–2015	*Philippines*
2002–	*Yemen*
2003–2011	*Iraq*
2004	Haiti
c. 2004–	Kenya
2011	Democratic Republic of the Congo
2011–2017	Uganda
2011–	*Libya*
c. 2012–	Central African Republic
c. 2012–	Mali
c. 2013–2016	South Sudan
c. 2013–	Burkina Faso
c. 2013–	Chad
c. 2013–	Mauritania
c. 2013–	Niger
c. 2013–	Nigeria
2014	Democratic Republic of the Congo
2014–	*Iraq*

2014–	*Syria*
2015	Democratic Republic of the Congo
c. 2015–	Cameroon
2016	Democratic Republic of the Congo
2017–	*Saudi Arabia*
c. 2017	Tunisia
2019–	Philippines

NOTES

PREFACE

1. Noweasels, "IGTNT: Remember Them," *Daily Kos,* June 27, 2010, www
.dailykos.com/story/2010/06/27/879698/-IGTNT-Remember-them#. Details
about Madden and his family come from interviews and phone conversations
with Peggy Madden Davitt, Mike Davitt, and other family and friends of Russell
Madden, Newport, KY, from 2012 to 2015.

2. Dan Blottenberger, "Soldier Killed in Afghanistan Remembered at Schwein-
furt Ceremony," *Stars and Stripes,* June 30, 2010, www.stripes.com/news
/europe/germany/soldier-killed-in-afghanistan-remembered-at-schweinfurt
-ceremony-1.109317; Scott Wartman, "Bellevue Buries a Fallen Son," *Kentucky
Enquirer,* July 9, 2010, A1; "Remembering Russell Madden," Facebook, accessed
February 18, 2020, www.facebook.com/pages/Remembering-Russell-Madden
/124071937634665?ref=search.

3. These details come from Russell Madden's official U.S. Army autopsy
report.

4. The countries are Afghanistan, Pakistan, the Philippines, Somalia, Yemen,
Iraq, Libya, Uganda, South Sudan, Burkina Faso, Chad, Niger, the Central African Republic, Syria, Kenya, Cameroon, Mali, Mauritania, Nigeria, the Democratic Republic of the Congo, Saudi Arabia, and Tunisia. Stephanie Savell and
5W Infographics, "This Map Shows Where in the World the U.S. Military
Is Combatting Terrorism," *Smithsonian Magazine,* January 2019, www

.smithsonianmag.com/history/map-shows-places-world-where-us-military-operates
-180970997/.

5. Nick Turse, "The U.S. Military Is Winning. No, Really, It Is!," TomDispatch, September 4, 2018, www.tomdispatch.com/post/176463/tomgram%3A_nick _turse%2C_victory_in_our_time; Andrew J. Bacevich, "Prisoners of War: Bob Woodward and All the President's Men (2010 Edition)," TomDispatch, September 26, 2010, www.tomdispatch.com/post/175300/tomgram%3A_andrew _bacevich,_the_washington_gossip_machine___/.

6. Aspen Institute, "Central Command: At the Center of the Action," Aspen Security Forum 2016, July 28, 2016, https://aspensecurityforum.org/wp -content/uploads/2016/07/central-command-at-the-center-of-the-action.pdf.

7. Barbara Salazar Torreon and Sofia Plagakis, *Instances of Use of United States Armed Forces Abroad, 1798–2018* (Washington, DC: Congressional Research Service, 2018). My list corrects for omissions, including wars with Native American nations, warfare in Canada in 1812–14, some Latin American invasions, recent combat in Africa, and the Greek civil war, when US officials were arming and directing the operations of Greek forces. I exclude evacuations, embassy deployments, humanitarian activities not involving combat, and deployments supporting military operations in third countries. The years without a war or invasion are 1796, 1797, 1897, 1935–40, 1977, and 1979. I date the U.S. war in Vietnam to the withdrawal of French military forces in 1955; without this early start date, one could count a total of fifteen years in U.S. history without war or military invasion by including 1957 and 1959–61. On the other hand, some would say there have been no years or almost no years without a military confrontation. Thank you to Monica Toft, Sidita Kushi, and Anna Ronnell for welcoming me at Tufts University's Center for Strategic Studies and for generously sharing and comparing data from your important Military Intervention Project.

8. Nikhil Pal Singh, *Race and America's Long War* (Oakland: University of California Press, 2017), 28.

9. Peter Carlson, "Raiding the Icebox: Behind Its Warm Front, the United States Made Cold Calculations to Subdue Canada," *Washington Post*, December 30, 2005, C1.

10. "American War and Military Operations Casualties: Lists and Statistics," Congressional Research Service, September 24, 2019, 1–3, https://fas.org/sgp /crs/natsec/RL32492.pdf; "Revolutionary War Facts," American Revolutionary War, 1775 to 1783, accessed February 16, 2020, https://revolutionarywar.us /facts/. For a list of sources, see Matthew White, "Statistics of Wars, Oppressions and Atrocities of the Eighteenth Century (the 1700s)," Necrometrics, accessed February 16, 2020, https://necrometrics.com/wars18c.htm. Although they are often left out of U.S. death statistics for World War II (typically listed at around 405,000), more than 1.1 million Filipino soldiers and civilians died in the war when the Philippines was still a U.S. colony. See Daniel Immerwahr,

How to Hide an Empire: A History of the Greater United States (New York: Farrar, Straus and Giroux, 2019), 212.

11. "US and Allied Killed and Wounded," Costs of War Project, Brown University, January 2020, https://watson.brown.edu/costsofwar/costs/human/military; Neta C. Crawford and Catherine Lutz, "Human Cost of Post-9/11 Wars: Direct War Deaths in Major War Zones, Afghanistan and Pakistan (October 2001–October 2019); Iraq (March 2003–October 2019); Syria (September 2014–October 2019); Yemen (October 2002–October 2019); and Other," Costs of War Project, Brown University, November 13, 2019, https://watson.brown.edu/costsofwar/files/cow/imce/papers/2019/Direct%20War%20Deaths%20COW%20Estimate%20November%2013%202019%20FINAL.pdf.

12. "US and Allied Killed."

13. Paul Thomas Chamberlin, *The Cold War's Killing Fields: Rethinking the Long Peace* (New York: Harper, 2018), 8; Will Dunham, "Deaths in Vietnam, Other Wars Undercounted: Study," Reuters, June 19, 2008, www.reuters.com/article/us-war-deaths/deaths-in-vietnam-other-wars-undercounted-study-idUSN1928547620080619.

14. Crawford and Lutz, "Human Cost of Post-9/11 Wars."

15. I expect to publish more precise estimates of deaths and displacement before this book is published. I will post links at https://davidvine.net. According to the Geneva Declaration's study of recent wars, there will be at least three and as many as fifteen "indirect deaths" for every direct combat death. This means the total human death toll in Afghanistan, Iraq, Syria, Pakistan, and Yemen could range between 3 million and 12.8 million. The study suggests that a ratio of four to one is a reasonable average estimate. See Geneva Declaration, *Global Burden of Armed Violence* (Geneva: Geneva Declaration Secretariat, 2008), 31–32.

16. Neta C. Crawford, "War-Related Death, Injury, and Displacement in Afghanistan and Pakistan, 2001–2014," Costs of War Project, Brown University, May 22, 2015, 7, https://watson.brown.edu/costsofwar/files/cow/imce/papers/2015/War%20Related%20Casualties%20Afghanistan%20and%20Pakistan%202001-2014%20FIN.pdf; Crawford, "Civilian Death and Injury in Iraq, 2003–2011," Costs of War Project, Brown University, September 2011, 10, https://watson.brown.edu/costsofwar/files/cow/imce/papers/2011/Civilian%20Death%20and%20Injury%20in%20Iraq%2C%202003-2011.pdf; Scott Harding and Kathryn Libal, "War and the Public Health Disaster in Iraq," in *The War Machine and Global Health: A Critical Medical Anthropological Examination of the Human Costs of Armed Conflict and the International Violence Industry*, ed. Merrill Singer and G. Derrick Hodge (Lanham, MD: AltaMira, 2010), 59–88; Office of the United Nations High Commissioner for Refugees, *Global Trends: Forced Displacement in 2018* (New York: United Nations, 2018).

17. The total includes money already spent on the wars and money that will be owed in the future, including veterans' health care costs and interest payments

on the borrowed money that has funded the wars. Neta C. Crawford, "United States Budgetary Costs and Obligations of the Post-9/11 Wars through FY2020: $6.4 Trillion Spent and Obligated," Costs of War Project, Brown University, November 13, 2019, https://watson.brown.edu/costsofwar/files/cow/imce/papers/2019 /US%20Budgetary%20Costs%20of%20Wars%20November%202019.pdf.

18. Trade-offs were calculated using fiscal year 2018 spending data. See "Trade-Offs: Your Money, Your Choices," National Priorities Project, last modified April 2019, www.nationalpriorities.org/interactive-data/trade-offs /?state=00&program=32.

A NOTE ON LANGUAGE AND TERMINOLOGY

1. Daniel Immerwahr, *How to Hide an Empire: A History of the Greater United States* (New York: Farrar, Straus and Giroux, 2019), 70.

2. Paul Thomas Chamberlin, *The Cold War's Killing Fields: Rethinking the Long Peace* (New York: Harper, 2018), 8, 2.

3. Roxanne Dunbar-Ortiz, *An Indigenous Peoples' History of the United States* (Boston: Beacon, 2014), 3–8.

INTRODUCTION

1. What one counts as a "base" is complicated. The estimate of 800 derives from the Pentagon's count of "base sites" in its annual *Base Structure Report.* See *Base Structure Report: Fiscal Year 2018 Baseline; A Summary of the Real Property Inventory Data* (Washington, DC: U.S. Department of Defense, 2018). There are obvious omissions and errors in the report, so I have created my own list, which I have updated and made public since 2014; see David Vine, "Lists of U.S. Military Bases Abroad, 1776–2020," American University Digital Research Archive, April 27, 2020, https://doi.org/10.17606/bbxc-4368; for a discussion, see notes introducing the list and David Vine, *Base Nation: How U.S. Military Bases Abroad Harm America and the World* (New York: Metropolitan Books, 2015), 342n5. The military has so many bases, it doesn't know the true total. It is telling—but not a good sign—that when a recent U.S. Army–funded study evaluated the effects of U.S. bases on conflict globally, the study relied on my list of bases rather than the Pentagon's. Angela O'Mahony et al., *U.S. Presence and Incidence of Conflict* (Santa Monica, CA: RAND Corporation, 2018).

The Pentagon's term *base site* means, in some cases, that an installation generally referred to as a single base, such as Aviano Air Base in Italy, actually consists of multiple base sites—in Aviano's case, at least eight. Counting each base site makes sense because sites with the same name are often in geographically disparate locations. Aviano's eight sites are in different parts of the town. Generally, too, each base site reflects distinct congressional appropriations of taxpayer funds. I include bases in U.S. colonies (territories) in my count of extraterritorial bases because these places lack full democratic incorporation into the United States. The Pentagon also considers these locations "overseas." (Like other scholars, I generally use the terms *extraterritorial bases, foreign bases, bases abroad,* and *overseas bases* synonymously.) Washington, DC, lacks full democratic rights, but, given that it is the nation's capital and is not overseas, I consider DC bases domestic. I explain in my list's introductory notes that while the list (and the maps in this book) conservatively indicate a current total of 752 base sites abroad, *around* 800 is a safe estimate given Pentagon reporting errors. There may be considerably more. For additional discussion, see the "Introduction and Notes" sheet in Vine, "Lists of U.S. Military Bases."

2. "Reversing the Roles, Revealing the Empire: Ecuador," *Nygaard Notes,* January 2, 2010, www.nygaardnotes.org/archive/issues/nn0445.html.

3. Editors, "U.S. Military Bases and Empire," *Monthly Review,* March 1, 2002, www.monthlyreview.org/0302editr.htm.

4. The U.S. Army study recommended interpreting its results "cautiously," emphasizing that its conclusions reflect "average associations." In addition to the previously noted finding, the study states that "on average, U.S. troop presence was associated with a higher likelihood of low-intensity interstate conflict (e.g., displays of military force and threats to use military force) but a lower likelihood of interstate war. . . . Nearby U.S. troop presence was associated with allies initiating fewer interstate disputes of all kinds. Conversely, a large nearby U.S. troop presence was associated with potential U.S. adversaries initiating more low- and high-intensity conflicts" (O'Mahony et al., *U.S. Presence and Incidence,* x–xi).

5. Andrew Bacevich, *Washington Rules: America's Path to Permanent War* (New York: Metropolitan Books, 2010), 22.

6. My deep thanks go to Catherine Lutz for her help in exploring these dynamics.

7. Quoted in *Standing Army,* directed by Thomas Fazi and Enrico Parenti (Rome: Effendemfilm and Takae Films, 2010).

8. For a discussion, including of the literature on deterrence, see Vine, *Base Nation,* chap. 17.

9. See, for example, George Washington, speech to officers at Newburgh, March 15, 1753, in *Rediscovering George Washington,* directed by Michael Pack (Chevy Chase, MD: Manifold Productions, 2002); and Daniel Webster Howe, *What Hath God Wrought: The Transformation of America, 1815–1848* (Oxford: Oxford University Press, 2007), 703. Paul Kramer rightly cautions against analyses that depend on isolated quotations from the Founding Fathers. See "How

Not to Write the History of U.S. Empire," *Diplomatic History* 42, no. 5 (2018): 919.

10. Paul Kennedy, quoted in Oliver Stone and Peter Kuznick, *The Untold History of the United States* (New York: Gallery Books, 2012), xv.

11. Carole McGranahan and John Collins, "Introduction: Ethnography and U.S. Empire," in *Ethnographies of Empire*, ed. Carole McGranahan and John Collins (Durham, NC: Duke University Press, 2018), 1.

12. Nikhil Pal Singh, *Race and America's Long War* (Oakland: University of California Press, 2017), 26.

13. G. John Ikenberry, "Illusions of Empire: Defining the New American Order," *Foreign Affairs* 83, no. 2 (2004): 144. For examples, see Michael Ignatieff, "American Empire: The Burden," *New York Times Magazine*, January 5, 2003, www.nytimes.com/2003/01/05/magazine/the-american-empire-the-burden.html; and Niall Ferguson, *Colossus: The Price of America's Empire* (New York: Penguin, 2004).

14. This comparison builds on David Vine, "War and Forced Migration in the Indian Ocean: The U.S. Military Base at Diego Garcia," *International Migration* 42, no. 3 (2004): 111–43.

15. See, for example, Neil Smith, *American Empire: Roosevelt's Geographer and the Prelude to Globalization* (Berkeley: University of California Press, 2003); Chalmers Johnson, *The Sorrows of Empire: Militarism, Secrecy, and the End of the Republic* (New York: Metropolitan, 2004); Chalmers Johnson, "America's Empire of Bases," TomDispatch, January 15, 2004, www.tomdispatch.com/post/1181/chalmers_johnson_on_garrisoning_the_planet; and Editors, "U.S. Military Bases."

16. Stephanie Savell and 5W Infographics, "This Map Shows Where in the World the U.S. Military Is Combatting Terrorism," *Smithsonian Magazine*, January 2019, www.smithsonianmag.com/history/map-shows-places-world-where-us-military-operates-180970997/. I add Pakistan, because of drone strikes, to the countries on Savell's map: Afghanistan, Iraq, Syria, Somalia, Libya, Yemen, Niger, Kenya, Central African Republic, Cameroon, Mali, Mauritania, Saudi Arabia, and Tunisia.

17. Greg Jaffe, "For Trump and His Generals, 'Victory' Has Different Meanings," *Washington Post*, April 5, 2018, www.washingtonpost.com/world/national-security/for-trump-and-his-generals-victory-has-different-meanings/2018/04/05/8d74eab0-381d-11e8-9c0a-85d477d9a226_story.html?utm_term=.f6371a958f99.

18. Mike Holmes, "2018 WEPTAC Conference Keynote Speaker: General Mike Holmes," Air Combat Command, February 13, 2018, www.acc.af.mil/News/Article-Display/Article/1440031/2018-weptac-conference-keynote-speaker-general-mike-holmes/.

19. See, for example, Walter LaFeber, *The New Empire: An Interpretation of American Expansion, 1860–1898* (Ithaca, NY: Cornell University Press, 1998), xvii.

20. Smith, *American Empire;* Johnson, *Sorrows of Empire;* Johnson, "America's Empire of Bases"; Editors, "U.S. Military Bases."

CHAPTER ONE. CONQUEST

1. BREMCOR is a joint venture between two large contractors, Burns and Roe and EMCOR. Jana K. Lipman, *Guantánamo: A Working-Class History between Empire and Revolution* (Berkeley: University of California Press, 2008), 228n90.

2. Larry Rohter, "Havana Journal: Remember the Maine? Cubans See an American Plot Continuing to This Day," *New York Times,* February 14, 1998, www.nytimes.com/1998/02/14/world/havana-journal-remember-maine-cubans-see-american-plot-continuing-this-day.html?pagewanted=all.

3. Quoted in Lipman, *Guantánamo,* 21. See also Stephen I. M. Schwab, *Guantánamo, USA: The Untold Story of America's Cuban Outpost* (Lawrence: University Press of Kansas, 2009), 36–60.

4. Theodore Roosevelt to John Hay, May 12, 1903, microfilm reel 416, Manuscript Division, Theodore Roosevelt Papers, Library of Congress, Washington, DC.

5. Lipman, *Guantánamo,* 23–24; Schwab, *Guantánamo, USA.*

6. Lipman, *Guantánamo,* 27–28.

7. Marion Emerson Murphy, *The History of Guantanamo Bay, 1494–1964,* U.S. Naval Station, Guantánamo Bay, Cuba, January 5, 1953, https://permanent.access.gpo.gov/lps17563/gtmohistorymurphy.htm, 2.

8. "Facts about the Transfer of Guantanamo Detainees," Human Rights First, October 10, 2018, www.humanrightsfirst.org/resource/facts-about-transfer-guantanamo-detainees.

9. See Mark L. Gillem, *America Town: Building the Outposts of Empire* (Minneapolis: University of Minnesota Press, 2007).

10. Amy Kaplan, "Where Is Guantánamo Bay?," *American Quarterly* 57, no. 3 (2005): 832.

11. Timothy Harrison, "The Lighthouse at Guantanamo Bay," *Lighthouse Digest,* March 2006, www.lighthousedigest.com/Digest/StoryPage.cfm?StoryKey=2426.

12. Dean C. Bartley, "Diary of Dean C. Bartley," n.d., Guantanamo Bay Lighthouse Museum, Guantanamo Bay Naval Base, Cuba.

13. Roxanne Dunbar-Ortiz, *An Indigenous Peoples' History of the United States* (Boston: Beacon, 2014), 4.

14. John J. Barry, *The Life of Christopher Columbus: From Authentic Spanish and Italian Documents* (Boston: Donohue, 1870), 292.

15. Washington Irving, *Life and Voyages of Christopher Columbus and the Voyages and Discoveries of the Companions of Columbus* (New York: Crowell, [1892?]), 136–46.

16. Frances Maclean, "The Lost Fort of Columbus," *Smithsonian*, January 2008, www.smithsonianmag.com/history/the-lost-fort-of-columbus-8026921/.

17. Translation mine. Jorge Ulloa Hung and Till F. Sonnemann, "Exploraciones arqueológicas en la Fortaleza de Santo Tomás de Jánico: Nuevos aportes a su comprensión histórica" [Archaeological explorations in the Fortress of Santo Tomás of Jánico: New contributions to its historical understanding], *Ciencia y Sociedad* 42, no. 3 (2017): 24.

18. Paul Farmer, *AIDS and Accusation: Haiti and the Geography of Blame* (Berkeley: University of California Press, 1992), 153.

19. Gillem, *America Town*, 3; Robert E. Harkavy, *Strategic Basing and the Great Powers, 1200–2000* (London: Routledge, 2007); Harkavy, *Bases Abroad: The Global Foreign Military Presence* (Oxford: Oxford University Press/SIPRI, 1989).

20. Gillem, *America Town*, 24.

21. Martin H. Brice, *Stronghold: A History of Military Architecture* (New York: Shocken Books, 1985), 13–45.

22. Brice, *Stronghold*, 48–55, 13–14.

23. "Pevensey Castle," English Heritage, accessed February 16, 2020, www.english-heritage.org.uk/visit/places/pevensey-castle/.

24. Brice, *Stronghold*, 48–55, 13–14.

25. Marc Morris, "Castles of the Conqueror," History Extra, August 11, 2012, www.historyextra.com/period/norman/castles-of-the-conqueror/.

26. Brice, *Stronghold*, 74–75.

27. Harkavy, *Strategic Basing*, 2.

28. Harkavy, *Strategic Basing*, 15.

29. Donald L. Berlin, "The 'Great Base Race' in the Indian Ocean Littoral: Conflict Prevention or Stimulation?," *Contemporary South Asia* 12, no. 3 (2004): 239.

30. Harkavy, *Strategic Basing*, 44–46, app. 2.

31. Kaplan, "Where Is Guantánamo Bay?," 831–58.

32. Harkavy, *Strategic Basing*, 15.

33. "Exploring 'the Buried Truth,'" Jamestown Rediscovery, accessed February 16, 2020, https://historicjamestowne.org/visit/plan-your-visit/fort-site/. For lists of bases cataloged by basing power, see Harkavy, *Strategic Basing*.

34. Carla M. Sinopoli, "Archaeology of Empires," *Annual Review of Anthropology* 23 (1994): 169.

35. Harkavy, *Strategic Basing*, 24.

36. Robert Scott, *Limuria: The Lesser Dependencies of Mauritius* (1961; repr., Westport, CT: Greenwood, 1976), 68.

37. Vytautas B. Bandjunis, *Diego Garcia: Creation of the Indian Ocean Base* (San Jose, CA: Writer's Showcase, 2001), 84.

38. Eric Wolf, *Europe and the People without History* (1982; repr., Berkeley: University of California Press, 1997), 5.

39. Harkavy, *Strategic Basing*, 2.

40. Robert B. Roberts, *Encyclopedia of Historic Forts: The Military, Pioneer, and Trading Posts of the United States* (New York: Macmillan, 1988), xii, 403-4; Harkavy, *Strategic Basing*, 1-3.

41. Benjamin Johnson, "Fort Independence," *Object of the Month*, Massachusetts Historical Society, June 2005, www.masshist.org/object-of-the-month /objects/fort-independence-2005-06-01.

CHAPTER TWO. OCCUPIED

1. Noel Rae, *People's War: Original Voices of the American Revolution* (Guilford, CT: Lyons, 2012), 71.

2. "Quartering Act (Amendment to Mutiny Act)," in *Founding Political Warfare Documents of the United States*, ed. J. Michael Waller (n.p.: Crossbow, 2009), 72.

3. Rae, *People's War*, 73.

4. Oliver Morton Dickerson, ed., *Boston under Military Rule, 1768-1769, as Revealed in a Journal of the Times* (Boston: Chapman and Grimes, 1936), 15, 42, 53.

5. Dickerson, *Boston under Military Rule*, 114. There is no way to verify this anonymous account.

6. Patrick Henry, "Debate in Virginia Ratifying Convention," June 16, 1788, *The Founders' Constitution*, vol. 5, amendment 3, doc. 8, University of Chicago Press, http://press-pubs.uchicago.edu/founders/documents/amendIIIs8.html.

7. Robert B. Roberts, *Encyclopedia of Historic Forts: The Military, Pioneer, and Trading Posts of the United States* (New York: Macmillan, 1988), xii, 403-4; Robert E. Harkavy, *Strategic Basing and the Great Powers, 1200-2000* (London: Routledge, 2007), 1-3.

8. "Revolutionary War Facts," American Revolutionary War, 1775 to 1783, accessed February 16, 2020, https://revolutionarywar.us/facts/. For a list of sources, see Matthew White, "Statistics of Wars, Oppressions and Atrocities of the Eighteenth Century (the 1700s)," Necrometrics, accessed February 16, 2020, https://necrometrics.com/wars18c.htm.

CHAPTER THREE. WHY ARE SO MANY PLACES NAMED *FORT*?

1. Data retrieved from U.S. Geological Survey, "Domestic Names," U.S. Board on Geographic Names, accessed February 16, 2020, www.usgs.gov/core -science-systems/ngp/board-on-geographic-names/domestic-names.

2. U.S. Geological Survey, "Domestic Names."

3. Catherine Lutz, "US Military Bases on Guam in Global Perspective," *Asia-Pacific Journal* 8, no. 30 (2010): https://apjjf.org/-Catherine-Lutz/3389/article.html.

4. The following works are still essential: James R. Blaker, *United States Overseas Basing: An Anatomy of the Dilemma* (New York: Praeger, 1990); Joseph Gerson, "The Sun Never Sets," in *The Sun Never Sets: Confronting the Network of Foreign U.S. Military Bases*, ed. Joseph Gerson and Bruce Birchard (Boston: South End, 1991), 3–34; Robert E. Harkavy, *Strategic Basing and the Great Powers, 1200-2000* (London: Routledge, 2007); and C. T. Sandars, *America's Overseas Garrisons: The Leasehold Empire* (Oxford: Oxford University Press, 2000). Cf. Catherine Lutz, "Introduction: Bases, Empire, and Global Response," in *Bases of Empire: The Global Struggle against U.S. Military Posts*, ed. Catherine Lutz (New York: New York University Press, 2009), 1–44; and Mark L. Gillem, *America Town: Building the Outposts of Empire* (Minneapolis: University of Minnesota Press, 2007).

5. Anni P. Baker, *American Soldiers Overseas: The Global Military Presence* (Westport, CT: Praeger, 2004), 4.

6. Richard W. Stewart, ed., *American Military History*, vol. 1, *The United States Army and the Forging of a Nation, 1775-1917*, 2nd ed. (Washington, DC: Center of Military History, 2005), 53; John Hancock, "To George Washington from John Hancock, 28 June 1775," *Founders Online*, National Archives, accessed February 16, 2020, https://founders.archives.gov/documents/Washington/03-01-02-0020.

7. Stewart, *American Military History*, 1:53–55.

8. John Grenier, *The First Way of War: American War Making on the Frontier, 1607-1814* (Cambridge: Cambridge University Press, 2005), 4.

9. Roxanne Dunbar-Ortiz, *An Indigenous Peoples' History of the United States* (Boston: Beacon, 2014), 58, 64–65.

10. William Earl Weeks, *Building the Continental Empire: American Expansion from the Revolution to the Civil War* (Chicago: Dee, 1996), ix; Richard W. Van Alstyne, *The Rising U.S. Empire* (New York: Norton Library, 1960), 8. See also Reginald Horsman, *Expansion and American Indian Policy, 1783-1812* (East Lansing: Michigan State University Press, 1967), viii, 5–6.

11. John Murray (Lord Dunmore), quoted in Dunbar-Ortiz, *Indigenous Peoples' History*, 71–72; see also pages 70–72.

12. Dunbar-Ortiz, *Indigenous Peoples' History*, 71.

13. Dunbar-Ortiz, *Indigenous Peoples' History*, 72–73.

14. Grenier, *First Way of War*, 161.

15. Grenier, *First Way of War*, 161, 11.

16. See, for example, Grenier, *First Way of War*, 159–62; and Dunbar-Ortiz, *Indigenous Peoples' History*, 71–77.

17. Dunbar-Ortiz, *Indigenous Peoples' History*, 75–76; Grenier, *First Way of War*, ix, 5.

18. Grenier, *First Way of War*, 21.

19. George Washington, "From George Washington to Major General John Sullivan, 31 May 1779," *Founders Online*, National Archives, accessed February 16, 2020, https://founders.archives.gov/documents/Washington/03-20-02-0661.

20. Quoted in Dunbar-Ortiz, *Indigenous Peoples' History*, 77.

21. Grenier, *First Way of War*, 11–12.

22. "Fort Harmar," Ohio History Central, accessed February 16, 2020, https://ohiohistorycentral.org/w/Fort_Harmar.

23. Stewart, *American Military History*, 1:116.

24. Emphasis in original. George Washington, "Washington's Sentiments on a Peace Establishment, 1 May 1783," *Founders Online*, National Archives, accessed February 16, 2020, http://founders.archives.gov/documents/Washington/99-01-02-11202.

25. Stewart, *American Military History*, 1:113–16.

26. This was especially the case following Congress's passage of the Northwest Ordinance of 1787, which created a path for U.S. territories to become states.

27. Francis Paul Prucha, *A Guide to the Military Posts of the United States, 1789-1895* (Madison: State Historical Society of Wisconsin, 1964), 2–7.

28. Grenier, *First Way of War*, 193–95; Stewart, *American Military History*, 1:113–17.

29. R. Douglas Hurt, *The Ohio Frontier: Crucible of the Old Northwest, 1720-1830* (Bloomington: Indian a University Press, 1998), 107.

30. Grenier, *First Way of War*, 194–96.

31. Grenier, *First Way of War*, 198.

32. Stewart, *American Military History*, 1:117–18.

33. Stewart, *American Military History*, 1:118–19.

34. Hurt, *Ohio Frontier*, 135–36.

35. Quoted in Grenier, *First Way of War*, 202; see also pages 200–202.

36. Dunbar-Ortiz, *Indigenous Peoples' History*, 80.

37. Stewart, *American Military History*, 1:119–20.

38. Stacie L. Pettyjohn, *U.S. Global Defense Posture, 1783-2011* (Santa Monica, CA: RAND Corporation, 2012), 16, 16n3; Stewart, *American Military History*, 1:121.

39. Horsman, *Expansion*, 141, 157; Gillem, *America Town*, 18–19.

40. Stewart, *American Military History*, 1:121.

41. David J. Wishart, *The Fur Trade of the American West, 1807-1840* (Lincoln: University of Nebraska Press, 1979), 215.

42. Neil Smith, *The New Urban Frontier: Gentrification and the Revanchist City* (New York: Routledge, 1996).

43. Thomas Jefferson, "President Thomas Jefferson's Confidential Message concerning Relations with the Indians," January 18, 1803, President's Messages from the Seventh Congress, Presidential Messages, 1791–1861, RG 233, Records of the U.S. House of Representatives, National Archives and Records Administration, Washington, DC, www.docsteach.org/documents/document/jefferson-confidential-message-relations-indians.

44. Stewart, *American Military History,* 1:126.

45. Stewart, *American Military History,* 1:124–26.

46. Emphasis mine. Jefferson, "Thomas Jefferson's Confidential Message."

47. Wishart, *Fur Trade,* 207–8, 18.

48. Stewart, *American Military History,* 1:124.

49. Wishart, *Fur Trade,* 207–8, 19, 22.

50. David Bernstein, "'We Are Not Now as We Once Were': Iowa Indians' Political and Economic Adaptations during U.S. Incorporation," *Ethnohistory* 42, no. 4 (2007): 614, 608, 629n9; Brooke L. Blower, "Nation of Outposts: Forts, Factories, Bases, and the Making of American Power," *Diplomatic History* 41, no. 3 (2017): 447.

51. Bernstein, "'We Are Not Now,'" 614.

52. Wishart, *Fur Trade,* 213–14.

53. Wishart, *Fur Trade,* 212, 213, 116–17.

54. Wishart, *Fur Trade,* 210–11, 214.

55. Stewart, *American Military History,* 1:126–27.

CHAPTER FOUR. INVADING YOUR NEIGHBORS

1. J. C. A. Stagg, *The War of 1812: Conflict for a Continent* (Cambridge: Cambridge University Press, 2012), 1.

2. Stephen J. Rauch, *The Campaign of 1812: The U.S. Army Campaigns of the War of 1812* (Washington, DC: Center of Military History, 2013), 9, 18, 21, 45–46, 56.

3. Daniel Webster Howe, *What Hath God Wrought: The Transformation of America, 1815–1848* (Oxford: Oxford University Press, 2007), 66.

4. Stagg, *War of 1812,* 4; Howe, *What Hath God Wrought,* 80.

5. Michael Beschloss, *Presidents of War: The Epic Story, from 1807 to Modern Times* (New York: Crown, 2018), 3–4.

6. Beschloss, *Presidents of War,* 5.

7. Carl Benn, "Aboriginal Peoples and Their Multiple Wars of 1812," in *The Routledge Handbook of the War of 1812,* ed. Donald R. Hickey and Conni D. Clark (London: Routledge, 2015), 132–33. See also Roxanne Dunbar-Ortiz, *An Indigenous Peoples' History of the United States* (Boston: Beacon, 2014); and

John Grenier, *The First Way of War: American War Making on the Frontier, 1607–1814* (Cambridge: Cambridge University Press, 2005).

8. Benn, "Aboriginal Peoples," 132–33.

9. Grenier, *First Way of War*, 213, 225; Reginald Horsman, *Expansion and American Indian Policy, 1783–1812* (East Lansing: Michigan State University Press, 1967), 141, 157.

10. Quoted in Richard W. Stewart, ed., *American Military History*, vol. 1, *The United States Army and the Forging of a Nation, 1775–1917*, 2nd ed. (Washington, DC: Center of Military History, 2005), 144.

11. William C. Davis, "The History of the Short-Lived Independent Republic of Florida," *Smithsonian Magazine*, May 2013, www.smithsonianmag.com/history /the-history-of-the-short-lived-independent-republic-of-florida-28056078/.

12. "Commission Planning for West Florida Republic Bicentennial," press release, Southeastern Louisiana University, July 6, 2009, www.southeastern .edu/news_media/news_releases/2009/july/west_fla.html.

13. "About the Fort," Fort of Colonial Mobile, accessed February 16, 2020, http://colonialmobile.com/about-the-fort/.

14. Steven J. Peach, "Creeks Organize to Resist White Expansion," National Park Service, accessed February 16, 2020, www.nps.gov/articles/creek -organize-to-resist-white-expansion.htm?utm_source=article&utm_medium= website&utm_campaign=experience_more; Greg O'Brien, "August 1813: The Attack on Fort Mims Prompts Choctaw Involvement," National Park Service, last modified August 14, 2017, www.nps.gov/articles/august-1813-fort-mims .htm; Stewart, *American Military History*, 1:144–46.

15. Howe, *What Hath God Wrought*, 71; Perkins, quoted in Howe, *What Hath God Wrought*, 71.

16. Howe, *What Hath God Wrought*, 70.

17. William McKee Evans, *Open Wound: The Long View of Race in America* (Champaign: University of Illinois Press, 2009), 71.

18. Howe, *What Hath God Wrought*, 76–77.

19. James E. Cherry, "Andrew Jackson: The Good, the Bad, the Ethnic Cleansing," *Jackson Sun*, March 22, 2017, www.jacksonsun.com/story/opinion /2017/03/22/andrew-jackson-good-bad-ethnic-cleansing/99409468/. (The *Jackson Sun* appears to have changed the title of this article since its original publication to remove the words "the Ethnic Cleansing." The URL still reflects the original title.)

20. Howe, *What Hath God Wrought*, 99–103; Stewart, *American Military History*, 1:161–63; Daniel Feller, "Andrew Jackson: Life before the Presidency," Miller Center, University of Virginia, accessed February 12, 2020, https:// millercenter.org/president/jackson/life-before-the-presidency.

21. Howe, *What Hath God Wrought*, 98–111.

22. See, for example, Cherry, "Andrew Jackson"; Michael Paul Rogin, *Fathers and Children: Andrew Jackson and the Subjugation of the American Indian* (1975; repr., New York: Routledge, 2017); Howe, *What Hath God Wrought,* 74–111; and Dunbar-Ortiz, *Indigenous Peoples' History,* 96–97.

23. Rogin, *Fathers and Children.*

24. Howe, *What Hath God Wrought,* 74–111.

25. Dunbar-Ortiz, *Indigenous Peoples' History,* 96–97.

26. Howe, *What Hath God Wrought,* 77–78. Pirates are generally private non-state actors seeking profits on the high seas.

27. "The XYZ Affair and the Quasi-War with France, 1798–1800," Office of the Historian, U.S. Department of State, accessed February 16, 2020, https://history.state.gov/milestones/1784-1800/xyz.

28. Andrew Krepinevich and Robert O. Work, *New US Global Defense Posture for the Transoceanic Era* (Washington, DC: Center for Strategic and Budgetary Assessments, 2007), 41–42.

29. Krepinevich and Work, *New US Global Defense,* 41–42.

30. Stacie L. Pettyjohn, *U.S. Global Defense Posture, 1783–2011* (Santa Monica, CA: RAND Corporation, 2012), 17–18.

31. William Francis Lynch, "Narrative of the United States' Expedition to the River Jordan and the Dead Sea," 1849, *Wikisource,* last modified January 17, 2018, https://en.wikisource.org/wiki/Narrative_Of_The_United_States_Expedition_To_The_River_Jordan_And_The_Dead_Sea.

32. Steven Hahn, *A Nation without Borders: The United States and Its World in an Age of Civil Wars, 1830–1910* (New York: Penguin, 2017), 238.

33. James Monroe, "Monroe Doctrine (1823)," Our Documents, December 2, 1823, www.ourdocuments.gov/doc.php?flash=false&doc=23. See also Howe, *What Hath God Wrought,* 113–16.

34. John Q. Adams, "She Goes Not Abroad in Search of Monsters to Destroy," *American Conservative,* July 4, 2013, www.theamericanconservative.com/repository/she-goes-not-abroad-in-search-of-monsters-to-destroy/.

35. Adams, "She Goes Not Abroad."

CHAPTER FIVE. THE PERMANENT INDIAN FRONTIER

1. Kelvin D. Crow, *Fort Leavenworth: Three Centuries of Service* (Fort Leavenworth, KS: Command History Office Combined Arms Center and Fort Leavenworth, n.d.), 2.

2. Richard W. Stewart, ed., *American Military History,* vol. 1, *The United States Army and the Forging of a Nation, 1775–1917,* 2nd ed. (Washington, DC: Center of Military History, 2005), 166.

3. Alison K. Hoagland, *Architecture in the West: Forts Laramie, Bridger, and D.A. Russell, 1849-1912* (Norman: University of Oklahoma Press, 2004), 6, ix, 3.

4. Hoagland, *Architecture in the West,* 7.

5. Francis Paul Prucha, *A Guide to the Military Posts of the United States, 1789-1895* (Madison: State Historical Society of Wisconsin, 1964), 10-11; Anni P. Baker, *American Soldiers Overseas: The Global Military Presence* (Westport, CT: Praeger, 2004), 5.

6. Alan Goodman, Yolanda T. Moses, and Joseph Jones, *Race: Are We So Different?* (Malden, MA: Wiley-Blackwell, 2012), 197.

7. Prucha, *Guide to the Military Posts,* 10-11.

8. Peleg Sprague, speech to the U.S. Senate, April 16-17, 1830, in *Speeches on the Passage of the Bill for the Removal of the Indians, Delivered in the Congress of the United States, April and May, 1830,* ed. Jeremiah Evarts (Boston: Perkins and Marvin, 1830).

9. Andrew Jackson, Second Annual Address to Congress, December 6, 1830, quoted in "A Century of Lawmaking for a New Nation: U.S. Congressional Documents and Debates, 1774-1875," Library of Congress, accessed February 16, 2020, https://memory.loc.gov/cgi-bin/ampage?collId=llrd&fileName=010/llrd010.db&recNum=438.

10. Quoted in Goodman, Moses, and Jones, *Race,* 198.

11. Stewart, *American Military History,* 1:168-72.

12. Stewart, *American Military History,* 1:172.

13. Stewart, *American Military History,* 1:173.

14. Crow, *Fort Leavenworth,* 22, 28.

15. Dee Brown, *Bury My Heart at Wounded Knee: An Indian History of the American West* (New York: Holt, 1970), 7; Prucha, *Guide to the Military Posts,* 32-34.

16. Stewart, *American Military History,* 1:173.

17. Steven Hahn, *A Nation without Borders: The United States and Its World in an Age of Civil Wars, 1830-1910* (New York: Penguin, 2017), 115-16.

18. Stewart, *American Military History,* 1:177-78; Hahn, *Nation without Borders,* 130.

19. Stewart, *American Military History,* 1:174, 180, 186-87.

20. Daniel Walker Howe, *What Hath God Wrought: The Transformation of America, 1815-1848* (Oxford: Oxford University Press, 2007), 708, 702.

21. Quoted in Howe, *What Hath God Wrought,* 703.

22. Howe, *What Hath God Wrought,* 704-5.

23. Quoted in Howe, *What Hath God Wrought,* 704.

24. Victor Bulmer-Thomas, *Empire in Retreat: The Past, Present, and Future of the United States* (New Haven, CT: Yale University Press, 2018), 56.

25. Ethan Allen Hitchcock, *Fifty Years in Camp and Field: Diary of Major-General Ethan Allen Hitchcock, U.S.A.*, ed. William Augustus Croffut (New York: Putnam's Sons, 1909), 212–13.

26. Quoted in Amy Greenberg, *A Wicked War: Polk, Clay, Lincoln, and the 1846 U.S. Invasion of Mexico* (New York: Knopf, 2012), vii.

27. "The Annexation of Texas, the Mexican-American War, and the Treaty of Guadalupe-Hidalgo, 1845–1848," Office of the Historian, U.S. Department of State, accessed February 16, 2020, https://history.state.gov/milestones/1830-1860/texas-annexation.

28. Hahn, *Nation without Borders*, 132.

29. Roxanne Dunbar-Ortiz, *Roots of Resistance: A History of Land Tenure in New Mexico* (Norman: University of Oklahoma Press, 2007), 98; Adrian G. Traas, *From the Golden Gate to Mexico City: The U.S. Army Topographical Engineers in the Mexican War, 1846–1848* (Washington, DC: United States Army, 1993), 63–66.

30. Stephen A. Carney, "The Occupation of Mexico: May 1846–July 1848," U.S. Army Center of Military History, 2005, https://history.army.mil/html/books/073/73-3/CMH_Pub_73-3.pdf, 12–13.

31. Quoted in Enrique Krauze, "The April Invasion of Veracruz," *New York Times*, April 20, 2014.

32. Hahn, *Nation without Borders*, 132, 136.

33. "On St. Patrick's Day, Mexico Remembers the Irishmen Who Fought for Mexico against the US," *World*, PRI, March 17, 2015, www.pri.org/stories/2015-03-17/st-patrick-s-day-mexico-remembers-irishmen-who-fought-mexico-against-us.

34. Carney, "Occupation of Mexico," 35–36.

35. Howe, *What Hath God Wrought*, 802–4.

36. Hoagland, *Architecture in the West*, 16.

37. Hoagland, *Architecture in the West*, 17, 9.

38. Quoted in Hoagland, *Architecture in the West*, 21.

39. Baker, *American Soldiers*, 5.

40. Hoagland, *Architecture in the West*, 16–17.

41. Hoagland, *Architecture in the West*, 17.

42. Prucha, *Guide to the Military Posts*, 14–18, 23, 28.

43. John Pope to Col. R. M. Sawyer, August 1, 1865, *United States Congressional Serial Set*, no. 3437 (1896): 1150–51.

44. Helen Hunt Jackson, *A Century of Dishonor* (New York: Harper's and Sons, 1881), 76–79.

45. H. Jackson, *Century of Dishonor*, 76–79.

46. "Freedom: A History of US," webisode, PBS, 2002, www.pbs.org/wnet/historyofus/web03/segment7_p.html.

47. "Civil War Defenses of Washington," National Park Service, accessed February 16, 2020, www.nps.gov/cwdw/index.htm.

48. Dunbar-Ortiz, *Indigenous Peoples' History*, 136.

49. Quoted in Tony Horwitz, "The Horrific Sand Creek Massacre Will Be Forgotten No More," *Smithsonian Magazine*, December 2014, www.smithsonianmag .com/history/horrific-sand-creek-massacre-will-be-forgotten-no-more-180953403/.

50. Horwitz, "Horrific Sand Creek Massacre"; Dunbar-Ortiz, *Indigenous Peoples' History*, 137–38.

51. Horwitz, "Horrific Sand Creek Massacre"; Dunbar-Ortiz, *Indigenous Peoples' History*, 137–38.

52. Horwitz, "Horrific Sand Creek Massacre"; Dunbar-Ortiz, *Indigenous Peoples' History*, 137–38.

53. Jon Wiener, "Largest Mass Execution in US History: 150 Years Ago Today," *Nation*, December 26, 2012, www.thenation.com/article/largest-mass -execution-us-history-150-years-ago-today/.

54. Wiener, "Largest Mass Execution."

55. Dunbar-Ortiz, *Indigenous Peoples' History*, 139, 144.

56. Dunbar-Ortiz, *Indigenous Peoples' History*, 144–53.

57. The number is 943, according to Col. R. Ernest Dupuy; see Sidney Lens, *The Forging of the American Empire: From the Revolution to Vietnam; A History of U.S. Imperialism* (1971; repr., London: Pluto, 2003), 7. Hoagland cites more than 1,200 between 1848 and 1890. See *Architecture in the West*, 6.

58. Pope to Sawyer, August 1, 1865, *Congressional Serial Set*, 1151–52. See also Stephen E. Ambrose, *Crazy Horse and Custer: The Parallel Lives of Two American Warriors* (1996; repr., New York: Anchor Books, 2014).

59. Howe, *What Hath God Wrought*, 810.

60. Quoted in Bulmer-Thomas, *Empire in Retreat*, 59.

61. Howe, *What Hath God Wrought*, 810–11; Bulmer-Thomas, *Empire in Retreat*, 59; Dunbar-Ortiz, *Indigenous Peoples' History*, 129.

62. Howe, *What Hath God Wrought*, 703.

63. House of Representatives, "Military Expedition against the Sioux Indians," Executive Document no. 184, *Congressional Serial Set* (Washington, DC: Government Printing Office, 1876), 3.

64. Crow, *Fort Leavenworth*, 22, 28; Dunbar-Ortiz, *Indigenous Peoples' History*, 149–50.

65. Daniel Immerwahr, *How to Hide an Empire: A History of the Greater United States* (New York: Farrar, Straus and Giroux, 2019), 42–44.

66. Hoagland, *Architecture in the West*, 203.

67. Prucha, *Guide to the Military Posts*, 23.

68. Hoagland, *Architecture in the West*, 14.

69. Hoagland, *Architecture in the West*, 7.

70. Robert M. Fogelson, *America's Armories: Architecture, Society, and Public Order* (Cambridge: MA: Harvard University Press, 1989).

71. Prucha, *Guide to the Military Posts*, 34; Robert M. Utley, *The Indian Frontier: 1860–1890* (Albuquerque: University of New Mexico Press, 1984), 92.

72. Hoagland *Architecture in the West*, xi.

73. Hoagland, *Architecture in the West*, 244.

74. David M. Delo, *Peddlers and Post Traders: The Army Sutler on the Frontier* (Salt Lake City: University of Utah Press, 1992), 209, 211.

75. Stephen A. Kinzer, *Overthrow: America's Century of Regime Change from Hawaii to Iraq* (New York: Times Books, 2006), 34.

76. "Fort Leavenworth Wayside Tour," pamphlet, U.S. Army Fort Leavenworth, [2014?], accessed February 16, 2020, https://home.army.mil/leavenworth/application/files/2215/6985/9495/PAO_Wayside_Tour.pdf.

77. "This Land Is Ours," Teaching Tolerance, Southern Poverty Law Center, n.d., accessed February 16, 2020, www.tolerance.org/classroom-resources/texts/this-land-is-ours.

78. Guenter Lewy, "Were American Indians the Victims of Genocide?," *Commentary*, September 2004, republished by History News Network, https://historynewsnetwork.org/article/7302.

79. Dunbar-Ortiz, *Indigenous Peoples' History*, 79.

CHAPTER SIX. GOING GLOBAL

1. "Spanish American War: 'A Splendid Little War,'" Presidio of San Francisco, National Park Service, February 28, 2015, www.nps.gov/prsf/learn/historyculture/spanish-american-war-a-splendid-little-war.htm.

2. Samuel Flagg Bemis, *A Diplomatic History of the United States* (New York: Holt, Rhinehart and Winston, 1965), chap. 26.

3. Thomas McCormick, "From Old Empire to New," in *Colonial Crucible: Empire in the Making of the Modern American State*, ed. Alfred W. McCoy and Francisco A. Scarano (Madison: University of Wisconsin Press, 2009), 73; see also 63–64.

4. McCormick, "Old Empire to New," in McCoy and Scarano, *Colonial Crucible*, 64.

5. Steven Hahn, *A Nation without Borders: The United States and Its World in an Age of Civil Wars, 1830–1910* (New York: Penguin, 2017), 117.

6. Brooke L. Blower, "Nation of Outposts: Forts, Factories, Bases, and the Making of American Power," *Diplomatic History* 41, no. 3 (2017): 447–49.

7. Andrew Krepinevich and Robert O. Work, *New US Global Defense Posture for the Transoceanic Era* (Washington, DC: Center for Strategic and Budgetary Assessments, 2007), 41–42.

8. Stacie L. Pettyjohn, *U.S. Global Defense Posture, 1783–2011* (Santa Monica, CA: RAND Corporation, 2012), 17–18; Barbara Salazar Torreon and Sofia Plagakis, *Instances of Use of United States Armed Forces Abroad, 1798–2018* (Washington, DC: Congressional Research Service, 2018); Blower, "Nation of Outposts," 450.

9. Edward P. Crapol, *John Tyler, the Accidental President* (Chapel Hill: University of North Carolina Press, 2006), 76–78. President John Tyler's Secretary of the Navy Abel P. Upshur was a naval evangelist who ironically had never been to sea or left the United States.

10. Shahan Cheong, "Chinatown Reversed: The Shanghai International Settlement," *Throughout History* (blog), October 15, 2011, www.throughout history.com/?p=1790.

11. Chris Ames, "Crossfire Couples: Marginality and Agency among Okinawan Women in Relationships with U.S. Military Men," in *Over There: Living with the U.S. Military Empire from World War Two to the Present*, ed. Maria Höhn and Seungsook Moon (Durham, NC: Duke University Press, 2010), 199n5; Blower, "Nation of Outposts," 451n37.

12. McCormick, "Old Empire to New," 65.

13. Thomas Jefferson to James Monroe, October 23, 1823, quoted in "What Thomas Jefferson Said about Annexing Cuba," *San Francisco Call*, April 10, 1898, 28, https://cdnc.ucr.edu/cgi-bin/cdnc?a=d&d=SFC18980410.2.132.2 6&e=-------en--20--1--txt-txIN--------1.

14. McCormick, "Old Empire to New," 65.

15. See, for example, William Earl Weeks, *Building the Continental Empire: American Expansion from the Revolution to the Civil War* (Chicago: Dee, 1996), 140–43; and McCormick, "Old Empire to New," 65–66.

16. Peter Carlson, "Raiding the Icebox: Behind Its Warm Front, the United States Made Cold Calculations to Subdue Canada," *Washington Post*, December 30, 2005, C1.

17. Carolyn Hall and Héctor Pérez Brignoli, *Historical Atlas of Central America* (Norman: University of Oklahoma Press, 2003), 184–85; Scott Martelle, *William Walker's Wars: How One Man's Private American Army Tried to Conquer Mexico, Nicaragua, and Honduras* (Chicago: Chicago Review Press, 2019); Victor Bulmer-Thomas, *Empire in Retreat: The Past, Present, and Future of the United States* (New Haven, CT: Yale University Press, 2018), 68; Ron Soodalter, "William Walker: King of the 19th Century Filibusters," History Net, March 2, 2010, www.historynet.com/william-walker-king-of-the-19th-century-filibusters .htm.

18. Weeks, *Building the Continental Empire*, 140–43; Hall and Pérez Brignoli, *Historical Atlas*, 184–85, 209.

19. Christina Duffy Burnett, "The Edges of Empire and the Limits of Sovereignty: American Guano Islands," *American Quarterly* 57, no. 3 (2005): 782.

20. Burnett, "Edges of Empire," 779–80, 788; A. M. Jackson to the Chief of Naval Operations, memorandum, December 7, 1964, folder 11000/1B, box 26, 00 Files, Naval History and Heritage Command Archives, Washington, DC, 2.

21. See Daniel Immerwahr, *How to Hide an Empire: A History of the Greater United States* (New York: Farrar, Straus and Giroux, 2019), 53–56; Burnett, "Edges of Empire," 788.

22. Daniel Immerwahr, "The Greater United States: Territory and Empire in U.S. History," *Diplomatic History* 40, no. 3 (2016): 385; Immerwahr, *Hide an Empire*, 52–53.

23. Burnett, "Edges of Empire," 779–803.

24. Burnett, "Edges of Empire," 798.

25. Richard D. Challener, *Admirals, Generals, and American Foreign Policy: 1898–1914* (Princeton, NJ: Princeton University Press, 1973), 5.

26. Blower, "Nation of Outposts," 451.

27. Fidel Tavárez, "'The Moral Miasma of the Tropics': American Imperialism and the Failed Annexation of the Dominican Republic, 1869–1871," *Nuevo Mundo/Mundos Nuevos*, July 13, 2011, https://journals.openedition.org /nuevomundo/61771?lang=en; Victor Bulmer-Thomas, *The Economic History of the Caribbean since the Napoleonic Wars* (Cambridge: Cambridge University Press, 2012), 25–26, 101.

28. Paul Farmer, *The Uses of Haiti*, 3rd ed. (1994; repr., Monroe, ME: Common Courage, 2006), 72–74, 418n43; Bulmer-Thomas, *Economic History*, 168–69.

29. Farmer, *Uses of Haiti*, 77–78.

30. William Appleman Williams, *The Tragedy of American Diplomacy*, rev. ed. (New York: Delta, 1962), 9, 24–25.

31. Alfred W. McCoy, "Gunboat Diplomacy and the Ghost of Captain Mahan, or How China and the U.S. Are Spawning a New Great Power Naval Rivalry," Tom-Dispatch, April 8, 2018, www.tomdispatch.com/blog/176408/tomgram%3A _alfred_mccoy%2C_a_new_age_of_sea_power.

32. Quoted in Philip A. Crowl, "Alfred Thayer Mahan: The Naval Historian," in *Makers of Modern Strategy from Machiavelli to the Nuclear Age*, ed. Peter Paret (Princeton, NJ: Princeton University Press, 1986), 455.

33. Quoted in McCoy, "Gunboat Diplomacy."

34. Quoted in McCoy, "Gunboat Diplomacy."

35. Alfred Thayer Mahan, "The United States Looking Outward," *Atlantic*, December 1890, www.theatlantic.com/magazine/archive/1890/12/the-united -states-looking-outward/306348/.

36. Mahan, "United States Looking Outward."

37. Quoted in Hahn, *Nation without Borders*, 491, 495.

38. Stephen A. Kinzer, *Overthrow: America's Century of Regime Change from Hawaii to Iraq* (New York: Times Books, 2006), 86–87; Krepinevich and Work,

New US Global Defense, 47–48; Hal M. Friedman, *Creating an American Lake: United States Imperialism and Strategic Security in the Pacific Basin, 1945–1947* (Westport, CT: Greenwood, 2001), 3.

39. Friedman, *Creating an American Lake*, 3; Kinzer, *Overthrow*, 33.

40. Richard W. Stewart, ed., *American Military History*, vol. 1, *The United States Army and the Forging of a Nation, 1775–1917*, 2nd ed. (Washington, DC: Center of Military History, 2005), 349.

41. J. Kēhaulani Kauanui, "Milking the Cow for All It's Worth: Settler Colonialism and the Politics of Imperialist Resentment in Hawai'i," in *Ethnographies of U.S. Empire*, ed. Carole McGranahan and John Collins (Durham, NC: Duke University Press, 2018), 53.

42. Quoted in Hahn, *Nation without Borders*, 493.

43. Pettyjohn, *U.S. Global Defense Posture*, 27n6; Kinzer, *Overthrow*, 18–19.

44. Quoted in Hahn, *Nation without Borders*, 495.

45. Hahn, *Nation without Borders*, 493.

46. Immerwahr, *Hide an Empire*, 66–67; McCoy, "Gunboat Diplomacy."

47. Quoted in Hahn, *Nation without Borders*, 493.

48. Jana K. Lipman, *Guantánamo: A Working-Class History between Empire and Revolution* (Berkeley: University of California Press, 2008), 23.

49. "El Hierro de la Casa," *Wikipedia*, uploaded September 14, 2013, http://en.wikipedia.org/wiki/File:Enmienda_Platt.JPG.

50. Quoted in Jack McCallum, *Leonard Wood: Rough Rider, Surgeon, Architect of American Imperialism* (New York: New York University Press, 2006), 187.

51. Quoted in Hahn, *Nation without Borders*, 494.

52. Hahn, *Nation without Borders*, 491.

53. Jana K. Lipman, "Guantánamo and the Case of Kid Chicle: Private Contract Labor and the Development of the U.S. Military," in McCoy and Scarano, *Colonial Crucible*, 453.

54. Stewart, *American Military History*, 1:360.

55. McCormick, "Old Empire to New," 73.

56. Quoted in Hahn, *Nation without Borders*, 495.

57. Quoted in Hahn, *Nation without Borders*, 496.

58. Eric T. L. Love, *Race over Empire: Racism and U.S. Imperialism, 1865–1900* (Chapel Hill: University of North Carolina Press, 2004), 159–95.

59. Quoted in "The Philippine War: A Conflict of Conscience for African Americans," Presidio of San Francisco, National Park Service, February 28, 2015, www.nps.gov/prsf/learn/historyculture/the-philippine-insurrectiothe-philippine-war-a-conflict-of-consciencen-a-war-of-controversy.htm.

60. Quoted in Hahn, *Nation without Borders*, 496.

61. McCormick, "Old Empire to New," 73.

62. Love, *Race over Empire*, 194–95.

63. Daniel Immerwahr, "Part 2: Empire State of Mind," interview, *On the Media*, WNYC, April 5, 2019, www.wnycstudios.org/story/on-the-media-empire -state-mind-part-2.

64. Quoted in Hahn, *Nation without Borders*, 494.

65. Brian McAllister Linn, "The Impact of the Philippine Wars (1898–1913) on the U.S. Army," in McCoy and Scarano, *Colonial Crucible*, 462.

66. Hahn, *Nation without Borders*, 495, 486.

67. Hahn, *Nation without Borders*, 485–89.

68. Death estimates vary widely. John M. Gates estimates between 128,000 and 360,000 total Filipino deaths; see "War-Related Deaths in the Philippines, 1898–1902," *Pacific Historical Review* 53, no. 3 (1984): 367–78. The U.S. Department of State cites 200,000 civilians, more than 20,000 Filipino combatants, and more than 4,200 US troops; see "The Philippine-American War, 1899–1902," Office of the Historian, accessed February 16, 2020, https://history .state.gov/milestones/1899-1913/war.

69. Patricio Abinales, "The U.S. Army as an Occupying Force in Muslim Mindanao, 1899–1913," in McCoy and Scarano, *Colonial Crucible*, 414–15. The quotations are from Russell Roth.

70. Joshua Gedacht, "'Mohammedan Religion Made It Necessary to Fire': Massacres on the American Imperial Frontier from South Dakota to the Southern Philippines," in McCoy and Scarano, *Colonial Crucible*, 397.

71. Samuel Clemens, "Comments on the Moro Massacre," March 12, 1906, *History Is a Weapon*, accessed January 6, 2020, www.historyisaweapon.com /defcon1/clemensmoromassacre.html.

72. Gedacht, "'Mohammedan Religion,'" 408.

73. Gedacht, "'Mohammedan Religion,'" 397–98.

74. Quoted in Walter L. Williams, "United States Indian Policy and the Debate over Philippine Annexation: Implications for the Origins of American Imperialism," *Journal of American History* 66, no. 4 (1980): 830–31.

75. Krepinevich and Work, *New US Global Defense*, 49.

CHAPTER SEVEN. THE MILITARY OPENS DOORS

1. LisaLinda Natividad and Gwyn Kirk, "Fortress Guam: Resistance to US Military Mega-Buildup," *Asia-Pacific Journal* 19, no. 1 (2010): https:// apjjf.org/-LisaLinda-Natividad/3356/article.html.

2. See, for example, William Appleman Williams, *The Tragedy of American Diplomacy*, rev. ed. (New York: Delta, 1962); Lloyd C. Gardner, Walter F. La Feber, and Thomas J. McCormick, *Creation of the U.S. Empire*, 2 vols. (Chicago: Rand McNally College, 1976); and Neil Smith, *American Empire: Roosevelt's Geographer and the Prelude to Globalization* (Berkeley: University of California Press, 2003).

3. See Christina Duffy Burnett, "The Edges of Empire and the Limits of Sovereignty: American Guano Islands," *American Quarterly* 57, no. 3 (2005): 779–803.

4. Thomas McCormick, "From Old Empire to New," in *Colonial Crucible: Empire in the Making of the Modern American State*, ed. Alfred W. McCoy and Francisco A. Scarano (Madison: University of Wisconsin Press, 2009), 77.

5. McCormick, "Old Empire to New," 77–78.

6. Andrew Krepinevich and Robert O. Work, *New US Global Defense Posture for the Transoceanic Era* (Washington, DC: Center for Strategic and Budgetary Assessments, 2007), 50.

7. Alfred W. McCoy, *In the Shadows of the American Century: The Rise and Decline of US Global Power* (Chicago: Haymarket Books, 2017), 49.

8. Steven Hahn, *A Nation without Borders: The United States and Its World in an Age of Civil Wars, 1830–1910* (New York: Penguin, 2017), 499.

9. John Lindsay-Poland, *Emperors in the Jungle: The Hidden History of the U.S. in Panama* (Durham, NC: Duke University Press, 2003), 27.

10. John Lindsay-Poland, note to author, January 24, 2019. See also Lindsay-Poland, *Emperors in the Jungle.*

11. Carolyn Hall and Héctor Pérez Brignoli, *Historical Atlas of Central America* (Norman: University of Oklahoma Press, 2003), 228; Lindsay-Poland, *Emperors in the Jungle*, 27.

12. C. T. Sandars, *America's Overseas Garrisons: The Leasehold Empire* (Oxford: Oxford University Press, 2000), 140.

13. Hahn, *Nation without Borders*, 498.

14. Theodore Roosevelt, "Roosevelt Corollary," State of the Union Address to Congress, *Modern Latin America*, web supplement for 8th ed., December 6, 1904, https://library.brown.edu/create/modernlatinamerica/chapters/chapter-14-the-united-states-and-latin-america/primary-documents-w-accompanying-discussion-questions/document-33-roosevelt-corollary-1904/.

15. Roosevelt, "Roosevelt Corollary."

16. Alan Brinkley, *American History: A Survey*, vol. 1, *To 1877*, 10th ed. (New York: McGraw-Hill, 1999), 767; Lindsay-Poland, *Emperors in the Jungle*, 16–17; Hall and Pérez Brignoli, *Historical Atlas*, 209.

17. Hall and Pérez Brignoli, *Historical Atlas*, 228.

18. Greg Grandin, *Empire's Workshop: Latin America, the United States, and the Rise of the New Imperialism* (New York: Metropolitan Books, 2006), 3, 20.

19. Victor Bulmer-Thomas, *Empire in Retreat: The Past, Present, and Future of the United States* (New Haven, CT: Yale University Press, 2018), 71.

20. McCormick, "Old Empire to New," 75–76.

21. Brinkley, *American History*, 767; Lindsay-Poland, *Emperors in the Jungle*, 16–17; Hall and Pérez Brignoli, *Historical Atlas*, 209.

22. McCormick, "Old Empire to New," 75–77.

23. Smedley Butler, "America's Armed Forces: 'In Time of Peace'; The Army," *Common Sense* 4, no. 11 (1935): 8–12.

24. Stephen A. Kinzer, *Overthrow: America's Century of Regime Change from Hawaii to Iraq* (New York: Times Books, 2006), 321.

25. Butler, "America's Armed Forces," 8–9.

26. Walter LaFeber, *Inevitable Revolutions: The United States in Central America* (New York: Norton, 1983), 42–46; Grandin, *Empire's Workshop*, 19.

27. LaFeber, *Inevitable Revolutions*, 42–46. See also Leo Panitch and Sam Gindin, *The Making of Global Capitalism: The Political Economy of American Empire* (New York: Verso, 2012).

28. LaFeber, *Inevitable Revolutions*, 9.

29. McCormick, "Old Empire to New," 75.

30. Ian Tyrrell, "Empire in American History," in McCoy and Scarano, *Colonial Crucible*, 551; Alfred W. McCoy, Francisco A. Scarano, and Courtney Johnson, "On the Tropic of Cancer: Transitions and Transformations in the U.S. Imperial State," in McCoy and Scarano, *Colonial Crucible*, 30–31.

31. Quoted in Eduardo Galeano, *Open Veins of Latin America: Five Centuries of the Pillage of a Continent* (New York: Monthly Review Press, 1973), 121.

32. Ibram X. Kendi, *Stamped from the Beginning: The Definitive History of Racist Ideas in America* (New York: Nation Books, 2016), 15–16.

33. McCoy, Scarano, and Johnson, "Tropic of Cancer," in McCoy and Scarano, *Colonial Crucible*, 31; Tyrrell, "Empire in American History," in McCoy and Scarano, *Colonial Crucible*, 551–53.

34. Ann Laura Stoler, "Refractions Off Empire: Untimely Comparisons in Harsh Times," with David Bond, *Radical History Review* 95 (2006): 95.

35. Richard W. Stewart, ed., *American Military History*, vol. 2, *The United States Army in a Global Era, 1917–2008*, 2nd ed. (Washington, DC: Center of Military History, 2010), 57–58.

36. Stewart, *American Military History*, 2:58.

37. Hal M. Friedman, *Creating an American Lake: United States Imperialism and Strategic Security in the Pacific Basin, 1945–1947* (Westport, CT: Greenwood, 2001), 3.

38. Paul Kramer, "A Useful Corner of the World: Guantánamo," *New Yorker*, July 31, 2013, www.newyorker.com/online/blogs/newsdesk/2013/07/a-useful-corner-of-the-world-a-history-of-guantanamo-base.html#slide_ss_0=1.

39. Daniel Immerwahr, *How to Hide an Empire: A History of the Greater United States* (New York: Farrar, Straus and Giroux, 2019), 203–12; "Research Starters: Worldwide Deaths in World War II," National World War II Museum, accessed February 16, 2020, www.nationalww2museum.org/students-teachers/student-resources/research-starters/research-starters-worldwide-deaths-world-war.

CHAPTER EIGHT. REOPENING THE FRONTIER

1. Quoted in "The Big Deal," *Time*, September 16, 1940, 11.

2. Francis Brown, "For America the Horizon Widens," *New York Times*, September 15, 1940, 19, 21.

3. Hanson W. Baldwin, "Our Deal with Britain Affects a World's Strategical Picture," *New York Times*, September 8, 1940, 77.

4. "Big Deal," 11; Brown, "For America," 109.

5. Quoted in C. T. Sandars, *America's Overseas Garrisons: The Leasehold Empire* (Oxford: Oxford University Press, 2000), See also States Bureau of Yards and Docks, *Building the Navy's Bases in World War II: History of the Bureau of Yards and Docks and the Civil Engineer Corps, 1940-1946*, vol. 2, pt. 3, *The Advance Bases* (Washington, DC: Government Printing Office, 1947).

6. Technically, bases in two of the colonies were gifts, while the others were exchanged for the destroyers. In practice it was a single deal with a single agreement.

7. Steven High, *Base Colonies in the Western Hemisphere, 1940-1967* (New York: Palgrave Macmillan, 2009), 2.

8. "Big Deal," 11.

9. Baldwin, "Our Deal with Britain," 77.

10. Brown, "For America," 3.

11. Robert E. Harkavy, *Great Power Competition for Overseas Bases: The Geopolitics of Access Diplomacy* (New York: Pergamon, 1982), 66.

12. James R. Blaker, *United States Overseas Basing: An Anatomy of the Dilemma* (New York: Praeger, 1990), 9.

13. Stetson Conn, Rose C. Engelman, and Byron Fairchild, *Guarding the United States and Its Outposts: U.S. Army in World War II* (Washington, D.C.: U.S. Army Center of Military History, 2000), 358-59.

14. High, *Base Colonies*, 1, 7.

15. Newspaper and colonial officer, quoted in High, *Base Colonies*, 8, 10.

16. Quoted in Jorge Rodríguez Beruff, "From Winship to Leahy: Crisis, War, and Transition in Puerto Rico," in *Colonial Crucible: Empire in the Making of the Modern American State*, ed. Alfred W. McCoy and Francisco A. Scarano (Madison: University of Wisconsin Press, 2009), 435.

17. Charlie Whitham, "On Dealing with Gangsters: The Limits of British 'Generosity' in the Leasing of Bases to the United States, 1940-1941," *Diplomacy and Statecraft* 7, no. 3 (1996): 592-93; High, *Base Colonies*, 21.

18. High, *Base Colonies*, 20.

19. Michael S. Sherry, *Preparing for the Next War: American Plans for Postwar Defense, 1941-45* (New Haven, CT: Yale University Press, 1977), 39-41.

20. Sherry, *Preparing*, 31-32.

21. High, *Base Colonies,* 20.

22. Beruff, "From Winship to Leahy," in McCoy and Scarano, *Colonial Crucible,* 436, 438.

23. Quoted in High, *Base Colonies,* 41.

24. Elliott V. Converse III, *Circling the Earth: United States Plans for a Postwar Overseas Military Base System, 1942-1948* (Maxwell Air Force Base, AL: Air University Press, 2005), xv.

25. Stacie L. Pettyjohn, *U.S. Global Defense Posture, 1783-2011* (Santa Monica, CA: RAND Corporation, 2012), 45-46.

26. James M. Lindsay, "Remembering the Destroyers-for-Bases Deal," *Global Public Square* (blog), CNN, September 2, 2011, http://globalpublicsquare.blogs .cnn.com/2011/09/02/destroyers-for-bases-fdr-churchill/.

27. High, *Base Colonies,* 23; Cordell Hull, "The Memoirs of Cordell Hull," *New York Times,* February 16, 1948, 23; Lindsay, citing Roosevelt biographer Jean Edward Smith, states that a "group of prominent Americans" interested in aiding Britain, including *Time* magazine publisher Henry Luce, first floated the idea at a New York country club in July ("Destroyers-for-Bases Deal").

28. Quoted in Lindsay, "Destroyers-for-Bases Deal."

29. Franklin D. Roosevelt, memorandum, August 2, 1940, in *Foreign Relations of the United States Diplomatic Papers, 1940: The British Commonwealth, the Soviet Union, the Near East and Africa,* vol. 3 (Washington, DC: Government Printing Office, 1958), doc. 51.

30. High, *Base Colonies,* 23-24.

31. "Our New Bases," editorial, *New York Times,* September 5, 1940.

32. Quoted in Lindsay, "Destroyers-for-Bases Deal."

33. Quoted in High, *Base Colonies,* 27.

34. Whitham, "On Dealing with Gangsters," 596.

35. Lindsay, "Destroyers-for-Bases Deal."

36. George A. Brownell to the Assistant Secretary of War for Air, "Airfields in Foreign Countries," memorandum, February 13, 1945, Office of the Assistant Secretary of War for Air, Plans, Policies and Agreements, 1943-47, A1 219/390/10/8/3m, boxes 199-200, RG 107, National Archives and Records Administration, Washington, DC, 3; High, *Base Colonies,* 10; Conn, Engelman, and Fairchild, *Guarding the United States,* 383.

37. Conn, Engelman, and Fairchild, *Guarding the United States,* 381, 376-78.

38. High, *Base Colonies,* 34.

39. "Lend-Lease and Military Aid to the Allies in the Early Years of World War II," *Milestones in the History of U.S. Foreign Relations,* Office of the Historian, U.S. Department of State, accessed February 16, 2020, https://history .state.gov/milestones/1937-1945/lend-lease.

40. High, *Base Colonies,* 34.

41. Previously, the East Coast had been relatively poorly defended, especially compared to the West Coast. Other than some coastal defenses and bases in Guantánamo Bay, Puerto Rico, and the U.S. Virgin Islands, the United States had quietly depended on the British navy's control of the Atlantic. High, *Base Colonies*, 18–19.

42. Hanson W. Baldwin, "U.S. Seen as Gainer in Destroyer Deal," *New York Times*, September 4, 1940, 14.

43. Alfred W. McCoy, "Gunboat Diplomacy and the Ghost of Captain Mahan, or How China and the U.S. Are Spawning a New Great Power Naval Rivalry," TomDispatch, April 8, 2018, www.tomdispatch.com/blog/176408/tomgram %3A_alfred_mccoy%2C_a_new_age_of_sea_power.

44. Quoted in McCoy, "Gunboat Diplomacy."

45. Baldwin, "Our Deal with Britain," 77.

46. Frederick J. Turner, "The Significance of the Frontier in American History (1893)," American Historical Association, accessed February 12, 2020, www.historians.org/about-aha-and-membership/aha-history-and-archives/historical -archives/the-significance-of-the-frontier-in-american-history.

47. Whitham, "On Dealing with Gangsters," 620.

48. Brown, "For America," 3.

CHAPTER NINE. EMPIRE OF BASES

1. Chalmers Johnson appears to have coined the phrase that provides the title for this chapter. "America's Empire of Bases," TomDispatch, January 15, 2004, www.tomdispatch.com/post/1181/chalmers_johnson_on_garrisoning _the_planet.

2. Neil Smith, *The New Urban Frontier: Gentrification and the Revanchist City* (New York: Routledge, 1996).

3. Neil Smith, *American Empire: Roosevelt's Geographer and the Prelude to Globalization* (Berkeley: University of California Press, 2003).

4. Franklin D. Roosevelt and Winston Churchill, "Atlantic Charter," August 14, 1941, Avalon Project, https://avalon.law.yale.edu/wwii/atlantic.asp.

5. Quoted in Steven High, *Base Colonies in the Western Hemisphere, 1940–1967* (New York: Palgrave Macmillan, 2009), 10.

6. N. Smith, *American Empire*, 351.

7. Quoted in N. Smith, *American Empire*, 351, 360.

8. Michael Desch, *When the Third World Matters: Latin America and United States Grand Strategy* (Baltimore: Johns Hopkins University Press, 1993), 183n123; John Lindsay-Poland, *Emperors in the Jungle: The Hidden History of the U.S. in Panama* (Durham, NC: Duke University Press, 2003), 45; Andrew Krepinevich and Robert O. Work, *New US Global Defense Posture for the*

Transoceanic Era (Washington, DC: Center for Strategic and Budgetary Assessments, 2007), 66-69.

9. Max Paul Friedman, *Nazis and Good Neighbors: The United States Campaign against the Germans of Latin America in World War II* (New York: Cambridge University Press, 2003), 82.

10. On Greenland, see Natalia Loukacheva, *The Arctic Promise: Legal and Political Autonomy of Greenland and Nunavut* (Toronto: University of Toronto Press, 2007), 132; Daniel Immerwahr, *How to Hide an Empire: A History of the Greater United States* (New York: Farrar, Straus and Giroux, 2019), 224.

11. Immerwahr, *Hide an Empire*, 217-18, 216-17.

12. Jeffery R. Macris, "The Persian Gulf Theater in World War II," *Journal of the Middle East and Africa* 1 (2010): 100.

13. Immerwahr, *Hide an Empire*, 284-86.

14. Hans W. Weigert, "U.S. Strategic Bases and Collective Security," *Foreign Affairs* 25, no. 2 (1947): 252.

15. David Hanlon, *Remaking Micronesia: Discourses over Development in a Pacific Territory, 1944-1982* (Honolulu: University of Hawai'i Press, 1998), 24-26.

16. Around ninety thousand Japanese and twelve thousand U.S. military personnel were killed. Gavan McCormack and Satoko Oka Norimatsu, *Resistant Islands: Okinawa Confronts Japan and the United States* (Lanham, MD: Rowman and Littlefield, 2012), 25-32, 47n60.

17. Weigert, "U.S. Strategic Bases," 257.

18. James R. Blaker, *United States Overseas Basing: An Anatomy of the Dilemma* (New York: Praeger, 1990), 9.

19. Weigert, "U.S. Strategic Bases," 252.

20. High, *Base Colonies*, 9, 72.

21. Andrew Friedman, "US Empire, World War 2 and the Racialising of Labour," *Race and Class* 58, no. 4 (2017): 27-29; Susan L. Carruthers, *The Good Occupation: American Soldiers and the Hazards of Peace* (Cambridge, MA: Harvard University Press, 2016), 302.

22. A. Friedman, "US Empire," 27.

23. A. Friedman, "US Empire," 28-29.

24. Quoted in C. T. Sandars, *America's Overseas Garrisons: The Leasehold Empire* (Oxford: Oxford University Press, 2000), 5-6.

25. Perry McCoy Smith, *The Air Force Plans for Peace, 1943-45* (Baltimore: Johns Hopkins University Press, 1970), 45, 48.

26. Michael S. Sherry, *Preparing for the Next War: American Plans for Postwar Defense, 1941-45* (New Haven, CT: Yale University Press, 1977), 42-43.

27. Elliott V. Converse III, *Circling the Earth: United States Plans for a Postwar Overseas Military Base System, 1942-1948* (Maxwell Air Force Base, AL: Air University Press, 2005), 1-10.

28. Melvyn P. Leffler, *A Preponderance of Power: National Security, the Truman Administration, and the Cold War* (Stanford, CA: Stanford University Press, 1992), 41.

29. Joint Staff Planners, "Over-all Examination of U.S. Requirements for Military Bases and Rights," October 23, 1945, enclosure C, JCS 570/40 report, Central Decimal File, 1942–45, box 272, sec. 9, no. 217, RG 218, National Archives and Records Administration (hereafter cited as NARA), Washington, DC.

30. Leffler, *Preponderance of Power*, 56, 41; Sherry, *Preparing*, 54, 56.

31. Sherry, *Preparing*, 52–53.

32. Joint Chiefs of Staff, "Statement of Problem," app. A in "United States Military Requirements for Airbases, Facilities, and Operating Rights in Foreign Territories," memorandum from Commanding General United States Army Air Forces, Secretary of War, Office of the Assistant Secretary of War for Air, Plans, Policies and Agreements 1943–47, A1 219/390/10/8/3, boxes 199–200, RG 107, NARA, 1.

33. Joint Staff Planners, "Over-all Examination," 218.

34. Franklin D. Roosevelt to the Joint Chiefs of Staff, "U.S. Requirements for Post-war Air Bases," memorandum, November 23, 1943, and "HCJ," Joint Chiefs of Staff Memorandum to Records, "U.S. Requirements for Post War Air Bases," December 30, 1943, both in Central Decimal File 1942–45, "Air Routes across the Pacific and Air Facilities for International Police Force," box 279, Records of the U.S. Joint Chiefs of Staff, RG 218, NARA; Converse, *Circling the Earth*, 34–36.

35. For the full list, see David Vine, "Table 1: 'US Requirements for Postwar Air Bases' according to the 'Base Bible,'" Base Nation, www.basenation.us /basestables.html.

36. Joint Chiefs of Staff, "U.S. Requirements for Post-War Air Bases," attachment, n.d., Secretary of War, Office of the Assistant Secretary of War for Air, Plans, Policies and Agreements, 1943–47, A1 219/390/10/8/3, boxes 199–200, RG 107, NARA; Joint Chiefs of Staff, "List of Air Bases in Foreign Territory Required by the United States," app. A, annex B, n.d., Central Decimal File 1942–45, "Air Routes Across the Pacific and Air Facilities for International Police Force," box 279, Records of the U.S. Joint Chiefs of Staff, RG 218, NARA, 15–19.

37. Roosevelt amended his instructions to the State Department three weeks after his first letter to reflect the enlarged scope of the plans. Secretary of the Navy James Forrestal to Secretary of State James F. Byrnes, Charles W. McCarthy, Alvin F. Richardson, and Raymond E. Cox, "Post-war Island Air Bases: Notes by the Secretaries," enclosure, October 4, 1945, State-War-Navy Coordinating Committee, SWNCC 38/20, Central Decimal File 1942–45, box 272, sec. 9, 217, RG 218, NARA, 65–68. See also Sherry, *Preparing*, 46–47.

38. For the full list, see David Vine, "Table 2: Island Locations Where the U.S. Navy Desired Bases or Rights to Build Bases," Base Nation, www.basenation.us /basestables.html.

39. Melvyn P. Leffler, "The American Conception of National Security and the Beginnings of the Cold War, 1945-1948," in *Safeguarding Democratic Capitalism: U.S. Foreign Policy and National Security, 1920-2015* (Princeton, NJ: Princeton University Press, 2017), 128. The essay was originally published in 1984 in *American Historical Review*.

40. Quoted in Leffler, "American Conception," 128-29.

41. N. Smith, *American Empire*, 409-10.

42. Converse, *Circling the Earth*, 39, 15.

43. P. Smith, *Air Force Plans*, 75.

44. P. Smith, *Air Force Plans*, 106, 82-83.

45. Quoted in Converse, *Circling the Earth*, 89. The second point appears in a copy of the memorandum from NARA. Location information is missing, but the copy is on file with the author. Other contemporaneous documents about the Dhahran base are at Secretary of the Army, Assistant Secretary of the Army, State Army-Navy-Air Coordinating Committee, entry 41, box 5, and entry 42, box 1, RG 335, NARA.

46. Macris, "Persian Gulf Theater," 104-5.

47. Leffler, *Preponderance of Power*, 80.

48. Quoted in Michael Klare, *Blood and Oil: The Dangers and Consequences of America's Growing Dependency on Imported Petroleum* (New York: Owl Books, 2004), 35.

49. Charlie Whitham, "On Dealing with Gangsters: The Limits of British 'Generosity' in the Leasing of Bases to the United States, 1940-1941," *Diplomacy and Statecraft* 7, no. 3 (1996): 620.

50. *Journal* article, quoted in High, *Base Colonies*, 22, 213n37.

51. Quoted in High, *Base Colonies*, 24.

52. Stetson Conn, Rose C. Engelman, and Byron Fairchild, *Guarding the United States and Its Outposts: U.S. Army in World War II* (Washington, DC: U.S. Army Center of Military History, 2000), 354.

53. N. Smith, *American Empire*, 360.

54. David Harvey, *The New Imperialism* (Oxford: Oxford University Press, 2003); Chalmers Johnson, *The Sorrows of Empire: Militarism, Secrecy, and the End of the Republic* (New York: Metropolitan, 2004).

55. N. Smith, *American Empire*, 361-62.

56. Almost as an afterthought, Truman said, "We will acquire them by arrangements consistent with the United Nations Charter." Quoted in Editors, "U.S. Military Bases and Empire," *Monthly Review*, March 1, 2002, www.monthlyreview.org/0302editr.htm.

57. Sherry, *Preparing*, 233.

58. Oliver Stone and Peter Kuznick, *The Untold History of the United States* (New York: Gallery Books, 2012), 138-43.

59. Quoted in Converse, *Circling the Earth*, 199.

60. Quoted in Stone and Kuznick, *Untold History*, 201.

61. Melvyn P. Leffler, *Safeguarding Democratic Capitalism: U.S. Foreign Policy and National Security, 1920–2015* (Princeton, NJ: Princeton University Press, 2017), 190–91, 210.

62. N. Smith, *American Empire*, 349, 360.

63. Editors, "U.S. Military Bases."

64. N. Smith, *American Empire;* Chalmers Johnson, *Blowback: The Costs and Consequences of U.S. Empire* (2000; repr., New York: Metropolitan, 2004); C. Johnson, "America's Empire of Bases"; Editors, "U.S. Military Bases."

65. Immerwahr, *Hide an Empire*, 226.

66. Editors, "U.S. Military Bases."

67. Immerwahr, *Hide an Empire*, 343.

68. The worldwide total may be many millions higher, given uncertainty around the number of Chinese who perished. See "Research Starters: Worldwide Deaths in World War II," National World War II Museum, accessed February 16, 2020, www.nationalww2museum.org/students-teachers/student-resources /research-starters/research-starters-worldwide-deaths-world-war.

69. Immerwahr, *Hide an Empire*, 226.

CHAPTER TEN. THE SPOILS OF WAR

1. Amy Holmes, *Social Unrest and American Military Bases in Turkey and Germany since 1945* (Cambridge: Cambridge University Press, 2014); Hans W. Weigert, "U.S. Strategic Bases and Collective Security," *Foreign Affairs* 25, no. 2 (1947): 259.

2. Daniel Immerwahr, *How to Hide an Empire: A History of the Greater United States* (New York: Farrar, Straus and Giroux, 2019), 356.

3. Joshua Freeman, *American Empire 1945–2000: The Rise of a Global Power, the Democratic Revolution at Home,* (New York: Penguin, 2012), 51.

4. Immerwahr, *Hide an Empire*, 356.

5. Quoted in John Lindsay-Poland, *Emperors in the Jungle: The Hidden History of the U.S. in Panama* (Durham, NC: Duke University Press, 2003), 60.

6. Because of "interdepartmental misunderstandings" borne of policy disagreements and interagency competition, U.S. officials did not finalize their plans until the following year. Melvyn P. Leffler, "The American Conception of National Security and the Beginnings of the Cold War, 1945–1948," in *Safeguarding Democratic Capitalism: U.S. Foreign Policy and National Security, 1920–2015* (Princeton, NJ: Princeton University Press, 2017), 117–63.

7. Michael S. Sherry, *Preparing for the Next War: American Plans for Postwar Defense, 1941–45* (New Haven, CT: Yale University Press, 1977), 204.

8. Melvyn P. Leffler, *A Preponderance of Power: National Security, the Truman Administration, and the Cold War* (Stanford, CA: Stanford University Press, 1992), 56–58.

9. Leffler, *Preponderance of Power,* 56.

10. Leffler, *Preponderance of Power,* 58.

11. Natalia Loukacheva, *The Arctic Promise: Legal and Political Autonomy of Greenland and Nunavut* (Toronto: University of Toronto Press, 2007), 132; Elliott V. Converse III, *Circling the Earth: United States Plans for a Postwar Overseas Military Base System, 1942–1948* (Maxwell Air Force Base, AL: Air University Press, 2005), 210.

12. Joseph Blocher and Mitu Gulati, "Sure, Trump Can Buy Greenland. But Why Does He Think It's Up to Denmark?," *Politico Magazine,* August 23, 2019, www.politico.com/magazine/story/2019/08/23/donald-trump-greenland-purchase-sovereignty-denmark-227859.

13. Weigert, "U.S. Strategic Bases," 258.

14. Catherine Lutz, *Homefront: A Military City and the American 20th Century* (Boston: Beacon, 2001), 47–48.

15. Quoted in Lutz, *Homefront,* 47–48.

16. Michael S. Sherry, *In the Shadow of War: The United States since the 1930s* (New Haven, CT: Yale University Press, 1995), 33, 30–44.

17. Lutz, *Homefront,* 86.

18. Quoted in Leffler, "American Conception," 125.

19. George Stambuk, *American Military Forces Abroad: Their Impact on the Western State System* (Columbus: Ohio State University Press, 1963), 13; Richard H. Immerman, *Empire for Liberty: A History of American Imperialism from Benjamin Franklin to Paul Wolfowitz* (Princeton, NJ: Princeton University Press, 2010), 18.

20. Hal M. Friedman, *Creating an American Lake: United States Imperialism and Strategic Security in the Pacific Basin, 1945–1947* (Westport, CT: Greenwood, 2001), 1–2.

21. Quoted in Peter Hayes, Lyuba Zarsky, and Walden Bello, *American Lake: Nuclear Peril in the Pacific* (Victoria, Australia: Penguin Books, 1986), 28.

22. Adm. Ernest King, quoted in Weigert, "U.S. Strategic Bases," 256.

23. Hayes, Zarsky, and Bello, *American Lake,* 23–24.

24. Quoted in Donald F. McHenry, *Micronesia: Trust Betrayed* (New York: Carnegie Endowment for International Peace, 1975), 67, 66.

25. Stanley de Smith, quoted in Roy H. Smith, *The Nuclear Free and Independent Pacific Movement: After Mururoa* (London: Tauris, 1997), 42.

26. Leffler, *Preponderance of Power,* 118, 123, 135–40, 108–12.

27. Leffler, *Preponderance of Power,* 78, 113.

28. Leffler, *Preponderance of Power,* 77, 112–13; John Lewis Gaddis, *We Now Know: Rethinking Cold War History* (Oxford: Oxford University Press, 1997), 165.

29. Weigert, "U.S. Strategic Bases," 253–54, 252.

30. Oliver Stone and Peter Kuznick, *The Untold History of the United States* (New York: Gallery Books, 2012), 199–200, 139.

31. Freeman, *American Empire*, 51.

32. Joint Chiefs of Staff, "Memorandum for the State-War-Navy Coordinating Committee," enclosure, June 4, 1946, SWNCC 38/35; Joint Chiefs of Staff, "Memorandum for the Under-secretary of War," September 16, 1947, both in 490/9/2/4–6, entry 41, box 5, Security Classified, 1944–49, State Army-Navy-Air Coordinating Committee Numbered Papers, Assistant Secretary of the Army, RG 335, National Archives and Records Administration, Washington, DC.

33. James R. Blaker, *United States Overseas Basing: An Anatomy of the Dilemma* (New York: Praeger, 1990), 32.

34. Stambuk, *American Military Forces Abroad*, 9.

35. Leffler, "American Conception," 127.

36. Leffler, *Preponderance of Power*, 113; John D. Rickerson to the Secretary of State, "U.S. Military Requirements in Iceland," memorandum, May 1, 1946, 490/9/2/4–6, entry 41, box 5, Security Classified, 1944–49, State Army-Navy-Air Coordinating Committee Numbered Papers, Assistant Secretary of the Army, RG 335, National Archives and Records Administration.

37. Leffler, "American Conception," 127. Quotation in Gretchen Heefner, "Military Power: Overseas Bases," in *Cambridge History of America and the World*, ed. David Engerman, Melani McAlister, and Max Paul Friedman, vol. 4 (Cambridge: Cambridge University Press, forthcoming).

38. Leffler, "American Conception," 127–28.

39. Gavin McCormack, *Client State: Japan in the American Embrace* (London: Verso Books, 2007), 156; Chalmers Johnson, *The Sorrows of Empire: Militarism, Secrecy, and the End of the Republic* (New York: Metropolitan, 2004), 201.

40. R. Smith, *Nuclear Free and Independent*, 42.

41. Leffler, *Preponderance of Power*, 171.

42. George Kennan, "Report by the Policy Planning Staff," February 24, 1948, in *Foreign Relations of the United States, 1948, General*, vol. 1, *The United Nations*, pt. 2, PPS/23, Office of the Historian, U.S. Department of State, https://history.state.gov/historicaldocuments/frus1948v01p2/d4.

43. John Lewis Gaddis, *Strategies of Containment: A Critical Appraisal of Postwar American National Security Policy* (Oxford: Oxford University Press, 1982).

44. Sherry, *Preparing*, 236–37.

45. Sherry, *Preparing*, 236–37.

46. Andrew Bacevich, *Washington Rules: America's Path to Permanent War* (New York: Metropolitan Books, 2010), 22–23.

47. Gaddis, *We Now Know*, 264.

48. Gaddis, *Strategies of Containment*, 90–91.

49. See, for example, Claude Ricketts to Chief of Naval Operations, "Study on Strategic Requirements for Guam," memorandum, February 21, 1963, folder 11000/1, tab B, 00 Files, Naval History and Heritage Command Archives, Washington, DC.

50. Kent E. Calder, *Embattled Garrisons: Comparative Base Politics and American Globalism* (Princeton, NJ: Princeton University Press, 2007), 239, 209.

51. Bacevich, *Washington Rules*, 22.

52. Quoted in *Standing Army*, directed by Thomas Fazi and Enrico Parenti (Rome: Effendemfilm and Takae Films, 2010).

53. Quoted in Leffler, *Preponderance of Power*, 114, 392.

CHAPTER ELEVEN. NORMALIZING OCCUPATION

1. Paul Thomas Chamberlin, *The Cold War's Killing Fields: Rethinking the Long Peace* (New York: Harper, 2018), 8.

2. Lt. Col. R. W. Lightfoot, "Military Rights Agreement regarding the Azores Islands," memorandum, August 30, 1951, 190/69/6/1–2, box 39, NM-15 341, General Records Relating to Overseas Bases, RG 341, National Archives and Records Administration, Washington, DC.

3. James R. Blaker, *United States Overseas Basing: An Anatomy of the Dilemma* (New York: Praeger, 1990), 32.

4. Peter Hayes, Lyuba Zarsky, and Walden Bello, *American Lake: Nuclear Peril in the Pacific* (Victoria, Australia: Penguin Books, 1986), 29–30, 45; Melvyn P. Leffler, *A Preponderance of Power: National Security, the Truman Administration, and the Cold War* (Stanford, CA: Stanford University Press, 1992), 392.

5. Joshua Freeman, *American Empire, 1945–2000: The Rise of a Global Power, the Democratic Revolution at Home* (New York: Penguin, 2012), 87.

6. Gretchen Heefner, "Military Power: Overseas Bases," in *Cambridge History of America and the World*, ed. David Engerman, Melani McAlister, and Max Paul Friedman, vol. 4 (Cambridge: Cambridge University Press, forthcoming); Leffler, *Preponderance of Power*, 480, 490–91; Freeman, *American Empire*, 87.

7. Walter Trohan, "U.S. Strategy Tied to World Air Superiority," *Chicago Daily Tribune*, February 14, 1955, 6.

8. Blaker, *United States Overseas*, 32.

9. Alfred W. McCoy, *In the Shadows of the American Century: The Rise and Decline of US Global Power* (Chicago: Haymarket Books, 2017), 52–53.

10. Amy Holmes, *Social Unrest and American Military Bases in Turkey and Germany since 1945* (Cambridge: Cambridge University Press, 2014), 6.

11. Col. L. C. Coddington, "(Top Secret) Proposed Agreement with Portugal for U.S. Military Operating Rights in the Azores Islands," Record and Routing Sheet, August 17, 1951, 190/69/6/1–2, box 39, NM-15 341, General Records

Relating to Overseas Bases, RG 341, National Archives and Records Administration.

12. Joseph Gerson, "The Sun Never Sets," in *The Sun Never Sets: Confronting the Network of Foreign U.S. Military Bases*, ed. Joseph Gerson and Bruce Birchard (Boston: South End, 1991), 16–17.

13. António José Telo, "Foreign Bases and Strategies in Contemporary Portugal," in *Military Bases: Historical Perspectives, Contemporary Challenges*, ed. Luís Rodrigues and Sergiy Glebov (Amsterdam: IOS, 2009), 155; Luís Nuno Rodrigues, "Azores or Angola? Military Bases and Self-Determination during the Kennedy Administration," in Rodrigues and Glebov, *Military Bases*, 69.

14. Alexander Cooley and Daniel H. Nexon, "'The Empire Will Compensate You': The Structural Dynamics of the U.S. Overseas Basing Network," *Perspectives on Politics* 11, no. 4 (2013): 1034–50.

15. Thanks to Stacy Pettyjohn and Andrew Yeo for their help in my thinking here. See also Cooley and Nexon, "'Empire Will Compensate,'" 1034–50; and Holmes, *Social Unrest*.

16. Cited in Holmes, *Social Unrest*, 6.

17. Telo, "Foreign Bases and Strategies," in Rodrigues and Glebov, *Military Bases*, 155.

18. Heefner, "Military Power," in Engerman, McAlister, and Friedman, *Cambridge History of America*.

19. Quoted in Rodrigues, "Azores or Angola?," 76.

20. Daniel J. Nelson, *A History of U.S. Military Forces in Germany* (Boulder, CO: Westview, 1987), 76–79.

21. "Off the Offset Era," editorial, *New York Times*, July 24, 1976, 22, www .nytimes.com/1976/07/24/archives/off-the-offset-era.html.

22. Alexander Cooley, *Base Politics: Democratic Change and the US Military Overseas* (Ithaca, NY: Cornell University Press, 2008), 208–9.

23. Walter LaFeber, *Inevitable Revolutions: The United States in Central America* (New York: Norton, 1983), 44–45.

24. Carole McGranahan, "Empire Out-of-Bounds: Tibet in the Era of Decolonization," in *Imperial Formations*, ed. Anna Laura Stoler, Carole McGranahan, and Peter C. Perdue (Santa Fe, NM: SAR, 2007), 180.

25. On cultural and scholarly funding to institutions such as the American Academy in Rome and the Rockefeller Foundation, as well as to jazz musicians, artists, and novelists, see Frances Stonor Saunders, *The Cultural Cold War: The CIA and the World of Arts and Letters* (1999; repr., New York: New Press, 2013).

26. Leffler, *Preponderance of Power*, 490–91.

27. McCoy, *In the Shadows*, 55.

28. McCoy, *In the Shadows*, 55.

29. John Lukacs, "American Nationalism," *Harper's Magazine*, May 2012, 57.

30. McCoy, *In the Shadows*, 55.

31. McCoy, *In the Shadows*, 55.

32. Cooley, *Base Politics*, 195–99, 199n88; C. T. Sandars, *America's Overseas Garrisons: The Leasehold Empire* (Oxford: Oxford University Press, 2000), 33. A subsequent treaty was signed in 1995 that adds to but does not invalidate the Bilateral Infrastructure Agreement.

33. "United States Army Africa (ASARAF); Southern European Task Force (SETAF)," GlobalSecurity.org, accessed February 17, 2020, www.globalsecurity.org /military/agency/army/setaf.htm.

34. Disarmiamoli!'s list counted 109 bases after the end of the "Cold War." "Basi USA-NATO ITALIA," *Disarmiamoli!*, accessed July 9, 2018, www.disarmiamoli .org/index.php?option=com_content&task=view&id=13&Itemid=69 (page discontinued).

35. Carla Monteleone, "Impact and Perspectives of American Bases in Italy," in Rodrigues and Glebov, *Military Bases*, 136.

36. Eric Schewe, paper presented in Local Meanings panel, U.S. Bases and the Construction of Hegemony symposium (Center for the Study of Force and Diplomacy, Temple University, Philadelphia, October 10, 2015).

37. In practice, after a crime, power dynamics, diplomatic politics, and on-the-ground maneuvering by military, embassy, and local officials can determine what happens no matter what a SOFA says.

38. My thanks to Joseph Gerson for pointing this out and for all the expertise he has generously shared.

39. John Willoughby, *Remaking the Conquering Heroes: The Postwar American Occupation of Germany* (London: Palgrave Macmillan, 2001), 150.

40. Maria H. Höhn, *GIs and Fräuleins: The German-American Encounter in 1950s West Germany* (Chapel Hill: University of North Carolina Press, 2002), 27. The following sections of this chapter owe a great debt to Maria Höhn and her important work.

41. Willoughby, *Remaking*, 25–28.

42. Quoted in Willoughby, *Remaking*, 138–39.

43. Willoughby, *Remaking*, 138–39, 46–49, 137, 140–41.

44. Quoted in Willoughby, *Remaking*, 118.

45. Anni Baker, *Life in the U.S. Armed Forces: (Not) Just Another Job* (Westport, CT: Praeger Security International, 2008), 119–20; Willoughby, *Remaking*.

46. Willoughby, *Remaking*, 118–21; Donna Alvah, "U.S. Military Families Abroad in the Post–Cold War Era and the 'New Global Posture,'" in *Over There: Living with the U.S. Military Empire from World War Two to the Present*, ed. Maria Höhn and Seungsook Moon (Durham, NC: Duke University Press, 2010), 154; Anni P. Baker, *American Soldiers Overseas: The Global Military Presence* (Westport, CT: Praeger, 2004), 53; Baker, *U.S. Armed Forces* 120.

47. Nelson, *History of U.S. Military,* 40–45, 81; Tim Kane, "Global U.S. Troop Deployment, 1950–2005," Heritage Foundation, May 24, 2006, www.heritage .org/defense/report/global-us-troop-deployment-1950-2005.

48. Baker, *U.S. Armed Forces,* 118–19; Baker, *American Soldiers,* 15.

49. Höhn, *GIs and Fräuleins,* 39–41.

50. See, for example, Mark L. Gillem, *America Town: Building the Outposts of Empire* (Minneapolis: University of Minnesota Press, 2007), 92–93; Felia Allum, *Camorristi, Politicians, and Businessmen: The Transformation of Organized Crime in Post-war Naples* (Leeds: Northern Universities Press, 2006), 99–100.

51. Höhn, *GIs and Fräuleins,* 8, 19, 33–34, 40–44, 52.

52. Baker, *American Soldiers,* 54.

53. See, for example, Höhn, *GIs and Fräuleins;* Baker, *American Soldiers;* and Willoughby, *Remaking.*

54. Willoughby, *Remaking,* 150; Nelson, *History of U.S. Military,* 55–56.

55. Holmes, *Social Unrest,* 11; Gerson, "Sun Never Sets," in Gerson and Birchard, *Sun Never Sets,* 16–17.

56. Holmes, *Social Unrest,* 6.

57. Kent E. Calder, *Embattled Garrisons: Comparative Base Politics and American Globalism* (Princeton, NJ: Princeton University Press, 2007), 9. Parts of this chapter derive from David Vine, "No Bases? How Social Movements against U.S. Military Bases Abroad Are Challenging Militarization and Militarism," in "Cultures of Militarism," ed. Catherine Besteman and Hugh Gusterson, supplemental issue, *Current Anthropology* 60, no. S19 (2019): S158–72.

58. See, for example, Gillem, *America Town;* Catherine Lutz, ed., *Bases of Empire: The Global Struggle against U.S. Military Posts* (New York: New York University Press, 2009); and David Vine, *Base Nation: How U.S. Military Bases Abroad Harm America and the World* (New York: Metropolitan, 2015).

59. Jana K. Lipman, *Guantánamo: A Working-Class History between Empire and Revolution* (Berkeley: University of California Press, 2008), 23–24; Stephen I. M. Schwab, *Guantánamo, USA: The Untold Story of America's Cuban Outpost* (Lawrence: University Press of Kansas, 2009).

60. Cooley, *Base Politics,* 147.

61. U.S. officials decided the expansion was "more trouble than it was worth." After two decades of protest, the U.S. Air Force moved to nearby Yokota Air Base and transferred Tachikawa to the Japanese Self-Defense Forces. Dustin Wright, "From Tokyo to Wounded Knee: Two Afterlives of the Sunagawa Struggle," *Sixties* 10, no. 2 (2017): 136–37.

62. Daniel Immerwahr, *How to Hide an Empire: A History of the Greater United States* (New York: Farrar, Straus and Giroux, 2019), 356.

63. Cooley, *Base Politics,* 159–68; Rodrigues, "Azores or Angola?," 70.

64. *The Pentagon Papers: The Defense Department History of United States Decision Making on Vietnam,* ed. Senator Gravel (Boston: Beacon, 1971), 53–75.

This edition is available at www.mtholyoke.edu/acad/intrel/pentagon/pent5.htm. All three editions are at https://nsarchive2.gwu.edu/NSAEBB/NSAEBB359 /index.htm.

65. Andrew Bacevich, *Washington Rules: America's Path to Permanent War* (New York: Metropolitan Books, 2010), 66.

66. Freeman, *American Empire*, 227.

67. *United States Security Agreements and Commitments Abroad: Hearings before the Senate Subcommittee on United States Security Agreements and Commitments Abroad of the Committee on Foreign Relations*, 91st Cong., vol. 2 (Washington, DC: Government Printing Office, 1971), 2417.

68. Freeman, *American Empire*, 227–28; Ziad Obermeyer, Christopher J. L. Murray, and Emmanuela Gakidou, "Fifty Years of Violent War Deaths from Vietnam to Bosnia: Analysis of Data from the World Health Survey Programme," *British Medical Journal* 336 (2008): www.bmj.com/content/336/7659/1482 .full.

CHAPTER TWELVE. ISLANDS OF IMPERIALISM

1. Horacio Rivero to Chief of Naval Operations, "Long Range Requirements for the Southern Oceans," enclosure to memorandum, May 21, 1960, folder 5710, box 8, 00 Files, Naval History and Heritage Command Archives, Washington, DC, 2. Rivero credited Barber with doing most of the writing for the Long Range Objectives Group, which produced this document. Parts of this chapter stem from David Vine, *Island of Shame: The Secret History of the U.S. Military Base on Diego Garcia* (Princeton, NJ: Princeton University Press, 2009).

2. Rivero, "Long Range Requirements"; Stuart B. Barber to Paul B. Ryan, April 26, 1982, private collection, 3. My thanks to Richard Barber for his help with details about his father's life and for providing this and other invaluable documents.

3. Barber to Ryan, April 26, 1982.

4. Daniel Immerwahr, *How to Hide an Empire: A History of the Greater United States* (New York: Farrar, Straus and Giroux, 2019), 342–43.

5. Robert Scott, *Limuria: The Lesser Dependencies of Mauritius* (1961; repr., Westport, CT: Greenwood, 1976), 68, 42–43, 48–50; Vijayalakshmi Teelock, *Mauritian History: From Its Beginnings to Modern Times* (Moka, Mauritius: Mahatma Gandhi Institute, 2000), 16–17.

6. J. Kēhaulani Kauanui, "Milking the Cow for All It's Worth: Settler Colonialism and the Politics of Imperialist Resentment in Hawai'i," in *Ethnographies of Empire*, ed. Carole McGranahan and John Collins (Durham, NC: Duke University Press, 2018), 54.

7. Chalmers Johnson, *The Sorrows of Empire: Militarism, Secrecy, and the End of the Republic* (New York: Metropolitan, 2004), 201; Roy H. Smith, *The Nuclear Free and Independent Pacific Movement: After Mururoa* (London: Tauris, 1997), 42.

8. Quoted in Immerwahr, *Hide an Empire*, 360.

9. C. Johnson, *Sorrows of Empire*, 50–53, 200; Chalmers Johnson, *Blowback: The Costs and Consequences of U.S. Empire* (2000; repr., New York: Metropolitan, 2004), 11; Kensei Yoshida, *Democracy Betrayed: Okinawa under U.S. Occupation* (Bellingham, WA: Western Washington University, [2001?]); Kozy K. Amemiya, "The Bolivian Connection: U.S. Bases and Okinawan Emigration," in *Okinawa: Cold War Island*, ed. Chalmers Johnson (Oakland, CA: Japan Policy Research Institute, 1999), 63.

10. Quoted in Michiyo Yonamine, "Economic Crisis Shakes US Forces Overseas: The Price of Base Expansion in Okinawa and Guam," *Asia-Pacific Journal* 9, no. 9 (2011): https://apjjf.org/2011/9/9/Yonamine-Michiyo/3494/article .html.

11. Beyond bases, U.S. support for ongoing French and British colonial rule became a key U.S. strategy of the early "Cold War"; the European militaries and their colonial regimes served as auxiliary forces to try to maintain U.S.-led NATO domination across most of the globe not controlled by the Soviet Union or China.

12. António José Telo, "Foreign Bases and Strategies in Contemporary Portugal," in *Military Bases: Historical Perspectives, Contemporary Challenges*, ed. Luís Rodrigues and Sergiy Glebov (Amsterdam: IOS, 2009), 159.

13. Vine, *Island of Shame*, chap. 3. I stress "perceived" because threats are a matter of subjective rather than objective assessment.

14. Barber to Ryan, April 26, 1982, 3.

15. Horacio Rivero to Chief of Naval Operations, "Assuring a Future Base Structure in the African-Indian Ocean Area," enclosure to memorandum, July 11, 1960, folder 5710, box 8, 00 Files, Naval History and Heritage Command Archives; Rivero, "Long Range Requirements."

16. Rivero, "Assuring a Future Base."

17. Roy L. Johnson to Deputy Chief of Naval Operations (Plans and Policy), memorandum, July 21, 1958, A4–2 Status of Shore Stations, box 4, 00 Files, U.S. Navy Archives, Washington, DC, 2–3. See also Vine, *Island of Shame*, introd., chap. 3. Barber was responsible for the memorandum signed by Johnson.

18. Vine, *Island of Shame*, chap. 3.

19. U.S. Embassy, London, to Secretary of State, telegram, February 27, 1964, folder 11000/1B, box 20, 00 Files, Naval History and Heritage Command Archives, 1–2.

20. John Pilger, *Freedom Next Time: Resisting the Empire* (New York: Nation Books, 2007), 25.

21. Vine, *Island of Shame*, chap. 4.

22. R. S. Leddick, "Memorandum for the Record," November 11, 1969, folder 11000, box 98, 00 Files, Naval History and Heritage Command Archives.

23. Anthony Aust, "Immigration Legislation for BIOT," memorandum, January 16, 1970, U.K. Lawyers for Chagossians Trial Bundle, on file with the author.

24. "Proposed Naval Communications Facility on Diego Garcia," attachment, Op-605E4, briefing sheet, [January?] 1970, folder 11000, box 111, 00 Files, Naval History and Heritage Command Archives. See also Vine, *Island of Shame*, chap. 6; John H. Chafee to Secretary of Defense, memorandum, January 31, 1970, folder 11000, box 111, 00 Files, Naval History and Heritage Command Archives.

25. Vine, *Island of Shame*, esp. chap. 5.

26. Parts of this section derive from Vine, *Island of Shame*, and David Vine, "Islands of Imperialism: Military Bases and the Ethnography of U.S. Empire," in McGranahan and Collins, *Ethnographies of Empire*, 249–69.

27. S. J. Dunn, "Shore Up the Indian Ocean," *U.S. Naval Institute Proceedings* 110, no. 9/979 (1984): 131.

28. David Vine, *Base Nation: How U.S. Military Bases Abroad Harm America and the World* (New York: Metropolitan Books, 2015), chap. 14.

29. Quoted in Robert D. Kaplan, *Hog Pilots, Blue Water Grunts: The American Military in the Air, at Sea, and on the Ground* (New York: Vintage, 2008), 60–61.

30. Quoted in Minagahet Chamorro, "Whether Cruel or Kind . . . ," *No Rest for the Awake* (blog), June 11, 2014, http://minagahet.blogspot.com/2014/06 /whether-cruel-or-kind.html; see also Immerwahr, *Hide an Empire*, 388.

31. Vine, *Base Nation*, chap. 16.

32. Immerwahr, *Hide an Empire*, 343.

33. Joseph Gerson, "The Sun Never Sets," in *The Sun Never Sets: Confronting the Network of Foreign U.S. Military Bases*, ed. Joseph Gerson and Bruce Birchard (Boston: South End, 1991), 14.

34. Catherine Lutz, "Empire Is in the Details," *American Ethnologist* 33, no. 4 (2006): 593–611.

35. Paul Kramer, "How Not to Write the History of U.S. Empire," *Diplomatic History* 42, no. 5 (2018): 919. U.S. officials also supported a violent counterinsurgency campaign against Filipino leftists.

36. Gretchen Heefner, "Military Power: Overseas Bases," in *Cambridge History of America and the World*, ed. David Engerman, Melani McAlister, and Max Paul Friedman, vol. 4 (Cambridge: Cambridge University Press, forthcoming).

CHAPTER THIRTEEN. THE COLONIAL PRESENT

1. David Vine, *Base Nation: How U.S. Military Bases Abroad Harm America and the World* (New York: Metropolitan Books, 2015), chap. 3.

2. Mark L. Gillem, *America Town: Building the Outposts of Empire* (Minneapolis: University of Minnesota Press, 2007), 36–37.

3. David Vine, *Island of Shame: The Secret History of the U.S. Military Base on Diego Garcia* (Princeton, NJ: Princeton University Press, 2009), 1–6.

4. Elmo Zumwalt to E. L. Cochrane Jr., attachment to memorandum for the Deputy Chief of Naval Operations (Plans and Policy), March 24, 1971, folder 11000, box 174, 00 Files, Naval History and Heritage Command Archives, Washington, DC.

5. Vine, *Island of Shame*, 113–14.

6. David Ottaway, "Islanders Were Evicted for U.S. Base," *Washington Post*, September 9, 1975, A1. See also "The Diego Garcians," editorial, *Washington Post*, September 11, 1975.

7. Vine, *Island of Shame*, chap. 10. See, for example, Benedict Carey, "Did Debbie Reynolds Die of a Broken Heart?," *New York Times*, December 29, 2016, www.nytimes.com/2016/12/29/health/did-debbie-reynolds-die-of-a-broken-heart .html.

8. Cheryl Lewis, "Kahoʻolawe and the Military," ICE case study 84, Spring 2001, http://mandalaprojects.com/ice/ice-cases/hawaiibombs.htm.

9. "Conference Report Filed in House (07/26/1988)," H. R. 442: Civil Liberties Act of 1987, accessed February 17, 2020, www.congress.gov/bill/100th -congress/house-bill/442.

10. Katherine T. McCaffrey, *Military Power and Popular Protest: The U.S. Navy in Vieques, Puerto Rico* (New Brunswick, NJ: Rutgers University Press, 2002), 38–39.

11. Aqqaluk Lynge, *The Right to Return: Fifty Years of Struggle by Relocated Inughuit in Greenland* (n.p.: Atuagkat, 2002).

12. Miyume Tanji, "Japanese Wartime Occupation, Reparation, and Guam's Chamorro Self-Determination," in *Under Occupation: Resistance and Struggle in a Militarised Asia-Pacific*, ed. Daniel Broudy, Peter Simpson, and Makoto Arakaki (Newcastle upon Tyne, U.K.: Cambridge Scholars, 2013), 162–67.

13. Leevin Camacho, "Resisting the Proposed Military Buildup on Guam," in Broudy, Simpson, and Arakaki, *Under Occupation*, 186. Some quote a figure as high as 82 percent. See LisaLinda Natividad and Gwyn Kirk, "Fortress Guam: Resistance to US Military Mega-buildup," *Asia-Pacific Journal* 19, no. 1 (2010): https://apjjf.org/-LisaLinda-Natividad/3356/article.html.

14. Timothy P. Maga, *Defending Paradise: The United States and Guam, 1898–1950* (New York: Garland, 1988), 203–7.

15. "Definitions of Insular Area Political Organizations," Office of Insular Affairs, U.S. Department of the Interior, accessed February 26, 2020, www.doi .gov/oia/islands/politicatypes.

16. See, for example, Chalmers Johnson, *The Sorrows of Empire: Militarism, Secrecy, and the End of the Republic* (New York: Metropolitan, 2004), 50–53,

200; and Alexander Cooley, *Base Politics: Democratic Change and the US Military Overseas* (Ithaca, NY: Cornell University Press, 2008), 146.

17. Barbara Rose Johnston and Holly M. Barker, *The Consequential Damages of Nuclear War: The Rongelap Report* (Walnut Creek, CA: Left Coast, 2008).

18. David Hanlon, *Remaking Micronesia: Discourses over Development in a Pacific Territory, 1944–1982* (Honolulu: University of Hawai'i Press, 1998), 193; Peter Marks, "Paradise Lost: The Americanization of the Pacific," *Newsday*, January 12, 1986, 10; Pacific Concerns Research Centre, "The Kwajalein Atoll and the New Arms Race: The US Anti-ballistic Weapons System and Consequences for the Marshall Islands of the Pacific," *Indigenous Affairs* 2 (2001): 38–43.

19. C. T. Sandars, *America's Overseas Garrisons: The Leasehold Empire* (Oxford: Oxford University Press, 2000), 36.

20. Catherine Lutz, "Introduction: Bases, Empire, and Global Response," in *Bases of Empire: The Global Struggle against U.S. Military Posts*, ed. Catherine Lutz (New York: New York University Press, 2009), 1–44.

21. Quoted in Vine, *Island of Shame*, 181.

22. McCaffrey, *Military Power*, 9–10.

23. Frances Fox Piven, conversation with the author, New York, 2002.

24. U.S. bases inside the United States have displaced locals of many races and ethnicities. There is reason to believe that most of the displaced have been disproportionately people of color and relatively poor. Catherine Lutz, *Homefront: A Military City and the American 20th Century* (Boston: Beacon, 2001), 26.

25. A. M. Jackson to Chief of Naval Operations, memorandum, December 7, 1964, folder 11000/1B, box 26, 00 Files, U.S. Navy Archives, Washington, DC, 3–4.

26. Regina (on the Application of Bancoult) v. Secretary of State for the Foreign and Commonwealth Office, (2006) EWHC 1038, para. 27.

27. W. E. B. DuBois, *The World and Africa*, exp. ed. (1946; repr., New York: International, 1965); Hannah Arendt, *The Origins of Totalitarianism*, pt. 2, *Imperialism* (New York: Harcourt, Brace and World, 1951).

28. Nancy Scheper-Hughes and Philippe Bourgois, "Introduction: Making Sense of Violence," in *Violence in War and Peace: An Anthology*, ed. Nancy Scheper-Hughes and Philippe Bourgois (Malden, MA: Blackwell, 2004), 19.

29. Phillip W. D. Martin, "Why So Many Iraqis Hate Us? Try 'Towel Head' on for Size," *Huffington Post*, April 11, 2008 (updated May 25, 2011), www.huffington post.com/phillip-martin/why-so-many-iraqis-hate-u_b_96330.html; Nikhil Pal Singh, *Race and America's Long War*, (Oakland: University of California Press, 2017), 24.

30. Scheper-Hughes and Bourgois, "Introduction," in Scheper-Hughes and Bourgois, *Violence in War*, 20–22.

31. See, for example, Gillem, *America Town*; Lutz, *Bases of Empire*; and Vine, *Base Nation*.

32. Scheper-Hughes and Bourgois, "Introduction," in Scheper-Hughes and Bourgois, *Violence in War,* 20.

33. Anthony Lake and Roger Morris, "Pentagon Papers (2): The Human Reality of Realpolitik," *Foreign Policy* 4 (1971): 159.

34. John Conroy, *Unspeakable Acts, Ordinary People: The Dynamics of Torture* (Berkeley: University of California Press, 2000); W. Fitzhugh Brundage, *Civilizing Torture: An American Tradition* (Cambridge, MA: Harvard University Press, 2018), 292, 328–30, 390n82; Natalie Y. Moore, "Payback," Marshall Project, October 30, 2018, www.themarshallproject.org/2018/10/30/payback.

35. Scheper-Hughes and Bourgois, "Introduction," in Scheper-Hughes and Bourgois, *Violence in War,* 21.

36. Quoted in Vine, *Island of Shame,* 197–98.

37. Quoted in Vine, *Island of Shame,* 195.

38. "Legal Consequences of the Separation of the Chagos Archipelago from Mauritius in 1965," General List 169, International Court of Justice, February 25, 2019, www.icj-cij.org/en/case/169.

CHAPTER FOURTEEN. BUILDING BLOWBACK

1. *United States Security Agreements and Commitments Abroad: Hearings before the Senate Subcommittee on United States Security Agreements and Commitments Abroad of the Committee on Foreign Relations,* 91st Cong., vol. 2 (Washington, DC: Government Printing Office, 1971), 2433–34. Parts of the conversation with Walter Pincus in this chapter stem from David Vine, *Base Nation: How U.S. Military Bases Abroad Harm America and the World* (New York: Metropolitan Books, 2015), 243–48.

2. James R. Blaker, *United States Overseas Basing: An Anatomy of the Dilemma* (New York: Praeger, 1990).

3. *United States Security Agreements,* 2433–34.

4. C. S. Minter Jr. to Chief of Naval Operations [Elmo Zumwalt], memorandum, July 20, 1972, folder 11000, box 161, 00 Files, Naval History and Heritage Command Archives, Washington, DC.

5. Vytautas B. Bandjunis, *Diego Garcia: Creation of the Indian Ocean Base* (San Jose, CA: Writer's Showcase, 2001), 49, 58.

6. Bandjunis, *Diego Garcia,* 64–71.

7. Melvyn P. Leffler, *A Preponderance of Power: National Security, the Truman Administration, and the Cold War* (Stanford, CA: Stanford University Press, 1992), 77, 112–13, 226, 238–40, 288, 352; Leffler, "American Conception," 164–85.

8. At the end of World War II and in the early postwar period, U.S. leaders strongly opposed Stalin's interest in establishing a base presence in the Turkish

Dardanelles Straits. Melvyn P. Leffler, "Strategy, Diplomacy, and the Cold War: The United States, Turkey, and NATO, 1945–1952," in *Safeguarding Democratic Capitalism: U.S. Foreign Policy and National Security, 1920–2015* (Princeton, NJ: Princeton University Press, 2017), 164–86; Victor Bulmer-Thomas, *Empire in Retreat: The Past, Present, and Future of the United States* (New Haven, CT: Yale University Press, 2018), 148–49, 193, 204.

9. Leffler, *Preponderance of Power*, 286.

10. Jimmy Carter, "State of the Union Address, 1980," January 23, 1980, Jimmy Carter Presidential Library and Museum, www.jimmycarterlibrary.gov /assets/documents/speeches/su80jec.phtml.

11. Joe Stork, "The Carter Doctrine and US Bases in the Middle East," *MERIP Reports*, September 1980, 3.

12. "Diego Garcia 'Camp Justice,'" GlobalSecurity.org, accessed February 13, 2020, www.globalsecurity.org/military/facility/diego-garcia.htm; David Vine, *Island of Shame: The Secret History of the U.S. Military Base on Diego Garcia* (Princeton, NJ: Princeton University Press, 2009), chap. 6.

13. Oliver Stone and Peter Kuznick, *The Untold History of the United States* (New York: Gallery Books, 2012), 413–14.

14. Tom Hayden, *Street Wars: Gangs and the Future of Violence* (New York: New Press, 2004), 57; William M. LeoGrande, *Our Own Backyard: The United States in Central America, 1977–1992* (Chapel Hill: University of North Carolina Press, 1998), 699nn119–20.

15. Trevor Paglen, *Blank Spots on the Map: The Dark Geography of the Pentagon's Secret World* (New York: Dalton, 2009), 218.

16. Todd Greentree, *Crossroads of Intervention: Insurgency and Counterinsurgency Lessons from Central America* (Westport, CT: Praeger Security International, 2008), 117; LeoGrande, *Our Own Backyard*, 150, 297.

17. Greentree, *Crossroads*, 117.

18. Richard W. Stewart, ed., *American Military History*, vol. 2, *The United States Army in a Global Era, 1917–2008*, 2nd ed. (Washington, DC: Center of Military History, 2010), 398.

19. Greentree, *Crossroads*, 121–22, 162.

20. LeoGrande, *Our Own Backyard*, 150, 297.

21. Glenn Garvin, *Everybody Had His Own Gringo: The CIA and the Contras* (Washington, DC: Brassey's, 1992), 40–41; LeoGrande, *Our Own Backyard*, 395.

22. U.S. General Accounting Office, *Honduras: Continuing U.S. Military Presence at Soto Cano Base Is Not Critical*, GAO/NSIAD-95-39 (Washington, DC: U.S. GAO, 1995), 2, www.gao.gov/assets/230/220840.pdf.

23. Eric L. Haney, "Inside Delta Force," in *American Soldier: Stories of Special Forces from Iraq to Afghanistan*, ed. Clint Willis (New York: Adrenaline, 2002), 28; Greentree, *Crossroads*, 116.

24. For details and source information on these bases, see Vine, *Base Nation*, chap. 5.

25. LeoGrande, *Our Own Backyard*, 331

26. LeoGrande, *Our Own Backyard*, 317, 587.

27. National Security Archive, *Chronology: The Documented Day-by-Day Account of the Secret Military Assistance to Iran and the Contras* (New York: Warner Books, 1987), 52–53.

28. LeoGrande, *Our Own Backyard*, 299.

29. Greentree, *Crossroads*, 7.

30. Haney, "Inside Delta Force," 34.

31. U.S. General Accounting Office, *Honduras*, 1.

32. Thanks and credit to Joe Masco for suggesting this line of analysis.

33. Chalmers Johnson, *Blowback: The Costs and Consequences of U.S. Empire* (2000; repr., New York: Metropolitan, 2004), xi.

34. Adrienne Pine, *Working Hard, Drinking Hard: On Violence and Survival in Honduras* (Berkeley: University of California Press, 2008), 35–38; T. W. Ward, *Gangsters without Borders: An Ethnography of a Salvadoran Street Gang* (Oxford: Oxford University Press, 2012).

35. Paglen, *Blank Spots*, 237, 211.

36. Thom Shanker, "Lessons of Iraq Help U.S. Fight a Drug War in Honduras," *New York Times*, May 5, 2012, 1.

37. United Nations Office on Drugs and Crime, G*lobal Study on Homicide 2013: Trends, Contexts, Data* (Vienna: UNODC, 2014), 24, 126.

38. Daniel Immerwahr, *How to Hide an Empire: A History of the Greater United States* (New York: Farrar, Straus and Giroux, 2019), 372–73; Enseng Ho, "Empire through Diasporic Eyes: A View from the Other Boat," *Comparative Studies in Society and History* 46, no. 2 (2004): 212–13.

CHAPTER FIFTEEN. DID THE "COLD WAR" END?

1. Andrew Hoehn, interviews with the author, Pentagon City, VA, April 29 and July 2, 2012.

2. "Strengthening U.S. Global Defense Posture," Department of Defense, September 17, 2004, 5, www.dmzhawaii.org/wp-content/uploads/2008/12/global_posture.pdf.

3. Keith B. Cunningham and Andreas Klemmer, *Restructuring the US Military Bases in Germany: Scope, Impacts, and Opportunities*, report 4 (Bonn, Germany: Bonn International Center for Conversion, 1995), 13, 20. There is a discrepancy in this report, which cites more than 92,000 acres (37,260 hectares) returned by the United States in total and more than 100,000 (40,500 hectares) returned by the U.S. Army alone.

4. Tim Kane, "Global U.S. Troop Deployment, 1950–2005," Heritage Foundation, May 24, 2006, www.heritage.org/defense/report/global-us-troop -deployment-1950-2005.

5. Joshua Freeman, *American Empire 1945–2000: The Rise of a Global Power, the Democratic Revolution at Home,* (New York: Penguin, 2012), 434.

6. Freeman, *American Empire,* 433–34.

7. Freeman, *American Empire,* 433–34.

8. Quoted in Andrew Bacevich, *Washington Rules: America's Path to Permanent War* (New York: Metropolitan Books, 2010), 148.

9. Catherine Lutz, "Warmaking as the American Way of Life," in *The Insecure American: How We Got Here and What We Should Do about It,* ed. Hugh Gusterson and Catherine Besteman (Berkeley: University of California Press, 2009), 50.

10. Roberto González, Hugh Gusterson, and David Price, "Introduction: War, Culture, and Counterinsurgency," in *The Counter-counterinsurgency Manual, or Notes on Demilitarizing American Society,* ed. Network of Concerned Anthropologists Steering Committee (Chicago: Prickly Paradigm, 2009), 5; Seymour Melman, *The Permanent War Economy: American Capitalism in Decline* (New York: Simon and Schuster, 1974).

11. Freeman, *American Empire,* 434.

12. U.S. General Accounting Office, *Honduras: Continuing U.S. Military Presence at Soto Cano Base Is Not Critical,* GAO/NSIAD-95-39 (Washington, DC: U.S. GAO, 1995), 4, 1, 8, www.gao.gov/assets/230/220840.pdf.

13. Scott M. Hines, "Joint Task Force—Bravo: The U.S. Military Presence in Honduras; U.S. Policy for an Evolving Region" (master's thesis, University of Maryland and National Defense University, 1994), 1.

14. William R. Meara, *Contra Cross: Insurgency and Tyranny in Central America, 1979–1989* (Annapolis, MD: Naval Institute Press, 2006), 32, 155.

15. Dana Priest, *The Mission: Waging Wars and Keeping Peace with America's Military* (New York: Norton, 2003), 199.

16. Priest, *Mission,* 200–206, 199, 77.

17. John Lindsay-Poland, "Pentagon Building Bases in Central America and Colombia Despite Constitutional Court Striking Down Base Agreement," *Fellowship of Reconciliation* (blog), January 27, 2011, http://forusa.org/blogs/john -lindsay-poland/pentagon-building-bases-central-america-colombia/8445 (blog discontinued); David Vine, *Base Nation: How U.S. Military Bases Abroad Harm America and the World* (New York: Metropolitan Books, 2015), chap. 5.

18. Associated Press, "U.S. Military Expands Its Drug War in Latin America," *USA Today,* February 3, 2013, www.usatoday.com/story/news/world /2013/02/03/us-expands-drug-war-latin-america/1887481/; John Lindsay-Poland, "Pentagon Continues Contracting U.S. Companies in Latin America,"

Fellowship of Reconciliation (blog), January 31, 2013, http://forusa.org
/blogs/john-lindsay-poland/pentagon-continues-contracting-us-companies-latin
-america/11782 (blog discontinued).

19. Vine, *Base Nation*, chap. 5.

20. Parts of this chapter draw on David Vine, "No Bases? How Social Movements against U.S. Military Bases Abroad Are Challenging Militarization and Militarism," in "Cultures of Militarism," ed. Catherine Besteman and Hugh Gusterson, supplemental issue, *Current Anthropology* 60, no. S19 (2019): S158–72. See also Amy Holmes, *Social Unrest and American Military Bases in Turkey and Germany since 1945* (Cambridge: Cambridge University Press, 2014); and Alexander Cooley, *Base Politics: Democratic Change and the US Military Overseas* (Ithaca, NY: Cornell University Press, 2008).

21. A communications station remained in Morocco after U.S. forces left Kenitra.

22. Bret Lortie, "And Then They Went Home," *Bulletin of the Atomic Scientists*, May–June 2000, 7.

23. Andrew Yeo, *Activists, Alliances, and Anti–U.S. Base Protests* (New York: Cambridge University Press, 2011), 186.

24. Joseph Gerson, "The Sun Never Sets," in *The Sun Never Sets: Confronting the Network of Foreign U.S. Military Bases*, ed. Joseph Gerson and Bruce Birchard (Boston: South End, 1991), 27; Andrew Yeo, "Not in Anyone's Backyard: The Emergence and Identity of a Transnational Anti-base Network," *International Studies Quarterly* 53, no. 3 (2009): 573.

25. Richard W. Stewart, ed., *American Military History*, vol. 2, *The United States Army in a Global Era, 1917–2008*, 2nd ed. (Washington, DC: Center of Military History, 2010), 401–6.

26. Michael Desch, *When the Third World Matters: Latin America and United States Grand Strategy* (Baltimore: Johns Hopkins University Press, 1993), 152.

27. Stewart, *American Military History*, 2:427.

28. Pratap Chatterjee, *Halliburton's Army: How a Well-Connected Texas Oil Company Revolutionized the Way America Makes War* (New York: Nation Books, 2009), 61–62.

29. P. W. Singer, *Corporate Warriors: The Rise of the Privatized Military Industry* (Ithaca, NY: Cornell University Press, 2003), 80.

30. Emma M. Ashford, "Better Balancing in the Middle East," in *US Grand Strategy in the 21st Century*, ed. Benjamin H. Friedman and A. Trevor Thrall (London: Routledge, 2018), 179.

31. Quoted in Peter L. Bergen, *The Osama Bin Laden I Know: An Oral History of Al Qaeda's Leader* (New York: Free Press, 2006), 165.

32. Bradley L. Bowman, "After Iraq: Future U.S. Military Posture in the Middle East," *Washington Quarterly* 31, no. 2 (2008): 85.

33. Matthew Evangelista, "Coping with 9/11: Alternatives to the War Paradigm," Costs of War Project, Brown University, June 16, 2011, https://watson .brown.edu/costsofwar/files/cow/imce/papers/2011/Coping%20with%20911.pdf. I am a board member of the Costs of War Project.

34. Michael O'Hanlon, "A Flawed Masterpiece," *Foreign Affairs* 81, no. 3 (2002): 47–53; Rebecca Grant, "The War Nobody Expected," *Air Force Magazine,* April 2002, 34–40.

35. Ann Jones, *Winter in Kabul: Life without Peace in Afghanistan* (New York: Metropolitan Books, 2006), 4.

36. Tom Englehardt, "The Wedding Crashers: A Short Till-Death-Do-Us-Part History of Bush's Wars," TomDispatch, July 13, 2008, www.tomdispatch.com /post/174954.

37. Rory Carroll, "Bloody Evidence of US Blunder," *Guardian,* January 6, 2002.

38. I regret being unable to conduct firsthand ethnographic research in Afghanistan, Pakistan, or Iraq or any extensive research with refugees from the wars in these countries. Details in this section come from *Afghanistan, Collateral Damage,* directed by Alberto Vendemmiati and Fabrizio Lazzaretti (Rome: Karousel Films/POV/RAI 3, 2002). See also *Jung (War) in the Land of the Mujaheddin (Nella Terra dei Mujaheddin),* directed by Fabrizio Lazzaretti and Alberto Vendemmiati (Rome: Elleti/Karousel Films, 2001).

39. *Afghanistan, Collateral Damage.*

40. Congressional Research Service, *United States Foreign Policy Objectives and Overseas Military Installations* (Washington, DC: Government Printing Office, 1979), 101–102.

41. Ken Adelman, "Cakewalk in Iraq," *Washington Post,* February 13, 2002, www.washingtonpost.com/archive/opinions/2002/02/13/cakewalk-in-iraq/cf09301c -c6c4-4f2e-8268-7c93017f5e93/?utm_term=.ec010bc2a1a9.

CHAPTER SIXTEEN. OUT-OF-CONTROL WAR

1. Amy Holmes, *Social Unrest and American Military Bases in Turkey and Germany since 1945* (Cambridge: Cambridge University Press, 2014), 183.

2. *Rebuilding America's Defenses: Strategy, Forces and Resources for a New Century* (Washington, DC: Project for a New American Century, 2000).

3. Nick Turse, "The Pentagon's Shadow Military Bases," *Nation,* January 9, 2019, www.thenation.com/article/syria-iraq-pentagon-overseas-military -bases/; David de Jong, email to the author, February 4, 2014, quoting a press officer for the Secretary of Defense: "Using October 2011 as a benchmark, we had about 800 facilities—ranging from very small checkpoints that have maybe

a squad or platoon of ISAF forces on it to bases that have several hundred to as many as a thousand ISAF members on them."

4. Tom Engelhardt, "How Permanent Are Those Bases?," TomDispatch, June 7, 2007, www.tomdispatch.com/post/174807/tom_engelhardt_how_permanent_are_those_bases.

5. Guy Raz, "U.S. Builds Air Base in Iraq for Long Haul," *All Things Considered,* National Public Radio, October 12, 2007, www.npr.org/templates/story/story.php?storyId=15184773; Tom Engelhardt, "Baseless Considerations," TomDispatch, November 5, 2007, www.tomdispatch.com/blog/174858/tomgram%3A__baseless_considerations.

6. "Diego Garcia 'Camp Justice,'" GlobalSecurity.org, accessed February 13, 2020, www.globalsecurity.org/military/facility/diego-garcia.htm.

7. David Vine, "Forty-Five Blows against Democracy: How U.S. Military Bases Back Dictators, Autocrats, and Military Regimes," TomDispatch, May 16, 2017, www.tomdispatch.com/blog/176281/.

8. David Vine, "The Bases of War in the Middle East: From Carter to the Islamic State, 35 Years of Building Bases and Sowing Disaster," TomDispatch, November 13, 2014, www.tomdispatch.com/blog/175922/tomgram%3A_david_vine,_a_permanent_infrastructure_for_permanent_war/; Robert F. Worth, Mark Mazzetti, and Scott Shane, "Drone Strikes' Risks to Get Rare Moment in the Public Eye," *New York Times,* February 5, 2013, www.nytimes.com/2013/02/06/world/middleeast/with-brennan-pick-a-light-on-drone-strikes-hazards.html?hp.

9. Matthew Wallin, "U.S. Military Bases and Facilities in the Middle East," fact sheet, American Security Project, June 2018, www.americansecurityproject.org/wp-content/uploads/2018/06/Ref-0213-US-Military-Bases-and-Facilities-Middle-East.pdf; Congressional Research Service, *The United Arab Emirates (UAE): Issues for U.S. Policy* (Washington, DC: CRS, 2019).

10. Leila Fadel, "U.S. Seeking 58 Bases in Iraq, Shiite Lawmakers Say," McClatchy DC, June 9, 2008, www.mcclatchydc.com/news/nation-world/world/article24486298.html.

11. Humeyra Pamuk and Phil Stewart, "U.S. Halts Secretive Drone Program with Turkey over Syria Incursion," Reuters, February 5, 2020, www.reuters.com/article/us-turkey-security-usa-drone-exclusive/exclusive-u-s-halts-secretive-drone-program-with-turkey-over-syria-incursion-idUSKBN1ZZ1AB.

12. Judah Ari Gross, "In First, US Establishes Permanent Military Base in Israel," *Times of Israel,* September 18, 2017, www.timesofisrael.com/in-first-us-establishes-permanent-military-base-in-israel/; "U.S. Navy Returns to Israeli Port in Sign of 'Deep Alliance,'" *Haaretz,* October 14, 2018, www.haaretz.com/israel-news/u-s-navy-returns-to-israeli-port-in-sign-of-deep-alliance-1.6554270. In Egypt there is at least one medical research facility (which may have other

functions) in Cairo. U.S. troops have occupied at least two bases on the Sinai Peninsula since 1982 as part of Camp David Accords peacekeeping.

13. *Quadrennial Defense Review, 2001* (Washington, DC: U.S. Department of Defense, 2001), 25.

14. Raymond F. DuBois, interview with the author, Washington, DC, April 29, 2012.

15. George W. Bush, "Statement on the Ongoing Review of the Overseas Force Posture," November 25, 2003, American Presidency Project, www.presidency .ucsb.edu/documents/statement-the-ongoing-review-the-overseas-force-posture.

16. David Vine, *Base Nation: How U.S. Military Bases Abroad Harm America and the World* (New York: Metropolitan Books, 2015), 52–59; Douglas J. Feith, "A Smarter Way to Use Our Troops," *Washington Post*, August 19, 2004, A25.

17. "Strengthening U.S. Global Defense Posture," Department of Defense, September 17, 2004, 5, www.dmzhawaii.org/wp-content/uploads/2008/12/global _posture.pdf.

18. "DOD Announces Plans to Adjust Posture of Land Forces in Europe," press release, U.S. Army Europe Public Affairs, February 16, 2012, https:// media.defense.gov/2018/May/03/2001911883/-1/-1/0/02162012%20DOD%20 ANNOUNCES%20PLANS%20TO%20ADJUST%20POSTURE%20OF%20 LAND%20FORCES%20IN%20EUROPE.PDF.

19. *National Defense Budget Estimates for FY 2014* (Washington, DC: U.S. Department of Defense, 2013), 146–48.

20. *National Defense Budget Estimates,* 143.

21. U.S. Senate Committee on Appropriations, Military Construction and Veterans Affairs, and Related Agencies Appropriation Bill, 2014, Senate Report 113-048 (113th Congress, 1st session, June 27, 2013).

22. "World Military Expenditure Grows to $1.8 Trillion in 2018," Stockholm International Peace Research Institute, April 29, 2019, www.sipri.org/media /press-release/2019/world-military-expenditure-grows-18-trillion-2018.

23. William Hartung and Mandy Smithberger, "Boondoggle, Inc.: Making Sense of the $1.25 Trillion National Security State Budget," TomDispatch, May 7, 2019, www.tomdispatch.com/blog/176561/tomgram%3A_hartung_and _smithberger%2C_a_dollar-by-dollar_tour_of_the_national_security_state.

24. Neta C. Crawford, "United States Budgetary Costs and Obligations of the Post-9/11 Wars through FY2020: $6.4 Trillion Spent and Obligated," Costs of War Project, Brown University, November 13, 2019, https://watson.brown.edu /costsofwar/files/cow/imce/papers/2019/US%20Budgetary%20Costs%20of%20 Wars%20November%202019.pdf.

25. R. Jeffrey Smith, "Pentagon's Accounting Shambles May Cost an Additional $1 Billion," Center for Public Integrity, October 13, 2011, https:// publicintegrity.org/national-security/pentagons-accounting-shambles-may-cost -an-additional-1-billion/; Barbara Lee, "Audit the Pentagon," *Daily Kos* (blog),

October 25, 2012, www.dailykos.com/story/2012/10/25/1150275/-Audit-the -Pentagon#.

26. Commission on Wartime Contracting in Iraq and Afghanistan, *Transforming Wartime Contracting: Controlling Costs, Reducing Risks; Final Report to Congress* (Arlington, VA: CWCIA, 2011).

27. Some of the contracts are for nonbase items like weapons procurement. Because thousands of contracts are believed to be omitted from these tallies thanks to accounting errors, $385 billion is a reasonable reflection of the funds flowing to private contractors to support the country's global base collection. Because of the Pentagon's poor accounting practices and secrecy, the true total may be significantly higher. For a full discussion and methodology, see Vine, *Base Nation*, chap. 12.

28. Vine, *Base Nation*, chap. 13.

29. *United States Department of Defense Fiscal Year 2015 Budget Amendment: Overview Overseas Contingency Operations* (Washington, DC: U.S. Department of Defense, June 2014), 5; *United States Department of Defense Fiscal Year 2015 Budget Request: Overview Overseas Contingency Operations Budget Amendment* (Washington, DC: November 2014).

30. "Defense: Long-Term Contribution Trends," Center for Responsive Politics, accessed February 17, 2020, www.opensecrets.org/industries/totals .php?cycle=2020&ind=D.

31. See "Adding It Up: The Top Players in Foreign Agent Lobbying," ProPublica, August 18, 2009, www.propublica.org/article/adding-it-up-the-top -players-in-foreign-agent-lobbying-718.

32. Vine, *Base Nation*, 244–51.

33. Dwight D. Eisenhower, "Military-Industrial Complex Speech, Dwight D. Eisenhower, 1961," January 17, 1961, Avalon Project, http://avalon.law.yale .edu/20th_century/eisenhower001.asp.

34. Gareth Porter, "The Permanent-War Complex," *American Conservative*, November–December, 2018, 32. There is some debate about whether Eisenhower called it the "Military Industrial Congressional Complex" in an early draft but shortened the name to avoid offending Congress.

35. Porter, "Permanent-War Complex," 28.

36. Heidi M. Peters, Moshe Schwartz, and Lawrence Kapp, *Department of Defense Contractor and Troop Levels in Iraq and Afghanistan: 2007-2017*, report R44116 (Washington, DC: Congressional Research Service, 2017).

37. Week Staff, "'Top Secret America': By the Numbers," *Washington Post*, July 19, 2010, https://theweek.com/articles/492600/secret-america-by-num-bers; Porter, "Permanent-War Complex," 28–29.

38. Quoted in Dana Priest and William M. Arkin, *Top Secret America: The Rise of the New American Security State* (New York: Little, Brown, 2011), 188.

CHAPTER SEVENTEEN. WAR IS THE MISSION

1. The description at the beginning of this chapter builds off David Vine, "The Lily-Pad Strategy: How the Pentagon Is Quietly Transforming Its Overseas Base Empire and Creating a Dangerous New Way of War," TomDispatch, July 16, 2012, www.tomdispatch.com/blog/175568.

2. Craig Whitlock, "Mysterious Fatal Crash Provides Rare Glimpse of U.S. Commandos in Mali," *Washington Post*, July 8, 2012, www.washingtonpost.com/world /national-security/mysterious-fatal-crash-provides-rare-glimpse-of-us-commandos -in-mali/2012/07/08/gJQAGO71WW_story.html; Thomas Gibbons-Neff et al., "Chaos as Militants Overran Airfield, Killing 3 Americans in Kenya," *New York Times*, January 22, 2020, www.nytimes.com/2020/01/22/world/africa/shabab -kenya-terrorism.html; Nick Turse, "U.S. Secret Wars in Africa Rage On, Despite Talk of Downsizing," *Intercept*, July 26, 2018, https://theintercept.com/2018/07/26 /us-special-operations-africa-green-berets-navy-seals/.

3. Quoted in Nick Turse, "The U.S. Has More Military Operations in Africa Than the Middle East," *Vice*, December 12, 2018, https://news.vice.com/en_us /article/a3my38/exclusive-the-us-has-more-military-operations-in-africa-than -the-middle-east.

4. Quoted in Nick Turse, "America's War-Fighting Footprint in Africa: Secret U.S. Military Documents Reveal a Constellation of American Military Bases across That Continent," TomDispatch, April 27, 2017, www.tomdispatch.com /blog/176272/tomgram%3A_nick_turse%2C_the_u.s._military_moves_deeper _into_africa/.

5. Stephen J. Townsend, "Statement of General Stephen J. Townsend, United States Army Commander, United States Africa Command before the Senate Armed Services Committee," U.S. Senate Armed Services Committee, January 30, 2020, 9, www.armed-services.senate.gov/imo/media/doc/Townsend_01-30-20 .pdf; Nick Turse, "Commandos sans Frontières: The Global Growth of U.S. Special Operations Forces," TomDispatch, July 17, 2018, www.tomdispatch.com /blog/176448/.

6. Turse, "Commandos sans Frontières."

7. Amedee Bollee, "Djibouti: From French Outpost to US Base," *Review of African Political Economy* 30, no. 97 (2003): 481–84.

8. Lauren Ploch, *Africa Command: U.S. Strategic Interests and the Role of the U.S. Military in Africa* (Washington, DC: Congressional Research Service, 2011), 9, 13; Benjamin A. Benson, AFRICOM, email to the author, November 13, 2014.

9. George W. Bush, "President Bush Creates a Department of Defense Unified Combatant Command for Africa," press release, White House, February 6, 2007, https://georgewbush-whitehouse.archives.gov/news/releases/2007/02/20070206 -3.html.

10. Catherine Besteman, "Counter AFRICOM," in *The Counter-counterinsurgency Manual, or Notes on Demilitarizing American Society,* ed. Network of Concerned Anthropologists Steering Committee (Chicago: Prickly Paradigm, 2009), 118–21.

11. Akil R. King, Zackary H. Moss, and Afi Y. Pittman, "Overcoming Logistics Challenges in East Africa," *Army Sustainment,* January–February 2014, 30.

12. Turse, "America's War-Fighting Footprint."

13. The following details rely heavily on Turse's important work, especially Nick Turse, "U.S. Military Says It Has a 'Light Footprint' in Africa: These Documents Show a Vast Network of Bases," *Intercept,* December 1, 2018, https://theintercept.com/2018/12/01/u-s-military-says-it-has-a-light-footprint-in-africa-these-documents-show-a-vast-network-of-bases/. I also benefited from the generous help of Adam Moore and the Costs of War Project (Stephanie Savell, emails to the author, November 9, 2018, and March 10, 2020). See also David Vine, *Base Nation: How U.S. Military Bases Abroad Harm America and the World* (New York: Metropolitan Books, 2015), chap. 16.

14. Quoted in Turse, "America's War-Fighting Footprint."

15. Quoted in Turse, "U.S. Military Says."

16. Richard Reeve and Zoë Pelter, *From New Frontier to New Normal: Counterterrorism Operations in the Sahel-Sahara* (London: Remote Control Group /Oxford Research Group, 2014), 25.

17. Turse, "U.S. Military Says"; "Al Shabaab," *Mapping Militant Organizations,* Stanford University, February 20, 2016, http://web.stanford.edu/group /mappingmilitants/cgi-bin/groups/view/61?highlightpal1shabaab; Catherine Besteman, "The Costs of War in Somalia," Costs of War Project, Brown University, September 5, 2019, https://watson.brown.edu/costsofwar/files/cow/imce /papers/2019/Costs%20of%20War%20in%20Somalia_Besteman.pdf; Gibbons-Neff et al., "Militants Overran Airfield."

18. See, for example, Nick Turse, "'What Does War Have to Do with Me?' Combat Viewed from the Rooftops and Beyond," TomDispatch, June 27, 2019, www.tomdispatch.com/blog/176580.

19. Turse, "U.S. Military Says"; Craig Whitlock, "U.S. to Airlift African Troops to Central African Republic," *Washington Post,* December 9, 2013.

20. Contractors have carried out significantly larger projects worldwide. Nick Turse, "U.S. Military Is Building a $100 Million Drone Base in Africa," *Intercept,* September 29, 2016, https://theintercept.com/2016/09/29/u-s-military-is -building-a-100-million-drone-base-in-africa/.

21. Turse, "U.S. Military Says."

22. "Statement of General Carter Ham, USA Commander: United States Africa Command before the Senate Armed Services Committee," United States Africa Command, March 7, 2013, www.africom.mil/Doc/10432. While some of

the Air Force and Navy construction could be for local military forces, building a base almost always involves inspection, "end-use monitoring," and usage rights, making it another effective way to disguise a U.S. presence. Thanks go to John Lindsay-Poland for making this point.

23. Nick Turse, "The Pivot to Africa: The Startling Size, Scope, and Growth of U.S. Military Operations on the African Continent," TomDispatch, September 5, 2013, www.tomdispatch.com/blog/175743; Reeve and Pelter, New Frontier, 22; Lalit Wadhwa, "The Society of American Military Engineers" (PowerPoint presentation, U.S. Army Corps of Engineers Europe District, April 12, 2013).

24. Amy Belasco, The Cost of Iraq, Afghanistan, and Other Global War on Terror Operations since 9/11 (Washington, DC: Congressional Research Service, 2011), 10; Chalmers Johnson, Nemesis: The Last Days of the American Republic (New York: Metropolitan Books, 2008), 147–48; Alexander Cooley, Base Politics: Democratic Change and the US Military Overseas (Ithaca, NY: Cornell University Press, 2008), 238, 242.

25. Reeve and Pelter, New Frontier, 16–18, 14.

26. Ploch, "Africa Command," 22–23.

27. Turse, "Pivot to Africa"; Oscar Nkala and Kim Helfrich, "US Army Looking to Contractors for African Operations," Defence Web, September 17, 2013, www.defenceweb.co.za/index.php?option=com_content&view=article&id=31919:us-army-looking-to-contractors-for-african-operations&catid=56:diplomacy-a-peace&Itemid=111.

28. Nick Turse, "Drug Wars, Missing Money, and a Phantom $500 Million: Pentagon Watchdog Calls Out Two Commands for Financial Malfeasance," TomDispatch, February 8, 2018, www.tomdispatch.com/post/176383/tomgram%3A_nick_turse%2C_the_u.s._military%27s_drug_of_choice/.

29. Herbert Docena, "The US Base in the Philippines," Inquirer, February 20, 2012, http://opinion.inquirer.net/23405/the-us-base-in-the-philippines; "Philippines: Security and Foreign Forces," Jane's Sentinel Security Assessment, May 14, 2009.

30. Robert D. Kaplan, Hog Pilots, Blue Water Grunts: The American Military in the Air, at Sea, and on the Ground (New York: Vintage, 2008), 315.

31. Robert D. Kaplan, Imperial Grunts: On the Ground with the American Military (New York: Vintage Departures, 2005), 131–84; Carlo Muñoz, "The Philippines Re-opens Military Bases to US Forces," June 6, 2012, http://thehill.com/blogs/defcon-hill/operations/231257-philippines-re-opens-military-bases-to-us-forces-.

32. Vine, Base Nation, chap. 16; Office of the Under Secretary of Defense (Policy), "Global Defense Posture and International Agreements Overview" (slide presentation, U.S. Department of Defense, April 27, 2009), 6, 9–10.

33. Chris Woods, "CIA Drones Quit One Pakistan Site—but US Keeps Access to Other Airbases," Bureau of Investigative Journalism, December 15, 2011, www.thebureauinvestigates.com/2011/12/15/cia-drones-quit-pakistan-site-but-us -keeps-access-to-other-airbases/.

34. Vine, *Base Nation*, chap. 16; David Vine, "Lists of U.S. Military Bases Abroad, 1776–2020," American University Digital Research Archive, April 27, 2020, https://doi.org/10.17606/bbxc-4368.

35. Vine, *Base Nation*, 53–59.

36. Turse, "U.S. Military Says."

37. David Vine, *Island of Shame: The Secret History of the U.S. Military Base on Diego Garcia* (Princeton, NJ: Princeton University Press, 2009), chap. 6.

38. *United States Security Agreements and Commitments Abroad: Hearings before the Senate Subcommittee on United States Security Agreements and Commitments Abroad of the Committee on Foreign Relations*, 91st Cong., vol. 2 (Washington, DC: Government Printing Office, 1971), 2433–34.

39. "Drone Bases Updates," Center for the Study of the Drone, Bard University, October 1, 2018, https://dronecenter.bard.edu/drone-bases-updates/.

40. Nick Turse, "The U.S. Is Building a Drone Base in Niger That Will Cost More Than $280 Million by 2024," *Intercept*, August 21, 2018, https:// theintercept.com/2018/08/21/us-drone-base-niger-africa/.

41. Carmela Fonbuena, "PH, US 'Close' to Signing Military Deal," *Rappler*, February 5, 2014, www.rappler.com/nation/49733-philippines-united-states-bases-access.

42. Docena, "US Base."

43. Quoted in Robert D. Kaplan, "What Rumsfeld Got Right: How Donald Rumsfeld Remade the U.S. Military for a More Uncertain World," *Atlantic*, July–August 2008, www.theatlantic.com/magazine/archive/2008/07/what-rumsfeld -got-right/306870/.

44. Kaplan, "What Rumsfeld Got Right."

45. Melvyn P. Leffler, *A Preponderance of Power: National Security, the Truman Administration, and the Cold War* (Stanford, CA: Stanford University Press, 1992), 41; Joint Staff Planners, "Over-all Examination of U.S. Requirements for Military Bases and Rights," enclosure C to "Over-all Examination of U.S. Requirements for Military Bases and Rights," JCS 570/40 report, October 23, 1945, Central Decimal File 1942–45, box 272, sec. 9, 217, RG 218, U.S. National Archives, Washington, DC.

46. George W. Bush, "Text of Bush's Speech at West Point," *New York Times*, June 1, 2002, www.nytimes.com/2002/06/01/international/text-of-bushs -speech-at-west-point.html.

47. Thomas Donnelly and Vance Serchuk, "Toward a Global Cavalry," American Enterprise Institute, July 1, 2003, www.aei.org/research-products/report /toward-a-global-cavalry/.

48. Kaplan, *Imperial Grunts*, 1–2.

49. Nikhil Pal Singh, *Race and America's Long War* (Oakland: University of California Press, 2017), 2; Byrd, quoted on 33.

50. Phillip W. D. Martin, "Why So Many Iraqis Hate Us? Try 'Towel Head' on for Size," *Huffington Post*, April 11, 2008 (updated May 25, 2011), www .huffingtonpost.com/phillip-martin/why-so-many-iraqis-hate-u_b_96330.html.

51. Townsend, "Statement," 10; Mark T. Esper, "In-Flight Media Availability by Secretary Esper," transcript, U.S. Department of Defense, January 22, 2020, www.defense.gov/Newsroom/Transcripts/Transcript/Article/2063275/in-flight -media-availability-by-secretary-esper/.

52. Paul C. Wright, "U.S. Military Intervention in Africa: The New Blueprint for Global Domination," Global Research, August 20, 2010, www.globalresearch .ca/PrintArticle.php?articleId=20708; "Sao Tome Sparks American Military Interest," Voice of America, October 28, 2009, www.voanews.com/archive/sao -tome-sparks-american-military-interest.

53. "US Naval Base to Protect Sao Tome Oil," BBC News, August 22, 2002, http://news.bbc.co.uk/2/hi/business/2210571.stm.

54. Joeva Rock, "Pythons and Lily Pads," *Africa Is a Country*, April 2, 2018, https://africasacountry.com/2018/04/pythons-and-lily-pads.

55. Quoted in James Bellamy Foster, "A Warning to Africa: The New U.S. Imperial Grand Strategy," *Monthly Review* 58, no. 2 (2006): www.monthlyreview .org/0606jbf.htm.

56. "Mapping Africa's Natural Resources," *Al Jazeera*, February 20, 2018, www .aljazeera.com/indepth/interactive/2016/10/mapping-africa-natural-resources -161020075811145.html.

57. "Mapping Africa's Natural Resources."

58. Michael Klare and Daniel Volman, "America, China and the Scramble for Africa's Oil," *Review of African Political Economy* 33, no. 108 (2006): 298–302.

59. Townsend, "Statement," 7.

60. Nick Turse, "The New Obama Doctrine, a Six-Point Plan for Global War: Special Ops, Drones, Spy Games, Civilian Soldiers, Proxy Fighters, and Cyber Warfare," TomDispatch, June 14, 2012, www.tomdispatch.com/archive/175557 /nick_turse_the_changing_face_of_empire.

61. Townsend, "Statement," 17–18.

62. Raymond F. DuBois, interview with the author, Washington, DC, April 29, 2012.

63. Lesley Gill, *The School of the Americas: Military Training and Political Violence in the Americas* (Durham, NC: Duke University Press, 2004), 235.

64. DuBois, interview.

65. Anonymous State Department official, interview with the author, Washington, DC, February 2011.

66. See Vine, *Base Nation*, 283–90; Keith B. Cunningham and Andreas Klemmer, *Restructuring the US Military Bases in Germany: Scope, Impacts, and Opportunities*, report 4 (Bonn, Germany: Bonn International Center for Conversion, 1995), 6.

67. Andrew Bacevich, *Washington Rules: America's Path to Permanent War* (New York: Metropolitan Books, 2010), 22.

68. U.S. Government Accountability Office, *Defense Headquarters: DOD Needs to Reassess Options for Permanent Location of U.S. Africa Command; Report to Congressional Committees* (Washington, DC: U.S. GAO, 2013).

69. Vine, *Base Nation*, 313; David M. Rodriguez, "Statement of General David M. Rodriguez, USA, Commander, United States Africa Command before the Senate Armed Services Committee Posture Hearing," March 6, 2014, 9, www.securityassistance.org/sites/default/files/Rodriguez_03-06-14.pdf.

70. Office of the Under Secretary of Defense (Comptroller)/Chief FinancialOfficer, *Operation and Maintenance Overview: Fiscal Year 2015 Budget Estimates*, U.S. Department of Defense, March 2014, 78, https://comptroller.defense.gov/Portals/45/Documents/defbudget/fy2015/fy2015_OM_Overview.pdf; Inspector General, Combined Joint Task Force-Horn of Africa Needed Better Guidance and Systems to Adequately Manage Civil-Military Operations (Alexandria, VA: U.S. Department of Defense, October 30, 2013).

71. Jonathan Kennedy, "How Drone Strikes and a Fake Vaccination Program Have Inhibited Polio Eradication in Pakistan: An Analysis of National Level Data," *International Journal of Health Services* 47, no. 4 (2017): 807–25.

72. Turse, "Drone Base in Niger."

73. Amnesty International, "Cameroon's Secret Torture Chambers: Human Rights Violations and War Crimes in the Fight against Boko Haram," July 19, 2017, www.amnestyusa.org/reports/cameroons-secret-torture/; Nick Turse, "New Video Shows More Atrocities by Cameroon, a Key U.S. Ally in Drone Warfare," *Intercept*, August 31, 2018, https://theintercept.com/2018/08/31/cameroon-video-execution-boko-haram/.

74. Reeve and Pelter, *New Frontier*, 3, 27.

75. Alex de Waal and Abdul Mohammed, "Handmaiden to Africa's Generals," *New York Times*, April 15, 2014, www.nytimes.com/2014/08/16/opinion/handmaiden-to-africas-generals.html. See also Adam Moore and James Walker, "Tracing the US Military's Presence in Africa," *Geopolitics* 21, no. 3 (2016): 686–716.

76. Klare and Volman, "Scramble for Africa's Oil," 306; Sandra T. Barnes, "Global Flows: Terror, Oil, and Strategic Philanthropy," *African Studies Review* 48, no. 1 (2005): 11.

77. Reeve and Pelter, *New Frontier*, 3.

78. Kofi Nsia-Pepra, "Militarization of U.S. Foreign Policy in Africa: Strategic Gain or Backlash," *Military Review*, January–February 2014, 58.

79. Nick Turse, "Special Ops at War: From Afghanistan to Somalia, Special Ops Achieves Less with More," TomDispatch, January 9, 2018, www .tomdispatch.com/post/176371/tomgram%3A_nick_turse%2C_the_coming _year_in_special_ops/; Seth G. Jones et al., *The Evolution of the Salafi-Jihadist Threat* (Washington, DC: Center for Strategic and International Studies, 2018).

80. Seth G. Jones and Martin C. Libicki, *How Terrorist Groups End: Lessons for Countering al Qa'ida* (Santa Monica, CA: RAND Corporation, 2008); Erik Goepner, "In Afghanistan, the Withdrawal of U.S. Troops Is Long Overdue," CATO Institute, September 29, 2017, www.cato.org/blog/afghanistan -withdrawal-us-troops-long-overdue.

81. The countries are France, China, Japan, Italy, Spain, Germany, the United States, and possibly Saudi Arabia. Neil Melvin, "The Foreign Military Presence in the Horn of Africa Region," SIPRI Background Paper, April 2019, 2, https:// sipri.org/sites/default/files/2019-04/sipribp1904.pdf.

82. Robert E. Harkavy, *Strategic Basing and the Great Powers, 1200–2000* (London: Routledge, 2007), chap. 6; Klare and Volman, "Scramble for Africa's Oil," 307.

83. Nick Turse, "The U.S. Will Invade West Africa in 2023 after an Attack in New York—according to Pentagon War Game," *Intercept*, October 22, 2017, https://theintercept.com/2017/10/22/the-u-s-will-invade-west-africa-in-2023-after -an-attack-in-new-york-according-to-pentagon-war-game/.

84. Peter Cronau, "The Base: Pine Gap's Role in US Warfighting," Australian Broadcasting Corporation Radio, August 20, 2017, www.abc.net.au /radionational/programs/backgroundbriefing/the-base-pine-gaps-role-in-us -warfighting/8813604.

85. Eric G. John to U.S. Secretary of Defense, cable, May 23, 2008, Bangkok, Thailand, WikiLeaks, http://wikileaks.org/cable/2008/05/08BANGKOK1611 .html; Kaplan, *Hog Pilots*, 79–82; Craig Whitlock, "U.S. Seeks Return to SE Asian Bases," *Washington Post*, June 22, 2012, www.washingtonpost.com/world /national-security/us-seeks-return-to-se-asian-bases/2012/06/22/gJQAKP83vV _story.html.

CONCLUSION

1. Anand Gopal cited "dozens" of bases in Syria alone in a 2017 interview. "Anand Gopal: As U.S. Continues Strikes in Afghanistan and Syria, Where Is Coverage of Civilian Deaths?," *Democracy Now!*, November 21, 2017, www .democracynow.org/2017/11/21/anand_gopal_as_us_continues_strikes; Tara Copp, "Pentagon Strips Iraq, Afghanistan, Syria Troop Numbers from Web," *Military Times*, April 9, 2018, www.militarytimes.com/news/your-military /2018/04/09/dod-strips-iraq-afghanistan-syria-troop-numbers-from-web/.

2. Oriana Pawlyk, "2 Years into Yemen War, US Ramps Up Refueling of Saudi Jets," *Military.com,* February 15, 2017, www.military.com/daily-news/2017 /02/15/2-years-yemen-war-us-ramps-up-refueling-saudi-jets.html.

3. There was a pause in CIA drone assassinations toward the end of the Obama administration, when the president transferred the killing exclusively to the military. Stephanie Savell and 5W Infographics, "This Map Shows Where in the World the U.S. Military Is Combatting Terrorism," *Smithsonian Magazine,* January 2019, www.smithsonianmag.com/history/map-shows-places-world-where -us-military-operates-180970997/.

4. Michael Horton, "Is China Waiting Us Out?," *American Conservative,* November–December 2018, 15.

5. Surgeon at Landstuhl Regional Medical Center, Germany, phone interview with the author, July 5, 2012. After we spoke the hospital lost its top-tier status, because it no longer sees a sufficient number of trauma patients to receive the top rating. Matt Millham, "With Fewer War Injuries, Landstuhl Becomes Level III Trauma Center," *Stars and Stripes,* May 28, 2014, www.stripes.com/news /with-fewer-war-injuries-landstuhl-becomes-level-iii-trauma-center-1.285819.

6. Walter Pincus, interview with the author, Washington, DC, August 24, 2012.

7. Catherine Lutz, "Warmaking as the American Way of Life," in *The Insecure American: How We Got Here and What We Should Do about It,* ed. Hugh Gusterson and Catherine Besteman (Berkeley: University of California Press, 2009), 50, 46.

8. Congressional Budget Office, *Funding for Overseas Contingency Operations and Its Impact on Defense Spending* (Washington, DC: CBO, 2018), 20.

9. Mike Holmes, "2018 WEPTAC Conference Keynote Speaker: General Mike Holmes," Air Combat Command, February 13, 2018, www.acc.af.mil/News /Article-Display/Article/1440031/2018-weptac-conference-keynote-speaker-general -mike-holmes/.

10. Andrew Cockburn, "The Military-Industrial Virus," *Harper's Magazine,* June 2019, 63–64.

11. Stephanie Savell, "Credit-Card Wars: Today's War-Financing Strategies Will Only Increase Inequality," TomDispatch, June 28, 2018, www.tomdispatch .com/blog/176442/tomgram%3A_stephanie_savell%2C_how_america%27s _wars_fund_inequality_at_home/.

12. Heidi Garrett-Peltier, "War Spending and Lost Opportunities," Costs of War Project, Brown University, March 2019, https://watson.brown.edu/costsofwar /files/cow/imce/papers/2019/March%202019%20Job%20Opportunity%20Cost %20of%20War.pdf.

13. Dwight D. Eisenhower, *Waging Peace, 1956–1961* (New York: Doubleday, 1965), 622.

14. For "peacetime crimes," see Nancy Scheper-Hughes and Philippe Bourgois, "Introduction: Making Sense of Violence," in *Violence in War and Peace: An*

Anthology, ed. Nancy Scheper-Hughes and Philippe Bourgois (Malden, MA: Blackwell, 2004), 20–22.

15. My thanks to Cara Flores-Mays for making this point so powerfully at a public meeting in Guam. See David Vine, *Base Nation: How U.S. Military Bases Abroad Harm America and the World* (New York: Metropolitan Books, 2015), 94–95.

16. Neta C. Crawford, "Human Cost of the Post-9/11 Wars: Lethality and the Need for Transparency," Costs of War Project, Brown University, November 2018, https://watson.brown.edu/costsofwar/files/cow/imce/papers/2018/Human%20Costs%2C%20Nov%208%202018%20CoW.pdf.

17. Falih Hassan and Rod Nordland, "Battered ISIS Keeps Grip on Last Piece of Territory for over a Year," *New York Times,* December 9, 2018, www.nytimes.com/2018/12/09/world/middleeast/isis-territory-syria-iraq.html.

18. Azmat Khan and Anand Gopal, "The Uncounted," *New York Times Magazine,* November 19, 2017, 42–53, 68–69.

19. Robert F. Worth, "How the War in Yemen Became a Bloody Stalemate—and the Worst Humanitarian Crisis in the World," *New York Times Magazine,* October 31, 2018, www.nytimes.com/interactive/2018/10/31/magazine/yemen-war-saudi-arabia.html.

20. "Yemen War Death Toll Exceeds 90,000 according to New ACLED Data for 2015," press release, Armed Conflict Location and Event Data Project, June 18, 2019, www.acleddata.com/2019/06/18/press-release-yemen-war-death-toll-exceeds-90000-according-to-new-acled-data-for-2015/.

21. Oriana Pawyk, "General Argues to Continue Refueling Saudi Planes in Yemen Fight," Military.com, March 13, 2018, www.military.com/daily-news/2018/03/13/general-argues-continue-refueling-saudi-planes-yemen-fight.html; Robert F. Worth, "They Break Us or We Break Them," *New York Times Magazine,* November 4, 2018, 50–51.

22. Dwight D. Eisenhower, "The Chance for Peace" (speech, American Society of Newspaper Editors, Washington, DC, April 16, 1953), https://babel.hathitrust.org/cgi/pt?id=umn.31951d03597166h&view=1up&seq=1.

23. Neta C. Crawford, "United States Budgetary Costs and Obligations of Post-9/11 Wars through FY2020: $6.4 Trillion," Costs of War Project, Brown University, November 13, 2019, https://watson.brown.edu/costsofwar/files/cow/imce/papers/2019/US%20Budgetary%20Costs%20of%20Wars%20November%202019.pdf.

24. Robert Pollin and Heidi Garrett-Peltier, *The U.S. Employment Effects of Military and Domestic Spending Priorities: 2011 Update* (Amherst, MA: Political Economy Research Institute, University of Massachusetts, 2011).

25. "Marilyn Young on the Exercise of American Power Abroad," Cornell Program on Ethics and Public Life, September 23, 2013, YouTube video, 1:28:04, www.youtube.com/watch?v=6CkxReOc7eA.

26. Craig Whitlock, "At War with the Truth," *Washington Post,* December 9, 2019, www.washingtonpost.com/graphics/2019/investigations/afghanistan-papers/afghanistan-war-confidential-documents/.

27. Claudia Grisales, "Senate Approves Legislation to Limit President's War Powers against Iran," National Public Radio, February 13, 2020, www.npr.org/2020/02/13/805594383/senate-approves-legislation-to-limit-presidents-war-powers-against-iran.

28. "We Must *End* the Forever War," Common Defense, accessed February 13, 2020, https://commondefense.us/end-the-forever-war/.

29. "About QI," Quincy Institute, accessed February 14, 2020, https://quincyinst.org/about/.

30. John Feffer, "After Trump," Foreign Policy in Focus, March 20, 2019, https://fpif.org/after-trump/; James Carden, "A New Poll Shows the Public Is Overwhelmingly Opposed to Endless US Military Interventions," *Nation,* January 9, 2019, www.thenation.com/article/new-poll-shows-public-overwhelmingly-opposed-to-endless-us-military-interventions/.

31. "Transcript: Donald Trump on NATO, Turkey's Coup Attempt and the World," *New York Times,* July 21, 2016, www.nytimes.com/2016/07/22/us/politics/donald-trump-foreign-policy-interview.html.

32. President Trump said of the U.S. war in Iraq and the fate of Iraqi oil: "It used to be to the victor belong the spoils. Now, there was no victor [in Iraq]. . . . But I always said, 'Take the oil.'" Ryan Teague Beckwith, "Read Hillary Clinton and Donald Trump's Remarks at a Military Forum," *Time,* September 8, 2016, https://time.com/4483355/commander-chief-forum-clinton-trump-intrepid/.

33. Vine, *Base Nation,* chaps. 15, 17.

34. Organizations and movements that provide plans for and movements toward significant military budget cuts include About Face: Veterans against the War, the Cato Institute, the Center for International Policy, Codepink, Common Defense, National Priorities Project/Institute for Policy Studies, #PeopleOverPentagon, the Poor People's Campaign, the Project on Government Oversight, the Quincy Institute, and Win without War. Shailly Gupta Barnes, Lindsay Koshgarian, and Ashik Siddique, eds., *Poor People's Moral Budget: Everybody Has the Right to Live* (Washington, DC: Poor People's Campaign/Institute for Policy Studies/Kairos Center/Repairers of the Breach, 2019).

35. Dan Grazier, "The F-35 and the Captured State," POGO, June 10, 2019, www.pogo.org/analysis/2019/06/the-f-35-and-the-captured-state/.

36. I believe that Chalmers Johnson deserves credit for identifying the Pentagon as the fourth branch of government.

37. See Vine, *Base Nation,* chap. 11.

38. See Kishore Mahbubani, "What China Threat?," *Harper's Magazine,* February 2019, 42; and Horton, "Is China Waiting?"

39. For "our liberties," see Dwight D. Eisenhower, "Military-Industrial Complex Speech, Dwight D. Eisenhower, 1961," January 17, 1961, Avalon Project, http://avalon.law.yale.edu/20th_century/eisenhower001.asp.

40. Martin Luther King Jr., "Beyond Vietnam: A Time to Break Silence, Declaration of Independence from the War in Vietnam" (speech, Riverside Church, New York, April 4, 1967), https://kinginstitute.stanford.edu/king-papers/documents/beyond-vietnam.

41. King, "Beyond Vietnam."

42. King, "Beyond Vietnam."

43. Rebecca Solnit, "Acts of Hope: Challenging Empire on the World Stage," *Orion Magazine*, January 2, 2004, www.orionmagazine.org/index.php/articles/article/211/.

44. Andrew Bacevich, "What Happens When a Few Volunteer and the Rest Just Watch: The American Military System Dissected," TomDispatch, April 10, 2018, www.tomdispatch.com/blog/176409/.

SUGGESTED RESOURCES

This is a highly abbreviated guide to resources I have found particularly helpful in conducting research about and attempting to understand the history of U.S. wars, U.S. Empire and imperialism, U.S. military bases, and related topics of militarism, militarization, and the Military Industrial Congressional Complex. The books, articles, films, videos, and other works cited in the book's endnotes provide a more exhaustive, but obviously still partial, list. The resources here and in the endnotes focus on English-language materials; there are many other important resources in other languages.

For current and historical lists of U.S. bases abroad, see my spreadsheets at www.basenation.us/learn-more.

Additional resources are on my websites www.basenation.us and www .davidvine.net.

Air Force Historical Research Agency: www.afhra.af.mil.
Antibase movements past and present, crowd-sourced list: https://bit.ly /2CUMcUg.
Center for Public Environmental Oversight, documenting military base contamination: www.cpeo.org/milit.html.
Coalition against U.S. Foreign Military Bases: https://noforeignbases.org.
CODEPINK, women-led organization working to end U.S. wars and support peace: www.codepink.org.

Congressional Research Service, reports on the U.S. military and war: www.fas
.org/sgp/crs/.

Costs of War Project, Brown University, reports on the human and financial
costs of the post-2001 U.S. wars: www.costsofwar.org.

COVID-19 Global Solidarity Coalition, Manifesto, and other information:
www.covidglobalsolidarity.org.

"Fifty-One US Military Outposts," satellite photographs of military bases
worldwide: https://mishkahenner.com/Fifty-One-US-Military-Outposts.

Global Campaign on Military Spending: http://demilitarize.org.

GlobalSecurity.org, data and information about militaries worldwide: https://
globalsecurity.org.

Government Accountability Office, reports on military and war-related issues:
www.gao.gov/browse/topic/National_Defense.

Guantánamo Public Memory Project: https://gitmomemory.org.

National Priorities Project, "Cost of National Security": www.nationalpriorities.org
/cost-of/; and "Trade-Offs: Your Money, Your Choices": www.nationalpriorities
.org/interactive-data/trade-offs.

Overseas Base Realignment and Closure Coalition: www.overseasbases.net.

Peace Action: www.peaceaction.org/what-we-do/campaigns/pentagon-
spending.

Radical Cartography, "U.S. Empire" maps: www.radicalcartography.net/index
.html?usempire.

Security Assistance Monitor, data on U.S. military and related aid abroad:
www.securityassistance.org.

Stockholm International Peace Research Institute, "SIPRI Military
Expenditure Database": www.sipri.org/databases/milex.

TomDispatch, articles on war, imperialism, the Military Industrial Congressional
Complex, other topics: www.tomdispatch.com.

Transnational Institute, primer on foreign military bases: www.tni.org/primer
/foreign-military-bases-and-global-campaign-close-them.

U.S. Army Center of Military History: www.history.army.mil.

U.S. Army Corps of Engineers, Office of History: www.usace.army.mil/About
/History.aspx.

U.S. Marine Corps History Division: www.usmcu.edu/Research/History-
Division/.

U.S. Navy Naval History and Heritage Command: www.history.navy.mil.

Women for Genuine Security: www.genuinesecurity.org.

INDEX

Note: Page references in *italics* refer to illustrations. Asterisks denote footnotes.

411

CALIFORNIA SERIES IN PUBLIC ANTHROPOLOGY

Founded in 1893,
UNIVERSITY OF CALIFORNIA PRESS
publishes bold, progressive books and journals
on topics in the arts, humanities, social sciences,
and natural sciences—with a focus on social
justice issues—that inspire thought and action
among readers worldwide.

The UC PRESS FOUNDATION
raises funds to uphold the press's vital role
as an independent, nonprofit publisher, and
receives philanthropic support from a wide
range of individuals and institutions—and from
committed readers like you. To learn more, visit
ucpress.edu/supportus.

1774–1783 SHAWNEE, DELAWARE ✪ 1776 CHEROKEE ✪ 1777–1781 IROQUOIS CONFE
1792–1793 MUSKOGEE (CREEK) ✪ 1798–1801 FRANCE (UNDECLARED WAR) ✪ 1801–18
FLORIDA ✪ 1810–1813 SHAWNEE CONFEDERACY ✪ 1812 SPANISH FLORIDA ✪ 1812–1815
CONFEDERACY (HAUDENOSAUNEE) ✪ 1813 SPANISH WEST FLORIDA ✪ 1813–1814 MAR
1814–1825 PIRATES ✪ 1815 ALGIERS ✪ 1815 TRIPOLI ✪ 1816 SPANISH FLORIDA ✪ 1
AFRICAN SLAVE TRADE PATROL ✪ 1822–1825 CUBA (SPAIN) ✪ 1824 PUERTO RICO (
1833 ARGENTINA ✪ 1835–1836 PERU ✪ 1835–1842 SEMINOLE ✪ 1836 MEXICO ✪ 18
1841 TABITEUEA ✪ 1842 MEXICO ✪ 1843 CHINA ✪ 1844 MEXICO ✪ 1846–1848 MEXICO ✪ 1
✪ 1852–1853 ARGENTINA ✪ 1853–1854 JAPAN ✪ 1853–1854 NICARAGUA ✪ 1853–1
1855–1856 ROGUE RIVER INDIGENOUS PEOPLES ✪ 1855–1856 YAKIMA, WALLA WAL
1857 NICARAGUA ✪ 1858 COEUR D'ALENE ALLIANCE ✪ 1858 FIJI ISLANDS ✪ 1858 URI
✪ 1860 COLOMBIA ✪ 1862 SIOUX ✪ 1863–1864 JAPAN ✪ 1864 CHEYENNE ✪ 1865
CHEYENNE, NORTHERN ARAPAHO ✪ 1867 FORMOSA (TAIWAN) ✪ 1867 NICARAGUA ✪
1870 MEXICO ✪ 1871 KOREA ✪ 1872–1873 MODOC ✪ 1873 COLOMBIA (PANAMA) ✪ 1873
✪ 1876–1877 SIOUX ✪ 1877 NEZ PERCE ✪ 1878 BANNOCK (BANA'KWUT) ✪ 1878–187
1888 KOREA ✪ 1888–1889 SAMOA ✪ 1889 HAWAI'I ✪ 1890 ARGENTINA ✪ 1890 LAKO
1894 NICARAGUA ✪ 1894–1895 CHINA ✪ 1894–1896 KOREA ✪ 1895 PANAMA (COLOMB
1898 PUERTO RICO (SPAIN) ✪ 1898–1899 CHINA ✪ 1899 NICARAGUA ✪ 1899 SAMOA ✪ 1
✪ 1903–1904 ABYSSINIA (ETHIOPIA) ✪ 1903 DOMINICAN REPUBLIC ✪ 1903–1914 PAN
✪ 1907 HONDURAS ✪ 1909–1910 NICARAGUA ✪ 1911–1912 HONDURAS ✪ 1911–194
REPUBLIC ✪ 1914 HAITI ✪ 1914–1919 MEXICO ✪ 1915–1934 HAITI ✪ 1916–1924 DOMIN
✪ 1918–1921 PANAMA ✪ 1919 DALMATIA ✪ 1919 TURKEY ✪ 1919–1920 HONDURAS (
1925 PANAMA ✪ 1932 EL SALVADOR ✪ 1941–1945 WORLD WAR II (EUROPE, NORTH A
✪ 1950 FORMOSA (TAIWAN) ✪ 1950–1953 KOREA ✪ 1953–1954 FORMOSA (TAIWAN)
1962–1975 LAOS ✪ 1964 CONGO (ZAIRE) ✪ 1965 DOMINICAN REPUBLIC ✪ 1965–19
1981 EL SALVADOR ✪ 1981 LIBYA ✪ 1981–1989 NICARAGUA ✪ 1982–1983 EGYPT ✪ 1982–
✪ 1988 PANAMA ✪ 1989 BOLIVIA ✪ 1989 COLOMBIA ✪ 1989 LIBYA ✪ 1989 PERU
✪ 1991–1992 KUWAIT ✪ 1991–1993 IRAQ ✪ 1992–1994 SOMALIA ✪ 1993–1994 MACED
✪ 1997–2003 IRAQ ✪ 1998 AFGHANISTAN ✪ 1998 SUDAN ✪ 1999–2000 KOSOVO ✪
✪ 2000–2016 COLOMBIA ✪ 2001– AFGHANISTAN ✪ 2001– PAKISTAN ✪ 2001– SOMALIA
✪ 2011 DEMOCRATIC REPUBLIC OF THE CONGO ✪ 2011–2017 UGANDA ✪ 2011– LIBYA
C. 2013– BURKINA FASO ✪ C. 2013– CHAD ✪ C. 2013– MAURITANIA ✪ C. 2013– NIGER (
✪ 2015 DEMOCRATIC REPUBLIC OF THE CONGO ✪ C. 2015– CAMEROON ✪ 2016 DEMOCR